Yarns and Stories of Abraham Lincoln

Yarns and Stories
of Abraham Lincoln

The Witty Anecdotes that made Lincoln Famous
as America's Greatest Storyteller

With Introduction and Anecdotes
by Alexander K. McClure

WAKING LION PRESS

ISBN 978-1-4341-0365-9

Published by Waking Lion Press, Salt Lake City, Utah.

www.wakinglionpress.com

editor@wakinglionpress.com

Contents

Contents

Preface

Dean Swift said that the man who makes two blades of grass grow where one grew before serves well of his kind. Considering how much grass there is in the world and comparatively how little fun, we think that a still more deserving person is the man who makes many laughs grow where none grew before.

Sometimes it happens that the biggest crop of laugh is produced by a man who ranks among the greatest and wisest. Such a man was Abraham Lincoln whose wholesome fun mixed with true philosophy made thousands laugh and think at the same time. He was a firm believer in the saying, "Laugh and the world laughs with you."

Whenever Abraham Lincoln wanted to make a strong point he usually began by saying, "Now, that reminds me of a story." And when he had told a story everyone saw the point and was put into a good humor.

The ancients had Aesop and his fables. The moderns had Abraham Lincoln and his stories.

Aesop's Fables have been printed in book form in almost every language and millions have read them with pleasure and profit. Lincoln's stories were scattered in the recollections of thousands of people in various parts of the country. The historians who wrote histories of Lincoln's life remembered only a few of them, but the most of Lincoln's stories and the best of them remained unwritten. More than five years ago the author of this book conceived the idea of collecting all the yarns and stories, the droll sayings, and witty and humorous anecdotes of Abraham Lincoln into one large book, and this volume is the result of that idea.

Before Lincoln was ever heard of as a lawyer or politician, he was famous as a story teller. As a politician, he always had a story to fit the other side; as a lawyer, he won many cases by telling the jury a story which showed them the justice of his side better than any argument could have done.

While nearly all of Lincoln's stories have a humorous side, they also contain a moral, which every good story should have.

They contain lessons that could be taught so well in no other way. Every one of them is a sermon. Lincoln, like the Man of Galilee, spoke to the people in parables.

Nothing that can be written about Lincoln can show his character in such a true light as the yarns and stories he was so fond of telling, and at which he would laugh as heartily as anyone.

For a man whose life was so full of great responsibilities, Lincoln had many hours of laughter when the humorous, fun-loving side of his great nature asserted itself.

Every person to keep healthy ought to have one good hearty laugh every day. Lincoln did, and the author hopes that the stories at which he laughed will continue to furnish laughter to all who appreciate good humor, with a moral point and spiced with that true philosophy bred in those who live close to nature and to the people around them.

The parables, yarns, stories, anecdotes and sayings of the "Immortal Abe" deserve a place beside Aesop's Fables, Bunyan's Pilgrim's Progress and all other books that have added to the happiness and wisdom of mankind.

Lincoln's stories are like Lincoln himself. The more we know of them the better we like them.

While Lincoln would have been great among the greatest of the land as a statesman and politician if like Washington, Jefferson and Jackson, he had never told a humorous story, his sense of humor was the most fascinating feature of his personal qualities.

He was the most exquisite humorist I have ever known in my life. His humor was always spontaneous, and that gave it a zest and elegance that the professional humorist never attains.

As a rule, the men who have become conspicuous in the country as humorists have excelled in nothing else. S. S. Cox, Proctor Knott, John P. Hale and others were humorists in Congress. When they arose to speak if they failed to be humorous they utterly failed, and they rarely strove to be anything but humorous. Such men often fail, for the professional humorist, however gifted, cannot always be at his best, and when not at his best he is grievously disappointing.

I remember Corwin, of Ohio, who was a great statesman as well as a great humorist, but whose humor predominated in his public speeches in Senate and House, warning a number of the younger Senators and Representatives on a social occasion when he had returned to Congress in his old age, against seeking to acquire the reputation of humorists. He said it was the mistake of his life. He loved it as did his hearers, but the temptation to be humorous was always uppermost, and while his speech on the Mexican War was the greatest ever delivered in the Senate, excepting Webster's reply to Hayne, he regretted that he was more known as a humorist than as a statesman.

His first great achievement in the House was delivered in 1840 in reply to General Crary, of Michigan, who had attacked General Harrison's military career. Corwin's reply in defense of Harrison is universally accepted as the most brilliant combination of humor and invective ever delivered in that body. The venerable John Quincy Adams a day or two after Corwin's speech, referred to Crary as "the late General Crary," and the justice of the remark from the "Old Man Eloquent" was accepted by all. Mr. Lincoln differed from the celebrated humorists of the country in the important fact that his humor was unstudied. He was not in any sense a professional humorist, but I have never in all my intercourse with public men, known one who was so apt in humorous illustration us Mr. Lincoln, and I have known him many times to silence controversy by a humorous story with pointed application to the issue.

His face was the saddest in repose that I have ever seen among accomplished and intellectual men, and his sympathies for the people, for the untold thousands who were suffering bereavement from the war, often made him speak with his heart upon his sleeve, about the sorrows which shadowed the homes of the land and for which his heart was freely bleeding.

I have many times seen him discussing in the most serious and heartfelt manner the sorrows and bereavements of the country, and when it would seem as though the tension was so strained that the brittle cord of life must break, his face would suddenly brighten like the sun escaping from behind the cloud to throw its effulgence upon the earth, and he would tell an appropriate story, and much as his stories were enjoyed by his hearers none enjoyed them more than Mr. Lincoln himself.

I have often known him within the space of a few minutes to be transformed from the saddest face I have ever looked upon to one of the brightest and most mirthful. It was well known that he had his great fountain of humor as a safety valve; as an escape and entire relief from the fearful exactions his endless duties put upon him. In the gravest consultations of the cabinet where he was usually a listener rather than a speaker, he would often end dispute by telling a story and none misunderstood it; and often when he was pressed to give expression on particular subjects, and his always abundant caution was baffled, he many times ended the interview by a story that needed no elaboration.

I recall an interview with Mr. Lincoln at the White House in the spring of 1865, just before Lee retreated from Petersburg. It was well understood that the military power of the Confederacy was broken, and that the question of reconstruction would soon be upon us.

Colonel Forney and I had called upon the President simply to pay our respects, and while pleasantly chatting with him General Benjamin F. Butler entered. Forney was a great enthusiast, and had intense hatred of the Southern leaders who had hindered his advancement when Buchanan was elected President, and he was bubbling over with resentment against them. He introduced the subject to the President of the treatment to be awarded to the leaders of the rebellion when its powers should be confessedly broken, and he was earnest in demanding that Davis and other conspicuous leaders of the Confederacy should be tried, condemned and executed as traitors.

General Butler joined Colonel Forney in demanding that treason must be made odious by the execution of those who had wantonly plunged the country into civil war. Lincoln heard them patiently, as he usually heard all, and none could tell, however carefully they scanned his countenance what impression the appeal made upon him.

I said to General Butler that, as a lawyer pre-eminent in his profession, he must know that the leaders of a government that had beleaguered our capital for four years, and was openly recognized as a belligerent power not only by our government but by all the leading governments of the world, could not be held to answer to the law for the crime of treason.

Butler was vehement in declaring that the rebellious leaders must be tried and executed. Lincoln listened to the discussion for half an hour or more and finally ended it by telling the story of a common drunkard out in Illinois who had been induced by his friends time and again to join the temperance society, but had always broken away. He was finally gathered up again and given notice that if he violated his pledge once more they would abandon him as an utterly hopeless vagrant. He made an earnest struggle to maintain his promise, and finally he called for lemonade and said to the man who was preparing it: "Couldn't you put just a drop of the cratur in unbeknownst to me?"

After telling the story Lincoln simply added: "If these men could get away from the country unbeknownst to us, it might save a world of trouble." All understood precisely what Lincoln meant, although he had given expression in the most cautious manner possible and the controversy was ended.

Lincoln differed from professional humorists in the fact that he never knew when he was going to be humorous. It bubbled up on the most unexpected occasions, and often unsettled the most carefully studied arguments. I have many times been with him when he gave no sign of humor, and those who saw him under such conditions would naturally suppose that he was incapable of a humorous expression. At other times he would effervesce with humor and always of the most exquisite and impressive nature. His humor was never strained; his stories never stale, and even if old, the application he made of them gave them the freshness of originality.

I recall sitting beside him in the White House one day when a message was brought to him telling of the capture of several brigadier-generals and a number of horses somewhere out in Virginia. He read the dispatch and then in an apparently soliloquizing mood, said: "Sorry for the horses; I can make brigadier-generals."

There are many who believe that Mr. Lincoln loved to tell obscene or profane stories, but they do great injustice to one of the purest and best men I have ever known. His humor must be judged by the environment that aided in its creation.

As a prominent lawyer who traveled the circuit in Illinois, he was much in the company of his fellow lawyers, who spent their evenings in the rude taverns of what was then almost frontier life. The Western people thus thrown together with but limited sources of culture and enjoyment, logically cultivated the story teller, and Lincoln proved to be the most accomplished in that line of all the members of the Illinois bar. They had no private rooms for study, and the evenings were always spent in the common barroom of the tavern, where Western wit, often vulgar or profane, was freely indulged in, and the best of them at times told stories which were somewhat "broad"; but even while thus indulging in humor that would grate harshly upon severely refined hearers, they despised the vulgarian; none despised vulgarity more than Lincoln.

I have heard him tell at one time or another almost or quite all of the stories he told during his Presidential term, and there were very few of them which might not have been repeated in a parlor and none descended to obscene, vulgar or profane expressions. I have never known a man of purer instincts than Abraham Lincoln, and his appreciation of all that was beautiful and good was of the highest order.

It was fortunate for Mr. Lincoln that he frequently sought relief from the fearfully oppressive duties which bore so heavily upon him. He had immediately about him a circle of men with whom he could be "at home" in the White House any evening as he was with his old time friends on the Illinois circuit.

David Davis was one upon whom he most relied as an adviser, and Leonard Swett was probably one of his closest friends, while Ward Lamon, whom he made Marshal of the District of Columbia to have him by his side, was one with whom he felt entirely "at home." Davis was of a more sober order but loved Lincoln's humor, although utterly incapable of a humorous expression himself. Swett was ready with Lincoln to give and take in storyland, as was Lamon, and either of them, and sometimes all of them, often dropped in upon Lincoln and gave him an hour's diversion from his exacting cares. They knew that he needed it and they sought him for the purpose of diverting him from what they feared was an excessive strain.

His devotion to Lamon was beautiful. I well remember at Harrisburg on the night of February 22, 1861, when at a dinner given by Governor Curtin to Mr. Lincoln, then on his way to Washington, we decided, against the protest of Lincoln, that he must change his route to Washington and make the memorable midnight journey to the capital. It was thought to be best that but one man should accompany him, and he was asked to choose. There were present of his suite Colonel Sumner, afterwards one of the heroic generals of the war, Norman B. Judd, who was chairman of the Republican State Committee of Illinois, Colonel Lamon and others, and he promptly chose Colonel Lamon, who alone accompanied him on his journey from Harrisburg to Philadelphia and thence to Washington.

Before leaving the room Governor Curtin asked Colonel Lamon whether he was armed, and he answered by exhibiting a brace of fine pistols, a huge bowie knife, a black jack, and a pair of brass knuckles. Curtin answered: "You'll do," and they were started on their journey after all the telegraph wires had been cut. We awaited through what seemed almost an endless night, until the east was purpled with the coming of another day, when Colonel Scott, who had managed the whole scheme, reunited the wires and soon received from Colonel Lamon this dispatch: "Plums delivered nuts safely," which gave us the intensely gratifying information that Lincoln had arrived in Washington.

Of all the Presidents of the United States, and indeed of all the great statesmen who have made their indelible impress upon the policy of the Republic, Abraham Lincoln stands out single and alone in his individual qualities. He had little experience in statesmanship when he was called to the Presidency. He had only a few years of service in the State Legislature of Illinois, and a single term in Congress ending twelve years before he became President, but he had to grapple with the gravest problems ever presented to the statesmanship of the nation for solution, and he met each and all of them in turn with the most consistent mastery, and settled them so successfully that all have stood unquestioned until the present time, and are certain to endure while the Republic lives.

In this he surprised not only his own cabinet and the leaders of his party who had little confidence in him when he first became President, but equally surprised the country and the world.

He was patient, tireless and usually silent when great conflicts raged about him to solve the appalling problems which were presented at various stages of the war for determination, and when he reached his conclusion he was inexorable. The wrangles of faction and the jostling of ambition were compelled to bow when Lincoln had determined upon his line of duty.

He was much more than a statesman; he was one of the most sagacious politicians I have ever known, although he was entirely unschooled in the machinery by which political results are achieved. His judgment of men was next to unerring, and when results were to be attained he knew the men who should be assigned to the task, and he rarely made a mistake.

I remember one occasion when he summoned Colonel Forney and myself to confer on some political problem, he opened the conversation by saying: "You know that I never was much of a conniver; I don't know the methods of political management, and I can only trust to the wisdom of leaders to accomplish what is needed."

Lincoln's public acts are familiar to every schoolboy of the nation, but his personal attributes, which are so strangely distinguished from the attributes of other great men, are now the most interesting study of young and old throughout our land, and I can conceive of no more acceptable presentation to the public than a compilation of anecdotes and incidents pertaining to the life of the greatest of all our Presidents.

Lincoln and McClure

Colonel Alexander K. McClure, the editorial director of the Philadelphia Times, which he founded in 1875, began his forceful career as a tanner's apprentice in the mountains of Pennsylvania threescore years ago. He tanned hides all day, and read exchanges nights in the neighboring weekly newspaper office. The learned tanner's boy also became the aptest Inner in the county, and the editor testified his admiration for young McClure's attainments by sending him to edit a new weekly paper which the exigencies of politics called into being in an adjoining county.

The lad was over six feet high, had the thews of Ajax and the voice of Boanerges, and knew enough about shoe-leather not to be afraid of any man that stood in it. He made his paper a success, went into politics, and made that a success, studied law with William McLellan, and made that a success, and actually went into the army—and made that a success, by an interesting accident which brought him into close personal relations with Abraham Lincoln, whom he had helped to nominate, serving as chairman of the Republican State Committee of Pennsylvania through the campaign.

In 1862 the government needed troops badly, and in each Pennsylvania county Republicans and Democrats were appointed to assist in the enrollment, under the State laws. McClure, working day and night at Harrisburg, saw conscripts coming in at the rate of a thousand a day, only to fret in idleness against the army red-tape which held them there instead of sending a regiment a day to the front, as McClure demanded should be done. The military officer continued to dispatch two companies a day—leaving the mass of the conscripts to be fed by the contractors.

McClure went to Washington and said to the President, "You must send a mustering officer to Harrisburg who will do as I say; I can't stay there any longer under existing conditions."

Lincoln sent into another room for Adjutant-General Thomas. "General," said he, "what is the highest rank of military officer at Harrisburg?" "Captain, sir," said Thomas. "Bring me a commission for an Assistant Adjutant-General of the United States Army," said Lincoln.

So Adjutant-General McClure was mustered in, and after that a regiment a day of boys in blue left Harrisburg for the front. Colonel McClure is one of the group of great Celt-American editors, which included Medill, McCullagh and McLean. (From Harper's Weekly, April 13, 1901.)

Chapter 1

"Abe" Lincoln's Yarns and Stories

"I Don't Want to Live"

Lincoln was, naturally enough, much surprised one day, when a man of rather forbidding countenance drew a revolver and thrust the weapon almost into his face. In such circumstances "Abe" at once concluded that any attempt at debate or argument was a waste of time and words.

"What seems to be the matter?" inquired Lincoln with all the calmness and self-possession he could muster.

"Well," replied the stranger, who did not appear at all excited, "some years ago I swore an oath that if I ever came across an uglier man than myself I'd shoot him on the spot."

A feeling of relief evidently took possession of Lincoln at this rejoinder, as the expression upon his countenance lost all suggestion of anxiety.

"Shoot me," he said to the stranger; "for if I am an uglier man than you I don't want to live."

Time Lost Didn't Count

Thurlow Weed, the veteran journalist and politician, once related how, when he was opposing the claims of Montgomery Blair, who aspired to a Cabinet appointment, that Mr. Lincoln inquired of Mr. Weed whom he would recommend. "Henry Winter Davis," was the response.

"David Davis, I see, has been posting you up on this question," retorted Lincoln. "He has Davis on the brain. I think Maryland must be a good State to move from."

The President then told a story of a witness in court in a neighboring county, who, on being asked his age, replied, "Sixty." Being satisfied he was much older the question was repeated, and on receiving the same answer the court admonished the witness, saying, "The court knows you to be much older than sixty."

"Oh, I understand now," was the rejoinder, "you're thinking of those ten years I spent on the eastern share of Maryland; that was so much time lost, and didn't count."

Blair was made Postmaster-General.

No Vices, No Virtues

Lincoln always took great pleasure in relating this yarn:

Riding at one time in a stage with an old Kentuckian who was returning from Missouri, Lincoln excited the old gentleman's surprise by refusing to accept either of tobacco or French brandy.

When they separated that afternoon—the Kentuckian to take another stage bound for Louisville—he shook hands warmly with Lincoln, and said, good-humoredly:

"See here, stranger, you're a clever but strange companion. I may never see you again, and I don't want to offend you, but I want to say this: My experience has taught me that a man who has no vices has d——d few virtues. Good-day."

Lincoln's Dues

Miss Todd (afterwards Mrs. Lincoln) had a keen sense of the ridiculous, and wrote several articles in the Springfield (Ill.) "Journal" reflecting severely upon General James Shields (who won fame in the Mexican and Civil Wars, and was United States Senator from three states), then Auditor of State.

Lincoln assumed the authorship, and was challenged by Shields to meet him on the "field of honor." Meanwhile Miss Todd increased Shields' ire by writing another letter to the paper, in which she said: "I hear the way of these fire-eaters is to give the challenged party the choice of weapons, which being the case, I'll tell you in confidence that I never fight with anything but broom-sticks, or hot water, or a shovelful of coals, the former of which, being somewhat like a shillalah, may not be objectionable to him."

Lincoln accepted the challenge, and selected broadswords as the weapons. Judge Herndon (Lincoln's law partner) gives the closing of this affair as follows:

"The laws of Illinois prohibited dueling, and Lincoln demanded that the meeting should be outside the state. Shields undoubtedly knew that Lincoln was opposed to fighting a duel—that his moral sense would revolt at the thought, and that he would not be likely to break the law by fighting in the state. Possibly he thought Lincoln would make a humble apology. Shields was brave, but foolish, and would not listen to overtures for explanation. It was arranged that the meeting should be in Missouri, opposite Alton. They proceeded to the place selected, but friends interfered, and there was no duel. There is little doubt that the man who had swung a beetle and driven iron wedges into gnarled hickory logs could have cleft the skull of his antagonist, but he had no such intention. He repeatedly said to the friends of Shields that in writing the first article he had no thought of anything personal. The Auditor's vanity had been sorely wounded by the second letter, in regard to which Lincoln could not make any explanation except that he had had no hand in writing it. The affair set all Springfield to laughing at Shields."

"Done with the Bible"

Lincoln sometimes told this story:

A country meeting-house, that was used once a month, was quite a distance from any other house.

The preacher, an old-line Baptist, was dressed in coarse linen pantaloons, and shirt of the same material. The pants, manufactured after the old fashion, with baggy legs, and a flap in the front, were made to attach to his frame without the aid of suspenders.

A single button held his shirt in position, and that was at the collar. He rose up in the pulpit, and with a loud voice announced his text thus: "I am the Christ whom I shall represent to-day."

About this time a little blue lizard ran up his roomy pantaloons. The old preacher, not wishing to interrupt the steady flow of his sermon, slapped away on his leg, expecting to arrest the intruder, but his efforts were unavailing, and the little fellow kept on ascending higher and higher.

Continuing the sermon, the preacher loosened the central button which graced the waistband of his pantaloons, and with a kick off came that easy-fitting garment.

But, meanwhile, Mr. Lizard had passed the equatorial line of the waistband, and was calmly exploring that part of the preacher's anatomy which lay underneath the back of his shirt.

Things were now growing interesting, but the sermon was still grinding on. The next movement on the preacher's part was for the collar button, and with one sweep of his arm off came the tow linen shirt.

The congregation sat for an instant as if dazed; at length one old lady in the rear part of the room rose up, and, glancing at the excited object in the pulpit, shouted at the top of her voice: "If you represent Christ, then I'm done with the Bible."

His Knowledge of Human Nature

Once, when Lincoln was pleading a case, the opposing lawyer had all the advantage of the law; the weather was warm, and his opponent, as was admissible in frontier courts, pulled off his coat and vest as he grew warm in the argument.

At that time, shirts with buttons behind were unusual. Lincoln took in the situation at once. Knowing the prejudices of the primitive people against pretension of all sorts, or any affectation of superior social rank, arising, he said: "Gentlemen of the jury, having justice on my side, I don't think you will be at all influenced by the gentleman's pretended knowledge of the law, when you see he does not even know which side of his shirt should be in front." There was a general laugh, and Lincoln's case was won.

A Mischievous Ox

President Lincoln once told the following story of Colonel W., who had been elected to the Legislature, and had also been judge of the County Court. His elevation, however, had made him somewhat pompous, and he became very fond of using big words. On his farm he had a very large and mischievous ox, called "Big Brindle," which very frequently broke down his neighbors' fences, and committed other depredations, much to the Colonel's annoyance.

One morning after breakfast, in the presence of Lincoln, who had stayed with him over night, and who was on his way to town, he called his overseer and said to him:

"Mr. Allen, I desire you to impound 'Big Brindle,' in order that I may hear no animadversions on his eternal depredations."

Allen bowed and walked off, sorely puzzled to know what the Colonel wanted him to do. After Colonel W. left for town, he went to his wife and asked her what the Colonel meant by telling him to impound the ox.

"Why, he meant to tell you to put him in a pen," said she.

Allen left to perform the feat, for it was no inconsiderable one, as the animal was wild and vicious, but, after a great deal of trouble and vexation, succeeded.

"Well," said he, wiping the perspiration from his brow and soliloquizing, "this is impounding, is it? Now, I am dead sure that the Colonel will ask me if I impounded 'Big Brindle,' and I'll bet I puzzle him as he did me."

The next day the Colonel gave a dinner party, and as he was not aristocratic, Allen, the overseer, sat down with the company. After the second or third glass was discussed, the Colonel turned to the overseer and said:

"Eh, Mr. Allen, did you impound 'Big Brindle,' sir?"

Allen straightened himself, and looking around at the company, replied:

"Yes, I did, sir; but 'Old Brindle' transcended the impanel of the impound, and scatterlophisticated all over the equanimity of the forest."

The company burst into an immoderate fit of laughter, while the Colonel's face reddened with discomfiture.

"What do you mean by that, sir?" demanded the Colonel.

"Why, I mean, Colonel," replied Allen, "that 'Old Brindle,' being prognosticated with an idea of the cholera, ripped and teared, snorted and pawed dirt, jumped the fence, tuck to the woods, and would not be impounded nohow."

This was too much; the company roared again, the Colonel being forced to join in the laughter, and in the midst of the jollity Allen left the table, saying to himself as he went, "I reckon the Colonel won't ask me to impound any more oxen."

The Presidential "Chin-Fly"

Some of Mr. Lincoln's intimate friends once called his attention to a certain member of his Cabinet who was quietly working to secure a nomination for the Presidency, although knowing that Mr. Lincoln was to be a candidate for re-election. His friends insisted that the

Cabinet officer ought to be made to give up his Presidential aspirations or be removed from office. The situation reminded Mr. Lincoln of a story:

"My brother and I," he said, "were once plowing corn, I driving the horse and he holding the plow. The horse was lazy, but on one occasion he rushed across the field so that I, with my long legs, could scarcely keep pace with him. On reaching the end of the furrow, I found an enormous chin-fly fastened upon him, and knocked him off. My brother asked me what I did that for. I told him I didn't want the old horse bitten in that way. 'Why,' said my brother, 'that's all that made him go.' Now," said Mr. Lincoln, "if Mr. —— has a Presidential chin-fly biting him, I'm not going to knock him off, if it will only make his department go."

'Squire Bagly's Precedent

Mr. T. W. S. Kidd, of Springfield, says that he once heard a lawyer opposed to Lincoln trying to convince a jury that precedent was superior to law, and that custom made things legal in all cases. When Lincoln arose to answer him he told the jury he would argue his case in the same way.

"Old 'Squire Bagly, from Menard, came into my office and said, 'Lincoln, I want your advice as a lawyer. Has a man what's been elected justice of the peace a right to issue a marriage license?' I told him he had not; when the old 'squire threw himself back in his chair very indignantly, and said, 'Lincoln, I thought you was a lawyer. Now Bob Thomas and me had a bet on this thing, and we agreed to let you decide; but if this is your opinion I don't want it, for I know a thundcrin' sight better, for I have been 'squire now for eight years and have done it all the time.'"

He'd Need His Gun

When the President, early in the War, was anxious about the defenses of Washington, he told a story illustrating his feelings in the case. General Scott, then Commander-in-Chief of the United States Army, had but 1,500 men, two guns and an old sloop of war, the latter anchored in the Potomac, with which to protect the National Capital, and the President was uneasy.

To one of his queries as to the safety of Washington, General Scott had replied, "It has been ordained, Mr. President, that the city shall not be captured by the Confederates."

"But we ought to have more men and guns here," was the Chief Executive's answer. "The Confederates are not such fools as to let a good chance to capture Washington go by, and even if it has been ordained that the city is safe, I'd feel easier if it were better protected. All this reminds me of the old trapper out in the West who had been assured by some 'city folks' who had hired him as a guide that all matters regarding life and death were prearranged.

"'It is ordained,' said one of the party to the old trapper, 'that you are to die at a certain time, and no one can kill you before that time. If you met a thousand Indians, and your death had not been ordained for that day, you would certainly escape.'

"'I don't exactly understand this "ordained" business,' was the trapper's reply. 'I don't care to run no risks. I always have my gun with me, so that if I come across some reds I can feel sure that I won't cross the Jordan 'thout taking some of 'em with me. Now, for instance, if I met an Indian in the woods; he drew a bead on me—sayin,' too, that he wasn't more'n ten feet away—an' I didn't have nothing to protect myself; say it was as bad as that, the redskin bein' dead ready to kill me; now, even if it had been ordained that the Indian (sayin' he was a good shot), was to die that very minute, an' I wasn't, what would I do 'thout my gun?'

"There you are," the President remarked; "even if it has been ordained that the city of Washington will never be taken by the Southerners, what would we do in case they made an attack upon the place, without men and heavy guns?"

Kept Up the Argument

Judge T. Lyle Dickey of Illinois related that when the excitement over the Kansas Nebraska bill first broke out, he was with Lincoln and several friends attending court. One evening several persons, including himself and Lincoln, were discussing the slavery question. Judge Dickey contended that slavery was an institution which the Constitution recognized, and which could not be disturbed. Lincoln argued that ultimately slavery must become extinct. "After awhile," said Judge Dickey, "we went upstairs to bed. There were two beds in our room, and I remember that Lincoln sat up in his night shirt on the edge of the bed arguing the point with me. At last we went to sleep. Early in the morning I woke up and there was Lincoln half sitting up in bed. 'Dickey,' said he, 'I tell you this nation cannot exist half slave and half free.' 'Oh, Lincoln,' said I, 'go to sleep.'"

Equine Ingratitude

President Lincoln, while eager that the United States troops should be supplied with the most modern and serviceable weapons, often took occasion to put his foot down upon the mania for experimenting with which some of his generals were afflicted. While engaged in these experiments much valuable time was wasted, the enemy was left to do as he thought best, no battles were fought, and opportunities for winning victories allowed to pass.

The President was an exceedingly practical man, and when an invention, idea or discovery was submitted to him, his first step was to ascertain how any or all of them could be applied in a way to be of benefit to the army. As to experimenting with "contrivances" which, to his mind, could never be put to practical use, he had little patience.

"Some of these generals," said he, "experiment so long and so much with newfangled, fancy notions that when they are finally brought to a head they are useless. Either the time to use them has gone by, or the machine, when put in operation, kills more than it cures.

"One of these generals, who has a scheme for 'condensing' rations, is willing to swear his life away that his idea, when carried to perfection, will reduce the cost of feeding the Union troops to almost nothing, while the soldiers themselves will get so fat that they'll 'bust out' of their uniforms. Of course, uniforms cost nothing, and real fat men are more active and vigorous than lean, skinny ones, but that is getting away from my story.

"There was once an Irishman—a cabman—who had a notion that he could induce his horse to live entirely on shavings. The latter he could get for nothing, while corn and oats were pretty high-priced. So he daily lessened the amount of food to the horse, substituting shavings for the corn and oats abstracted, so that the horse wouldn't know his rations were being cut down.

"However, just as he had achieved success in his experiment, and the horse had been taught to live without other food than shavings, the ungrateful animal 'up and died,' and he had to buy another.

"So far as this general referred to is concerned, I'm afraid the soldiers will all be dead at the time when his experiment is demonstrated as thoroughly successful."

'Twas "Moving Day"

Speed, who was a prosperous young merchant of Springfield, reports that Lincoln's personal effects consisted of a pair of saddle-bags, containing two or three lawbooks, and a few pieces of clothing. Riding on a borrowed horse, he thus made his appearance in Springfield. When he discovered that a single bedstead would cost seventeen dollars he said, "It is probably cheap enough, but I have not enough money to pay for it." When Speed offered to trust him, he said: "If I fail here as a lawyer, I will probably never pay you at all." Then Speed offered to share his large double bed with him.

"Where is your room?" Lincoln asked.

"Upstairs," said Speed, pointing from the store leading to his room.

Without saying a word, he took his saddle-bags on his arm, went upstairs, set them down on the floor, came down again, and with a face beaming with pleasure and smiles, exclaimed: "Well, Speed, I'm moved."

"Abe's" Hair Needed Combing

"By the way," remarked President Lincoln one day to Colonel Cannon, a close personal friend, "I can tell you a good story about my hair. When I was nominated at Chicago, an enterprising fellow thought that a great many people would like to see how 'Abe' Lincoln looked, and, as I had not long before sat for a photograph, the fellow, having seen it, rushed over and bought the negative.

"He at once got no end of wood-cuts, and so active was their circulation they were soon selling in all parts of the country.

"Soon after they reached Springfield, I heard a boy crying them for sale on the streets. 'Here's your likeness of "Abe" Lincoln!' he shouted. 'Buy one; price only two shillings! Will look a great deal better when he gets his hair combed!'"

Would "Take to the Woods"

Secretary of State Seward was bothered considerably regarding the complication into which Spain had involved the United States government in connection with San Domingo, and related his troubles to the President. Negotiations were not proceeding satisfactorily, and things were mixed generally. We wished to conciliate Spain, while the negroes had appealed against Spanish oppression.

The President did not, to all appearances, look at the matter seriously, but, instead of treating the situation as a grave one, remarked that Seward's dilemma reminded him of an interview between two negroes in Tennessee.

One was a preacher, who, with the crude and strange notions of his ignorant race, was endeavoring to admonish and enlighten his brother African of the importance of religion and the danger of the future.

"Dar are," said Josh, the preacher, "two roads befo' you, Joe; be ca'ful which ob dese you take. Narrow am de way dat leads straight to destruction; but broad am de way dat leads right to damnation."

Joe opened his eyes with affright, and under the spell of the awful danger before him, exclaimed, "Josh, take which road you please; I shall go troo de woods."

"I am not willing," concluded the President, "to assume any new troubles or responsibilities at this time, and shall therefore avoid going to the one place with Spain, or with the negro to the other, but shall 'take to the woods.' We will maintain an honest and strict neutrality."

Lincoln Carried Her Trunk

"My first strong impression of Mr. Lincoln," says a lady of Springfield, "was made by one of his kind deeds. I was going with a little friend for my first trip alone on the railroad cars. It was an epoch of my life. I had planned for it and dreamed of it for weeks. The day I was to go came, but as the hour of the train approached, the hackman, through some neglect, failed to call for my trunk. As the minutes went on, I realized, in a panic of grief, that I should miss the train. I was standing by the gate, my hat and gloves on, sobbing as if my heart would break, when Mr. Lincoln came by.

"'Why, what's the matter?' he asked, and I poured out all my story.

"'How big's the trunk? There's still time, if it isn't too big.' And he pushed through the gate and up to the door. My mother and I took him up to my room, where my little old-fashioned trunk stood, locked and tied. 'Oh, ho,' he cried, 'wipe your eyes and come on quick.' And before I knew what he was going to do, he had shouldered the trunk, was down stairs, and striding out of the yard. Down the street he went fast as his long legs could carry him, I trotting behind, drying my tears as I went. We reached the station in time. Mr. Lincoln put me on the train, kissed me good-bye, and told me to have a good time. It was just like him."

Boat Had to Stop

Lincoln never failed to take part in all political campaigns in Illinois, as his reputation as a speaker caused his services to be in great demand. As was natural, he was often the target at which many of the "Smart Alecks" of that period shot their feeble bolts, but Lincoln was so ready with his answers that few of them cared to engage him a second time.

In one campaign Lincoln was frequently annoyed by a young man who entertained the idea that he was a born orator. He had a loud voice, was full of language, and so conceited that he could not understand why the people did not recognize and appreciate his abilities.

This callow politician delighted in interrupting public speakers, and at last Lincoln determined to squelch him. One night while addressing a large meeting at Springfield, the fellow became so offensive that "Abe" dropped the threads of his speech and turned his attention to the tormentor.

"I don't object," said Lincoln, "to being interrupted with sensible questions, but I must say that my boisterous friend does not always make inquiries which properly come under that head. He says he is afflicted with headaches, at which I don't wonder, as it is a well-known fact that nature abhors a vacuum, and takes her own way of demonstrating it.

"This noisy friend reminds me of a certain steamboat that used to run on the Illinois river. It was an energetic boat, was always busy. When they built it, however, they made one serious mistake, this error being in the relative sizes of the boiler and the whistle. The latter was usually busy, too, and people were aware that it was in existence.

"This particular boiler to which I have reference was a six-foot one, and did all that was required of it in the way of pushing the boat along; but as the builders of the vessel had made the whistle a six-foot one, the consequence was that every time the whistle blew the boat had to stop."

McClellan's "Special Talent"

President Lincoln one day remarked to a number of personal friends who had called upon him at the White House:

"General McClellan's tardiness and unwillingness to fight the enemy or follow up advantages gained, reminds me of a man back in Illinois who knew a few law phrases but whose lawyer lacked aggressiveness. The man finally lost all patience and springing to his feet vociferated, 'Why don't you go at him with a fi. fa., a demurrer, a capias, a surrebutter, or a ne exeat, or something; or a nundam pactum or a non est?'

"I wish McClellan would go at the enemy with something—I don't care what. General McClellan is a pleasant and scholarly gentleman. He is an admirable engineer, but he seems to have a special talent for a stationary engine."

How "Jake" Got Away

One of the last, if not the very last story told by President Lincoln, was to one of his Cabinet who came to see him, to ask if it would be proper to permit "Jake" Thompson to slip through Maine in disguise and embark for Portland.

The President, as usual, was disposed to be merciful, and to permit the arch-rebel to pass unmolested, but Secretary Stanton urged that he should be arrested as a traitor.

"By permitting him to escape the penalties of treason," persisted the War Secretary, "you sanction it."

"Well," replied Mr. Lincoln, "let me tell you a story. There was an Irish soldier here last summer, who wanted something to drink stronger than water, and stopped at a drug-shop, where he espied a soda-fountain. 'Mr. Doctor,' said he, 'give me, plase, a glass of soda-wather, an' if yez can put in a few drops of whiskey unbeknown to any one, I'll be obleeged.' Now," continued Mr. Lincoln, "if 'Jake' Thompson is permitted to go through Maine unbeknown to any one, what's the harm? So don't have him arrested."

More Light and Less Noise

The President was bothered to death by those persons who bois-terously demanded that the War be pushed vigorously; also, those who shouted their advice and opinions into his weary ears, but who never suggested anything practical. These fellows were not in the army, nor did they ever take any interest, in a personal way, in mili-tary matters, except when engaged in dodging drafts.

"That reminds me," remarked Mr. Lincoln one day, "of a farmer who lost his way on the Western frontier. Night came on, and the embarrassments of his position were increased by a furious tempest which suddenly burst upon him. To add to his discomfort, his horse had given out, leaving him exposed to all the dangers of the pitiless storm.

"The peals of thunder were terrific, the frequent flashes of light-ning affording the only guide on the road as he resolutely trudged onward, leading his jaded steed. The earth seemed fairly to tremble beneath him in the war of elements. One bolt threw him suddenly upon his knees.

"Our traveler was not a prayerful man, but finding himself invol-untarily brought to an attitude of devotion, he addressed himself to the Throne of Grace in the following prayer for his deliverance:

"'O God! hear my prayer this time, for Thou knowest it is not often that I call upon Thee. And, O Lord! if it is all the same to Thee, give us a little more light and a little less noise.'

"I wish," the President said, sadly, "there was a stronger dispo-sition manifested on the part of our civilian warriors to unite in suppressing the rebellion, and a little less noise as to how and by whom the chief executive office shall be administered."

One Bullet and a Hatful

Lincoln made the best of everything, and if he couldn't get what he wanted he took what he could get. In matters of policy, while President he acted according to this rule. He would take perilous chances, even when the result was, to the minds of his friends, not worth the risk he had run.

One day at a meeting of the Cabinet, it being at the time when it seemed as though war with England and France could not be avoided, Secretary of State Seward and Secretary of War Stanton warmly advocated that the United States maintain an attitude, the result of which would have been a declaration of hostilities by the European Powers mentioned.

"Why take any more chances than are absolutely necessary?" asked the President.

"We must maintain our honor at any cost," insisted Secretary Seward.

"We would be branded as cowards before the entire world," Secretary Stanton said.

"But why run the greater risk when we can take a smaller one?" queried the President calmly. "The less risk we run the better for us. That reminds me of a story I heard a day or two ago, the hero of which was on the firing line during a recent battle, where the bullets were flying thick.

"Finally his courage gave way entirely, and throwing down his gun, he ran for dear life.

"As he was flying along at top speed he came across an officer who drew his revolver and shouted, 'Go back to your regiment at once or I will shoot you!'

"'Shoot and be hanged,' the racer exclaimed. 'What's one bullet to a whole hatful?'"

Lincoln's Story to Peace Commissioners

Among the reminiscences of Lincoln left by Editor Henry J. Raymond, is the following:

Among the stories told by Lincoln, which is freshest in my mind, one which he related to me shortly after its occurrence, belongs to the history of the famous interview on board the River Queen, at Hampton Roads, between himself and Secretary Seward and the rebel Peace Commissioners. It was reported at the time that the President told a "little story" on that occasion, and the inquiry went around among the newspapers, "What was it?"

The New York Herald published what purported to be a version of it, but the "point" was entirely lost, and it attracted no attention. Being in Washington a few days subsequent to the interview with the Commissioners (my previous sojourn there having terminated about the first of last August), I asked Mr. Lincoln one day if it was true that he told Stephens, Hunter and Campbell a story.

"Why, yes," he replied, manifesting some surprise, "but has it leaked out? I was in hopes nothing would be said about it, lest some over-sensitive people should imagine there was a degree of levity in the intercourse between us." He then went on to relate the circumstances which called it out.

"You see," said he, "we had reached and were discussing the slavery question. Mr. Hunter said, substantially, that the slaves, always accustomed to an overseer, and to work upon compulsion, suddenly freed, as they would be if the South should consent to peace on the basis of the 'Emancipation Proclamation,' would precipitate not only themselves, but the entire Southern society, into irremediable ruin. No work would be done, nothing would be cultivated, and both blacks and whites would starve!"

Said the President: "I waited for Seward to answer that argument, but as he was silent, I at length said: 'Mr. Hunter, you ought to know a great deal better about this argument than I, for you have always lived under the slave system. I can only say, in reply to your statement of the case, that it reminds me of a man out in Illinois, by the name of Case, who undertook, a few years ago, to raise a very large herd of hogs. It was a great trouble to feed them, and how to get around this was a puzzle to him. At length he hit on the plan of planting an immense field of potatoes, and, when they were sufficiently grown, he turned the whole herd into the field, and let them have full swing, thus saving not only the labor of feeding the hogs, but also that of digging the potatoes. Charmed with his sagacity, he stood one day leaning against the fence, counting his hogs, when a neighbor came along.

"'Well, well,' said he, 'Mr. Case, this is all very fine. Your hogs are doing very well just now, but you know out here in Illinois the frost comes early, and the ground freezes for a foot deep. Then what you going to do?'

"This was a view of the matter which Mr. Case had not taken into account. Butchering time for hogs was 'way on in December or January! He scratched his head, and at length stammered: 'Well, it may come pretty hard on their snouts, but I don't see but that it will be "root, hog, or die."'"

"Abe" Got the Worst of It

When Lincoln was a young lawyer in Illinois, he and a certain Judge once got to bantering one another about trading horses; and it was agreed that the next morning at nine o'clock they should make a trade, the horses to be unseen up to that hour, and no backing out, under a forfeiture of $25. At the hour appointed, the Judge came up, leading the sorriest-looking specimen of a horse ever seen in those parts. In a few minutes Mr. Lincoln was seen approaching with a wooden saw-horse upon his shoulders.

Great were the shouts and laughter of the crowd, and both were greatly increased when Lincoln, on surveying the Judge's animal, set down his saw-horse, and exclaimed:

"Well, Judge, this is the first time I ever got the worst of it in a horse trade."

It Depended Upon His Condition

The President had made arrangements to visit New York, and was told that President Garrett, of the Baltimore and Ohio Railroad, would be glad to furnish a special train.

"I don't doubt it a bit," remarked the President, "for I know Mr. Garrett, and like him very well, and if I believed—which I don't, by any means—all the things some people say about his 'secesh' principles, he might say to you as was said by the Superintendent of a certain railroad to a son of one my predecessors in office. Some two years after the death of President Harrison, the son of his successor in this office wanted to take his father on an excursion somewhere or other, and went to the Superintendent's office to order a special train.

"This Superintendent was a Whig of the most uncompromising sort, who hated a Democrat more than all other things on the earth, and promptly refused the young man's request, his language being to the effect that this particular railroad was not running special trains for the accommodation of Presidents of the United States just at that season.

"The son of the President was much surprised and exceedingly annoyed. 'Why,' he said, 'you have run special Presidential trains, and I know it. Didn't you furnish a special train for the funeral of President Harrison?'

"'Certainly we did,' calmly replied the Superintendent, with no relaxation of his features, 'and if you will only bring your father here in the same shape as General Harrison was, you shall have the best train on the road.'"

When the laughter had subsided, the President said: "I shall take pleasure in accepting Mr. Garrett's offer, as I have no doubts whatever as to his loyalty to the United States government or his respect for the occupant of the Presidential office."

"Got Down to the Raisins"

A. B. Chandler, chief of the telegraph office at the War Department, occupied three rooms, one of which was called "the President's room," so much of his time did Mr. Lincoln spend there. Here he would read over the telegrams received for the several heads of departments. Three copies of all messages received were made— one for the President, one for the War Department records and one for Secretary Stanton.

Mr. Chandler told a story as to the manner in which the President read the despatches:

"President Lincoln's copies were kept in what we called the 'President's drawer' of the 'cipher desk.' He would come in at any time of the night or day, and go at once to this drawer, and take out a file of telegrams, and begin at the top to read them. His position in running over these telegrams was sometimes very curious.

"He had a habit of sitting frequently on the edge of his chair, with his right knee dragged down to the floor. I remember a curious expression of his when he got to the bottom of the new telegrams and began on those that he had read before. It was, 'Well, I guess I have got down to the raisins.'

"The first two or three times he said this he made no explanation, and I did not ask one. But one day, after he had made the remark, he looked up under his eyebrows at me with a funny twinkle in his eyes, and said: 'I used to know a little girl out West who sometimes was inclined to eat too much. One day she ate a good many more raisins than she ought to, and followed them up with a quantity of other goodies. They made her very sick. After a time the raisins began to come.

"She gasped and looked at her mother and said: 'Well, I will be better now I guess, for I have got down to the raisins.'"

"Honest Abe" Swallows His Enemies

"'Honest Abe' Taking Them on the Half-Shell" was one of the cartoons published in 1860 by one of the illustrated periodicals. It represents Lincoln in a "Political Oyster House," preparing to swallow two of his Democratic opponents for the Presidency—Douglas and Breckinridge. He performed the feat at the November election. The Democratic party was hopelessly split in 1860 The Northern wing nominated Stephen A. Douglas, of Illinois, as their candidate, the Southern wing naming John C. Breckinridge, of Kentucky; the Constitutional Unionists (the old American of Know-Nothing party) placed John Bell, of Tennessee, in the field, and against these was put Abraham Lincoln, who received the support of the Abolitionists.

Lincoln made short work of his antagonists when the election came around. He received a large majority in the Electoral College, while nearly every Northern State voted majorities for him at the polls. Douglas had but twelve votes in the Electoral College, while Bell had thirty-nine. The votes of the Southern States, then preparing to secede, were, for the most part, thrown for Breckinridge. The popular vote was: Lincoln, 1,857,610; Douglas, 1,365,976; Breckinridge, 847,953; Bell, 590,631; total vote, 4,662,170. In the Electoral College Lincoln received 180; Douglas, 12; Breckinridge, 72; Bell, 39; Lincoln's majority over all, 57.

Saving His Wind

Judge H. W. Beckwith of Danville, Ill., said that soon after the Ottawa debate between Lincoln and Douglas he passed the Chenery House, then the principal hotel in Springfield. The lobby was crowded with partisan leaders from various sections of the state, and Mr. Lincoln, from his greater height, was seen above the surging mass that clung about him like a swarm of bees to their ruler. The day was warm, and at the first chance he broke away and came out for a little fresh air, wiping the sweat from his face.

"As he passed the door he saw me," said Judge Beckwith, "and, taking my hand, inquired for the health and views of his 'friends over in Vermillion county.' He was assured they were wide awake, and further told that they looked forward to the debate between him and Senator Douglas with deep concern. From the shadow that went quickly over his face, the pained look that came to give way quickly to a blaze of eyes and quiver of lips, I felt that Mr. Lincoln had gone beneath my mere words and caught my inner and current fears as to the result. And then, in a forgiving, jocular way peculiar to him, he said: 'Sit down; I have a moment to spare, and will tell you a story.' Having been on his feet for some time, he sat on the end of the stone step leading into the hotel door, while I stood closely fronting him.

"'You have,' he continued, 'seen two men about to fight?'

"'Yes, many times.'

"'Well, one of them brags about what he means to do. He jumps high in the air, cracking his heels together, smites his fists, and wastes his breath trying to scare somebody. You see the other fellow, he says not a word,'—here Mr. Lincoln's voice and manner changed to great earnestness, and repeating—'you see the other man says not a word. His arms are at his sides, his fists are closely doubled up, his head is drawn to the shoulder, and his teeth are set firm together. He is saving his wind for the fight, and as sure as it comes off he will win it, or die a-trying.'"

Right for, Once, Anyhow

Where men bred in courts, accustomed to the world, or versed in diplomacy, would use some subterfuge, or would make a polite speech, or give a shrug of the shoulders, as the means of getting out of an embarrassing position, Lincoln raised a laugh by some bold west-country anecdote, and moved off in the cloud of merriment produced by the joke. When Attorney-General Bates was remonstrating apparently against the appointment of some indifferent lawyer to a place of judicial importance, the President interposed with: "Come now, Bates, he's not half as bad as you think. Besides that, I must tell you, he did me a good turn long ago. When I took to the law, I was going to court one morning, with some ten or twelve miles of bad road before me, and I had no horse.

"The judge overtook me in his carriage.

"'Hallo, Lincoln! are you not going to the court-house? Come in and I will give you a seat!'

"Well, I got in, and the Judge went on reading his papers. Presently the carriage struck a stump on one side of the road, then it hopped off to the other. I looked out, and I saw the driver was jerking from side to side in his seat, so I says:

"'Judge, I think your coachman has been taking a little too much this morning.'

"'Well, I declare, Lincoln,' said he, 'I should not much wonder if you were right, for he has nearly upset me half a dozen times since starting.'

"So, putting his head out of the window, he shouted, 'Why, you infernal scoundrel, you are drunk!'

"Upon which, pulling up his horses, and turning round with great gravity, the coachman said:

"'Begorra! that's the first rightful decision that you have given for the last twelvemonth.'"

While the company were laughing, the President beat a quiet retreat from the neighborhood.

"Pity the Poor Orphan"

After the War was well on, and several battles had been fought, a lady from Alexandria asked the President for an order to release a certain church which had been taken for a Federal hospital. The President said he could do nothing, as the post surgeon at Alexandria was immovable, and then asked the lady why she did not donate money to build a hospital.

"We have been very much embarrassed by the war," she replied, "and our estates are much hampered."

"You are not ruined?" asked the President.

"No, sir, but we do not feel that we should give up anything we have left."

The President, after some reflection, then said: "There are more battles yet to be fought, and I think God would prefer that your church be devoted to the care and alleviation of the sufferings of our poor fellows. So, madam, you will excuse me. I can do nothing for you."

Afterward, in speaking of this incident, President Lincoln said that the lady, as a representative of her class in Alexandria, reminded him of the story of the young man who had an aged father and mother owning considerable property. The young man being an only son, and believing that the old people had outlived their usefulness, assassinated them both. He was accused, tried and convicted of the murder. When the judge came to pass sentence upon him, and called upon him to give any reason he might have why the sentence of death should not be passed upon him, he with great promptness replied that he hoped the court would be lenient upon him because he was a poor orphan!

"Bap." McNabb's Booster

It is true that Lincoln did not drink, never swore, was a stranger to smoking and lived a moral life generally, but he did like horse-racing and chicken fighting. New Salem, Illinois, where Lincoln was "clerking," was known the neighborhood around as a "fast" town, and the average young man made no very desperate resistance when tempted to join in the drinking and gambling bouts.

"Bap." McNabb was famous for his ability in both the raising and the purchase of roosters of prime fighting quality, and when his birds fought the attendance was large. It was because of the "flunking" of one of "Bap.'s" roosters that Lincoln was enabled to make a point when criticising McClellan's unreadiness and lack of energy.

One night there was a fight on the schedule, one of "Bap." McNabb's birds being a contestant. "Bap." brought a little red rooster, whose fighting qualities had been well advertised for days in advance, and much interest was manifested in the outcome. As the result of these contests was generally a quarrel, in which each man, charging foul play, seized his victim, they chose Lincoln umpire, relying not only on his fairness but his ability to enforce his decisions. Judge Herndon, in his "Abraham Lincoln," says of this notable event:

"I cannot improve on the description furnished me in February, 1865, by one who was present.

"They formed a ring, and the time having arrived, Lincoln, with one hand on each hip and in a squatting position, cried, 'Ready.' Into the ring they toss their fowls, 'Bap.'s' red rooster along with the rest. But no sooner had the little beauty discovered what was to be done than he dropped his tail and ran.

"The crowd cheered, while 'Bap.,' in disappointment, picked him up and started away, losing his quarter (entrance fee) and carrying home his dishonored fowl. Once arrived at the latter place he threw his pet down with a feeling of indignation and chagrin.

"The little fellow, out of sight of all rivals, mounted a woodpile and proudly flirting out his feathers, crowed with all his might. 'Bap.' looked on in disgust.

"'Yes, you little cuss,' he exclaimed, irreverently, 'you're great on dress parade, but not worth a darn in a fight.'"

It is said, according to Judge Herndon, that Lincoln considered McClellan as "great on dress parade," but not so much in a fight.

A Low-Down Trick

When Lincoln was a candidate of the Know Nothings for the State Legislature, the party was over-confident, and the Democrats pursued a still-hunt. Lincoln was defeated. He compared the situation to one of the camp-followers of General Taylor's army, who had secured a barrel of cider, erected a tent, and commenced selling it to the thirsty soldiers at twenty-five cents a drink, but he had sold but little before another sharp one set up a tent at his back, and tapped the barrel so as to flow on his side, and peddled out No. 1 cider at five cents a drink, of course, getting the latter's entire trade on the borrowed capital.

"The Democrats," said Mr. Lincoln, "had played Knownothing on a cheaper scale than had the real devotees of Sam, and had raked down his pile with his own cider!"

End for End

Judge H. W. Beckwith, of Danville, Ill., in his "Personal Recollections of Lincoln," tells a story which is a good example of Lincoln's way of condensing the law and the facts of an issue in a story: "A man, by vile words, first provoked and then made a bodily attack upon another. The latter, in defending himself, gave the other much the worst of the encounter. The aggressor, to get even, had the one who thrashed him tried in our Circuit Court on a charge of an assault and battery. Mr. Lincoln defended, and told the jury that his client was in the fix of a man who, in going along the highway with a pitchfork on his shoulder, was attacked by a fierce dog that ran out at him from a farmer's dooryard. In parrying off the brute with the fork, its prongs stuck into the brute and killed him.

"'What made you kill my dog?' said the farmer.

"'What made him try to bite me?'

"'But why did you not go at him with the other end of the pitchfork?'

"'Why did he not come after me with his other end?'

"At this Mr. Lincoln whirled about in his long arms an imaginary dog, and pushed its tail end toward the jury. This was the defensive plea of 'son assault demesne'—loosely, that 'the other fellow brought on the fight,'—quickly told, and in a way the dullest mind would grasp and retain."

Let Six Skunks Go

The President had decided to select a new War Minister, and the Leading Republican Senators thought the occasion was opportune to change the whole seven Cabinet ministers. They, therefore, earnestly advised him to make a clean sweep, and select seven new men, and so restore the waning confidence of the country.

The President listened with patient courtesy, and when the Senators had concluded, he said, with a characteristic gleam of humor in his eye:

"Gentlemen, your request for a change of the whole Cabinet because I have made one change reminds me of a story I once heard in Illinois, of a farmer who was much troubled by skunks. His wife insisted on his trying to get rid of them.

"He loaded his shotgun one moonlight night and awaited developments. After some time the wife heard the shotgun go off, and in a few minutes the farmer entered the house.

"'What luck have you?' asked she.

"'I hid myself behind the wood-pile,' said the old man, 'with the shotgun pointed towards the hen roost, and before long there appeared not one skunk, but seven. I took aim, blazed away, killed one, and he raised such a fearful smell that I concluded it was best to let the other six go.'"

The Senators laughed and retired.

How He Got Blackstone

The following story was told by Mr. Lincoln to Mr. A. J. Conant, the artist, who painted his portrait in Springfield in 1860:

"One day a man who was migrating to the West drove up in front of my store with a wagon which contained his family and household plunder. He asked me if I would buy an old barrel for which he had no room in his wagon, and which he said contained nothing of special value. I did not want it, but to oblige him I bought it, and paid him, I think, half a dollar for it. Without further examination, I put it away in the store and forgot all about it. Some time after, in overhauling things, I came upon the barrel, and, emptying it upon the floor to see what it contained, I found at the bottom of the rubbish a complete edition of Blackstone's Commentaries. I began to read those famous works, and I had plenty of time; for during the long summer days, when the farmers were busy with their crops, my customers were few and far between. The more I read"—this he said with unusual emphasis—"the more intensely interested I became.

Never in my whole life was my mind so thoroughly absorbed. I read until I devoured them."

A Job for the New Cabinetmaker

A cartoon labeled "A Job for the New Cabinetmaker" was printed in "Frank Leslie's Illustrated Newspaper" on February 2d, 1861, a month and two days before Abraham Lincoln was inaugurated President of the United States. The Southern states had seceded from the Union, the Confederacy was established, with Jefferson Davis as its President, the Union had been split in two, and the task Lincoln had before him was to glue the two parts of the Republic together. In his famous speech, delivered a short time before his nomination for the Presidency by the Republican National Convention at Chicago, in 1860, Lincoln had said: "A house divided against itself cannot stand; this nation cannot exist half slave and half free." After his inauguration as President, Mr. Lincoln went to work to glue the two pieces together, and after four years of bloody war, and at immense cost, the job was finished; the house of the Great American Republic was no longer divided; the severed sections—the North and the South—were cemented tightly; the slaves were freed, peace was firmly established, and the Union of states was glued together so well that the nation is stronger now than ever before. Lincoln was just the man for that job, and the work he did will last for all time. "The New Cabinetmaker" knew his business thoroughly, and finished his task of glueing in a workmanlike manner. At the very moment of its completion, five days after the surrender of Lee to Grant at Appomattox, the Martyr President fell at the hands of the assassin, J. Wilkes Booth.

"I Can Stand It If They Can"

United States Senator Benjamin Wade, of Ohio, Henry Winter Davis, of Maryland, and Wendell Phillips were strongly opposed to President Lincoln's re-election, and Wade and Davis issued a manifesto. Phillips made several warm speeches against Lincoln and his policy.

When asked if he had read the manifesto or any of Phillips' speeches, the President replied:

"I have not seen them, nor do I care to see them. I have seen enough to satisfy me that I am a failure, not only in the opinion of the people in rebellion, but of many distinguished politicians of my own party. But time will show whether I am right or they are right, and I am content to abide its decision.

"I have enough to look after without giving much of my time to the consideration of the subject of who shall be my successor in office. The position is not an easy one; and the occupant, whoever he may be, for the next four years, will have little leisure to pluck a thorn or plant a rose in his own pathway."

It was urged that this opposition must be embarrassing to his Administration, as well as damaging to the party. He replied: "Yes, that is true; but our friends, Wade, Davis, Phillips, and others are hard to please. I am not capable of doing so. I cannot please them without wantonly violating not only my oath, but the most vital principles upon which our government was founded.

"As to those who, like Wade and the rest, see fit to depreciate my policy and cavil at my official acts, I shall not complain of them. I accord them the utmost freedom of speech and liberty of the press, but shall not change the policy I have adopted in the full belief that I am right.

"I feel on this subject as an old Illinois farmer once expressed himself while eating cheese. He was interrupted in the midst of his repast by the entrance of his son, who exclaimed, 'Hold on, dad! there's skippers in that cheese you're eating!'

"'Never mind, Tom,' said he, as he kept on munching his cheese, 'if they can stand it I can.'"

Lincoln Mistaken for Once

President Lincoln was compelled to acknowledge that he made at least one mistake in "sizing up" men. One day a very dignified man called at the White House, and Lincoln's heart fell when his visitor approached. The latter was portly, his face was full of apparent anxiety, and Lincoln was willing to wager a year's salary that he represented some Society for the Easy and Speedy Repression of Rebellions.

The caller talked fluently, but at no time did he give advice or suggest a way to put down the Confederacy. He was full of humor, told a clever story or two, and was entirely self-possessed.

At length the President inquired, "You are a clergyman, are you not, sir?"

"Not by a jug full," returned the stranger heartily.

Grasping him by the hand Lincoln shook it until the visitor squirmed. "You must lunch with us. I am glad to see you. I was afraid you were a preacher."

"I went to the Chicago Convention," the caller said, "as a friend of Mr. Seward. I have watched you narrowly ever since your inauguration, and I called merely to pay my respects. What I want to say is this: I think you are doing everything for the good of the country that is in the power of man to do. You are on the right track. As one of your constituents I now say to you, do in future as you d—— please, and I will support you!"

This was spoken with tremendous effect.

"Why," said Mr. Lincoln in great astonishment, "I took you to be a preacher. I thought you had come here to tell me how to take Richmond," and he again grasped the hand of his strange visitor.

Accurate and penetrating as Mr. Lincoln's judgment was concerning men, for once he had been wholly mistaken. The scene was comical in the extreme. The two men stood gazing at each other. A smile broke from the lips of the solemn wag and rippled over the wide expanse of his homely face like sunlight overspreading a continent, and Mr. Lincoln was convulsed with laughter.

He stayed to lunch.

Forgot Everything He Knew

President Lincoln, while entertaining a few friends, is said to have related the following anecdote of a man who knew too much:

During the administration of President Jackson there was a singular young gentleman employed in the Public Postoffice in Washington.

His name was G.; he was from Tennessee, the son of a widow, a neighbor of the President, on which account the old hero had a kind feeling for him, and always got him out of difficulties with some of the higher officials, to whom his singular interference was distasteful.

Among other things, it is said of him that while employed in the General Postoffice, on one occasion he had to copy a letter to Major H., a high official, in answer to an application made by an old gentleman in Virginia or Pennsylvania, for the establishment of a new postoffice.

The writer of the letter said the application could not be granted, in consequence of the applicant's "proximity" to another office.

When the letter came into G.'s hand to copy, being a great stickler for plainness, he altered "proximity" to "nearness to."

Major H. observed it, and asked G. why he altered his letter.

"Why," replied G., "because I don't think the man would understand what you mean by proximity."

"Well," said Major H., "try him; put in the 'proximity' again."

In a few days a letter was received from the applicant, in which he very indignantly said that his father had fought for liberty in the second war for independence, and he should like to have the name of the scoundrel who brought the charge of proximity or anything else wrong against him.

"There," said G., "did I not say so?"

G. carried his improvements so far that Mr. Berry, the Postmaster-General, said to him: "I don't want you any longer; you know too much."

Poor G. went out, but his old friend got him another place.

This time G.'s ideas underwent a change. He was one day very busy writing, when a stranger called in and asked him where the Patent Office was.

"I don't know," said G.

"Can you tell me where the Treasury Department is?" said the stranger.

"No," said G.

"Nor the President's house?"

"No."

The stranger finally asked him if he knew where the Capitol was.

"No," replied G.

"Do you live in Washington, sir."

"Yes, sir," said G.

"Good Lord! and don't you know where the Patent Office, Treasury, President's House and Capitol are?"

"Stranger," said G., "I was turned out of the postoffice for knowing too much. I don't mean to offend in that way again.

"I am paid for keeping this book.

"I believe I know that much; but if you find me knowing anything more you may take my head."

"Good morning," said the stranger.

He Loved a Good Story

Judge Breese, of the Supreme bench, one of the most distinguished of American jurists, and a man of great personal dignity, was about to open court at Springfield, when Lincoln called out in his hearty way: "Hold on, Breese! Don't open court yet! Here's Bob Blackwell just going to tell a story!" The judge passed on without replying, evidently regarding it as beneath the dignity of the Supreme Court to delay proceedings for the sake of a story.

Heels Ran Away with Them

In an argument against the opposite political party at one time during a campaign, Lincoln said: "My opponent uses a figurative expression to the effect that 'the Democrats are vulnerable in the heel, but they are sound in the heart and head.' The first branch of the figure—that is the Democrats are vulnerable in the heel—I admit is not merely figuratively but literally true. Who that looks but for a moment at their hundreds of officials scampering away with the public money to Texas, to Europe, and to every spot of the earth where a villain may hope to find refuge from justice, can at all doubt that they are most distressingly affected in their heels with a species of running itch?

"It seems that this malady of their heels operates on the sound-headed and honest-hearted creatures very much as the cork leg in the comic song did on its owner, which, when he once got started on it, the more he tried to stop it, the more it would run away.

"At the hazard of wearing this point threadbare, I will relate an anecdote the situation calls to my mind, which seems to be too strikingly in point to be omitted. A witty Irish soldier, who was always boasting of his bravery when no danger was near, but who invariably retreated without orders at the first charge of the engagement, being asked by his captain why he did so, replied, 'Captain, I have as brave a heart as Julius Caesar ever had, but somehow or other, whenever danger approaches, my cowardly legs will run away with it.'

"So with the opposite party—they take the public money into their hands for the most laudable purpose that wise heads and honest hearts can dictate; but before they can possibly get it out again, their rascally, vulnerable heels will run away with them."

Wanted to Burn Him Down to the Stump

Preston King once introduced A. J. Bleeker to the President, and the latter, being an applicant for office, was about to hand Mr. Lincoln his vouchers, when he was asked to read them. Bleeker had not read very far when the President disconcerted him by the exclamation, "Stop a minute! You remind me exactly of the man who killed the dog; in fact, you are just like him."

"In what respect?" asked Bleeker, not feeling he had received a compliment.

"Well," replied the President, "this man had made up his mind to kill his dog, an ugly brute, and proceeded to knock out his brains with a club. He continued striking the dog after the latter was dead until a friend protested, exclaiming, 'You needn't strike him any more; the dog is dead; you killed him at the first blow.'

"'Oh, yes,' said he, 'I know that; but I believe in punishment after death.' So, I see, you do."

Bleeker acknowledged it was possible to overdo a good thing, and then came back at the President with an anecdote of a good priest who converted an Indian from heathenism to Christianity; the only difficulty he had with him was to get him to pray for his enemies. "This Indian had been taught to overcome and destroy all his friends he didn't like," said Bleeker, "but the priest told him that while that might be the Indian method, it was not the doctrine of Christianity or the Bible. 'Saint Paul distinctly says,' the priest told him, 'If thine enemy hunger, feed him; if he thirst, give him drink.'

"The Indian shook his head at this, but when the priest added, 'For in so doing thou shalt heap coals of fire on his head,' Poor Lo was overcome with emotion, fell on his knees, and with outstretched hands and uplifted eyes invoked all sorts of blessings on the heads of all his enemies, supplicating for pleasant hunting-grounds, a large supply of friends, lots of children, and all other Indian comforts.

"Finally the good priest interrupted him (as you did me, Mr. President), exclaiming, 'Stop, my son! You have discharged your Christian duty, and have done more than enough.'

"'Oh, no, father,' replied the Indian; 'let me pray! I want to burn him down to the stump!'"

Had a "Kick" Coming

During the war, one of the Northern Governors, who was able, earnest and untiring in aiding the administration, but always complaining, sent dispatch after dispatch to the War Office, protesting against the methods used in raising troops. After reading all his papers, the President said, in a cheerful and reassuring tone to the Adjutant-General:

"Never mind, never mind; those dispatches don't mean anything. Just go right ahead. The Governor is like a boy I once saw at a launching. When everything was ready, they picked out a boy and sent him under the ship to knock away the trigger and let her go.

"At the critical moment everything depended on the boy. He had to do the job well by a direct, vigorous blow, and then lie flat and keep still while the boat slid over him.

"The boy did everything right, but he yelled as if he were being murdered from the time he got under the keel until he got out. I thought the hide was all scraped off his back, but he wasn't hurt at all.

"The master of the yard told me that this boy was always chosen for that job; that he did his work well; that he never had been hurt, but that he always squealed in that way.

"That's just the way with Governor—. Make up your mind that he is not hurt, and that he is doing the work right, and pay no attention to his squealing. He only wants to make you understand how hard his task is, and that he is on hand performing it."

The Case of Betsy Ann Dougherty

Many requests and petitions made to Mr. Lincoln when he was President were ludicrous and trifling, but he always entered into them with that humor-loving spirit that was such a relief from the grave duties of his great office.

Once a party of Southerners called on him in behalf of one Betsy Ann Dougherty. The spokesman, who was an ex-Governor, said:

"Mr. President, Betsy Ann Dougherty is a good woman. She lived in my county and did my washing for a long time. Her husband went off and joined the rebel army, and I wish you would give her a protection paper." The solemnity of this appeal struck Mr. Lincoln as uncommonly ridiculous.

The two men looked at each other—the Governor desperately earnest, and the President masking his humor behind the gravest exterior. At last Mr. Lincoln asked, with inimitable gravity, "Was Betsy Ann a good washerwoman?" "Oh, yes, sir, she was, indeed."

"Was your Betsy Ann an obliging woman?" "Yes, she was certainly very kind," responded the Governor, soberly. "Could she do other things than wash?" continued Mr. Lincoln with the same portentous gravity.

"Oh, yes; she was very kind—very."

"Where is Betsy Ann?"

"She is now in New York, and wants to come back to Missouri, but she is afraid of banishment."

"Is anybody meddling with her?"

"No; but she is afraid to come back unless you will give her a protection paper."

Thereupon Mr. Lincoln wrote on a visiting card the following:

"Let Betsy Ann Dougherty alone as long as she behaves herself.

"A. LINCOLN."

He handed this card to her advocate, saying, "Give this to Betsy Ann."

"But, Mr. President, couldn't you write a few words to the officers that would insure her protection?"

"No," said Mr. Lincoln, "officers have no time now to read letters. Tell Betsy Ann to put a string in this card and hang it around her neck. When the officers see this, they will keep their hands off your Betsy Ann."

Had to Wear a Wooden Sword

Captain "Abe" Lincoln and his company (in the Black Hawk War) were without any sort of military knowledge, and both were forced to acquire such knowledge by attempts at drilling. Which was the more awkward, the "squad" or the commander, it would have been difficult to decide.

In one of Lincoln's earliest military problems was involved the process of getting his company "endwise" through a gate. Finally he shouted, "This company is dismissed for two minutes, when it will fall in again on the other side of the gate!"

Lincoln was one of the first of his company to be arraigned for unmilitary conduct. Contrary to the rules he fired a gun "within the limits," and had his sword taken from him. The next infringement of rules was by some of the men, who stole a quantity of liquor, drank it, and became unfit for duty, straggling out of the ranks the next day, and not getting together again until late at night.

For allowing this lawlessness the captain was condemned to wear a wooden sword for two days. These were merely interesting but trivial incidents of the campaign. Lincoln was from the very first popular with his men, although one of them told him to "go to the devil."

"Abe" Stirring the "Black" Coals

Under the caption, "The American Difficulty," "Punch" printed on May 11th, 1861, a cartoon. The following text was placed beneath the illustration: PRESIDENT ABE: "What a nice White House this would be, if it were not for the blacks!" It was the idea in England, and, in fact, in all the countries on the European continent, that the War of the Rebellion was fought to secure the freedom of the negro slaves. Such was not the case. The freedom of the slaves was one of the necessary consequences of the Civil War, but not the cause of that bloody four years' conflict. The War was the result of the secession of the states of the South from the Union, and President

"Abe's" main aim was to compel the seceding states to resume their places in the Federal Union of states.

The blacks did not bother President "Abe" in the least as he knew he would be enabled to give them their freedom when the proper time came. He had the project of freeing them in his mind long before he issued his Emancipation Proclamation, the delay in promulgating that document being due to the fact that he did not wish to estrange the hundreds of thousands of patriots of the border states who were fighting for the preservation of the Union, and not for the freedom of the negro slaves. President "Abe" had patience, and everything came out all right in the end.

Getting Rid of an Elephant

Charles A. Dana, who was Assistant Secretary of War under Mr. Stanton, relates the following: A certain Thompson had been giving the government considerable trouble. Dana received information that Thompson was about to escape to Liverpool.

Calling upon Stanton, Dana was referred to Mr. Lincoln.

"The President was at the White House, business hours were over, Lincoln was washing his hands. 'Hallo, Dana,' said he, as I opened the door, 'what is it now?' 'Well, sir,' I said, 'here is the Provost Marshal of Portland, who reports that Jacob Thompson is to be in town to-night, and inquires what orders we have to give.' 'What does Stanton say?' he asked. 'Arrest him,' I replied. 'Well,' he continued, drawling his words, 'I rather guess not. When you have an elephant on your hands, and he wants to run away, better let him run.'"

Grotesque, Yet Frightful

The nearest Lincoln ever came to a fight was when he was in the vicinity of the skirmish at Kellogg's Grove, in the Black Hawk War. The rangers arrived at the spot after the engagement and helped bury the five men who were killed.

Lincoln told Noah Brooks, one of his biographers, that he "remembered just how those men looked as we rode up the little hill where their camp was. The red light of the morning sun was streaming upon them as they lay, heads toward us, on the ground. And every man had a round, red spot on the top of his head about as big as a dollar, where the redskins had taken his scalp. It was frightful, but it was grotesque; and the red sunlight seemed to paint everything all over."

Lincoln paused, as if recalling the vivid picture, and added, somewhat irrelevantly, "I remember that one man had on buckskin breeches."

"Abe" Was No Dude

Always indifferent in matters of dress, Lincoln cut but small figure in social circles, even in the earliest days of Illinois. His trousers were too short, his hat too small, and, as a rule, the buttons on the back of his coat were nearer his shoulder blades than his waist.

No man was richer than his fellows, and there was no aristocracy; the women wore linsey-woolsey of home manufacture, and dyed them in accordance with the tastes of the wearers; calico was rarely seen, and a woman wearing a dress of that material was the envy of her sisters.

There being no shoemakers the women wore moccasins, and the men made their own boots. A hunting shirt, leggins made of skins, buckskin breeches, dyed green, constituted an apparel no maiden could withstand.

Characteristic of Lincoln

One man who knew Lincoln at New Salem, says the first time he saw him he was lying on a trundle-bed covered with books and papers and rocking a cradle with his foot.

The whole scene was entirely characteristic—Lincoln reading and studying, and at the same time helping his landlady by quieting her child.

A gentleman who knew Mr. Lincoln well in early manhood says: "Lincoln at this period had nothing but plenty of friends."

After the customary hand-shaking on one occasion in the White House at Washington several gentlemen came forward and asked the President for his autograph. One of them gave his name as "Cruikshank." "That reminds me," said Mr. Lincoln, "of what I used to be called when a young man—'Long-shanks!'"

"Plough All 'Round Him"

Governor Blank went to the War Department one day in a towering rage:

"I suppose you found it necessary to make large concessions to him, as he returned from you perfectly satisfied," suggested a friend.

"Oh, no," the President replied, "I did not concede anything. You have heard how that Illinois farmer got rid of a big log that was too big to haul out, too knotty to split, and too wet and soggy to burn.

"'Well, now,' said he, in response to the inquiries of his neighbors one Sunday, as to how he got rid of it, 'well, now, boys, if you won't divulge the secret, I'll tell you how I got rid of it—I ploughed around it.'

"Now," remarked Lincoln, in conclusion, "don't tell anybody, but that's the way I got rid of Governor Blank. I ploughed all round him, but it took me three mortal hours to do it, and I was afraid every minute he'd see what I was at."

"I've Lost My Apple"

During a public "reception," a farmer from one of the border counties of Virginia told the President that the Union soldiers, in passing his farm, had helped themselves not only to hay, but his horse, and he hoped the President would urge the proper officer to consider his claim immediately.

Mr. Lincoln said that this reminded him of an old acquaintance of his, "Jack" Chase, a lumberman on the Illinois, a steady, sober man, and the best raftsman on the river. It was quite a trick to take the logs over the rapids; but he was skilful with a raft, and always kept her straight in the channel. Finally a steamer was put on, and

"Jack" was made captain of her. He always used to take the wheel, going through the rapids. One day when the boat was plunging and wallowing along the boiling current, and "Jack's" utmost vigilance was being exercised to keep her in the narrow channel, a boy pulled his coat-tail and hailed him with:

"Say, Mister Captain! I wish you would just stop your boat a minute—I've lost my apple overboard!"

Lost His Certificate of Character

Mr. Lincoln prepared his first inaugural address in a room over a store in Springfield. His only reference works were Henry Clay's great compromise speech of 1850, Andrew Jackson's Proclamation against Nullification, Webster's great reply to Hayne, and a copy of the Constitution.

When Mr. Lincoln started for Washington, to be inaugurated, the inaugural address was placed in a special satchel and guarded with special care. At Harrisburg the satchel was given in charge of Robert T. Lincoln, who accompanied his father. Before the train started from Harrisburg the precious satchel was missing. Robert thought he had given it to a waiter at the hotel, but a long search failed to reveal the missing satchel with its precious document. Lincoln was annoyed, angry, and finally in despair. He felt certain that the address was lost beyond recovery, and, as it only lacked ten days until the inauguration, he had no time to prepare another. He had not even preserved the notes from which the original copy had been written.

Mr. Lincoln went to Ward Lamon, his former law partner, then one of his bodyguards, and informed him of the loss in the following words:

"Lamon, I guess I have lost my certificate of moral character, written by myself. Bob has lost my gripsack containing my inaugural address." Of course, the misfortune reminded him of a story.

"I feel," said Mr. Lincoln, "a good deal as the old member of the Methodist Church did when he lost his wife at the camp meeting, and went up to an old elder of the church and asked him if he could tell him whereabouts in h—l his wife was. In fact, I am in a worse fix than my Methodist friend, for if it were only a wife that were missing, mine would be sure to bob up somewhere."

The clerk at the hotel told Mr. Lincoln that he would probably find his missing satchel in the baggage-room. Arriving there, Mr. Lincoln saw a satchel which he thought was his, and it was passed out to him. His key fitted the lock, but alas! when it was opened the satchel contained only a soiled shirt, some paper collars, a pack of cards and a bottle of whisky. A few minutes later the satchel containing the inaugural address was found among the pile of baggage.

The recovery of the address also reminded Mr. Lincoln of a story, which is thus narrated by Ward Lamon in his "Recollections of Abraham Lincoln":

The loss of the address and the search for it was the subject of a great deal of amusement. Mr. Lincoln said many funny things in connection with the incident. One of them was that he knew a fellow once who had saved up fifteen hundred dollars, and had placed it in a private banking establishment. The bank soon failed, and he afterward received ten per cent of his investment. He then took his one hundred and fifty dollars and deposited it in a savings bank, where he was sure it would be safe. In a short time this bank also failed, and he received at the final settlement ten per cent on the amount deposited. When the fifteen dollars was paid over to him, he held it in his hand and looked at it thoughtfully; then he said, "Now, darn you, I have got you reduced to a portable shape, so I'll put you in my pocket." Suiting the action to the word, Mr. Lincoln took his address from the bag and carefully placed it in the inside pocket of his vest, but held on to the satchel with as much interest as if it still contained his "certificate of moral character."

Note Presented for Payment

The great English funny paper, London "Punch," printed a cartoon on September 27th, 1862, intended to convey the idea that Lincoln, having asserted that the war would be over in ninety days, had not redeemed his word: The text under the cartoon in Punch was:

MR. SOUTH TO MR. NORTH: "Your 'ninety-day' promissory note isn't taken up yet, sirree!"

The tone of the cartoon is decidedly unfriendly. The North finally took up the note, but the South had to pay it. "Punch" was not pleased with the result, but "Mr. North" did not care particularly what this periodical thought about it. The United States, since then, has been prepared to take up all of its obligations when due, but it must be acknowledged that at the time this cartoon was published the outlook was rather dark and gloomy. Lincoln did not despair, however; but although business was in rather bad shape for a time, the financial skies finally cleared, business was resumed at the old stand, and Uncle Sam's credit is now as good, or better, than other nations' cash in hand.

Dog Was a "Leetle Bit Ahead"

Lincoln could not sympathize with those Union generals who were prone to indulge in high-sounding promises, but whose performances did not by any means come up to their predictions as to what they would do if they ever met the enemy face to face. He said one day, just after one of these braggarts had been soundly thrashed by the Confederates:

"These fellows remind me of the fellow who owned a dog which, so he said, just hungered and thirsted to combat and eat up wolves. It was a difficult matter, so the owner declared, to keep that dog from devoting the entire twenty-four hours of each day to the destruction of his enemies. He just 'hankered' to get at them.

"One day a party of this dog-owner's friends thought to have some sport. These friends heartily disliked wolves, and were anxious to see the dog eat up a few thousand. So they organized a hunting party and invited the dog-owner and the dog to go with them. They desired to be personally present when the wolf-killing was in progress.

"It was noticed that the dog-owner was not over-enthusiastic in the matter; he pleaded a 'business engagement,' but as he was the most notorious and torpid of the town loafers, and wouldn't have recognized a 'business engagement' had he met it face to face, his excuse was treated with contempt. Therefore he had to go.

"The dog, however, was glad enough to go, and so the party started out. Wolves were in plenty, and soon a pack was discovered, but when the 'wolf-hound' saw the ferocious animals he lost heart, and, putting his tail between his legs, endeavored to slink away. At last—after many trials—he was enticed into the small growth of underbrush where the wolves had secreted themselves, and yelps of terror betrayed the fact that the battle was on.

"Away flew the wolves, the dog among them, the hunting party following on horseback. The wolves seemed frightened, and the dog was restored to public favor. It really looked as if he had the savage creatures on the run, as he was fighting heroically when last sighted.

"Wolves and dog soon disappeared, and it was not until the party arrived at a distant farmhouse that news of the combatants was gleaned.

"'Have you seen anything of a wolf-dog and a pack of wolves around here?' was the question anxiously put to the male occupant of the house, who stood idly leaning upon the gate.

"'Yep,' was the short answer.

"'How were they going?'

"'Purty fast.'

"'What was their position when you saw them?'

"'Well,' replied the farmer, in a most exasperatingly deliberate way, 'the dog was a leetle bit ahead.'

"Now, gentlemen," concluded the President, "that's the position in which you'll find most of these bragging generals when they get into a fight with the enemy. That's why I don't like military orators."

"Abe's" Fight with Negroes

When Lincoln was nineteen years of age, he went to work for a Mr. Gentry, and, in company with Gentry's son, took a flatboat load of provisions to New Orleans. At a plantation six miles below Baton Rouge, while the boat was tied up to the shore in the dead hours of the night, and Abe and Allen were fast asleep in the bed, they were startled by footsteps on board. They knew instantly that it was a gang of negroes come to rob and perhaps murder them. Allen, thinking to frighten the negroes, called out, "Bring guns, Lincoln, and shoot them!" Abe came without the guns, but fell among the negroes with a huge bludgeon and belabored them most cruelly, following them onto the bank. They rushed back to their boat and hastily put out into the stream. It is said that Lincoln received a scar in this tussle which he carried with him to his grave. It was on this trip that he saw the workings of slavery for the first time. The sight of New Orleans was like a wonderful panorama to his eyes, for never before had he seen wealth, beauty, fashion and culture. He returned home with new and larger ideas and stronger opinions of right and justice.

Noise Like a Turnip

"Every man has his own peculiar and particular way of getting at and doing things," said President Lincoln one day, "and he is often criticised because that way is not the one adopted by others. The great idea is to accomplish what you set out to do. When a man is successful in whatever he attempts, he has many imitators, and the methods used are not so closely scrutinized, although no man who is of good intent will resort to mean, underhanded, scurvy tricks.

"That reminds me of a fellow out in Illinois, who had better luck in getting prairie chickens than any one in the neighborhood. He had a rusty old gun no other man dared to handle; he never seemed to exert himself, being listless and indifferent when out after game, but he always brought home all the chickens he could carry, while

some of the others, with their finely trained dogs and latest improved fowling-pieces, came home alone.

"'How is it, Jake?' inquired one sportsman, who, although a good
shot, and knew something about hunting, was often unfortunate,
'that you never come home without a lot of birds?'

"Jake grinned, half closed his eyes, and replied: 'Oh, I don't know
that there's anything queer about it. I jes' go ahead an' git 'em.'

"'Yes, I know you do; but how do you do it?'

"'You'll tell.'

"'Honest, Jake, I won't say a word. Hope to drop dead this
minute.'

"'Never say nothing, if I tell you?'

"'Cross my heart three times.'

"This reassured Jake, who put his mouth close to the ear of his
eager questioner, and said, in a whisper:

"'All you got to do is jes' to hide in a fence corner an' make a noise
like a turnip. That'll bring the chickens every time.'"

Warding Off God's Vengeance

When Lincoln was a candidate for re-election to the Illinois Legislature in 1836, a meeting was advertised to be held in the court-
house in Springfield, at which candidates of opposing parties were
to speak. This gave men of spirit and capacity a fine opportunity to
show the stuff of which they were made.

George Forquer was one of the most prominent citizens; he had
been a Whig, but became a Democrat—possibly for the reason that
by means of the change he secured the position of Government land
register, from President Andrew Jackson. He had the largest and
finest house in the city, and there was a new and striking appendage
to it, called a lightning-rod! The meeting was very large. Seven Whig
and seven Democratic candidates spoke.

Lincoln closed the discussion. A Kentuckian (Joshua F. Speed),
who had heard Henry Clay and other distinguished Kentucky orators, stood near Lincoln, and stated afterward that he "never heard
a more effective speaker; . . . the crowd seemed to be swayed by

him as he pleased." What occurred during the closing portion of this meeting must be given in full, from Judge Arnold's book:

"Forquer, although not a candidate, asked to be heard for the Democrats, in reply to Lincoln. He was a good speaker, and well known throughout the county. His special task that day was to attack and ridicule the young countryman from Salem.

"Turning to Lincoln, who stood within a few feet of him, he said: 'This young man must be taken down, and I am truly sorry that the task devolves upon me.' He then proceeded, in a very overbearing way, and with an assumption of great superiority, to attack Lincoln and his speech. He was fluent and ready with the rough sarcasm of the stump, and he went on to ridicule the person, dress and arguments of Lincoln with so much success that Lincoln's friends feared that he would be embarrassed and overthrown."

"The Clary's Grove boys were present, and were restrained with difficulty from 'getting up a fight' in behalf of their favorite (Lincoln), they and all his friends feeling that the attack was ungenerous and unmanly.

"Lincoln, however, stood calm, but his flashing eye and pale cheek indicated his indignation. As soon as Forquer had closed he took the stand, and first answered his opponent's arguments fully and triumphantly. So impressive were his words and manner that a hearer (Joshua F. Speed) believes that he can remember to this day and repeat some of the expressions.

"Among other things he said: 'The gentleman commenced his speech by saying that "this young man," alluding to me, "must be taken down." I am not so young in years as I am in the tricks and the trades of a politician, but,' said he, pointing to Forquer, 'live long or die young, I would rather die now than, like the gentleman, change my politics, and with the change receive an office worth $3,000 a year, and then,' continued he, 'feel obliged to erect a lightning-rod over my house, to protect a guilty conscience from an offended God!'"

Jeff Davis and Charles the First

Jefferson Davis insisted on being recognized by his official title as commander or President in the regular negotiation with the Government. This Mr. Lincoln would not consent to.

Mr. Hunter thereupon referred to the correspondence between King Charles the First and his Parliament as a precedent for a negotiation between a constitutional ruler and rebels. Mr. Lincoln's face then wore that indescribable expression which generally preceded his hardest hits, and he remarked: "Upon questions of history, I must refer you to Mr. Seward, for he is posted in such things, and I don't profess to be; but my only distinct recollection of the matter is, that Charles lost his head."

Loved Soldiers' Humor

Lincoln loved anything that savored of wit or humor among the soldiers. He used to relate two stories to show, he said, that neither death nor danger could quench the grim humor of the American soldier:

"A soldier of the Army of the Potomac was being carried to the rear of battle with both legs shot off, who, seeing a pie-woman, called out, 'Say, old lady, are them pies sewed or pegged?'

"And there was another one of the soldiers at the battle of Chancellorsville, whose regiment, waiting to be called into the fight, was taking coffee. The hero of the story put to his lips a crockery mug which he had carried with care through several campaigns. A stray bullet, just missing the tinker's head, dashed the mug into fragments and left only the handle on his finger. Turning his head in that direction, he scowled, 'Johnny, you can't do that again!'"

Bad Time for a Barbecue

Captain T. W. S. Kidd of Springfield was the crier of the court in the days when Mr. Lincoln used to ride the circuit.

"I was younger than he," says Captain Kidd, "but he had a sort of admiration for me, and never failed to get me into his stories. I was a story-teller myself in those days, and he used to laugh very heartily at some of the stories I told him.

"Now and then he got me into a good deal of trouble. I was a Democrat, and was in politics more or less. A good many of our Democratic voters at that time were Irishmen. They came to Illinois in the days of the old canal, and did their honest share in making that piece of internal improvement an accomplished fact.

"One time Mr. Lincoln told the story of one of those important young fellows—not an Irishman—who lived in every town, and have the cares of state on their shoulders. This young fellow met an Irishman on the street, and called to him, officiously: 'Oh, Mike, I'm awful glad I met you. We've got to do something to wake up the boys. The campaign is coming on, and we've got to get out voters. We've just had a meeting up here, and we're going to have the biggest barbecue that ever was heard of in Illinois. We are going to roast two whole oxen, and we're going to have Douglas and Governor Cass and someone from Kentucky, and all the big Democratic guns, and we're going to have a great big time.'

"'By dad, that's good!' says the Irishman. 'The byes need stirrin' up.'

"'Yes, and you're on one of the committees, and you want to hustle around and get them waked up, Mike.'

"'When is the barbecue to be?' asked Mike.

"'Friday, two weeks.'

"'Friday, is it? Well, I'll make a nice committeeman, settin' the barbecue on a day with half of the Dimocratic party of Sangamon county can't ate a bite of mate. Go on wid ye.'

"Lincoln told that story in one of his political speeches, and when the laugh was over he said: 'Now, gentlemen, I know that story is true, for Tom Kidd told it to me.' And then the Democrats would make trouble for me for a week afterward, and I'd have to explain."

He'd See It Again

About two years before Lincoln was nominated for the Presidency he went to Bloomington, Illinois, to try a case of some importance. His opponent—who afterward reached a high place in his profession—was a young man of ability, sensible but sensitive, and one to whom the loss of a case was a great blow. He therefore studied hard and made much preparation.

This particular case was submitted to the jury late at night, and, although anticipating a favorable verdict, the young attorney spent a sleepless night in anxiety. Early next morning he learned, to his great chagrin, that he had lost the case.

Lincoln met him at the court-house some time after the jury had come in, and asked him what had become of his case.

With lugubrious countenance and in a melancholy tone the young man replied, "It's gone to hell."

"Oh, well," replied Lincoln, "then you will see it again."

Call Another Witness

When arguing a case in court, Mr. Lincoln never used a word which the dullest juryman could not understand. Rarely, if ever, did a Latin term creep into his arguments. A lawyer, quoting a legal maxim one day in court, turned to Lincoln, and said: "That is so, is it not, Mr. Lincoln?"

"If that's Latin." Lincoln replied, "you had better call another witness."

A Contest with Little "Tad"

Mr. Carpenter, the artist, relates the following incident: "Some photographers came up to the White House to make some stereoscopic studies for me of the President's office. They requested a dark closet in which to develop the pictures, and, without a thought that I was infringing upon anybody's rights, I took them to an unoccupied room of which little 'Tad' had taken possession a few days before, and, with the aid of a couple of servants, had fitted up a minia-ture theater, with stage, curtains, orchestra, stalls, parquette and all. Knowing that the use required would interfere with none of his arrangements, I led the way to this apartment.

"Everything went on well, and one or two pictures had been taken, when suddenly there was an uproar. The operator came back to the office and said that 'Tad' had taken great offense at the oc-cupation of his room without his consent, and had locked the door, refusing all admission.

"The chemicals had been taken inside, and there was no way of getting at them, he having carried off the key. In the midst of this conversation 'Tad' burst in, in a fearful passion. He laid all the blame upon me—said that I had no right to use his room, and the men should not go in even to get their things. He had locked the door and they should not go there again—'they had no business in his room!'

"Mr. Lincoln was sitting for a photograph, and was still in the chair. He said, very mildly, 'Tad, go and unlock the door.' Tad went off muttering into his mother's room, refusing to obey. I followed him into the passage, but no coaxing would pacify him. Upon my return to the President, I found him still patiently in the chair, from which he had not risen. He said: 'Has not the boy opened the door?' I replied that we could do nothing with him—he had gone off in a great pet. Mr. Lincoln's lips came together firmly, and then, suddenly rising, he strode across the passage with the air of one bent on pun-ishment, and disappeared in the domestic apartments. Directly he returned with the key to the theater, which he unlocked himself.

"'Tad,' said he, half apologetically, 'is a peculiar child. He was vi olently excited when I went to him. I said, "Tad, do you know that you are making your father a great deal of trouble?" He burst into tears, instantly giving me up the key.'"

Reminded Him of "a Little Story"

When Lincoln's attention was called to the fact that, at one time in his boyhood, he had spelled the name of the Deity with a small "g," he replied:

"That reminds me of a little story. It came about that a lot of Confederate mail was captured by the Union forces, and, while it was not exactly the proper thing to do, some of our soldiers opened several letters written by the Southerners at the front to their people at home.

"In one of these missives the writer, in a postscript, jotted down this assertion:

"'We'll lick the Yanks termorrer, if goddlemity (God Almighty) spares our lives.'

"That fellow was in earnest, too, as the letter was written the day before the second battle of Manassas."

"Fetched Several Short Ones"

"The first time I ever remember seeing 'Abe' Lincoln," is the testimony of one of his neighbors, "was when I was a small boy and had gone with my father to attend some kind of an election. One of the neighbors, James Larkins, was there.

"Larkins was a great hand to brag on anything he owned. This time it was his horse. He stepped up before 'Abe,' who was in a crowd, and commenced talking to him, boasting all the while of his animal.

"'I have got the best horse in the country,' he shouted to his young listener. 'I ran him nine miles in exactly three minutes, and he never fetched a long breath.'

"'I presume,' said 'Abe,' rather dryly, 'he fetched a good many short ones, though.'"

Lincoln Lugs the Old Man

On May 3rd, 1862, "Frank Leslie's Illustrated Newspaper" printed a cartoon over the title of "Sandbag Lincoln and the Old Man of the Sea, Secretary of the Navy Welles." It was intended to demonstrate that the head of the Navy Department was incompetent to manage the affairs of the Navy; also that the Navy was not doing as good work as it might.

When this cartoon was published, the United States Navy had cleared and had under control the Mississippi River as far south as Memphis; had blockaded all the cotton ports of the South; had assisted in the reduction of a number of Confederate forts; had aided Grant at Fort Donelson and the battle of Shiloh; the Monitor had whipped the ironclad terror, Merrimac (the Confederates called her the Virginia); Admiral Farragut's fleet had compelled the surrender of the city of New Orleans, the great forts which had defended it, and the Federal Government obtained control of the lower Mississippi.

"The Old Man of the Sea" was therefore, not a drag or a weight upon President Lincoln, and the Navy was not so far behind in making a good record as the picture would have the people of the world believe. It was not long after the Monitor's victory that the United States Navy was the finest that ever plowed the seas. The building of the Monitor also revolutionized naval warfare.

Mcclellan Was "Intrenching"

About a week after the Chicago Convention, a gentleman from New York called upon the President, in company with the Assistant Secretary of War, Mr. Dana.

In the course of conversation, the gentleman said: "What do you think, Mr. President, is the reason General McClellan does not reply to the letter from the Chicago Convention?"

"Oh!" replied Mr. Lincoln, with a characteristic twinkle of the eye, "he is intrenching!"

Make Something Out of It, Anyway

From the day of his nomination by the Chicago convention, gifts poured in upon Lincoln. Many of these came in the form of wearing apparel. Mr. George Lincoln, of Brooklyn, who brought to Springfield, in January, 1861, a handsome silk hat to the President-elect, the gift of a New York hatter, told some friends that in receiving the hat Lincoln laughed heartily over the gifts of clothing, and remarked to Mrs. Lincoln: "Well, wife, if nothing else comes out of this scrape, we are going to have some new clothes, are we not?"

Vicious Oxen Have Short Horns

In speaking of the many mean and petty acts of certain members of Congress, the President, while talking on the subject one day with friends, said:

"I have great sympathy for these men, because of their temper and their weakness; but I am thankful that the good Lord has given to the vicious ox short horns, for if their physical courage were equal to their vicious disposition, some of us in this neck of the woods would get hurt."

Lincoln's Name for "Weeping Water"

"I was speaking one time to Mr. Lincoln," said Governor Saunders, "of Nebraska, of a little Nebraskan settlement on the Weeping Water, a stream in our State."

"'Weeping Water!' said he.

"Then with a twinkle in his eye, he continued.

"'I suppose the Indians out there call Minneboohoo, don't they? They ought to, if Laughing Water is Minnehaha in their language.'"

Peter Cartwright's Description of Lincoln

Peter Cartwright, the famous and eccentric old Methodist preacher, who used to ride a church circuit, as Mr. Lincoln and others did the court circuit, did not like Lincoln very well, probably because Mr. Lincoln was not a member of his flock, and once defeated the preacher for Congress. This was Cartwright's description of Lincoln: "This Lincoln is a man six feet four inches tall, but so angular that if you should drop a plummet from the center of his head it would cut him three times before it touched his feet."

No Deaths in His House

A gentleman was relating to the President how a friend of his had been driven away from New Orleans as a Unionist, and how, on his expulsion, when he asked to see the writ by which he was expelled, the deputation which called on him told him the Government would do nothing illegal, and so they had issued no illegal writs, and simply meant to make him go of his own free will.

"Well," said Mr. Lincoln, "that reminds me of a hotel-keeper down at St. Louis, who boasted that he never had a death in his hotel, for whenever a guest was dying in his house he carried him out to die in the gutter."

Painted His Principles

The day following the adjournment of the Baltimore Convention, at which President Lincoln was renominated, various political organizations called to pay their respects to the President. While the Philadelphia delegation was being presented, the chairman of that body, in introducing one of the members, said:

"Mr. President, this is Mr. S., of the second district of our State,—a most active and earnest friend of yours and the cause. He has, among other things, been good enough to paint, and present to our league rooms, a most beautiful portrait of yourself."

President Lincoln took the gentleman's hand in his, and shaking it cordially said, with a merry voice, "I presume, sir, in painting your beautiful portrait, you took your idea of me from my principles and not from my person."

Dignifying the Statute

Lincoln was married—he balked at the first date set for the ceremony and did not show up at all—November 4, 1842, under most
happy auspices. The officiating clergyman, the Rev. Mr. Dresser, used
the Episcopal church service for marriage. Lincoln placed the ring
upon the bride's finger, and said, "With this ring I now thee wed,
and with all my worldly goods I thee endow."

Judge Thomas C. Browne, who was present, exclaimed, "Good
gracious, Lincoln! the statute fixes all that!"

"Oh, well," drawled Lincoln, "I just thought I'd add a little dignity
to the statute."

Lincoln Campaign Mottoes

The joint debates between Lincoln and Douglas were attended by
crowds of people, and the arrival of both at the places of speaking were in the nature of a triumphal procession. In these processions there were many banners bearing catch-phrases and mottoes
expressing the sentiment of the people on the candidates and the
issues.

The following were some of the mottoes on the Lincoln banners:

Westward the star of empire takes its way;
The girls link on to Lincoln, their mothers were for Clay.

Abe, the Giant-Killer.

Edgar County for the Tall Sucker.

Free Territories and Free Men,
Free Pulpits and Free Preachers,
Free Press and a Free Pen,
Free Schools and Free Teachers.

Giving Away the Case

Between the first election and inauguration of Mr. Lincoln the disunion sentiment grew rapidly in the South, and President Buchanan's failure to stop the open acts of secession grieved Mr. Lincoln sorely. Mr. Lincoln had a long talk with his friend, Judge Gillespie, over the state of affairs. One incident of the conversation is thus narrated by the Judge:

"When I retired, it was the master of the house and chosen ruler of the country who saw me to my room. 'Joe,' he said, as he was about to leave me, 'I am reminded and I suppose you will never forget that trial down in Montgomery county, where the lawyer associated with you gave away the whole case in his opening speech. I saw you signaling to him, but you couldn't stop him.

"'Now, that's just the way with me and Buchanan. He is giving away the case, and I have nothing to say, and can't stop him. Goodnight.'"

Posing with a Broomstick

Mr. Leonard Volk, the artist, relates that, being in Springfield when Lincoln's nomination for President was announced, he called upon Mr. Lincoln, whom he found looking smiling and happy. "I exclaimed, 'I am the first man from Chicago, I believe, who has had the honor of congratulating you on your nomination for President.' Then those two great hands took both of mine with a grasp never to be forgotten, and while shaking, I said, 'Now that you will doubtless be the next President of the United States, I want to make a statue of you, and shall try my best to do you justice.'

"Said he, 'I don't doubt it, for I have come to the conclusion that you are an honest man,' and with that greeting, I thought my hands in a fair way of being crushed.

"On the Sunday following, by agreement, I called to make a cast of Mr. Lincoln's hands. I asked him to hold something in his hands, and told him a stick would do. Thereupon he went to the woodshed, and I heard the saw go, and he soon returned to the dining-room, whittling off the end of a piece of broom handle. I remarked to him that he need not whittle off the edges. 'Oh, well,' said he, 'I thought I would like to have it nice.'"

"Both Length and Breadth"

During Lincoln's first and only term in Congress—he was elected in 1846—he formed quite a cordial friendship with Stephen A. Douglas, a member of the United States Senate from Illinois, and the beaten one in the contest as to who should secure the hand of Miss Mary Todd. Lincoln was the winner; Douglas afterwards beat him for the United States Senate, but Lincoln went to the White House.

During all of the time that they were rivals in love and in politics they remained the best of friends personally. They were always glad to see each other, and were frequently together. The disparity in their size was always the more noticeable upon such occasions, and they well deserved their nicknames of "Long Abe" and the "Little Giant." Lincoln was the tallest man in the National House of Representatives, and Douglas the shortest (and perhaps broadest) man the Senate, and when they appeared on the streets together much merriment was created. Lincoln, when joked about the matter, replied, in a very serious tone, "Yes, that's about the length and breadth of it."

"Abe" Recites a Song

Lincoln couldn't sing, and he also lacked the faculty of musical adaptation. He had a liking for certain ballads and songs, and while he memorized and recited their lines, someone else did the singing. Lincoln often recited for the delectation of his friends, the following, the authorship of which is unknown:

> *The first factional fight in old Ireland, they say,*
> *Was all on account of St. Patrick's birthday;*
> *It was somewhere about midnight without any*
> > *doubt,*

And certain it is, it made a great rout.

On the eighth day of March, as some people say,
St. Patrick at midnight he first saw the day;
While others assert 'twas the ninth he was born—
'Twas all a mistake—between midnight and morn.

Some blamed the baby, some blamed the clock;
Some blamed the doctor, some the crowing cock.
With all these close questions sure no one could
        know,
Whether the babe was too fast or the clock was too
        slow.

Some fought for the eighth, for the ninth some
        would die;
He who wouldn't see right would have a black eye.
At length these two factions so positive grew,
They each had a birthday, and Pat he had two.

Till Father Mulcahay who showed them their sins,
He said none could have two birthdays but as
        twins.
"Now boys, don't be fighting for the eight or the
        nine;
Don't quarrel so always, now why not combine."

Combine eight with nine. It is the mark;
Let that be the birthday. Amen! said the clerk.
So all got blind drunk, which completed their bliss,
And they've kept up the practice from that day to
        this.

"Manage to Keep House"

Senator John Sherman, of Ohio, introduced his brother, William T. Sherman (then a civilian) to President Lincoln in March, 1861. Sherman had offered his services, but, as in the case of Grant, they had been refused.

After the Senator had transacted his business with the President, he said: "Mr. President, this is my brother, Colonel Sherman, who is just up from Louisiana; he may give you some information you want."

To this Lincoln replied, as reported by Senator Sherman himself: "Ah! How are they getting along down there?"

Sherman answered: "They think they are getting along swimmingly; they are prepared for war."

To which Lincoln responded: "Oh, well, I guess we'll manage to keep the house."

"Tecump," whose temper was not the mildest, broke out on "Brother John" as soon as they were out of the White House, cursed the politicians roundly, and wound up with, "You have got things in a h—l of a fix, and you may get out as best you can."

Sherman was one of the very few generals who gave Lincoln little or no worry.

Grant "Tumbled" Right Away

General Grant told this story about Lincoln some years after the War:

"Just after receiving my commission as lieutenant-general the President called me aside to speak to me privately. After a brief reference to the military situation, he said he thought he could illustrate what he wanted to say by a story. Said he:

"'At one time there was a great war among the animals, and one side had great difficulty in getting a commander who had sufficient confidence in himself. Finally they found a monkey by the name of Jocko, who said he thought he could command their army if his tail could be made a little longer. So they got more tail and spliced it on to his caudal appendage.

"'He looked at it admiringly, and then said he thought he ought to have still more tail. This was added, and again he called for more. The splicing process was repeated many times until they had coiled Jocko's tail around the room, filling all the space.

"'Still he called for more tail, and, there being no other place to coil it, they began wrapping it around his shoulders. He continued his call for more, and they kept on winding the additional tail around him until its weight broke him down.'

"I saw the point, and, rising from my chair, replied, 'Mr. President, I will not call for any more assistance unless I find it impossible to do with what I already have.'"

"Don't Kill Him with Your Fist"

Ward Lamon, Marshal of the District of Columbia during Lincoln's time in Washington, was a powerful man; his strength was phenomenal, and a blow from his fist was like unto that coming from the business end of a sledge.

Lamon tells this story, the hero of which is not mentioned by name, but in all probability his identity can be guessed:

"On one occasion, when the fears of the loyal element of the city (Washington) were excited to fever-heat, a free fight near the old National Theatre occurred about eleven o'clock one night. An officer, in passing the place, observed what was going on, and seeing the great number of persons engaged, he felt it to be his duty to command the peace.

"The imperative tone of his voice stopped the fighting for a moment, but the leader, a great bully, roughly pushed back the officer and told him to go away or he would whip him. The officer again advanced and said, 'I arrest you,' attempting to place his hand on the man's shoulder, when the bully struck a fearful blow at the officer's face.

"This was parried, and instantly followed by a blow from the fist of the officer, striking the fellow under the chin and knocking him senseless. Blood issued from his mouth, nose and ears. It was believed that the man's neck was broken. A surgeon was called, who pronounced the case a critical one, and the wounded man was hurried away on a litter to the hospital.

"There the physicians said there was concussion of the brain, and that the man would die. All the medical skill that the officer could procure was employed in the hope of saving the life of the man. His conscience smote him for having, as he believed, taken the life of a fellow-creature, and he was inconsolable.

"Being on terms of intimacy with the President, about two o'clock that night the officer went to the White House, woke up Mr. Lincoln, and requested him to come into his office, where he told him his story. Mr. Lincoln listened with great interest until the narrative was completed, and then asked a few questions, after which he remarked:

"'I am sorry you had to kill the man, but these are times of war, and a great many men deserve killing. This one, according to your story, is one of them; so give yourself no uneasiness about the matter. I will stand by you.'

"'That is not why I came to you. I knew I did my duty, and had no fears of your disapproval of what I did,' replied the officer; and then he added: 'Why I came to you was, I felt great grief over the unfortunate affair, and I wanted to talk to you about it.'

"Mr. Lincoln then said, with a smile, placing his hand on the officer' shoulder: 'You go home now and get some sleep; but let me give you this piece of advice—hereafter, when you have occasion to strike a man, don't hit him with your fist; strike him with a club, a crowbar, or with something that won't kill him.'"

Could Be Arbitrary

Lincoln could be arbitrary when occasion required. This is the letter he wrote to one of the Department heads:

"You must make a job of it, and provide a place for the bearer of this, Elias Wampole. Make a job of it with the collector and have it done. You can do it for me, and you must."

There was no delay in taking action in this matter. Mr. Wampole, or "Eli," as he was thereafter known, "got there."

A General Bustification

Many amusing stories are told of President Lincoln and his gloves. At about the time of his third reception he had on a tight-fitting pair of white kids, which he had with difficulty got on. He saw approaching in the distance an old Illinois friend named Simpson, whom he welcomed with a genuine Sangamon county (Illeenoy) shake, which resulted in bursting his white kid glove, with an audible sound. Then, raising his brawny hand up before him, looking at it with an indescribable expression, he said, while the whole procession was checked, witnessing this scene:

"Well, my old friend, this is a general bustification. You and I were never intended to wear these things. If they were stronger they might do well enough to keep out the cold, but they are a failure to shake hands with between old friends like us. Stand aside, Captain, and I'll see you shortly."

Simpson stood aside, and after the unwelcome ceremony was terminated he rejoined his old Illinois friend in familiar intercourse.

Making Quartermasters

H. C. Whitney wrote in 1866: "I was in Washington in the Indian service for a few days before August, 1861, and I merely said to President Lincoln one day: 'Everything is drifting into the war, and I guess you will have to put me in the army.'

"The President looked up from his work and said, good-humoredly: 'I'm making generals now; in a few days I will be making quartermasters, and then I'll fix you.'"

No Postmasters in His Pocket

In the "Diary of a Public Man" appears this jocose anecdote:

"Mr. Lincoln walked into the corridor with us; and, as he bade us good-by and thanked Blank for what he had told him, he again brightened up for a moment and asked him in an abrupt kind of way, laying his hand as he spoke with a queer but not uncivil familiarity on his shoulder, 'You haven't such a thing as a postmaster in your pocket, have you?'

"Blank stared at him in astonishment, and I thought a little in alarm, as if he suspected a sudden attack of insanity; then Mr. Lincoln went on:

'You see it seems to me kind of unnatural that you shouldn't have at least a postmaster in your pocket. Everybody I've seen for days past has had foreign ministers and collectors, and all kinds, and I thought you couldn't have got in here without having at least a postmaster get into your pocket!'"

He "Skewed" the Line

When a surveyor, Mr. Lincoln first platted the town of Petersburg, Ill. Some twenty or thirty years afterward the property-owners along one of the outlying streets had trouble in fixing their boundaries. They consulted the official plat and got no relief. A committee was sent to Springfield to consult the distinguished surveyor, but he failed to recall anything that would give them aid, and could only refer them to the record. The dispute therefore went into the courts. While the trial was pending, an old Irishman named McGuire, who had worked for some farmer during the summer, returned to town for the winter. The case being mentioned in his presence, he promptly said: "I can tell you all about it. I helped carry the chain when Abe Lincoln laid out this town. Over there where they are quarreling about the lines, when he was locating the street, he straightened up from his instrument and said: 'If I run that street right through, it will cut three or four feet off the end of ——'s house. It's all he's got in the world and he never could get another. I reckon it won't hurt anything out here if I skew the line a little and miss him.'"

The line was "skewed," and hence the trouble, and more testimony furnished as to Lincoln's abounding kindness of heart, that would not willingly harm any human being.

"Whereas," He Stole Nothing

One of the most celebrated courts-martial during the War was that of Franklin W. Smith and his brother, charged with defrauding the government. These men bore a high character for integrity. At this time, however, courts-martial were seldom invoked for any other purpose than to convict the accused, and the Smiths shared the usual fate of persons whose cases were submitted to such arbitrament. They were kept in prison, their papers seized, their business destroyed, and their reputations ruined, all of which was followed by a conviction.

The finding of the court was submitted to the President, who, after a careful investigation, disapproved the judgment, and wrote the following endorsement upon the papers:

"Whereas, Franklin W. Smith had transactions with the Navy Department to the amount of a million and a quarter of dollars; and:

"Whereas, he had a chance to steal at least a quarter of a million and was only charged with stealing twenty-two hundred dollars, and the question now is about his stealing one hundred, I don't believe he stole anything at all.

"Therefore, the record and the findings are disapproved, declared null and void, and the defendants are fully discharged."

Not Like the Pope's Bull

President Lincoln, after listening to the arguments and appeals of a committee which called upon him at the White House not long before the Emancipation Proclamation was issued, said:

"I do not want to issue a document that the whole world will see must necessarily be inoperative, like the Pope's bull against the comet."

Could He Tell?

A "high" private of the One Hundred and Fortieth Infantry Regiment, Pennsylvania Volunteers, wounded at Chancellorsville, was taken to Washington. One day, as he was becoming convalescent, a whisper ran down the long row of cots that the President was in the building and would soon pass by. Instantly every boy in blue who was able arose, stood erect, hands to the side, ready to salute his Commander-in-Chief.

The Pennsylvanian stood six feet seven inches in his stockings. Lincoln was six feet four. As the President approached this giant towering above him, he stopped in amazement, and casting his eyes from head to foot and from foot to head, as if contemplating the immense distance from one extremity to the other, he stood for a moment speechless.

At length, extending his hand, he exclaimed, "Hello, comrade, do you know when your feet get cold?"

Darned Uncomfortable Sitting

"Frank Leslie's Illustrated Newspaper" of March 2nd, 1861, two days previous to the inauguration of President-elect Lincoln, contained the caricature reproduced here. It was intended to convey the idea that the National Administration would thereafter depend upon the support of bayonets to uphold it, and the text underneath the picture ran as follows:

OLD ABE: "Oh, it's all well enough to say that I must support the dignity of my high office by force—but it's darned uncomfortable sitting, I can tell yer."

This journal was not entirely friendly to the new Chief Magistrate, but it could not see into the future. Many of the leading publications of the East, among them some of those which condemned slavery and were opposed to secession, did not believe Lincoln was the man for the emergency, but instead of doing what they could do to help him along, they attacked him most viciously. No man, save Washington, was more brutally lied about than Lincoln, but he bore all the slurs and thrusts, not to mention the open, cruel antagonism of those who should have been his warmest friends, with a fortitude and patience few men have ever shown. He was on the right road, and awaited the time when his course should receive the approval it merited.

"What's-His-Name" Got There

General James B. Fry told a good one on Secretary of War Stanton, who was worsted in a contention with the President. Several brigadier-generals were to be selected, and Lincoln maintained that "something must be done in the interest of the Dutch." Many complaints had come from prominent men, born in the Fatherland, but who were fighting for the Union.

"Now, I want Schimmelpfennig given one of those brigadierships."

Stanton was stubborn and headstrong, as usual, but his manner and tone indicated that the President would have his own way in the end. However, he was not to be beaten without having made a fight.

"But, Mr. President," insisted the Iron War Secretary, "it may be that this Mr. Schim—what's-his-name—has no recommendations showing his fitness. Perhaps he can't speak English."

"That doesn't matter a bit, Stanton," retorted Lincoln, "he may be deaf and dumb for all I know, but whatever language he speaks, if any, we can furnish troops who will understand what he says. That name of his will make up for any differences in religion, politics or understanding, and I'll take the risk of his coming out all right."

Then, slamming his great hand upon the Secretary's desk, he said, "Schim-mel-fen-nig must be appointed."

And he was, there and then.

A Really Great General

"Do you know General A—?" queried the President one day to a friend who had "dropped in" at the White House.

"Certainly; but you are not wasting any time thinking about him, are you?" was the rejoinder.

"You wrong him," responded the President, "he is a really great man, a philosopher."

"How do you make that out? He isn't worth the powder and ball necessary to kill him so I have heard military men say," the friend remarked.

"He is a mighty thinker," the President returned, "because he has mastered that ancient and wise admonition, 'Know thyself;' he has formed an intimate acquaintance with himself, knows as well for what he is fitted and unfitted as any man living. Without doubt he is a remarkable man. This War has not produced another like him."

"How is it you are so highly pleased with General A—— all at once?"

"For the reason," replied Mr. Lincoln, with a merry twinkle of the eye, "greatly to my relief, and to the interests of the country, he has resigned. The country should express its gratitude in some substantial way."

"Shrunk Up North"

There was no member of the Cabinet from the South when Attorney-General Bates handed in his resignation, and President Lincoln had a great deal of trouble in making a selection. Finally Titian F. Coffey consented to fill the vacant place for a time, and did so until the appointment of Mr. Speed.

In conversation with Mr. Coffey the President quaintly remarked:

"My Cabinet has shrunk up North, and I must find a Southern man. I suppose if the twelve Apostles were to be chosen nowadays, the shrieks of locality would have to be heeded."

Lincoln Adopted the Suggestion

It is not generally known that President Lincoln adopted a suggestion made by Secretary of the Treasury Salmon P. Chase in regard to the Emancipation Proclamation, and incorporated it in that famous document.

After the President had read it to the members of the Cabinet he asked if he had omitted anything which should be added or inserted to strengthen it. It will be remembered that the closing paragraph of the Proclamation reads in this way:

"And upon this act, sincerely believed to be an act of justice warranted by the Constitution, I invoke the considerate judgment of mankind, and the gracious favor of Almighty God!" President Lincoln's draft of the paper ended with the word "mankind," and the words, "and the gracious favor of Almighty God," were those suggested by Secretary Chase.

Something for Everyone

It was the President's overweening desire to accommodate all persons who came to him soliciting favors, but the opportunity was never offered until an untimely and unthinking disease, which possessed many of the characteristics of one of the most dreaded maladies, confined him to his bed at the White House.

The rumor spread that the President was afflicted with this disease, while the truth was that it was merely a very mild attack of varioloid. The office-seekers didn't know the facts, and for once the Executive Mansion was clear of them.

One day, a man from the West, who didn't read the papers, but wanted the postoffice in his town, called at the White House. The President, being then practically a well man, saw him. The caller was engaged in a voluble endeavor to put his capabilities in the most favorable light, when the President interrupted him with the remark that he would be compelled to make the interview short, as his doctor was due.

"Why, Mr. President, are you sick?" queried the visitor.

"Oh, nothing much," replied Mr. Lincoln, "but the physician says he fears the worst."

"What worst, may I ask?"

"Smallpox," was the answer; "but you needn't be scared. I'm only in the first stages now."

The visitor grabbed his hat, sprang from his chair, and without a word bolted for the door.

"Don't be in a hurry," said the President placidly; "sit down and talk awhile."

"Thank you, sir; I'll call again," shouted the Westerner, as he disappeared through the opening in the wall.

"Now, that's the way with people," the President said, when relating the story afterward. "When I can't give them what they want, they're dissatisfied, and say harsh things about me; but when I've something to give to everybody they scamper off."

Too Many Pigs for the Teats

An applicant for a sutlership in the army relates this story: "In the winter of 1864, after serving three years in the Union Army, and being honorably discharged, I made application for the post sutlership at Point Lookout. My father being interested, we made application to Mr. Stanton, the Secretary of War. We obtained an audience, and were ushered into the presence of the most pompous man I ever met. As I entered he waved his hand for me to stop at a given distance from him, and then put these questions, viz.:

"'Did you serve three years in the army?'

"'I did, sir.'

"'Were you honorably discharged?'

"'I was, sir.'

"'Let me see your discharge.'

"I gave it to him. He looked it over, then said:

'Were you ever wounded?' I told him yes, at the battle of Williamsburg, May 5, 1861.

"He then said: 'I think we can give this position to a soldier who has lost an arm or leg, he being more deserving; and he then said I looked hearty and healthy enough to serve three years more. He would not give me a chance to argue my case.

"The audience was at an end. He waved his hand to me. I was then dismissed from the august presence of the Honorable Secretary of War.

"My father was waiting for me in the hallway, who saw by my countenance that I was not successful. I said to my father:

"'Let us go over to Mr. Lincoln; he may give us more satisfaction.'

"He said it would do me no good, but we went over. Mr. Lincoln's reception room was full of ladies and gentlemen when we entered.

"My turn soon came. Lincoln turned to my father and said:

"'Now, gentlemen, be pleased to be as quick as possible with your business, as it is growing late.'

"My father then stepped up to Lincoln and introduced me to him. Lincoln then said:

"'Take a seat, gentlemen, and state your business as quickly as possible.'

"There was but one chair by Lincoln, so he motioned my father to sit, while I stood. My father stated the business to him as stated above. He then said:

"'Have you seen Mr. Stanton?'

"We told him yes, that he had refused. He (Mr. Lincoln) then said:

"'Gentlemen, this is Mr. Stanton's business; I cannot interfere with him; he attends to all these matters and I am sorry I cannot help you.'

"He saw that we were disappointed, and did his best to revive our spirits. He succeeded well with my father, who was a Lincoln man, and who was a staunch Republican.

"Mr. Lincoln then said:

"'Now, gentlemen, I will tell you, what it is; I have thousands of applications like this every day, but we cannot satisfy all for this reason, that these positions are like office seekers—there are too many pigs for the teats.'

"The ladies who were listening to the conversation placed their handkerchiefs to their faces and turned away. But the joke of 'Old Abe' put us all in a good humor. We then left the presence of the greatest and most just man who ever lived to fill the Presidential chair.'"

Greeley Carries Lincoln to the Lunatic Asylum

No sooner was Abraham Lincoln made the candidate for the Presidency of the Republican Party, in 1860, than the opposition began to lampoon and caricature him. In a cartoon given the title of "The Republican Party Going to the Right House," Lincoln is represented as entering the Lunatic Asylum, riding on a rail, carried by Horace Greeley, the great Abolitionist; Lincoln, followed by his "fellow-cranks," is assuring the latter that the millennium is "going to begin," and that all requests will be granted.

Lincoln's followers are depicted as those men and women composing the "free love" element; those who want religion abolished; negroes, who want it understood that the white man has no rights his black brother is bound to respect; women suffragists, who demand that men be made subject to female authority; tramps, who insist upon free lodging-houses; criminals, who demand the right to steal from all they meet; and toughs, who want the police forces abolished, so that "the b'hoys" can "run wid de masheen," and have "a muss" whenever they feel like it, without interference by the authorities.

The Last Time He Saw Douglas

Speaking of his last meeting with Judge Douglas, Mr. Lincoln said: "One day Douglas came rushing in and said he had just got a telegraph dispatch from some friends in Illinois urging him to come out and help set things right in Egypt, and that he would go, or stay in Washington, just where I thought he could do the most good.

"I told him to do as he chose, but that probably he could do best in Illinois. Upon that he shook hands with me, and hurried away to catch the next train. I never saw him again."

Hurt His Legs Less

Lincoln was one of the attorneys in a case of considerable importance, court being held in a very small and dilapidated schoolhouse out in the country; Lincoln was compelled to stoop very much in order to enter the door, and the seats were so low that he doubled up his legs like a jackknife.

Lincoln was obliged to sit upon a school bench, and just in front of him was another, making the distance between him and the seat in front of him very narrow and uncomfortable.

His position was almost unbearable, and in order to carry out his preference which he secured as often as possible, and that was "to sit as near to the jury as convenient," he took advantage of his discomfort and finally said to the Judge on the "bench":

"Your Honor, with your permission, I'll sit up nearer to the gentlemen of the jury, for it hurts my legs less to rub my calves against the bench than it does to skin my shins."

A Little Shy or Grammar

When Mr. Lincoln had prepared his brief letter accepting the Presidential nomination he took it to Dr. Newton Bateman, the State Superintendent of Education.

"Mr. Schoolmaster," he said, "here is my letter of acceptance. I am not very strong on grammar and I wish you to see if it is all right. I wouldn't like to have any mistakes in it.."

The doctor took the letter and after reading it, said:

"There is only one change I should suggest, Mr. Lincoln, you have written 'It shall be my care to not violate or disregard it in any part,' you should have written 'not to violate.' Never split an infinitive, is the rule."

Mr. Lincoln took the manuscript, regarding it a moment with a puzzled air, "So you think I better put those two little fellows end to end, do you?" he said as he made the change.

His First Satirical Writing

Reuben and Charles Grigsby were married in Spencer county, Indiana, on the same day to Elizabeth Ray and Matilda Hawkins, respectively. They met the next day at the home of Reuben Grigsby, Sr., and held a double infare, to which most of the county was invited, with the exception of the Lincolns. This Abraham duly resented, and it resulted in his first attempt at satirical writing, which he called "The Chronicles of Reuben."

The manuscript was lost, and not recovered until 1865, when a house belonging to one of the Grigsbys was torn down. In the loft a boy found a roll of musty old papers, and was intently reading them, when he was asked what he was doing.

"Reading a portion of the Scriptures that haven't been revealed yet," was the response. This was Lincoln's "Chronicles," which is herewith given:

"THE CHRONICLES OF REUBEN."

"Now, there was a man whose name was Reuben, and the same was very great in substance, in horses and cattle and swine, and a very great household.

"It came to pass when the sons of Reuben grew up that they were desirous of taking to themselves wives, and, being too well known as to honor in their own country, they took a journey into a far country and there procured for themselves wives.

"It came to pass also that when they were about to make the return home they sent a messenger before them to bear the tidings to their parents.

"These, inquiring of the messenger what time their sons and wives would come, made a great feast and called all their kinsmen and neighbors in, and made great preparation.

"When the time drew nigh, they sent out two men to meet the grooms and their brides, with a trumpet to welcome them, and to accompany them.

"When they came near unto the house of Reuben, the father, the messenger came before them and gave a shout, and the whole multitude ran out with shouts of joy and music, playing on all kinds of instruments.

"Some were playing on harps, some on viols, and some blowing on rams' horns.

"Some also were casting dust and ashes toward Heaven, and chief among them all was Josiah, blowing his bugle and making sounds so great the neighboring hills and valleys echoed with the resounding acclamation.

"When they had played and their harps had sounded till the grooms and brides approached the gates, Reuben, the father, met them and welcomed them to his house.

"The wedding feast being now ready, they were all invited to sit down and eat, placing the bridegrooms and their brides at each end of the table.

"Waiters were then appointed to serve and wait on the guests. When all had eaten and were full and merry, they went out again and played and sung till night.

"And when they had made an end of feasting and rejoicing the multitude dispersed, each going to his own home.

"The family then took seats with their waiters to converse while preparations were being made in two upper chambers for the brides and grooms.

"This being done, the waiters took the two brides upstairs, placing one in a room at the right hand of the stairs and the other on the left.

"The waiters came down, and Nancy, the mother, then gave directions to the waiters of the bridegrooms, and they took them upstairs, but placed them in the wrong rooms.

"The waiters then all came downstairs.

"But the mother, being fearful of a mistake, made inquiry of the waiters, and learning the true facts, took the light and sprang upstairs.

"It came to pass she ran to one of the rooms and exclaimed, 'O Lord, Reuben, you are with the wrong wife.'

"The young men, both alarmed at this, ran out with such violence against each other, they came near knocking each other down.

"The tumult gave evidence to those below that the mistake was certain.

"At last they all came down and had a long conversation about who made the mistake, but it could not be decided.

"So ended the chapter."

The original manuscript of "The Chronicles of Reuben" was last in the possession of Redmond Grigsby, of Rockport, Indiana. A newspaper which had obtained a copy of the "Chronicles," sent a reporter to interview Elizabeth Grigsby, or Aunt Betsy, as she was called, and asked her about the famous manuscript and the mistake made at the double wedding.

"Yes, they did have a joke on us," said Aunt Betsy. "They said my man got into the wrong room and Charles got into my room. But it wasn't so. Lincoln just wrote that for mischief. Abe and my man often laughed about that."

Likely to Do It

An officer, having had some trouble with General Sherman, being very angry, presented himself before Mr. Lincoln, who was visiting the camp, and said, "Mr. President, I have a cause of grievance. This morning I went to General Sherman and he threatened to shoot me."

"Threatened to shoot you?" asked Mr. Lincoln. "Well, (in a stage whisper) if I were you I would keep away from him; if he threatens to shoot, I would not trust him, for I believe he would do it."

"The Enemy Are 'Ourn'"

Early in the Presidential campaign of 1864, President Lincoln said one night to a late caller at the White House:

"We have met the enemy and they are 'ourn!' I think the cabal of obstructionists 'am busted.' I feel certain that, if I live, I am going to be re-elected. Whether I deserve to be or not, it is not for me to say; but on the score even of remunerative chances for speculative service, I now am inspired with the hope that our disturbed country further requires the valuable services of your humble servant. 'Jordan has been a hard road to travel,' but I feel now that, notwithstanding the enemies I have made and the faults I have committed, I'll be dumped on the right side of that stream.

"I hope, however, that I may never have another four years of such anxiety, tribulation and abuse. My only ambition is and has been to put down the rebellion and restore peace, after which I want to resign my office, go abroad, take some rest, study foreign governments, see something of foreign life, and in my old age die in peace with all of the good of God's creatures."

"And—Here I Am!"

An old acquaintance of the President visited him in Washington. Lincoln desired to give him a place. Thus encouraged, the visitor, who was an honest man, but wholly inexperienced in public affairs or business, asked for a high office, Superintendent of the Mint.

The President was aghast, and said: "Good gracious! Why didn't he ask to be Secretary of the Treasury, and have done with it?"

Afterward, he said: "Well, now, I never thought Mr. —— had anything more than average ability, when we were young men together. But, then, I suppose he thought the same thing about me, and—here I am!"

Safe as Long as They Were Good

At the celebrated Peace Conference, whereat there was much "pow-wow" and no result, President Lincoln, in response to certain remarks by the Confederate commissioners, commented with some severity upon the conduct of the Confederate leaders, saying they had plainly forfeited all right to immunity from punishment for their treason.

Being positive and unequivocal in stating his views concerning individual treason, his words were of ominous import. There was a pause, during which Commissioner Hunter regarded the speaker with a steady, searching look. At length, carefully measuring his words, Mr. Hunter said:

"Then, Mr. President, if we understand you correctly, you think that we of the Confederacy have committed treason; are traitors to your Government; have forfeited our rights, and are proper subjects for the hangman. Is not that about what your words imply?"

"Yes," replied President Lincoln, "you have stated the proposition better than I did. That is about the size of it!"

Another pause, and a painful one succeeded, and then Hunter, with a pleasant smile remarked:

"Well, Mr. Lincoln, we have about concluded that we shall not be hanged as long as you are President—if we behave ourselves."

And Hunter meant what he said.

"Smelt No Royalty in Our Carriage"

On one occasion, in going to meet an appointment in the southern part of the Sucker State—that section of Illinois called Egypt—Lincoln, with other friends, was traveling in the "caboose" of a freight train, when the freight was switched off the main track to allow a special train to pass.

Lincoln's more aristocratic rival (Stephen A. Douglas) was being conveyed to the same town in this special. The passing train was decorated with banners and flags, and carried a band of music, which was playing "Hail to the Chief."

As the train whistled past, Lincoln broke out in a fit of laughter, and said: "Boys, the gentleman in that car evidently smelt no royalty in our carriage."

Hell a Mile from the White House

Ward Lamon told this story of President Lincoln, whom he found one day in a particularly gloomy frame of mind. Lamon said:

"The President remarked, as I came in, 'I fear I have made Senator Wade, of Ohio, my enemy for life.'

"'How?' I asked.

"'Well,' continued the President, 'Wade was here just now urging me to dismiss Grant, and, in response to something he said, I remarked, "Senator, that reminds me of a story."'

"'What did Wade say?' I inquired of the President.

"'He said, in a petulant way,' the President responded, "'It is with you, sir, all story, story! You are the father of every military blunder that has been made during the war. You are on your road to hell, sir, with this government, by your obstinacy, and you are not a mile off this minute.'"

"'What did you say then?'

"'I good-naturedly said to him,' the President replied, "'Senator, that is just about from here to the Capitol, is it not?" He was very angry, grabbed up his hat and cane, and went away.'"

His "Glass Hack"

President Lincoln had not been in the White House very long before Mrs. Lincoln became seized with the idea that a fine new barouche was about the proper thing for "the first lady in the land." The President did not care particularly about it one way or the other, and told his wife to order whatever she wanted.

Lincoln forgot all about the new vehicle, and was overcome with astonishment one afternoon when, having acceded to Mrs. Lincoln's desire to go driving, he found a beautiful barouche standing in front of the door of the White House.

His wife watched him with an amused smile, but the only remark he made was, "Well, Mary, that's about the slickest 'glass hack' in town, isn't it?"

Leave Him Kicking

Lincoln, in the days of his youth, was often unfaithful to his Quaker traditions. On the day of election in 1840, word came to him that one Radford, a Democratic contractor, had taken possession of one of the polling places with his workmen, and was preventing the Whigs from voting. Lincoln started off at a gait which showed his interest in the matter in hand.

He went up to Radford and persuaded him to leave the polls, remarking at the same time: "Radford, you'll spoil and blow, if you live much longer."

Radford's prudence prevented an actual collision, which, it is said, Lincoln regretted. He told his friend Speed he wanted Radford to show fight so that he might "knock him down and leave him kicking."

"Who Commenced This Fuss?"

President Lincoln was at all times an advocate of peace, provided it could be obtained honorably and with credit to the United States. As to the cause of the Civil War, which side of Mason and Dixon's line was responsible for it, who fired the first shots, who were the aggressors, etc., Lincoln did not seem to bother about; he wanted to preserve the Union, above all things. Slavery, he was assured, was dead, but he thought the former slaveholders should be recompensed.

To illustrate his feelings in the matter he told this story:

"Some of the supporters of the Union cause are opposed to accommodate or yield to the South in any manner or way because the Confederates began the war; were determined to take their States out of the Union, and, consequently, should be held responsible to the last stage for whatever may come in the future. Now this reminds me of a good story I heard once, when I lived in Illinois.

"A vicious bull in a pasture took after everybody who tried to cross the lot, and one day a neighbor of the owner was the victim. This man was a speedy fellow and got to a friendly tree ahead of the bull, but not in time to climb the tree. So he led the enraged animal a merry race around the tree, finally succeeding in seizing the bull by the tail.

"The bull, being at a disadvantage, not able to either catch the man or release his tail, was mad enough to eat nails; he dug up the earth with his feet, scattered gravel all around, bellowed until you could hear him for two miles or more, and at length broke into a dead run, the man hanging onto his tail all the time.

"While the bull, much out of temper, was legging it to the best of his ability, his tormentor, still clinging to the tail, asked, 'Darn you, who commenced this fuss?'

"It's our duty to settle this fuss at the earliest possible moment, no matter who commenced it. That's my idea of it."

"Abe's" Little Joke

When General W. T. Sherman, November 12th, 1864, severed all communication with the North and started for Savannah with his magnificent army of sixty thousand men, there was much anxiety for a month as to his whereabouts. President Lincoln, in response to an inquiry, said: "I know what hole Sherman went in at, but I don't know what hole he'll come out at."

Colonel McClure had been in consultation with the President one day, about two weeks after Sherman's disappearance, and in this connection related this incident:

"I was leaving the room, and just as I reached the door the President turned around, and, with a merry twinkling of the eye, inquired, 'McClure, wouldn't you like to hear something from Sherman?'

"The inquiry electrified me at the instant, as it seemed to imply that Lincoln had some information on the subject. I immediately answered, 'Yes, most of all, I should like to hear from Sherman.'

"To this President Lincoln answered, with a hearty laugh: 'Well, I'll be hanged if I wouldn't myself.'"

What Summer Thought

Although himself a most polished, even a fastidious, gentleman, Senator Sumner never allowed Lincoln's homely ways to hide his great qualities. He gave him a respect and esteem at the start which others accorded only after experience. The Senator was most tactful, too, in his dealings with Mrs. Lincoln, and soon had a firm footing in the household. That he was proud of this, perhaps a little boastful, there is no doubt.

Lincoln himself appreciated this. "Sumner thinks he runs me," he said, with an amused twinkle, one day.

A Useless Dog

When Hood's army had been scattered into fragments, President Lincoln, elated by the defeat of what had so long been a menacing force on the borders of Tennessee was reminded by its collapse of the fate of a savage dog belonging to one of his neighbors in the frontier settlements in which he lived in his youth. "The dog," he said, "was the terror of the neighborhood, and its owner, a churlish and quarrelsome fellow, took pleasure in the brute's forcible attitude.

"Finally, all other means having failed to subdue the creature, a man loaded a lump of meat with a charge of powder, to which was attached a slow fuse; this was dropped where the dreaded dog would find it, and the animal gulped down the tempting bait.

"There was a dull rumbling, a muffled explosion, and fragments of the dog were seen flying in every direction. The grieved owner, picking up the shattered remains of his cruel favorite, said: 'He was a good dog, but as a dog, his days of usefulness are over.' Hood's army was a good army," said Lincoln, by way of comment, "and we were all afraid of it, but as an army, its usefulness is gone."

Origin of the "Influence" Story

Judge Baldwin, of California, being in Washington, called one day on General Halleck, then Commander-in-Chief of the Union forces, and, presuming upon a familiar acquaintance in California a few years since, solicited a pass outside of our lines to see a brother in Virginia, not thinking that he would meet with a refusal, as both his brother and himself were good Union men.

"We have been deceived too often," said General Halleck, "and I regret I can't grant it."

Judge B. then went to Stanton, and was very briefly disposed of with the same result. Finally, he obtained an interview with Mr. Lincoln, and stated his case.

"Have you applied to General Halleck?" inquired the President.

"Yes, and met with a flat refusal," said Judge B.

"Then you must see Stanton," continued the President.

"I have, and with the same result," was the reply.

"Well, then," said Mr. Lincoln, with a smile, "I can do nothing; for you must know that I have very little influence with this Administration, although I hope to have more with the next."

Felt Sorry for Both

Many ladies attended the famous debates between Lincoln and Douglas, and they were the most unprejudiced listeners. "I can recall only one fact of the debates," says Mrs. William Crotty, of Seneca, Illinois, "that I felt so sorry for Lincoln while Douglas was speaking, and then to my surprise I felt so sorry for Douglas when Lincoln replied."

The disinterested to whom it was an intellectual game, felt the power and charm of both men.

Where Did It Come from?

"What made the deepest impression upon you?" inquired a friend one day, "when you stood in the presence of the Falls of Niagara, the greatest of natural wonders?"

"The thing that struck me most forcibly when I saw the Falls," Lincoln responded, with characteristic deliberation, "was, where in the world did all that water come from?"

"Long Abe" Four Years Longer

The second election of Abraham Lincoln to the Presidency of the United States was the reward of his courage and genius bestowed upon him by the people of the Union States. General George B. McClellan was his opponent in 1864 upon the platform that "the War is a failure," and carried but three States—New Jersey, Delaware and Kentucky. The States which did not think the War was a failure were those in New England, New York, Pennsylvania, all the Western commonwealths, West Virginia, Tennessee, Louisiana, Arkansas and the new State of Nevada, admitted into the Union on October 31st. President Lincoln's popular majority over McClellan, who never did much toward making the War a success, was more than four hundred thousand. Underneath a cartoon in "Harper's Weekly" of November 26th, 1864, were the words, "Long Abraham Lincoln a Little Longer."

But the beloved President's time upon earth was not to be much longer, as he was assassinated just one month and ten days after his second inauguration. Indeed, the words, "a little longer," printed below the cartoon, were strangely prophetic, although not intended to be such.

The people of the United States had learned to love "Long Abe," their affection being of a purely personal nature, in the main. No other Chief Executive was regarded as so sincerely the friend of the great mass of the inhabitants of the Republic as Lincoln. He was, in truth, one of "the common people," having been born among them, and lived as one of them.

Lincoln's great height made him an easy subject for the cartoonist, and they used it in his favor as well as against him.

"All Sicker'n Your Man"

A Commissioner to the Hawaiian Islands was to be appointed, and eight applicants had filed their papers, when a delegation from the South appeared at the White House on behalf of a ninth. Not only was their man fit—so the delegation urged—but was also in bad health, and a residence in that balmy climate would be of great benefit to him.

The President was rather impatient that day, and before the members of the delegation had fairly started in, suddenly closed the interview with this remark:

"Gentlemen, I am sorry to say that there are eight other applicants for that place, and they are all 'sicker'n' your man."

Easier to Empty the Potomac

An officer of low volunteer rank persisted in telling and re-telling his troubles to the President on a summer afternoon when Lincoln was tired and careworn.

After listening patiently, he finally turned upon the man, and, looking wearily out upon the broad Potomac in the distance, said in a peremptory tone that ended the interview:

"Now, my man, go away, go away. I cannot meddle in your case. I could as easily bail out the Potomac River with a teaspoon as attend to all the details of the army."

He Wanted a Steady Hand

When the Emancipation Proclamation was taken to Mr. Lincoln by Secretary Seward, for the President's signature, Mr. Lincoln took a pen, dipped it in the ink, moved his hand to the place for the signature, held it a moment, then removed his hand and dropped the pen. After a little hesitation, he again took up the pen and went through the same movement as before. Mr. Lincoln then turned to Mr. Seward and said:

"I have been shaking hands since nine o'clock this morning, and my right arm is almost paralyzed. If my name ever goes into history, it will be for this act, and my whole soul is in it. If my hand trembles when I sign the Proclamation, all who examine the document hereafter will say, 'He hesitated.'"

He then turned to the table, took up the pen again, and slowly, firmly wrote "Abraham Lincoln," with which the whole world is now familiar.

He then looked up, smiled, and said, "That will do."

Lincoln Saw Stanton About It

Mr. Lovejoy, heading a committee of Western men, discussed an important scheme with the President, and the gentlemen were then directed to explain it to Secretary of War Stanton.

Upon presenting themselves to the Secretary, and showing the President's order, the Secretary said: "Did Lincoln give you an order of that kind?"

"He did, sir."

"Then he is a d—d fool," said the angry Secretary.

"Do you mean to say that the President is a d—d fool?" asked Lovejoy, in amazement.

"Yes, sir, if he gave you such an order as that."

The bewildered Illinoisan betook himself at once to the President and related the result of the conference.

"Did Stanton say I was a d—d fool?" asked Lincoln at the close of the recital.

"He did, sir, and repeated it."

After a moment's pause, and looking up, the President said: "If Stanton said I was a d—d fool, then I must be one, for he is nearly always right, and generally says what he means. I will slip over and see him."

Mrs. Lincoln's Surprise

A good story is told of how Mrs. Lincoln made a little surprise for her husband.

In the early days it was customary for lawyers to go from one county to another on horseback, a journey which often required several weeks. On returning from one of these trips, late one night, Mr. Lincoln dismounted from his horse at the familiar corner and then turned to go into the house, but stopped; a perfectly unknown structure was before him. Surprised, and thinking there must be some mistake, he went across the way and knocked at a neighbor's door. The family had retired, and so called out:

"Who's there?"

"Abe Lincoln," was the reply. "I am looking for my house. I thought it was across the way, but when I went away a few weeks ago there was only a one-story house there and now there is a two-story house in its place. I think I must be lost."

The neighbors then explained that Mrs. Lincoln had added another story during his absence. And Mr. Lincoln laughed and went to his remodeled house.

Menace to the Government

The persistence of office-seekers nearly drove President Lincoln wild. They slipped in through the half-opened doors of the Executive Mansion; they dogged his steps if he walked; they edged their way through the crowds and thrust their papers in his hands when he rode; and, taking it all in all, they well-nigh worried him to death.

He once said that if the Government passed through the Rebellion without dismemberment there was the strongest danger of its falling a prey to the rapacity of the office-seeking class.

"This human struggle and scramble for office, for a way to live without work, will finally test the strength of our institutions," were the words he used.

Troops Couldn't Fly over It

On April 20th a delegation from Baltimore appeared at the White House and begged the President that troops for Washington be sent around and not through Baltimore.

President Lincoln replied, laughingly: "If I grant this concession, you will be back tomorrow asking that no troops be marched 'around' it."

The President was right. That afternoon, and again on Sunday and Monday, committees sought him, protesting that Maryland soil should not be "polluted" by the feet of soldiers marching against the South.

The President had but one reply: "We must have troops, and as they can neither crawl under Maryland nor fly over it, they must come across it."

Pat Was "Forninst the Government"

The Governor-General of Canada, with some of his principal officers, visited President Lincoln in the summer of 1864.

They had been very troublesome in harboring blockade runners, and they were said to have carried on a large trade from their ports with the Confederates. Lincoln treated his guests with great courtesy.

After a pleasant interview, the Governor, alluding to the coming Presidential election said, jokingly, but with a grain of sarcasm: "I understand Mr. President, that everybody votes in this country. If we remain until November, can we vote?"

"You remind me," replied the President, "of a countryman of yours, a green emigrant from Ireland. Pat arrived on election day, and perhaps was as eager as your Excellency to vote, and to vote early, and late and often.

"So, upon landing at Castle Garden, he hastened to the nearest voting place, and as he approached, the judge who received the ballots inquired, 'Who do you want to vote for? On which side are you?' Poor Pat was embarrassed; he did not know who were the candidates. He stopped, scratched his head, then, with the readiness of his countrymen, he said:

"'I am forninst the Government, anyhow. Tell me, if your Honor plase: which is the rebellion side, and I'll tell you haw I want to vote. In ould Ireland, I was always on the rebellion side, and, by Saint Patrick, I'll do that same in America.' Your Excellency," said Mr. Lincoln, "would, I should think, not be at all at a loss on which side to vote!"

"Can't Spare This Man"

One night, about eleven o'clock, Colonel A. K. McClure, whose intimacy with President Lincoln was so great that he could obtain admittance to the Executive Mansion at any and all hours, called at the White House to urge Mr. Lincoln to remove General Grant from command.

After listening patiently for a long time, the President, gathering himself up in his chair, said, with the utmost earnestness:

"I can't spare this man; he fights!"

In relating the particulars of this interview, Colonel McClure said:

"That was all he said, but I knew that it was enough, and that Grant was safe in Lincoln's hands against his countless hosts of enemies. The only man in all the nation who had the power to save Grant was Lincoln, and he had decided to do it. He was not influenced by any personal partiality for Grant, for they had never met.

"It was not until after the battle of Shiloh, fought on the 6th and 7th of April, 1862, that Lincoln was placed in a position to exercise a controlling influence in shaping the destiny of Grant. The first reports from the Shiloh battle-field created profound alarm throughout the entire country, and the wildest exaggerations were spread in a floodtide of vituperation against Grant.

"The few of to-day who can recall the inflamed condition of public sentiment against Grant caused by the disastrous first day's battle at Shiloh will remember that he was denounced as incompetent for his command by the public journals of all parties in the North, and with almost entire unanimity by Senators and Congressmen, regardless of political affinities.

"I appealed to Lincoln for his own sake to remove Grant at once, and in giving my reasons for it I simply voiced the admittedly overwhelming protest from the loyal people of the land against Grant's continuance in command.

"I did not forget that Lincoln was the one man who never allowed himself to appear as wantonly defying public sentiment. It seemed to me impossible for him to save Grant without taking a crushing load of condemnation upon himself; but Lincoln was wiser than all those around him, and he not only saved Grant, but he saved him by such well-concerted effort that he soon won popular applause from those who were most violent in demanding Grant's dismissal."

His Teeth Chattered

During the Lincoln-Douglas joint debates of 1858, the latter accused Lincoln of having, when in Congress, voted against the appropriation for supplies to be sent the United States soldiers in Mexico. In reply, Lincoln said: "This is a perversion of the facts. I was opposed to the policy of the administration in declaring war against Mexico; but when war was declared I never failed to vote for the support of any proposition looking to the comfort of our poor fellows who were maintaining the dignity of our flag in a war that I thought unnecessary and unjust."

He gradually became more and more excited; his voice thrilled and his whole frame shook. Sitting on the stand was O. B. Ficklin, who had served in Congress with Lincoln in 1847. Lincoln reached back, took Ficklin by the coat-collar, back of his neck, and in no gentle manner lifted him from his seat as if he had been a kitten, and roared: "Fellow-citizens, here is Ficklin, who was at that time in Congress with me, and he knows it is a lie."

He shook Ficklin until his teeth chattered. Fearing he would shake Ficklin's head off, Ward Lamon grasped Lincoln's hand and broke his grip.

After the speaking was over, Ficklin, who had warm personal friendship with him, said: "Lincoln, you nearly shook all the Democracy out of me to-day."

"Aaron Got His Commission"

President Lincoln was censured for appointing one that had zealously opposed his second term.

He replied: "Well, I suppose Judge E., having been disappointed before, did behave pretty ugly, but that wouldn't make him any less fit for the place; and I think I have Scriptural authority for appointing him.

"You remember when the Lord was on Mount Sinai getting out a commission for Aaron, that same Aaron was at the foot of the mountain making a false god for the people to worship. Yet Aaron got his commission, you know."

Lincoln and the Ministers

At the time of Lincoln's nomination, at Chicago, Mr. Newton Bateman, Superintendent of Public Instruction for the State of Illinois, occupied a room adjoining and opening into the Executive Chamber at Springfield. Frequently this door was open during Mr. Lincoln's receptions, and throughout the seven months or more of his occupation he saw him nearly every day. Often, when Mr. Lincoln was tired, he closed the door against all intruders, and called Mr. Bateman into his room for a quiet talk. On one of these occasions, Mr. Lincoln took up a book containing canvass of the city of Springfield, in which he lived, showing the candidate for whom each citizen had declared it his intention to vote in the approaching election. Mr. Lincoln's friends had, doubtless at his own request, placed the result of the canvass in his hands. This was towards the close of October, and only a few days before election. Calling Mr. Bateman to a seat by his side, having previously locked all the doors, he said:

"Let us look over this book; I wish particularly to see how the ministers if Springfield are going to vote." The leaves were turned, one by one, and as the names were examined Mr. Lincoln frequently asked if this one and that one was not a minister, or an elder, or a member of such and such a church, and sadly expressed his surprise on receiving an affirmative answer. In that manner he went through the book, and then he closed it, and sat silently for some minutes regarding a memorandum in pencil which lay before him. At length he turned to Mr. Bateman, with a face full of sadness, and said:

"Here are twenty-three ministers of different denominations, and all of them are against me but three, and here are a great many prominent members of churches, a very large majority are against me. Mr. Bateman, I am not a Christian—God knows I would be one—but I have carefully read the Bible, and I do not so understand this book," and he drew forth a pocket New Testament.

"These men well know," he continued, "that I am for freedom in the Territories, freedom everywhere, as free as the Constitution and the laws will permit, and that my opponents are for slavery. They know this, and yet, with this book in their hands, in the light of which human bondage cannot live a moment, they are going to vote against me; I do not understand it at all."

Here Mr. Lincoln paused—paused for long minutes, his features surcharged with emotion. Then he rose and walked up and down the reception-room in the effort to retain or regain his self-possession. Stopping at last, he said, with a trembling voice and cheeks wet with tears:

"I know there is a God, and that He hates injustice and slavery. I see the storm coming, and I know that His hand is in it. If He has a place and work for me, and I think He has, I believe I am ready. I am nothing, but Truth is everything. I know I am right, because I know that liberty is right, for Christ teaches it, and Christ is God. I have told them that a house divided against itself cannot stand; and Christ and Reason say the same, and they will find it so.

"Douglas doesn't care whether slavery is voted up or down, but God cares, and humanity cares, and I care; and with God's help I shall not fail. I may not see the end, but it will come, and I shall be vindicated; and these men will find they have not read their Bible right."

Much of this was uttered as if he were speaking to himself, and with a sad, earnest solemnity of manner impossible to be described. After a pause he resumed:

"Doesn't it seem strange that men can ignore the moral aspect of this contest? No revelation could make it plainer to me that slavery or the Government must be destroyed. The future would be something awful, as I look at it, but for this rock on which I stand" (alluding to the Testament which he still held in his hand), "especially with the knowledge of how these ministers are going to vote. It seems as if God had borne with this thing (slavery) until the teachers of religion have come to defend it from the Bible, and to claim for it a divine character and sanction; and now the cup of iniquity is full, and the vials of wrath will be poured out."

Everything he said was of a peculiarly deep, tender, and religious tone, and all was tinged with a touching melancholy. He repeatedly referred to his conviction that the day of wrath was at hand, and that he was to be an actor in the terrible struggle which would issue in the overthrow of slavery, although he might not live to see the end.

After further reference to a belief in the Divine Providence and the fact of God in history, the conversation turned upon prayer. He freely stated his belief in the duty, privilege, and efficacy of prayer, and intimated, in no unmistakable terms, that he had sought in that way Divine guidance and favor. The effect of this conversation upon the mind of Mr. Bateman, a Christian gentleman whom Mr. Lincoln profoundly respected, was to convince him that Mr. Lincoln had, in a quiet way, found a path to the Christian standpoint—that he had found God, and rested on the eternal truth of God. As the two men were about to separate, Mr. Bateman remarked:

"I have not supposed that you were accustomed to think so much upon this class of subjects; certainly your friends generally are ignorant of the sentiments you have expressed to me."

He replied quickly: "I know they are, but I think more on these subjects than upon all others, and I have done so for years; and I am willing you should know it."

Hardtack Better Than Generals

Secretary of War Stanton told the President the following story, which greatly amused the latter, as he was especially fond of a joke at the expense of some high military or civil dignitary.

Stanton had little or no sense of humor.

When Secretary Stanton was making a trip up the Broad River in North Carolina, in a tugboat, a Federal picket yelled out, "What have you got on board of that tug?"

The severe and dignified answer was, "The Secretary of War and Major-General Foster."

Instantly the picket roared back, "We've got Major-Generals enough up here. Why don't you bring us up some hardtack?"

Got the Preacher

A story told by a Cabinet member tended to show how accurately Lincoln could calculate political results in advance—a faculty which remained with him all his life.

"A friend, who was a Democrat, had come to him early in the canvass and told him he wanted to see him elected, but did not like to vote against his party; still he would vote for him, if the contest was to be so close that every vote was needed.

"A short time before the election Lincoln said to him: 'I have got the preacher, and I don't want your vote.'"

Big Joke on Halleck

When General Halleck was Commander-in-Chief of the Union forces, with headquarters at Washington, President Lincoln unconsciously played a big practical joke upon that dignified officer. The President had spent the night at the Soldiers' Home, and the next morning asked Captain Derickson, commanding the company of Pennsylvania soldiers, which was the Presidential guard at the White House and the Home—wherever the President happened to be—to go to town with him.

Captain Derickson told the story in a most entertaining way:

"When we entered the city, Mr. Lincoln said he would call at General Halleck's headquarters and get what news had been received from the army during the night. I informed him that General Cullum, chief aid to General Halleck, was raised in Meadville, and that I knew him when I was a boy.

"He replied, 'Then we must see both the gentlemen.' When the carriage stopped, he requested me to remain seated, and said he would bring the gentlemen down to see me, the office being on the second floor. In a short time the President came down, followed by the other gentlemen. When he introduced them to me, General Cullum recognized and seemed pleased to see me.

"In General Halleck I thought I discovered a kind of quizzical look, as much as to say, 'Isn't this rather a big joke to ask the Commander-in-Chief of the army down to the street to be introduced to a country captain?'"

Stories Better Than Doctors

A gentleman, visiting a hospital at Washington, heard an occupant of one of the beds laughing and talking about the President, who had been there a short time before and gladdened the wounded with some of his stories. The soldier seemed in such good spirits that the gentleman inquired:

"You must be very slightly wounded?"

"Yes," replied the brave fellow, "very slightly—I have only lost one leg, and I'd be glad enough to lose the other, if I could hear some more of 'Old Abe's' stories."

Short, but Exciting

William B. Wilson, employed in the telegraph office at the War Department, ran over to the White House one day to summon Mr. Lincoln. He described the trip back to the War Department in this manner:

"Calling one of his two younger boys to join him, we then started from the White House, between stately trees, along a gravel path which led to the rear of the old War Department building. It was a warm day, and Mr. Lincoln wore as part of his costume a faded gray linen duster which hung loosely around his long gaunt frame; his kindly eye was beaming with good nature, and his ever-thoughtful brow was unruffled.

"We had barely reached the gravel walk before he stooped over, picked up a round smooth pebble, and shooting it off his thumb, challenged us to a game of 'followings,' which we accepted. Each in

turn tried to hit the outlying stone, which was being constantly pro-
jected onward by the President. The game was short, but exciting;
the cheerfulness of childhood, the ambition of young manhood, and
the gravity of the statesman were all injected into it.

"The game was not won until the steps of the War Department
were reached. Every inch of progression was toughly contested, and
when the President was declared victor, it was only by a hand span.
He appeared to be as much pleased as if he had won a battle."

Mr. Bull Didn't Get His Cotton

Because of the blockade, by the Union fleets, of the Southern cotton ports, England was deprived of her supply of cotton, and scores
of thousands of British operatives were thrown out of employment
by the closing of the cotton mills at Manchester and other cities in
Great Britain. England (John Bull) felt so badly about this that the
British wanted to go to war on account of it, but when the United
States eagle ruffled up its wings the English thought over the business and concluded not to fight.

"Harper's Weekly" of May 16th, 1863, contained a cartoon which
shows John Bull as manifesting much anxiety regarding the cotton he had bought from the Southern planters, but which the latter
could not deliver. Beneath the cartoon is this bit of dialogue between
John Bull and President Lincoln: MR. BULL (confiding creature): "Hi
want my cotton, bought at fi'pence a pound."

MR. LINCOLN: "Don't know anything about it, my dear sir. Your
friends, the rebels, are burning all the cotton they can find, and I
confiscate the rest. Good-morning, John!"

As President Lincoln has a big fifteen-inch gun at his side, the
black muzzle of which is pressed tightly against Mr. Bull's waistcoat,
the President, to all appearances, has the best of the argument "by a
long shot." Anyhow, Mr. Bull had nothing more to say, but gave the
cotton matter up as a bad piece of business, and pocketed the loss.

Stick to American Principles

President Lincoln's first conclusion (that Mason and Slidell should be released) was the real ground on which the Administration submitted. "We must stick to American principles concerning the rights of neutrals." It was to many, as Secretary of the Treasury Chase declared it was to him, "gall and wormwood." James Russell Lowell's verse expressed best the popular feeling:

We give the critters back, John, Cos Abram thought 'twas right; It warn't your bullyin' clack, John, Provokin' us to fight.

The decision raised Mr. Lincoln immeasurably in the view of thoughtful men, especially in England.

Used "Rude Tact"

General John C. Fremont, with headquarters at St. Louis, astonished the country by issuing a proclamation declaring, among other things, that the property, real and personal, of all the persons in the State of Missouri who should take up arms against the United States, or who should be directly proved to have taken an active part with its enemies in the field, would be confiscated to public use and their slaves, if they had any, declared freemen.

The President was dismayed; he modified that part of the proclamation referring to slaves, and finally replaced Fremont with General Hunter.

Mrs. Fremont (daughter of Senator T. H. Benton), her husband's real chief of staff, flew to Washington and sought Mr. Lincoln. It was midnight, but the President gave her an audience. Without waiting for an explanation, she violently charged him with sending an enemy to Missouri to look into Fremont's case, and threatening that if Fremont desired to he could set up a government for himself.

"I had to exercise all the rude tact I have to avoid quarreling with her," said Mr. Lincoln afterwards.

"Abe" on a Woodpile

Lincoln's attempt to make a lawyer of himself under adverse and unpromising circumstances—he was a bare-footed farm-hand—excited comment. And it was not to be wondered. One old man, who was yet alive as late as 1901, had often employed Lincoln to do farm work for him, and was surprised to find him one day sitting barefoot on the summit of a woodpile and attentively reading a book.

"This being an unusual thing for farm-hands in that early day to do," said the old man, when relating the story, "I asked him what he was reading.

"'I'm not reading,' he answered. 'I'm studying.'

"'Studying what?' I inquired.

"'Law, sir,' was the emphatic response.

"It was really too much for me, as I looked at him sitting there proud as Cicero. 'Great God Almighty!' I exclaimed, and passed on." Lincoln merely laughed and resumed his "studies."

Taking Down a Dandy

In a political campaign, Lincoln once replied to Colonel Richard Taylor, a self-conceited, dandified man, who wore a gold chain and ruffled shirt. His party at that time was posing as the hard-working bone and sinew of the land, while the Whigs were stigmatized as aristocrats, ruffled-shirt gentry. Taylor making a sweeping gesture, his overcoat became torn open, displaying his finery. Lincoln in reply said, laying his hand on his jeans-clad breast:

"Here is your aristocrat, one of your silk-stocking gentry, at your service." Then, spreading out his hands, bronzed and gaunt with toil: "Here is your rag-basin with lily-white hands. Yes, I suppose, according to my friend Taylor, I am a bloated aristocrat."

When Old Abe Got Mad

Soon after hostilities broke out between the North and South, Congress appointed a Committee on the Conduct of the War. This committee beset Mr. Lincoln and urged all sorts of measures. Its members were aggressive and patriotic, and one thing they determined upon was that the Army of the Potomac should move. But it was not until March that they became convinced that anything would be done.

One day early in that month, Senator Chandler, of Michigan, a member of the committee, met George W. Julian. He was in high glee. "'Old' Abe is mad," said Julian, "and the War will now go on."

Wanted to "Borrow" the Army

During one of the periods when things were at a standstill, the Washington authorities, being unable to force General McClellan to assume an aggressive attitude, President Lincoln went to the general's headquarters to have a talk with him, but for some reason he was unable to get an audience.

Mr. Lincoln returned to the White House much disturbed at his failure to see the commander of the Union forces, and immediately sent for two general officers, to have a consultation. On their arrival, he told them he must have someone to talk to about the situation, and as he had failed to see General McClellan, he wished their views as to the possibility or probability of commencing active operations with the Army of the Potomac.

"Something's got to be done," said the President, emphatically, "and done right away, or the bottom will fall out of the whole thing. Now, if McClellan doesn't want to use the army for awhile, I'd like to borrow it from him and see if I can't do something or other with it.

"If McClellan can't fish, he ought at least to be cutting bait at a time like this."

Young "Sucker" Visitors

After Mr. Lincoln's nomination for the Presidency, the Executive Chamber, a large, fine room in the State House at Springfield, was set apart for him, where he met the public until after his election.

As illustrative of the nature of many of his calls, the following incident was related by Mr. Holland, an eye-witness: "Mr. Lincoln being in conversation with a gentleman one day, two raw, plainly-dressed young 'Suckers' entered the room, and bashfully lingered near the door. As soon as he observed them, and saw their embarrassment, he rose and walked to them, saying: 'How do you do, my good fellows? What can I do for you? Will you sit down?' The spokesman of the pair, the shorter of the two, declined to sit, and explained the object of the call thus: He had had a talk about the relative height of Mr. Lincoln and his companion, and had asserted his belief that they were of exactly the same height. He had come in to verify his judgment. Mr. Lincoln smiled, went and got his cane, and, placing the end of it upon the wall, said" 'Here, young man, come under here.' "The young man came under the cane as Mr. Lincoln held it, and when it was perfectly adjusted to his height, Mr. Lincoln said:

"'Now, come out, and hold the cane.'

"This he did, while Mr. Lincoln stood under. Rubbing his head back and forth to see that it worked easily under the measurement, he stepped out, and declared to the sagacious fellow who was curiously looking on, that he had guessed with remarkable accuracy— that he and the young man were exactly the same height. Then he shook hands with them and sent them on their way. Mr. Lincoln would just as soon have thought of cutting off his right hand as he would have thought of turning those boys away with the impression that they had in any way insulted his dignity."

"And You Don't Wear Hoopskirts"

An Ohio Senator had an appointment with President Lincoln at six o'clock, and as he entered the vestibule of the White House his attention was attracted toward a poorly clad young woman, who was violently sobbing. He asked her the cause of her distress. She said she had been ordered away by the servants, after vainly waiting many hours to see the President about her only brother, who had been condemned to death. Her story was this:

She and her brother were foreigners, and orphans. They had been in this country several years. Her brother enlisted in the army, but, through bad influences, was induced to desert. He was captured, tried and sentenced to be shot—the old story.

The poor girl had obtained the signatures of some persons who had formerly known him, to a petition for a pardon, and alone had come to Washington to lay the case before the President. Thronged as the waiting-rooms always were, she had passed the long hours of two days trying in vain to get an audience, and had at length been ordered away.

The gentleman's feelings were touched. He said to her that he had come to see the President, but did not know as he should succeed. He told her, however, to follow him upstairs, and he would see what could be done for her.

Just before reaching the door, Mr. Lincoln came out, and, meeting his friend, said good-humoredly, "Are you not ahead of time?" The gentleman showed him his watch, with the hand upon the hour of six.

"Well," returned Mr. Lincoln, "I have been so busy to-day that I have not had time to get a lunch. Go in and sit down; I will be back directly."

The gentleman made the young woman accompany him into the office, and when they were seated, said to her: "Now, my good girl, I want you to muster all the courage you have in the world. When the President comes back, he will sit down in that armchair. I shall get up to speak to him, and as I do so you must force yourself between us, and insist upon his examination of your papers, telling him it is a case of life and death, and admits of no delay." These instructions were carried out to the letter. Mr. Lincoln was at first somewhat surprised at the apparent forwardness of the young woman, but observing her distressed appearance, he ceased conversation with his friend, and commenced an examination of the document she had placed in his hands.

Glancing from it to the face of the petitioner, whose tears had broken forth afresh, he studied its expression for a moment, and then his eye fell upon her scanty but neat dress. Instantly his face lighted up.

"My poor girl," said he, "you have come here with no Governor, or Senator, or member of Congress to plead your cause. You seem honest and truthful; and you don't wear hoopskirts—and I will be whipped but I will pardon your brother." And he did.

Lieutenant Tad Lincoln's Sentinels

President Lincoln's favorite son, Tad, having been sportively commissioned a lieutenant in the United States Army by Secretary Stanton, procured several muskets and drilled the men-servants of the house in the manual of arms without attracting the attention of his father. And one night, to his consternation, he put them all on duty, and relieved the regular sentries, who, seeing the lad in full uniform, or perhaps appreciating the joke, gladly went to their quarters. His brother objected; but Tad insisted upon his rights as an officer. The President laughed but declined to interfere, but when the lad had lost his little authority in his boyish sleep, the Commander-in-Chief of the Army and Navy of the United States went down and personally discharged the sentries his son had put on the post.

Douglas Held Lincoln's Hat

When Mr. Lincoln delivered his first inaugural he was introduced by his friend, United States Senator E. D. Baker, of Oregon. He carried a cane and a little roll—the manuscript of his inaugural address. There was moment's pause after the introduction, as he vainly looked for a spot where he might place his high silk hat.

Stephen A. Douglas, the political antagonist of his whole public life, the man who had pressed him hardest in the campaign of 1860, was seated just behind him. Douglas stepped forward quickly, and took the hat which Mr. Lincoln held helplessly in his hand.

"If I can't be President," Douglas whispered smilingly to Mrs. Brown, a cousin of Mrs. Lincoln and a member of the President's party, "I at least can hold his hat."

The Dead Man Spoke

Mr. Lincoln once said in a speech: "Fellow-citizens, my friend, Mr. Douglas, made the startling announcement to-day that the Whigs are all dead.

"If that be so, fellow-citizens, you will now experience the novelty of hearing a speech from a dead man; and I suppose you might properly say, in the language of the old hymn:

"'Hark! from the tombs a doleful sound.'"

Military Snails Not Speedy

President Lincoln—as he himself put it in conversation one day with a friend—"fairly ached" for his generals to "get down to business." These slow generals he termed "snails."

Grant, Sherman and Sheridan were his favorites, for they were aggressive. They did not wait for the enemy to attack. Too many of the others were "lingerers," as Lincoln called them. They were magnificent in defense, and stubborn and brave, but their names figured too much on the "waiting list."

The greatest fault Lincoln found with so many of the commanders on the Union side was their unwillingness to move until everything was exactly to their liking.

Lincoln could not understand why these leaders of Northern armies hesitated.

Outran the Jack-Rabbit

When the Union forces were routed in the first battle of Bull Run, there were many civilians present, who had gone out from Washington to witness the battle. Among the number were several Congressmen. One of these was a tall, long-legged fellow, who wore a long-tailed coat and a high plug hat. When the retreat began, this Congressman was in the lead of the entire crowd fleeing toward Washington. He outran all the rest, and was the first man to arrive in the city. No person ever made such good use of long legs as this Congressman. His immense stride carried him yards at every bound. He went over ditches and gullies at a single leap, and cleared a six-foot fence with a foot to spare. As he went over the fence his plug hat blew off, but he did not pause. With his long coat-tails flying in the wind, he continued straight ahead for Washington.

Many of those behind him were scared almost to death, but the flying Congressman was such a comical figure that they had to laugh in spite of their terror.

Mr. Lincoln enjoyed the description of how this Congressman led the race from Bull's Run, and laughed at it heartily.

"I never knew but one fellow who could run like that," he said, "and he was a young man out in Illinois. He had been sparking a girl, much against the wishes of her father. In fact, the old man took such a dislike to him that he threatened to shoot him if he ever caught him around his premises again.

"One evening the young man learned that the girl's father had gone to the city, and he ventured out to the house. He was sitting in the parlor, with his arm around Betsy's waist, when he suddenly spied the old man coming around the corner of the house with a shotgun. Leaping through a window into the garden, he started down a path at the top of his speed. He was a long-legged fellow, and could run like greased lightning. Just then a jack-rabbit jumped up in the path in front of him. In about two leaps he overtook the rabbit. Giving it a kick that sent it high in the air, he exclaimed: 'Git out of the road, gosh dern you, and let somebody run that knows how.'

"I reckon," said Mr. Lincoln, "that the long-legged Congressman, when he saw the rebel muskets, must have felt a good deal like that young fellow did when he saw the old man's shot-gun."

"Fooling" the People

Lincoln was a strong believer in the virtue of dealing honestly with the people.

"If you once forfeit the confidence of your fellow-citizens," he said to a caller at the White House, "you can never regain their respect and esteem.

"It is true that you may fool all the people some of the time; you can even fool some of the people all the time; but you can't fool all of the people all the time."

"Abe, You Can't Play That on Me"

The night President-elect Lincoln arrived at Washington, one man was observed watching Lincoln very closely as he walked out of the railroad station. Standing a little to one side, the man looked very sharply at Lincoln, and, as the latter passed, seized hold of his hand, and said in a loud tone of voice, "Abe, you can't play that on me!"

Ward Lamon and the others with Lincoln were instantly alarmed, and would have struck the stranger had not Lincoln hastily said, "Don't strike him! It is Washburne. Don't you know him?"

Mr. Seward had given Congressman Washburne a hint of the time the train would arrive, and he had the right to be at the station when the train steamed in, but his indiscreet manner of loudly addressing the President-elect might have led to serious consequences to the latter.

His "Broad" Stories

Mrs. Rose Linder Wilkinson, who often accompanied her father, Judge Linder, in the days when he rode circuit with Mr. Lincoln, tells the following story:

"At night, as a rule, the lawyers spent awhile in the parlor, and permitted the women who happened to be along to sit with them. But after half an hour or so we would notice it was time for us to leave them. I remember traveling the circuit one season when the young wife of one of the lawyers was with him. The place was so crowded that she and I were made to sleep together. When the time came for banishing us from the parlor, we went up to our room and sat there till bed-time, listening to the roars that followed each ether swiftly while those lawyers down-stairs told stories and laughed till the rafters rang.

"In the morning Mr. Lincoln said to me: 'Rose, did we disturb your sleep last night?' I answered, 'No, I had no sleep'—which was not entirely true but the retort amused him. Then the young lawyer's wife complained to him that we were not fairly used. We came along with them, young women, and when they were having the best time we were sent away like children to go to bed in the dark.

"'But, Madame,' said Mr. Lincoln, 'you would not enjoy the things we laugh at.' And then he entered into a discussion on what have been termed his 'broad' stories. He deplored the fact that men seemed to remember them longer and with less effort than any others.

"My father said: 'But, Lincoln, I don't remember the "broad" part of your stories so much as I do the moral that is in them,' and it was a thing in which they were all agreed."

Sorry for the Horses

When President Lincoln heard of the Confederate raid at Fairfax, in which a brigadier-general and a number of valuable horses were captured, he gravely observed:

"Well, I am sorry for the horses."

"Sorry for the horses, Mr. President!" exclaimed the Secretary of War, raising his spectacles and throwing himself back in his chair in astonishment.

"Yes," replied Mr., Lincoln, "I can make a brigadier-general in five minutes, but it is not easy to replace a hundred and ten horses."

Mild Rebuke to a Doctor

Dr. Jerome Walker, of Brooklyn, told how Mr. Lincoln once administered to him a mild rebuke. The doctor was showing Mr. Lincoln through the hospital at City Point.

"Finally, after visiting the wards occupied by our invalid and convalescing soldiers," said Dr. Walker, "we came to three wards occupied by sick and wounded Southern prisoners. With a feeling of patriotic duty, I said: 'Mr. President, you won't want to go in there; they are only rebels.'

"I will never forget how he stopped and gently laid his large hand upon my shoulder and quietly answered, 'You mean Confederates!' And I have meant Confederates ever since.

"There was nothing left for me to do after the President's remark but to go with him through these three wards; and I could not see but that he was just as kind, his hand-shakings just as hearty, his interest just as real for the welfare of the men, as when he was among our own soldiers."

Cold Molasses Was Swifter

"Old Pap," as the soldiers called General George H. Thomas, was aggravatingly slow at a time when the President wanted him to "get a move on"; in fact, the gallant "Rock of Chickamauga" was evidently entered in a snail-race.

"Some of my generals are so slow," regretfully remarked Lincoln one day, "that molasses in the coldest days of winter is a race horse compared to them.

"They're brave enough, but somehow or other they get fastened in a fence corner, and can't figure their way out."

Lincoln Calls Medill a Coward

Joseph Medill, for many years editor of the Chicago Tribune, not long before his death, told the following story regarding the "talking to" President Lincoln gave himself and two other Chicago gentlemen who went to Washington to see about reducing Chicago's quota of troops after the call for extra men was made by the President in 1864:

"In 1864, when the call for extra troops came, Chicago revolted. She had already sent 22,000 troops up to that time, and was drained. When the call came there were no young men to go, and no aliens except what were bought. The citizens held a mass meeting and appointed three persons, of whom I was one, to go to Washington and ask Stanton to give Cook County a new enrollment. On reaching Washington, we went to Stanton with our statement. He refused entirely to give us the desired aid. Then we went to Lincoln. 'I cannot do it,' he said, 'but I will go with you to the War Department, and Stanton and I will hear both sides.'

"So we all went over to the War Department together. Stanton and General Frye were there, and they, of course, contended that the quota should not be changed. The argument went on for some time, and was finally referred to Lincoln, who had been sitting silently listening.

"I shall never forget how he suddenly lifted his head and turned on us a black and frowning face.

"'Gentlemen,' he said, in a voice full of bitterness, 'after Boston, Chicago has been the chief instrument in bringing war on this country. The Northwest has opposed the South as New England has opposed the South. It is you who are largely responsible for making blood flow as it has.

"'You called for war until we had it. You called for Emancipation, and I have given it to you. Whatever you have asked, you have had. Now you come here begging to be let off from the call for men, which I have made to carry out the war which you demanded. You ought to be ashamed of yourselves. I have a right to expect better things of you.

"'Go home and raise your six thousand extra men. And you,

Medill, you are acting like a coward. You and your Tribune have had more influence than any paper in the Northwest in making this war. You can influence great masses, and yet you cry to be spared at a moment when your cause is suffering. Go home and send us those men!'

"I couldn't say anything. It was the first time I ever was whipped, and I didn't have an answer. We all got up and went out, and when the door closed one of my colleagues said:

"'Well, gentlemen, the old man is right. We ought to be ashamed of ourselves. Let us never say anything about this, but go home and raise the men.'

"And we did—six thousand men—making twenty-eight thousand in the War from a city of one hundred and fifty-six thousand. But there might have been crape on every door, almost, in Chicago, for every family had lost a son or a husband. I lost two brothers. It was hard for the mothers."

They Didn't Build It

In 1862 a delegation of New York millionaires waited upon President Lincoln to request that he furnish a gunboat for the protection of New York harbor.

Mr. Lincoln, after listening patiently, said: "Gentlemen, the credit of the Government is at a very low ebb; greenbacks are not worth more than forty or fifty cents on the dollar; it is impossible for me, in the present condition of things, to furnish you a gunboat, and, in this condition of things, if I was worth half as much as you, gentlemen, are represented to be, and as badly frightened as you seem to be, I would build a gunboat and give it to the Government."

Stanton's Abuse of Lincoln

President Lincoln's sense of duty to the country, together with his keen judgment of men, often led to the appointment of persons unfriendly to him. Some of these appointees were, as well, not loyal to the National Government, for that matter.

Regarding Secretary of War Stanton's attitude toward Lincoln, Colonel A. K. McClure, who was very close to President Lincoln, said:

"After Stanton's retirement from the Buchanan Cabinet when Lincoln was inaugurated, he maintained the closest confidential relations with Buchanan, and wrote him many letters expressing the utmost contempt for Lincoln, the Cabinet, the Republican Congress, and the general policy of the Administration.

"These letters speak freely of the 'painful imbecility of Lincoln,' of the 'venality and corruption' which ran riot in the government, and expressed the belief that no better condition of things was possible 'until Jeff Davis turns out the whole concern.'

"He was firmly impressed for some weeks after the battle of Bull Run that the government was utterly overthrown, as he repeatedly refers to the coming of Davis into the National Capital.

"In one letter he says that 'in less than thirty days Davis will be in possession of Washington;' and it is an open secret that Stanton advised the revolutionary overthrow of the Lincoln government, to be replaced by General McClellan as military dictator. These letters, bad as they are, are not the worst letters written by Stanton to Buchanan. Some of them were so violent in their expressions against Lincoln and the administration that they have been charitably withheld from the public, but they remain in the possession of the surviving relatives of President Buchanan.

"Of course, Lincoln had no knowledge of the bitterness exhibited by Stanton to himself personally and to his administration, but if he had known the worst that Stanton ever said or wrote about him, I doubt not that he would have called him to the Cabinet in January, 1862. The disasters the army suffered made Lincoln forgetful of everything but the single duty of suppressing the rebellion.

"Lincoln was not long in discovering that in his new Secretary of War he had an invaluable but most troublesome Cabinet officer, but he saw only the great and good offices that Stanton was performing for the imperilled Republic.

"Confidence was restored in financial circles by the appointment of Stanton, and his name as War Minister did more to strengthen the faith of the people in the government credit than would have been probable from the appointment of any other man of that day.

"He was a terror to all the hordes of jobbers and speculators and camp-followers whose appetites had been whetted by a great war, and he enforced the strictest discipline throughout our armies.

"He was seldom capable of being civil to any officer away from the army on leave of absence unless he had been summoned by the government for conference or special duty, and he issued the strictest orders from time to time to drive the throng of military idlers from the capital and keep them at their posts. He was stern to savagery in his enforcement of military law. The wearied sentinel who slept at his post found no mercy in the heart of Stanton, and many times did Lincoln's humanity overrule his fiery minister.

"Any neglect of military duty was sure of the swiftest punishment, and seldom did he make even just allowance for inevitable military disaster. He had profound, unfaltering faith in the Union cause, and, above all, he had unfaltering faith in himself.

"He believed that he was in all things except in name Commander-in-Chief of the armies and the navy of the nation, and it was with unconcealed reluctance that he at times deferred to the authority of the President."

Lincoln Was Ready to Fight

On one occasion, Colonel Baker was speaking in a court-house, which had been a storehouse, and, on making some remarks that were offensive to certain political rowdies in the crowd, they cried: "Take him off the stand!"

Immediate confusion followed, and there was an attempt to carry the demand into execution. Directly over the speaker's head was an old skylight, at which it appeared Mr. Lincoln had been listening to the speech. In an instant, Mr. Lincoln's feet came through the skylight, followed by his tall and sinewy frame, and he was standing by Colonel Baker's side. He raised his hand and the assembly subsided into silence. "Gentlemen," said Mr. Lincoln, "let us not disgrace the age and country in which we live. This is a land where freedom of speech is guaranteed. Mr. Baker has a right to speak, and ought to be permitted to do so. I am here to protect him, and no man shall take him from this stand if I can prevent it." The suddenness of his appearance, his perfect calmness and fairness, and the knowledge that he would do what he had promised to do, quieted all disturbance, and the speaker concluded his remarks without difficulty.

It Was Up-Hill Work

Two young men called on the President from Springfield, Illinois. Lincoln shook hands with them, and asked about the crops, the weather, etc.

Finally one of the young men said, "Mother is not well, and she sent me up to inquire of you how the suit about the Wells property is getting on."

Lincoln, in the same even tone with which he had asked the question, said: "Give my best wishes and respects to your mother, and tell her I have so many outside matters to attend to now that I have put that case, and others, in the hands of a lawyer friend of mine, and if you will call on him (giving name and address) he will give you the information you want."

After they had gone, a friend, who was present, said: "Mr. Lincoln, you did not seem to know the young men?"

He laughed and replied: "No, I had never seen them before, and I had to beat around the bush until I found who they were. It was up-hill work, but I topped it at last."

Lee's Slim Animal

President Lincoln wrote to General Hooker on June 5, 1863, warning Hooker not to run any risk of being entangled on the Rappahannock "like an ox jumped half over a fence and liable to be torn by dogs, front and rear, without a fair chance to give one way or kick the other." On the 10th he warned Hooker not to go south of the Rappahannock upon Lee's moving north of it. "I think Lee's army and not Richmond is your true objective power. If he comes toward the upper Potomac, follow on his flank, and on the inside track, shortening your lines while he lengthens his. Fight him, too, when opportunity offers. If he stay where he is, fret him, and fret him."

On the 14th again he says: "So far as we can make out here, the enemy have Milroy surrounded at Winchester, and Tyler at Martinsburg. If they could hold out for a few days, could you help them? If the head of Lee's army is at Martinsburg, and the tail of it on the flank road between Fredericksburg and Chancellorsville, the animal must be very slim somewhere; could you not break him?"

"Mrs. North and Her Attorney"

In the issue of London "Punch" of September 24th, 1864, President Lincoln is pictured as sitting at a table in his law office, while in a chair to his right is a client, Mrs. North. The latter is a fine client for any attorney to have on his list, being wealthy and liberal, but as the lady is giving her counsel, who has represented her in a legal way for four years, notice that she proposes to put her legal business in the hands of another lawyer, the dejected look upon the face of Attorney Lincoln is easily accounted for. "Punch" puts these words in the lady's mouth:

MRS. NORTH: "You see, Mr. Lincoln, we have failed utterly in our course of action; I want peace, and so, if you cannot effect an amicable arrangement, I must put the case into other hands."

In this cartoon, "Punch" merely reflected the idea, or sentiment, current in England in 1864, that the North was much dissatisfied with the War policy of President Lincoln; and would surely elect General McClellan to succeed the Westerner in the White House. At the election McClellan carried but one Northern State—New Jersey, where he was born—President Lincoln sweeping the country like a prairie fire.

"Punch" had evidently been deceived by some bold, bad man, who wanted a little spending money, and sold the prediction to the funny journal with a certificate of character attached, written by— possibly—a member of the Horse Marines. "Punch," was very much disgusted to find that its credulity and faith in mankind had been so imposed upon, especially when the election returns showed that "the-War-is-a-failure" candidate ran so slowly that Lincoln passed him as easily as though the Democratic nominee was tied to a post.

Satisfaction to the Soul

In the far-away days when "Abe" went to school in Indiana, they had exercises, exhibitions and speaking-meetings in the schoolhouse or the church, and "Abe" was the "star." His father was a Democrat, and at that time "Abe" agreed with his parent. He would frequently make political and other speeches to the boys and explain tangled questions.

Booneville was the county seat of Warrick county, situated about fifteen miles from Gentryville. Thither "Abe" walked to be present at the sittings of the court, and listened attentively to the trials and the speeches of the lawyers.

One of the trials was that of a murderer. He was defended by Mr. John Breckinridge, and at the conclusion of his speech "Abe" was so enthusiastic that he ventured to compliment him. Breckinridge looked at the shabby boy, thanked him, and passed on his way.

Many years afterwards, in 1862, Breckinridge called on the President, and he was told, "It was the best speech that I, up to that time, had ever heard. If I could, as I then thought, make as good a speech as that, my soul would be satisfied."

Withdrew the Colt

Mr. Alcott, of Elgin, Ill., tells of seeing Mr. Lincoln coming away from church unusually early one Sunday morning. "The sermon could not have been more than half way through," says Mr. Alcott. "'Tad' was slung across his left arm like a pair of saddlebags, and Mr. Lincoln was striding along with long, deliberate steps toward his home. On one of the street corners he encountered a group of his fellow-townsmen. Mr. Lincoln anticipated the question which was about to be put by the group, and, taking his figure of speech from practices with which they were only too familiar, said: 'Gentlemen, I entered this colt, but he kicked around so I had to withdraw him.'"

"Tad" Got His Dollar

No matter who was with the President, or how intently absorbed, his little son "Tad" was always welcome. He almost always accompanied his father.

Once, on the way to Fortress Monroe, he became very troublesome. The President was much engaged in conversation with the party who accompanied him, and he at length said:

"'Tad,' if you will be a good boy, and not disturb me any more until we get to Fortress Monroe, I will give you a dollar."

The hope of reward was effectual for awhile in securing silence, but, boylike, "Tad" soon forgot his promise, and was as noisy as ever. Upon reaching their destination, however, he said, very promptly: "Father, I want my dollar." Mr. Lincoln looked at him half-reproachfully for an instant, and then, taking from his pocketbook a dollar note, he said "Well, my son, at any rate, I will keep my part of the bargain."

Tells an Editor About Nasby

Henry J. Raymond, the famous New York editor, thus tells of Mr. Lincoln's fondness for the Nasby letters:

"It has been well said by a profound critic of Shakespeare, and it occurs to me as very appropriate in this connection, that the spirit which held the woe of Lear and the tragedy of "Hamlet" would have broken had it not also had the humor of the "Merry Wives of Windsor" and the merriment of the "Midsummer Night's Dream."

"This is as true of Mr. Lincoln as it was of Shakespeare. The capacity to tell and enjoy a good anecdote no doubt prolonged his life.

"The Saturday evening before he left Washington to go to the front, just previous to the capture of Richmond, I was with him from seven o'clock till nearly twelve. It had been one of his most trying days. The pressure of office-seekers was greater at this juncture than I ever knew it to be, and he was almost worn out.

"Among the callers that evening was a party composed of two Senators, a Representative, an ex-Lieutenant-Governor of a Western State, and several private citizens. They had business of great importance, involving the necessity of the President's examination of voluminous documents. Pushing everything aside, he said to one of the party:

"'Have you seen the Nasby papers?'

"'No, I have not,' was the reply; 'who is Nasby?'

"'There is a chap out in Ohio,' returned the President, 'who has been writing a series of letters in the newspapers over the signature of Petroleum V. Nasby. Someone sent me a pamphlet collection of them the other day. I am going to write to "Petroleum" to come down here, and I intend to tell him if he will communicate his talent to me, I will swap places with him!'

"Thereupon he arose, went to a drawer in his desk, and, taking out the 'Letters,' sat down and read one to the company, finding in their enjoyment of it the temporary excitement and relief which another man would have found in a glass of wine. The instant he had ceased, the book was thrown aside, his countenance relapsed into its habitual serious expression, and the business was entered upon with the utmost earnestness."

Long and Short of It

On the occasion of a serenade, the President was called for by the crowd assembled. He appeared at a window with his wife (who was somewhat below the medium height), and made the following "brief remarks":

"Here I am, and here is Mrs. Lincoln. That's the long and the short of it."

More Pegs Than Holes

Some gentlemen were once finding fault with the President because certain generals were not given commands.

"The fact is," replied President Lincoln, "I have got more pegs than I have holes to put them in."

"Webster Couldn't Have Done More"

Lincoln "got even" with the Illinois Central Railroad Company, in 1855, in a most substantial way, at the same time secured sweet revenge for an insult, unwarranted in every way, put upon him by one of the officials of that corporation.

Lincoln and Herndon defended the Illinois Central Railroad in an action brought by McLean County, Illinois, in August, 1853, to recover taxes alleged to be due the county from the road. The Legislature had granted the road immunity from taxation, and this was a case intended to test the constitutionality of the law. The road sent a retainer fee of $250.

In the lower court the case was decided in favor of the railroad. An appeal to the Supreme Court followed, was argued twice, and finally decided in favor of the road. This last decision was rendered some time in 1855. Lincoln then went to Chicago and presented the bill for legal services. Lincoln and Herndon only asked for $2,000 more.

The official to whom he was referred, after looking at the bill, expressed great surprise.

"Why, sir," he exclaimed, "this is as much as Daniel Webster himself would have charged. We cannot allow such a claim."

"Why not?" asked Lincoln.

"We could have hired first-class lawyers at that figure," was the response.

"We won the case, didn't we?" queried Lincoln.

"Certainly," replied the official.

"Daniel Webster, then," retorted Lincoln in no amiable tone, "couldn't have done more," and "Abe" walked out of the official's office.

Lincoln withdrew the bill, and started for home. On the way he stopped at Bloomington, where he met Grant Goodrich, Archibald Williams, Norman B. Judd, O. H. Browning, and other attorneys, who, on learning of his modest charge for the valuable services rendered the railroad, induced him to increase the demand to $5,000, and to bring suit for that sum.

This was done at once. On the trial six lawyers certified that the bill was reasonable, and judgment for that sum went by default; the judgment was promptly paid, and, of course, his partner, Herndon, got "your half Billy," without delay.

Lincoln Met Clay

When a member of Congress, Lincoln went to Lexington, Kentucky, to hear Henry Clay speak. The Westerner, a Kentuckian by birth, and destined to reach the great goal Clay had so often sought, wanted to meet the "Millboy of the Slashes." The address was a tame affair, as was the personal greeting when Lincoln made himself known. Clay was courteous, but cold. He may never have heard of the man, then in his presence, who was to secure, without solicitation, the prize which he for many years had unsuccessfully sought. Lincoln was disenchanted; his ideal was shattered. One reason why Clay had not realized his ambition had become apparent.

Clay was cool and dignified; Lincoln was cordial and hearty. Clay's hand was bloodless and frosty, with no vigorous grip in it; Lincoln's was warm, and its clasp was expressive of kindliness and sympathy.

Reminded "Abe" of a Little Joke

President Lincoln had a little joke at the expense of General George B. McClellan, the Democratic candidate for the Presidency in opposition to the Westerner in 1864. McClellan was nominated by the Democratic National Convention, which assembled at Chicago, but after he had been named, and also during the campaign, the military candidate was characteristically slow in coming to the front.

President Lincoln had his eye upon every move made by General

McClellan during the campaign, and when reference was made one day, in his presence, to the deliberation and caution of the New Jerseyite, Mr. Lincoln remarked, with a twinkle in his eye, "Perhaps he is intrenching."

A cartoon in "Harper's Weekly," September 17th, 1864, shows General McClellan, with his little spade in hand, being subjected to the scrutiny of the President—the man who gave McClellan, when the latter was Commander-in-Chief of the Union forces, every opportunity in the world to distinguish himself. There is a smile on the face of "Honest Abe," which shows conclusively that he does not regard his political opponent as likely to prove formidable in any way. President Lincoln "sized up" McClellan in 1861-2, and knew, to a fraction, how much of a man he was, what he could do, and how he went about doing it. McClellan was no politician, while the President was the shrewdest of political diplomats.

His Dignity Saved Him

When Washington had become an armed camp, and full of soldiers, President Lincoln and his Cabinet officers drove daily to one or another of these camps. Very often his outing for the day was attending some ceremony incident to camp life: a military funeral, a camp wedding, a review, a flag-raising. He did not often make speeches. "I have made a great many poor speeches," he said one day, in excusing himself, "and I now feel relieved that my dignity does not permit me to be a public speaker."

The Man He Was Looking For

Judge Kelly, of Pennsylvania, who was one of the committee to advise Lincoln of his nomination, and who was himself a great many feet high, had been eyeing Lincoln's lofty form with a mixture of admiration and possibly jealousy.

This had not escaped Lincoln, and as he shook hands with the judge he inquired, "What is your height?"

"Six feet three. What is yours, Mr. Lincoln?"

"Six feet four."

"Then," said the judge, "Pennsylvania bows to Illinois. My dear man, for years my heart has been aching for a President that I could look up to, and I've at last found him."

His Cabinet Chances Poor

Mr. Jeriah Bonham, in describing a visit he paid Lincoln at his room in the State House at Springfield, where he found him quite alone, except that two of his children, one of whom was "Tad," were with him.

"The door was open.

"We walked in and were at once recognized and seated—the two boys still continuing their play about the room. "Tad" was spinning his top; and Lincoln, as we entered, had just finished adjusting the string for him so as to give the top the greatest degree of force. He remarked that he was having a little fun with the boys."

At another time, at Lincoln's residence, "Tad" came into the room, and, putting his hand to his mouth, and his mouth to his father's ear, said, in a boy's whisper: "Ma says come to supper."

All heard the announcement; and Lincoln, perceiving this, said: "You have heard, gentlemen, the announcement concerning the interesting state of things in the dining-room. It will never do for me, if elected, to make this young man a member of my Cabinet, for it is plain he cannot be trusted with secrets of state."

The General Was "Headed in"

A Union general, operating with his command in West Virginia, allowed himself and his men to be trapped, and it was feared his force would be captured by the Confederates. The President heard the report read by the operator, as it came over the wire, and remarked:

"Once there was a man out West who was 'heading' a barrel, as they used to call it. He worked like a good fellow in driving down the hoops, but just about the time he thought he had the job done, the head would fall in. Then he had to do the work all over again.

"All at once a bright idea entered his brain, and he wondered how it was he hadn't figured it out before. His boy, a bright, smart lad, was standing by, very much interested in the business, and, lifting the young one up, he put him inside the barrel, telling him to hold the head in its proper place, while he pounded down the hoops on the sides. This worked like a charm, and he soon had the 'heading' done.

"Then he realized that his boy was inside the barrel, and how to get him out he couldn't for his life figure out. General Blank is now inside the barrel, 'headed in,' and the job now is to get him out."

Sugar-Coated

Government Printer Defrees, when one of the President's messages was being printed, was a good deal disturbed by the use of the term "sugar-coated," and finally went to Mr. Lincoln about it.

Their relations to each other being of the most intimate character, he told the President frankly that he ought to remember that a message to Congress was a different affair from a speech at a mass meeting in Illinois; that the messages became a part of history, and should be written accordingly.

"What is the matter now?" inquired the President.

"Why," said Defrees, "you have used an undignified expression in the message"; and, reading the paragraph aloud, he added, "I would alter the structure of that, if I were you."

"Defrees," replied the President, "that word expresses exactly my idea, and I am not going to change it. The time will never come in this country when people won't know exactly what 'sugar-coated' means."

Could Make "Rabbit-Tracks"

When a grocery clerk at New Salem, the annual election came around. A Mr. Graham was clerk, but his assistant was absent, and it was necessary to find a man to fill his place. Lincoln, a "tall young man," had already concentrated on himself the attention of the people of the town, and Graham easily discovered him. Asking him if he could write, "Abe" modestly replied, "I can make a few rabbit-tracks." His rabbit-tracks proving to be legible and even graceful, he was employed.

The voters soon discovered that the new assistant clerk was honest and fair, and performed his duties satisfactorily, and when, the work done, he began to "entertain them with stories," they found that their town had made a valuable personal and social acquisition.

Lincoln Protected Currency Issues

Marshal Ward Lamon was in President Lincoln's office in the White House one day, and casually asked the President if he knew how the currency of the country was made. Greenbacks were then under full headway of circulation, these bits of paper being the representatives of United State money.

"Our currency," was the President's answer, "is made, as the lawyers would put it, in their legal way, in the following manner, to-wit: The official engraver strikes off the sheets, passes them over to the Register of the Currency, who, after placing his earmarks upon them, signs the same; the Register turns them over to old Father Spinner, who proceeds to embellish them with his wonderful signature at the bottom; Father Spinner sends them to Secretary of the Treasury Chase, and he, as a final act in the matter, issues them to the public as money—and may the good Lord help any fellow that doesn't take all he can honestly get of them!"

Taking from his pocket a $5 greenback, with a twinkle in his eye, the President then said: "Look at Spinner's signature! Was there ever anything like it on earth? Yet it is unmistakable; no one will ever be able to counterfeit it!"

Lamon then goes on to say:

"'But,' I said, 'you certainly don't suppose that Spinner actually wrote his name on that bill, do you?'

"'Certainly, I do; why not?' queried Mr. Lincoln.

"I then asked, 'How much of this currency have we afloat?'

"He remained thoughtful for a moment, and then stated the amount.

"I continued: 'How many times do you think a man can write a signature like Spinner's in the course of twenty-four hours?'

"The beam of hilarity left the countenance of the President at once. He put the greenback into his vest pocket, and walked the floor; after awhile he stopped, heaved a long breath and said: 'This thing frightens me!' He then rang for a messenger and told him to ask the Secretary of the Treasury to please come over to see him.

"Mr. Chase soon put in an appearance; President Lincoln stated the cause of his alarm, and asked Mr. Chase to explain in detail the operations, methods, system of checks, etc., in his office, and a lengthy discussion followed, President Lincoln contending there were not sufficient safeguards afforded in any degree in the money-making department, and Secretary Chase insisting that every protection was afforded he could devise."

Afterward the President called the attention of Congress to this important question, and devices were adopted whereby a check was put upon the issue of greenbacks that no spurious ones ever came out of the Treasury Department, at least. Counterfeiters were busy, though, but this was not the fault of the Treasury.

Lincoln's Apology to Grant

"General Grant is a copious worker and fighter," President Lincoln wrote to General Burnside in July, 1863, "but a meagre writer or telegrapher."

Grant never wrote a report until the battle was over.

President Lincoln wrote a letter to General Grant on July 13th, 1863, which indicated the strength of the hold the successful fighter had upon the man in the White House.

It ran as follows:

"I do not remember that you and I ever met personally.

"I write this now as a grateful acknowledgment for the almost inestimable service you have done the country.

"I write to say a word further.

"When you first reached the vicinity of Vicksburg, I thought you should do what you finally did—march the troops across the neck, run the batteries with the transports, and thus go below; and I never had any faith, except a general hope, that you knew better than I, that the Yazoo Pass expedition, and the like, could succeed.

"When you got below and took Port Gibson, Grand Gulf and vicinity, I thought you should go down the river and join General Banks; and when you turned northward, east of Big Black, I feared it was a mistake.

"I now wish to make the personal acknowledgment that you were right and I was wrong."

Lincoln Said "by Jing"

Lincoln never used profanity, except when he quoted it to illustrate a point in a story. His favorite expressions when he spoke with emphasis were "By dear!" and "By jing!"

Just preceding the Civil War he sent Ward Lamon on a ticklish mission to South Carolina.

When the proposed trip was mentioned to Secretary Seward, he opposed it, saying, "Mr. President, I fear you are sending Lamon to his grave. I am afraid they will kill him in Charleston, where the people are excited and desperate. We can't spare Lamon, and we shall feel badly if anything happens to him."

Mr. Lincoln said in reply: "I have known Lamon to be in many a close place, and he has never, been in one that he didn't get out of, somehow. By jing! I'll risk him. Go ahead, Lamon, and God bless you! If you can't bring back any good news, bring a palmetto." Lamon brought back a palmetto branch, but no promise of peace.

It Tickled the Little Woman

Lincoln had been in the telegraph office at Springfield during the casting of the first and second ballots in the Republican National Convention at Chicago, and then left and went over to the office of the State Journal, where he was sitting conversing with friends while the third ballot was being taken.

In a few moments came across the wires the announcement of the result. The superintendent of the telegraph company wrote on a scrap of paper: "Mr. Lincoln, you are nominated on the third ballot," and a boy ran with the message to Lincoln.

He looked at it in silence, amid the shouts of those around him; then rising and putting it in his pocket, he said quietly: "There's a little woman down at our house would like to hear this; I'll go down and tell her."

"Shall All Fall Together"

After Lincoln had finished that celebrated speech in "Egypt" (as a section of Southern Illinois was formerly designated), in the course of which he seized Congressman Ficklin by the coat collar and shook him fiercely, he apologized. In return, Ficklin said Lincoln had "nearly shaken the Democracy out of him." To this Lincoln replied:

"That reminds me of what Paul said to Agrippa, which, in language and substance, was about this: 'I would to God that such Democracy as you folks here in Egypt have were not only almost, but altogether, shaken out of, not only you, but all that heard me this day, and that you would all join in assisting in shaking off the shackles of the bondmen by all legitimate means, so that this country may be made free as the good Lord intended it.'"

Said Ficklin in rejoinder: "Lincoln, I remember of reading somewhere in the same book from which you get your Agrippa story, that Paul, whom you seem to desire to personate, admonished all servants (slaves) to be obedient to them that are their masters according to the flesh, in fear and trembling.

"It would seem that neither our Savior nor Paul saw the iniquity of slavery as you and your party do. But you must not think that where you fail by argument to convince an old friend like myself and win him over to your heterodox abolition opinions, you are justified in resorting to violence such as you practiced on me to-day.

"Why, I never had such a shaking up in the whole course of my life. Recollect that that good old book that you quote from somewhere says in effect this: 'Woe be unto him who goeth to Egypt for help, for he shall fall. The holpen shall fall, and they shall all fall together.'"

Dead Dog No Cure

Lincoln's quarrel with Shields was his last personal encounter. In later years it became his duty to give an official reprimand to a young officer who had been court-martialed for a quarrel with one of his associates. The reprimand is probably the gentlest on record:

"Quarrel not at all. No man resolved to make the most of himself can spare time for personal contention. Still less can he afford to take all the consequences, including the vitiating of his temper and the loss of self-control. Yield larger things to which you can show no more than equal right; and yield lesser ones, though clearly your own.

"Better give your path to a dog than be bitten by him in contesting for the right. Even killing the dog would not cure the bite."

"Thorough" Is a Good Word

Someone came to the President with a story about a plot to accomplish some mischief in the Government. Lincoln listened to what was a very superficial and ill-formed story, and then said: "There is one thing that I have learned, and that you have not. It is only one word—'thorough.'"

Then, bringing his hand down on the table with a thump to emphasize his meaning, he added, "thorough!"

The Cabinet Was a-Settin'

Being in Washington one day, the Rev. Robert Collyer thought he'd take a look around. In passing through the grounds surrounding the White House, he cast a glance toward the Presidential residence, and was astonished to see three pairs of feet resting on the ledge of an open window in one of the apartments of the second story. The divine paused for a moment, calmly surveyed the unique spectacle, and then resumed his walk toward the War Department.

Seeing a laborer at work not far from the Executive Mansion, Mr. Collyer asked him what it all meant. To whom did the feet belong, and, particularly, the mammoth ones? "You old fool," answered the workman, "that's the Cabinet, which is a-settin,' an' them thar big feet belongs to 'Old Abe.'"

A Bullet through His Hat

A soldier tells the following story of an attempt upon the life of Mr. Lincoln "One night I was doing sentinel duty at the entrance to the Soldiers' Home. This was about the middle of August, 1864. About eleven o'clock I heard a rifle shot, in the direction of the city, and shortly afterwards I heard approaching hoof-beats. In two or three minutes a horse came dashing up. I recognized the belated President. The President was bareheaded. The President simply thought that his horse had taken fright at the discharge of the firearms.

"On going back to the place where the shot had been heard, we found the President's hat. It was a plain silk hat, and upon examination we discovered a bullet hole through the crown.

"The next day, upon receiving the hat, the President remarked that it was made by some foolish marksman, and was not intended for him; but added that he wished nothing said about the matter.

"The President said, philosophically: 'I long ago made up my mind that if anybody wants to kill me, he will do it. Besides, in this case, it seems to me, the man who would succeed me would be just as objectionable to my enemies—if I have any.'

"One dark night, as he was going out with a friend, he took along a heavy cane, remarking, good-naturedly: 'Mother (Mrs. Lincoln) has got a notion into her head that I shall be assassinated, and to please her I take a cane when I go over to the War Department at night—when I don't forget it.'"

No Kind to Get to Heaven on

Two ladies from Tennessee called at the White House one day and begged Mr. Lincoln to release their husbands, who were rebel prisoners at Johnson's Island. One of the fair petitioners urged as a reason for the liberation of her husband that he was a very religious man, and rang the changes on this pious plea.

"Madam," said Mr. Lincoln, "you say your husband is a religious man. Perhaps I am not a good judge of such matters, but in my opinion the religion that makes men rebel and fight against their government is not the genuine article; nor is the religion the right sort which reconciles them to the idea of eating their bread in the sweat of other men's faces. It is not the kind to get to heaven on."

Later, however, the order of release was made, President Lincoln remarking, with impressive solemnity, that he would expect the ladies to subdue the rebellious spirit of their husbands, and to that end he thought it would be well to reform their religion. "True patriotism," said he, "is better than the wrong kind of piety."

The Only Real Peacemaker

During the Presidential campaign of 1864 much ill-feeling was displayed by the opposition to President Lincoln. The Democratic managers issued posters of large dimensions, picturing the Washington Administration as one determined to rule or ruin the country, while the only salvation for the United States was the election of McClellan.

One of these 1864 campaign posters was titled "The True Issue; or 'That's What's the Matter.'"

The dominant idea or purpose of the cartoon-poster was to demonstrate McClellan's availability. Lincoln, the Abolitionist, and

Davis, the Secessionist, are pictured as bigots of the worst sort, who were determined that peace should not be restored to the distracted country, except upon the lines laid down by them. McClellan, the patriotic peacemaker, is shown as the man who believed in the preservation of the Union above all things—a man who had no fads nor vagaries.

This peacemaker, McClellan, standing upon "the War-is-a-failure" platform, is portrayed as a military chieftain, who would stand no nonsense; who would compel Mr. Lincoln and Mr. Davis to cease their quarreling; who would order the soldiers on both sides to quit their blood-letting and send the combatants back to the farm, workshop and counting-house; and the man whose election would restore order out of chaos, and make everything bright and lovely.

The Apple Woman's Pass

One day when President Lincoln was receiving callers a buxom Irish woman came into the office, and, standing before the President, with her hands on her hips, said:

"Mr. Lincoln, can't I sell apples on the railroad?"

President Lincoln replied: "Certainly, madam, you can sell all you wish."

"But," she said, "you must give me a pass, or the soldiers will not let me."

President Lincoln then wrote a few lines and gave them to her.

"Thank you, sir; God bless you!" she exclaimed as she departed joyfully.

Split Rails by the Yard

It was in the spring of 1830 that "Abe" Lincoln, "wearing a jean jacket, shrunken buckskin trousers, a coonskin cap, and driving an ox-team," became a citizen of Illinois. He was physically and mentally equipped for pioneer work. His first desire was to obtain a new and decent suit of clothes, but, as he had no money, he was glad to arrange with Nancy Miller to make him a pair of trousers, he to split four hundred fence rails for each yard of cloth—fourteen hundred rails in all. "Abe" got the clothes after awhile.

It was three miles from his father's cabin to her wood-lot, where he made the forest ring with the sound of his ax. "Abe" had helped his father plow fifteen acres of land, and split enough rails to fence it, and he then helped to plow fifty acres for another settler.

The Question of Legs

Whenever the people of Lincoln's neighborhood engaged in dispute; whenever a bet was to be decided; when they differed on points of religion or politics; when they wanted to get out of trouble, or desired advice regarding anything on the earth, below it, above it, or under the sea, they went to "Abe."

Two fellows, after a hot dispute lasting some hours, over the problem as to how long a man's legs should be in proportion to the size of his body, stamped into Lincoln's office one day and put the question to him.

Lincoln listened gravely to the arguments advanced by both contestants, spent some time in "reflecting" upon the matter, and then, turning around in his chair and facing the disputants, delivered his opinion with all the gravity of a judge sentencing a fellow-being to death.

"This question has been a source of controversy," he said, slowly and deliberately, "for untold ages, and it is about time it should be definitely decided. It has led to bloodshed in the past, and there is no reason to suppose it will not lead to the same in the future.

"After much thought and consideration, not to mention mental worry and anxiety, it is my opinion, all side issues being swept aside, that a man's lower limbs, in order to preserve harmony of proportion, should be at least long enough to reach from his body to the ground."

Too Many Widows Already

A Union officer in conversation one day told this story:

"The first week I was with my command there were twenty-four deserters sentenced by court-martial to be shot, and the warrants for their execution were sent to the President to be signed. He refused.

"I went to Washington and had an interview. I said:

"'Mr. President, unless these men are made an example of, the army itself is in danger. Mercy to the few is cruelty to the many.'

"He replied: 'Mr. General, there are already too many weeping widows in the United States. For God's sake, don't ask me to add to the number, for I won't do it.'"

God Needed That Church

In the early stages of the war, after several battles had been fought, Union troops seized a church in Alexandria, Va., and used it as a hospital.

A prominent lady of the congregation went to Washington to see Mr. Lincoln and try to get an order for its release.

"Have you applied to the surgeon in charge at Alexandria?" inquired Mr. Lincoln.

"Yes, sir, but I can do nothing with him," was the reply.

"Well, madam," said Mr. Lincoln, "that is an end of it, then. We put him there to attend to just such business, and it is reasonable to suppose that he knows better what should be done under the circumstances than I do."

The lady's face showed her keen disappointment. In order to learn her sentiment, Mr. Lincoln asked:

"How much would you be willing to subscribe toward building a hospital there?"

She said that the war had depreciated Southern property so much that she could afford to give but little.

"This war is not over yet," said Mr. Lincoln, "and there will likely be another fight very soon. That church may be very useful in which to house our wounded soldiers. It is my candid opinion that God needs that church for our wounded fellows; so, madam, I can do nothing for you."

The Man Down South

An amusing instance of the President's preoccupation of mind occurred at one of his levees, when he was shaking hands with a host of visitors passing him in a continuous stream.

An intimate acquaintance received the usual conventional handshake and salutation, but perceiving that he was not recognized, kept his ground instead of moving on, and spoke again, when the President, roused to a dim consciousness that something unusual had happened, perceived who stood before him, and, seizing his friend's hand, shook it again heartily, saying:

"How do you do? How do you do? Excuse me for not noticing you. I was thinking of a man down South."

"The man down South" was General W. T. Sherman, then on his march to the sea.

Couldn't Let Go the Hog

When Governor Curtin of Pennsylvania described the terrible butchery at the battle of Fredericksburg, Mr. Lincoln was almost broken-hearted.

The Governor regretted that his description had so sadly affected the President. He remarked: "I would give all I possess to know how to rescue you from this terrible war." Then Mr. Lincoln's wonderful recuperative powers asserted themselves and this marvelous man was himself.

Lincoln's whole aspect suddenly changed, and he relieved his mind by telling a story.

"This reminds me, Governor," he said, "of an old farmer out in Illinois that I used to know.

"He took it into his head to go into hog-raising. He sent out to Europe and imported the finest breed of hogs he could buy.

"The prize hog was put in a pen, and the farmer's two mischievous boys, James and John, were told to be sure not to let it out. But James, the worst of the two, let the brute out the next day. The hog went straight for the boys, and drove John up a tree, then the hog went for the seat of James' trousers, and the only way the boy could save himself was by holding on to the hog's tail.

"The hog would not give up his hunt, nor the boy his hold! After they had made a good many circles around the tree, the boy's courage began to give out, and he shouted to his brother, 'I say, John, come down, quick, and help me let go this hog!'

"Now, Governor, that is exactly my case. I wish someone would come and help me to let the hog go."

The Cabinet Lincoln Wanted

Judge Joseph Gillespie, of Chicago, was a firm friend of Mr. Lincoln, and went to Springfield to see him shortly before his departure for the inauguration.

"It was," said judge Gillespie, "Lincoln's Gethsemane. He feared he was not the man for the great position and the great events which confronted him. Untried in national affairs, unversed in international diplomacy, unacquainted with the men who were foremost in the politics of the nation, he groaned when he saw the inevitable War of the Rebellion coming on. It was in humility of spirit that he told me he believed that the American people had made a mistake in selecting him.

"In the course of our conversation he told me if he could select his cabinet from the old bar that had traveled the circuit with him in the early days, he believed he could avoid war or settle it without a battle, even after the fact of secession.

"'But, Mr. Lincoln,' said I, 'those old lawyers are all Democrats.'

"'I know it,' was his reply. 'But I would rather have Democrats whom I know than Republicans I don't know.'"

Ready for "Butcher-Day"

Leonard Swett told this eminently characteristic story:

"I remember one day being in his room when Lincoln was sitting at his table with a large pile of papers before him, and after a pleasant talk he turned quite abruptly and said: 'Get out of the way, Swett; to-morrow is butcher-day, and I must go through these papers and see if I cannot find some excuse to let these poor fellows off.'

"The pile of papers he had were the records of courts-martial of men who on the following day were to be shot."

"The Bad Bird and the Mudsill"

It took quite a long time, as well as the lives of thousands of men, to say nothing of the cost in money, to take Richmond, the Capital City of the Confederacy. In a cartoon in "Frank Leslie's Illustrated Newspaper," of February 21, 1863, Jeff Davis is sitting upon the Secession eggs in the "Richmond" nest, smiling down upon President Lincoln, who is up to his waist in the Mud of Difficulties.

The President finally waded through the morass, in which he had become immersed, got to the tree, climbed its trunk, reached the limb, upon which the "bad bird" had built its nest, threw the mother out, destroyed the eggs of Secession and then took the nest away with him, leaving the "bad bird" without any home at all.

The "bad bird" had its laugh first, but the last laugh belonged to the "mudsill," as the cartoonist was pleased to call the President of the United States. It is true that the President got his clothes and hat all covered with mud, but as the job was a dirty one, as well as one that had to be done, the President didn't care. He was able to get another suit of clothes, as well as another hat, but the "bad bird" couldn't, and didn't, get another nest.

The laugh was on the "bad bird" after all.

Gave the Soldier His Fish

Once, when asked what he remembered about the war with Great Britain, Lincoln replied: "Nothing but this: I had been fishing one day and caught a little fish, which I was taking home. I met a soldier in the road, and, having been always told at home that we must be good to the soldiers, I gave him my fish."

This must have been about 1814, when "Abe" was five years of age.

A Peculiar Lawyer

Lincoln was once associate counsel for a defendant in a murder case. He listened to the testimony given by witness after witness against his client, until his honest heart could stand it no longer; then, turning to his associate, he said: "The man is guilty; you defend him—I can't," and when his associate secured a verdict of acquittal, Lincoln refused to share the fee to the extent of one cent.

Lincoln would never advise clients to enter into unwise or unjust lawsuits, always preferring to refuse a retainer rather than be a party to a case which did not commend itself to his sense of justice.

If They'd Only "Skip"

General Creswell called at the White House to see the President the day of the latter's assassination. An old friend, serving in the Confederate ranks, had been captured by the Union troops and sent to prison. He had drawn an affidavit setting forth what he knew about the man, particularly mentioning extenuating circumstances.

Creswell found the President very happy. He was greeted with: "Creswell, old fellow, everything is bright this morning. The War is over. It has been a tough time, but we have lived it out,—or some of us have," and he dropped his voice a little on the last clause of the sentence. "But it is over; we are going to have good times now, and a united country."

General Creswell told his story, read his affidavit, and said, "I know the man has acted like a fool, but he is my friend, and a good fellow; let him out; give him to me, and I will be responsible that he won't have anything more to do with the rebs."

"Creswell," replied Mr. Lincoln, "you make me think of a lot of young folks who once started out Maying. To reach their destination, they had to cross a shallow stream, and did so by means of an old flatboat. When the time came to return, they found to their dismay that the old scow had disappeared. They were in sore trouble, and thought over all manner of devices for getting over the water, but without avail.

"After a time, one of the boys proposed that each fellow should pick up the girl he liked best and wade over with her. The masterly proposition was carried out, until all that were left upon the island was a little short chap and a great, long, gothic-built, elderly lady.

"Now, Creswell, you are trying to leave me in the same predicament. You fellows are all getting your own friends out of this scrape; and you will succeed in carrying off one after another, until nobody but Jeff Davis and myself will be left on the island, and then I won't know what to do. How should I feel? How should I look, lugging him over?

"I guess the way to avoid such an embarrassing situation is to let them all out at once."

He made a somewhat similar illustration at an informal Cabinet meeting, at which the disposition of Jefferson Davis and other prominent Confederates was discussed. Each member of the Cabinet gave his opinion; most of them were for hanging the traitors, or for some severe punishment. President Lincoln said nothing.

Finally, Joshua F. Speed, his old and confidential friend, who had been invited to the meeting, said, "I have heard the opinion of your Ministers, and would like to hear yours."

"Well, Josh," replied President Lincoln, "when I was a boy in Indiana, I went to a neighbor's house one morning and found a boy of my own size holding a coon by a string. I asked him what he had and what he was doing.

"He says, 'It's a coon. Dad cotched six last night, and killed all but this poor little cuss. Dad told me to hold him until he came back, and I'm afraid he's going to kill this one too; and oh, "Abe," I do wish he would get away!'

"'Well, why don't you let him loose?'

"'That wouldn't be right; and if I let him go, Dad would give me h—. But if he got away himself, it would be all right.'

"Now," said the President, "if Jeff Davis and those other fellows will only get away, it will be all right. But if we should catch them, and I should let them go, 'Dad would give me h—!'"

Father of the "Greenback"

Don Piatt, a noted journalist of Washington, told the story of the first proposition to President Lincoln to issue interest-bearing notes as currency, as follows:

"Amasa Walker, a distinguished financier of New England, suggested that notes issued directly from the Government to the people, as currency, should bear interest. This for the purpose, not only of making the notes popular, but for the purpose of preventing inflation, by inducing people to hoard the notes as an investment when the demands of trade would fail to call them into circulation as a currency.

"This idea struck David Taylor, of Ohio, with such force that he sought Mr. Lincoln and urged him to put the project into immediate execution. The President listened patiently, and at the end said, 'That is a good idea, Taylor, but you must go to Chase. He is running that end of the machine, and has time to consider your proposition.'

"Taylor sought the Secretary of the Treasury, and laid before him Amasa Walker's plan. Secretary Chase heard him through in a cold, unpleasant manner, and then said: 'That is all very well, Mr. Taylor; but there is one little obstacle in the way that makes the plan impracticable, and that is the Constitution.'

"Saying this, he turned to his desk, as if dismissing both Mr. Taylor and his proposition at the same moment.

"The poor enthusiast felt rebuked and humiliated. He returned to the President, however, and reported his defeat. Mr. Lincoln looked at the would-be financier with the expression at times so peculiar to his homely face, that left one in doubt whether he was jesting or in earnest. 'Taylor!' he exclaimed, 'go back to Chase and tell him not to bother himself about the Constitution. Say that I have that sacred instrument here at the White House, and I am guarding it with great care.'

"Taylor demurred to this, on the ground that Secretary Chase showed by his manner that he knew all about it, and didn't wish to be bored by any suggestion.

"'We'll see about that,' said the President, and taking a card from the table, he wrote upon it:

"'The Secretary of the Treasury will please consider Mr. Taylor's proposition. We must have money, and I think this a good way to get it.

"'A. LINCOLN.'"

Major Anderson's Bad Memory

Among the men whom Captain Lincoln met in the Black Hawk campaign were Lieutenant-Colonel Zachary Taylor, Lieutenant Jefferson Davis, President of the Confederacy, and Lieutenant Robert Anderson, all of the United States Army.

Judge Arnold, in his "Life of Abraham Lincoln," relates that Lincoln and Anderson did not meet again until some time in 1861. After Anderson had evacuated Fort Sumter, on visiting Washington, he called at the White House to pay his respects to the President. Lincoln expressed his thanks to Anderson for his conduct at Fort Sumter, and then said:

"Major, do you remember of ever meeting me before?"

"No, Mr. President, I have no recollection of ever having had that pleasure."

"My memory is better than yours," said Lincoln; "you mustered me into the service of the United States in 1832, at Dixon's Ferry, in the Black Hawk war."

No Vanderbilt

In February, 1860, not long before his nomination for the Presidency, Lincoln made several speeches in Eastern cities. To an Illinois acquaintance, whom he met at the Astor House, in New York, he said: "I have the cottage at Springfield, and about three thousand dollars in money. If they make me Vice-President with Seward, as some say they will, I hope I shall be able to increase it to twenty thousand, and that is as much as any man ought to want."

Squashed a Brutal Lie

In September, 1864, a New York paper printed the following brutal story:

"A few days after the battle of Antietam, the President was driving over the field in an ambulance, accompanied by Marshal Lamon, General McClellan and another officer. Heavy details of men were engaged in the task of burying the dead. The ambulance had just reached the neighborhood of the old stone bridge, where the dead were piled highest, when Mr. Lincoln, suddenly slapping Marshal Lamon on the knee, exclaimed: 'Come, Lamon, give us that song about "Picayune Butler"; McClellan has never heard it.'

"'Not now, if you please,' said General McClellan, with a shudder; 'I would prefer to hear it some other place and time.'"

President Lincoln refused to pay any attention to the story, would not read the comments made upon it by the newspapers, and would permit neither denial nor explanation to be made. The National election was coming on, and the President's friends appealed to him to settle the matter for once and all. Marshal Lamon was particularly insistent, but the President merely said:

"Let the thing alone. If I have not established character enough to give the lie to this charge, I can only say that I am mistaken in my own estimate of myself. In politics, every man must skin his own skunk. These fellows are welcome to the hide of this one. Its body has already given forth its unsavory odor."

But Lamon would not "let the thing alone." He submitted to Lincoln a draft of what he conceived to be a suitable explanation, after reading which the President said:

"Lamon, your 'explanation' is entirely too belligerent in tone for so grave a matter. There is a heap of 'cussedness' mixed up with your usual amiability, and you are at times too fond of a fight. If I were you, I would simply state the facts as they were. I would give the statement as you have here, without the pepper and salt. Let me try my hand at it."

The President then took up a pen and wrote the following, which was copied and sent out as Marshal Lamon's refutation of the shameless slander:

"The President has known me intimately for nearly twenty years, and has often heard me sing little ditties. The battle of Antietam was fought on the 17th day of September, 1862. On the first day of October, just two weeks after the battle, the President, with some others, including myself, started from Washington to visit the Army, reaching Harper's Ferry at noon of that day.

"In a short while General McClellan came from his headquarters near the battleground, joined the President, and with him reviewed the troops at Bolivar Heights that afternoon, and at night returned to his headquarters, leaving the President at Harper's Ferry.

"On the morning of the second, the President, with General Sumner, reviewed the troops respectively at Loudon Heights and Maryland Heights, and at about noon started to General McClellan's headquarters, reaching there only in time to see very little before night.

"On the morning of the third all started on a review of the Third Corps and the cavalry, in the vicinity of the Antietam battle-ground. After getting through with General Burnside's corps, at the suggestion of General McClellan, he and the President left their horses to be led, and went into an ambulance to go to General Fitz John Porter's corps, which was two or three miles distant.

"I am not sure whether the President and General McClellan were in the same ambulance, or in different ones; but myself and some others were in the same with the President. On the way, and on no part of the battleground, and on what suggestions I do not remember, the President asked me to sing the little sad song that follows ("Twenty Years Ago, Tom"), which he had often heard me sing, and had always seemed to like very much.

"After it was over, someone of the party (I do not think it was the President) asked me to sing something else; and I sang two or three little comic things, of which 'Picayune Butler' was one. Porter's corps was reached and reviewed; then the battle-ground was passed over, and the most noted parts examined; then, in succession, the cavalry and Franklin's corps were reviewed, and the President and party returned to General McClellan's headquarters at the end of a very hard, hot and dusty day's work.

"Next day (the 4th), the President and General McClellan visited such of the wounded as still remained in the vicinity, including the now lamented General Richardson; then proceeded to and examined the South-Mountain battle-ground, at which point they parted, General McClellan returning to his camp, and the President returning to Washington, seeing, on the way, General Hartsoff, who lay wounded at Frederick Town.

"This is the whole story of the singing and its surroundings. Neither General McClellan nor any one else made any objections to the singing; the place was not on the battle-field; the time was sixteen days after the battle; no dead body was seen during the whole time the President was absent from Washington, nor even a grave that had not been rained on since the time it was made."

"One War at a Time"

Nothing in Lincoln's entire career better illustrated the surprising resources of his mind than his manner of dealing with "The Trent Affair." The readiness and ability with which he met this perilous emergency, in a field entirely new to his experience, was worthy the most accomplished diplomat and statesman. Admirable, also, was his cool courage and self-reliance in following a course radically opposed to the prevailing sentiment throughout the country and in Congress, and contrary to the advice of his own Cabinet.

Secretary of the Navy Welles hastened to approve officially the act of Captain Wilkes in apprehending the Confederate Commissioners Mason and Slidell, Secretary Stanton publicly applauded, and even Secretary of State Seward, whose long public career had made him especially conservative, stated that he was opposed to any concession or surrender of Mason and Slidell.

But Lincoln, with great sagacity, simply said, "One war at a time."

President Lincoln's Last Public Address

The President made his last public address on the evening of April 11th, 1865, to a gathering at the White House. Said he:

"We meet this evening not in sorrow, but in gladness of heart.

"The evacuation of Petersburg and Richmond, and the surrender of the principal insurgent army, give hope of a righteous and speedy peace, whose joyous expression cannot be restrained.

"In the midst of this, however, He from whom all blessings flow must not be forgotten.

"Nor must those whose harder part gives us the cause of rejoicing be overlooked; their honors must not be parceled out with others.

"I myself was near the front, and had the high pleasure of transmitting the good news to you; but no part of the honor, for plan or execution, is mine.

"To General Grant, his skillful officers and brave men, all belongs."

No Others Like Them

One day an old lady from the country called on President Lincoln, her tanned face peering up to his through a pair of spectacles. Her errand was to present Mr. Lincoln a pair of stockings of her own make a yard long. Kind tears came to his eyes as she spoke to him, and then, holding the stockings one in each hand, dangling wide apart for general inspection, he assured her that he should take them with him to Washington, where (and here his eyes twinkled) he was sure he should not be able to find any like them.

Quite a number of well-known men were in the room with the

President when the old lady made her presentation. Among them was George S. Boutwell, who afterwards became Secretary of the Treasury.

The amusement of the company was not at all diminished by Mr. Boutwell's remark, that the lady had evidently made a very correct estimate of Mr. Lincoln's latitude and longitude.

Cash Was at Hand

Lincoln was appointed postmaster at New Salem by President Jackson. The office was given him because everybody liked him, and because he was the only man willing to take it who could make out the returns. Lincoln was pleased, because it gave him a chance to read every newspaper taken in the vicinity. He had never been able to get half the newspapers he wanted before.

Years after the postoffice had been discontinued and Lincoln had become a practicing lawyer at Springfield, an agent of the Postoffice Department entered his office and inquired if Abraham Lincoln was within. Lincoln responded to his name, and was informed that the agent had called to collect the balance due the Department since the discontinuance of the New Salem office.

A shade of perplexity passed over Lincoln's face, which did not escape the notice of friends present. One of them said at once:

"Lincoln, if you are in want of money, let us help you."

He made no reply, but suddenly rose, and pulled out from a pile of books a little old trunk, and, returning to the table, asked the agent how much the amount of his debt was.

The sum was named, and then Lincoln opened the trunk, pulled out a little package of coin wrapped in a cotton rag, and counted out the exact sum, amounting to more than seventeen dollars.

After the agent had left the room, he remarked quietly that he had never used any man's money but his own. Although this sum had been in his hands during all those years, he had never regarded it as available, even for any temporary use of his own.

Welcomed the Little Girls

At a Saturday afternoon reception at the White House, many persons noticed three little girls, poorly dressed, the children of some mechanic or laboring man, who had followed the visitors into the White House to gratify their curiosity. They passed around from room to room, and were hastening through the reception-room, with some trepidation, when the President called to them:

"Little girls, are you going to pass me without shaking hands?"

Then he bent his tall, awkward form down, and shook each little girl warmly by the hand. Everybody in the apartment was spellbound by the incident, so simple in itself.

"Don't Swap Horses"

Uncle Sam was pretty well satisfied with his horse, "Old Abe," and, as shown at the Presidential election of 1864, made up his mind to keep him, and not "swap" the tried and true animal for a strange one. "Harper's Weekly" of November 12th, 1864, had a cartoon which illustrated how the people of the United States felt about the matter better than anything published at the time. Beneath the picture was this text:

JOHN BULL: "Why don't you ride the other horse a bit? He's the best animal." (Pointing to McClellan in the bushes at the rear.)

BROTHER JONATHAN: "Well, that may be; but the fact is, OLD ABE is just where I can put my finger on him; and as for the other—though they say he's somewhere out in the scrub yonder—I never know where to find him."

Most Valuable Political Attribute

"One time I remember I asked Mr. Lincoln what attribute he considered most valuable to the successful politician," said Captain T. W. S. Kidd, of Springfield.

"He laid his hand on my shoulder and said, very earnestly:

"'To be able to raise a cause which shall produce an effect, and then fight the effect.'

"The more you think about it, the more profound does it become."

"Abe" Resented the Insult

A cashiered officer, seeking to be restored through the power of the executive, became insolent, because the President, who believed the man guilty, would not accede to his repeated requests, at last said, "Well, Mr. President, I see you are fully determined not to do me justice!"

This was too aggravating even for Mr. Lincoln; rising he suddenly seized the disgraced officer by the coat collar, and marched him forcibly to the door, saying as he ejected him into the passage:

"Sir, I give you fair warning never to show your face in this room again. I can bear censure, but not insult. I never wish to see your face again."

One Man Isn't Missed

Salmon P. Chase, when Secretary of the Treasury, had a disagreement with other members of the Cabinet, and resigned.

The President was urged not to accept it, as "Secretary Chase is to-day a national necessity," his advisers said.

"How mistaken you are!" Lincoln quietly observed. "Yet it is not strange; I used to have similar notions. No! If we should all be turned out to-morrow, and could come back here in a week, we should find our places filled by a lot of fellows doing just as well as we did, and in many instances better.

"Now, this reminds me of what the Irishman said. His verdict was that 'in this country one man is as good as another; and, for the matter of that, very often a great deal better.' No; this Government does not depend upon the life of any man."

"Stretched the Facts"

George B. Lincoln, a prominent merchant of Brooklyn, was traveling through the West in 1855-56, and found himself one night in a town on the Illinois River, by the name of Naples. The only tavern of the place had evidently been constructed with reference to business on a small scale. Poor as the prospect seemed, Mr. Lincoln had no alternative but to put up at the place.

The supper-room was also used as a lodging-room. Mr. Lincoln told his host that he thought he would "go to bed."

"Bed!" echoed the landlord. "There is no bed for you in this house unless you sleep with that man yonder. He has the only one we have to spare."

"Well," returned Mr. Lincoln, "the gentleman has possession, and perhaps would not like a bed-fellow."

Upon this a grizzly head appeared out of the pillows, and said:

"What is your name?"

"They call me Lincoln at home," was the reply.

"Lincoln!" repeated the stranger; "any connection of our Illinois Abraham?"

"No," replied Mr. Lincoln. "I fear not."

"Well," said the old gentleman, "I will let any man by the name of 'Lincoln' sleep with me, just for the sake of the name. You have heard of Abe?" he inquired.

"Oh, yes, very often," replied Mr. Lincoln. "No man could travel far in this State without hearing of him, and I would be very glad to claim connection if I could do so honestly."

"Well," said the old gentleman, "my name is Simmons. 'Abe' and I used to live and work together when young men. Many a job of woodcutting and rail-splitting have I done up with him. Abe Lincoln was the likeliest boy in God's world. He would work all day as hard as any of us and study by firelight in the log-house half the night; and in this way he made himself a thorough, practical surveyor. Once, during those days, I was in the upper part of the State, and I met General Ewing, whom President Jackson had sent to the Northwest to make surveys. I told him about Abe Lincoln, what a student he was, and that I wanted he should give him a job. He looked over his memorandum, and, holding out a paper, said:

"'There is County must be surveyed; if your friend can do the work properly, I shall be glad to have him undertake it—the compensation will be six hundred dollars.'

"Pleased as I could be, I hastened to Abe, after I got home, with an account of what I had secured for him. He was sitting before the fire in the log-cabin when I told him; and what do you think was his answer? When I finished, he looked up very quietly, and said:

"'Mr. Simmons, I thank you very sincerely for your kindness, but I don't think I will undertake the job.'

"'In the name of wonder,' said I, 'why? Six hundred does not grow upon every bush out here in Illinois.'

"'I know that,' said Abe, 'and I need the money bad enough, Simmons, as you know; but I have never been under obligation to a Democratic Administration, and I never intend to be so long as I can get my living another way. General Ewing must find another man to do his work.'"

A friend related this story to the President one day, and asked him if it were true.

"Pollard Simmons!" said Lincoln. "Well do I remember him. It is correct about our working together, but the old man must have stretched the facts somewhat about the survey of the county. I think I should have been very glad of the job at the time, no matter what Administration was in power."

It Lengthened the War

President Lincoln said, long before the National political campaign of 1864 had opened:

"If the unworthy ambition of politicians and the jealousy that exists in the army could be repressed, and all unite in a common aim and a common endeavor, the rebellion would soon be crushed."

His Theory of the Rebellion

The President once explained to a friend the theory of the Rebellion by the aid of the maps before him.

Running his long fore-finger down the map, he stopped at Virginia.

"We must drive them away from here" (Manassas Gap), he said, "and clear them out of this part of the State so that they cannot threaten us here (Washington) and get into Maryland.

"We must keep up a good and thorough blockade of their ports. We must march an army into East Tennessee and liberate the Union sentiment there. Finally we must rely on the people growing tired and saying to their leaders, 'We have had enough of this thing, we will bear it no longer.'"

Such was President Lincoln's plan for heading off the Rebellion in the summer of 1861. How it enlarged as the War progressed, from a call for seventy thousand volunteers to one for five hundred thousand men and $500,000,000 is a matter of well-known history.

Ran Away When Victorious

Three or four days after the battle of Bull Run, some gentlemen who had been on the field called upon the President.

He inquired very minutely regarding all the circumstances of the affair, and, after listening with the utmost attention, said, with a touch of humor: "So it is your notion that we whipped the rebels and then ran away from them!"

Wanted Stanton Spanked

Old Dennis Hanks was sent to Washington at one time by persons interested in securing the release from jail of several men accused of being copperheads. It was thought Old Dennis might have some influence with the President.

The latter heard Dennis' story and then said: "I will send for Mr. Stanton. It is his business."

Secretary Stanton came into the room, stormed up and down, and said the men ought to be punished more than they were. Mr. Lincoln sat quietly in his chair and waited for the tempest to subside, and then quietly said to Stanton he would like to have the papers next day.

When he had gone, Dennis said:

"'Abe,' if I was as big and as ugly as you are, I would take him over my knee and spank him."

The President replied: "No, Stanton is an able and valuable man for this Nation, and I am glad to bear his anger for the service he can give the Nation."

Stanton Was Out of Town

The quaint remark of the President to an applicant, "My dear sir, I have not much influence with the Administration," was one of Lincoln's little jokes.

Mr. Stanton, Secretary of War, once replied to an order from the President to give a colonel a commission in place of the resigning brigadier:

"I shan't do it, sir! I shan't do it! It isn't the way to do it, sir, and I shan't do it. I don't propose to argue the question with you, sir."

A few days after, the friend of the applicant who had presented the order to Secretary Stanton called upon the President and related his reception. A look of vexation came over the face of the President, and he seemed unwilling to talk of it, and desired the friend to see him another day. He did so, when he gave his visitor a positive order for the promotion. The latter told him he would not speak to Secretary Stanton again until he apologized.

"Oh," said the President, "Stanton has gone to Fortress Monroe, and Dana is acting. He will attend to it for you."

This he said with a manner of relief, as if it was a piece of good luck to find a man there who would obey his orders.

The nomination was sent to the Senate and confirmed.

Identified the Colored Man

Many applications reached Lincoln as he passed to and from the White House and the War Department. One day as he crossed the park he was stopped by a negro, who told him a pitiful story. The President wrote him out a check, which read. "Pay to colored man with one leg five dollars."

Office Seekers Worse Than War

When the Republican party came into power, Washington swarmed with office-seekers. They overran the White House and gave the President great annoyance. The incongruity of a man in his position, and with the very life of the country at stake, pausing to appoint postmasters, struck Mr. Lincoln forcibly. "What is the matter, Mr. Lincoln," said a friend one day, when he saw him looking particularly grave and dispirited. "Has anything gone wrong at the front?" "No," said the President, with a tired smile. "It isn't the war; it's the postoffice at Brownsville, Missouri."

He "Set 'Em Up"

Immediately after Mr. Lincoln's nomination for President at the Chicago Convention, a committee, of which Governor Morgan, of New York, was chairman, visited him in Springfield, Ill., where he was officially informed of his nomination.

After this ceremony had passed, Mr. Lincoln remarked to the company that as a fit ending to an interview so important and interesting as that which had just taken place, he supposed good manners would require that he should treat the committee with something to drink; and opening the door that led into the rear, he called out, "Mary! Mary!" A girl responded to the call, to whom Mr. Lincoln spoke a few words in an undertone, and, closing the door, returned again and talked with his guests. In a few minutes the maid entered, bearing a large waiter, containing several glass tumblers, and a large pitcher, and placed them upon the center-table. Mr. Lincoln arose, and, gravely addressing the company, said: "Gentlemen, we must pledge our mutual health in the most healthy beverage that God has given to man—it is the only beverage I have ever used or allowed my family to use, and I cannot conscientiously depart from it on the present occasion. It is pure Adam's ale from the spring." And, taking the tumbler, he touched it to his lips, and pledged them his highest respects in a cup of cold water. Of course, all his guests admired his consistency, and joined in his example.

Wasn't Stanton's Say

A few days before the President's death, Secretary Stanton tendered his resignation as Secretary of War. He accompanied the act with a most heartfelt tribute to Mr. Lincoln's constant friendship and faithful devotion to the country, saying, also, that he, as Secretary, had accepted the position to hold it only until the war should end, and that now he felt his work was done, and his duty was to resign.

Mr. Lincoln was greatly moved by the Secretary's words, and, tearing in pieces the paper containing the resignation, and throwing his arms about the Secretary, he said:

"Stanton, you have been a good friend and a faithful public servant, and it is not for you to say when you will no longer be needed here."

Several friends of both parties were present on the occasion, and there was not a dry eye that witnessed the scene.

"Jeffy" Threw Up the Sponge

When the War was fairly on, many people were astonished to find that "Old Abe" was a fighter from "way back." No one was the victim of greater amazement than Jefferson Davis, President of the Confederate States of America. Davis found out that "Abe" was not only a hard hitter, but had staying qualities of a high order. It was a fight to a "finish" with "Abe," no compromises being accepted. Over the title, "North and South," the issue of "Frank Leslie's Illustrated Newspaper" of December 24th, 1864, contained a cartoon, underneath which were these lines:

"Now, Jeffy, when you think you have had enough of this, say so, and I'll leave off." (See President's message.) In his message to Congress, December 6th,

President Lincoln said: "No attempt at negotiation with the insurgent leader could result in any good. He would accept of nothing short of the severance of the Union."

Therefore, Father Abraham, getting "Jeffy's" head "in chancery," proceeded to change the appearance and size of the secessionist's countenance, much to the grief and discomfort of the Southerner. It was Lincoln's idea to re-establish the Union, and he carried out his purpose to the very letter. But he didn't "leave off" until "Jeffy" cried "enough."

Didn't Know Grant's Preference

In October, 1864, President Lincoln, while he knew his re-election to the White House was in no sense doubtful, knew that if he lost New York and with it Pennsylvania on the home vote, the moral effect of his triumph would be broken and his power to prosecute the war and make peace would be greatly impaired. Colonel A. K. McClure was with Lincoln a good deal of the time previous to the November election, and tells this story:

"His usually sad face was deeply shadowed with sorrow when I told him that I saw no reasonable prospect of carrying Pennsylvania on the home vote, although we had about held our own in the hand-to-hand conflict through which we were passing.

"'Well, what is to be done?' was Lincoln's inquiry, after the whole situation had been presented to him. I answered that the solution of the problem was a very simple and easy one—that Grant was idle in front of Petersburg; that Sheridan had won all possible victories in the Valley; and that if five thousand Pennsylvania soldiers could be furloughed home from each army, the election could be carried without doubt.

"Lincoln's face' brightened instantly at the suggestion, and I saw that he was quite ready to execute it. I said to him: 'Of course, you can trust want to make the suggestion to him to furlough five thousand Pennsylvania troops for two weeks?'

"'To my surprise, Lincoln made no answer, and the bright face of a few moments before was instantly shadowed again. I was much disconcerted, as I supposed that Grant was the one man to whom Lincoln could turn with absolute confidence as his friend. I then said, with some earnestness: 'Surely, Mr. President, you can trust Grant with a confidential suggestion to furlough Pennsylvania troops?'

"Lincoln remained silent and evidently distressed at the proposition I was pressing upon him. After a few moments, and speaking with emphasis, I said: 'It can't be possible that Grant is not your friend; he can't be such an ingrate?'

"Lincoln hesitated for some time, and then answered in these words: 'Well, McClure, I have no reason to believe that Grant prefers my election to that of McClellan.'

"I believe Lincoln was mistaken in his distrust of Grant."

Justice vs. Numbers

Lincoln was constantly bothered by members of delegations of "goody-goodies," who knew all about running the War, but had no inside information as to what was going on. Yet, they poured out their advice in streams, until the President was heartily sick of the whole business, and wished the War would find some way to kill off these nuisances.

"How many men have the Confederates now in the field?" asked one of these bores one day.

"About one million two hundred thousand," replied the President.

"Oh, my! Not so many as that, surely, Mr. Lincoln."

"They have fully twelve hundred thousand, no doubt of it. You see, all of our generals when they get whipped say the enemy outnumbers them from three or five to one, and I must believe them. We have four hundred thousand men in the field, and three times four make twelve,—don't you see it? It is as plain to be seen as the nose on a man's face; and at the rate things are now going, with the great amount of speculation and the small crop of fighting, it will take a long time to overcome twelve hundred thousand rebels in arms.

"If they can get subsistence they have everything else, except a just cause. Yet it is said that 'thrice is he armed that hath his quarrel just.' I am willing, however, to risk our advantage of thrice in justice against their thrice in numbers."

No False Pride in Lincoln

General McClellan had little or no conception of the greatness of Abraham Lincoln. As time went on, he began to show plainly his contempt of the President, frequently allowing him to wait in the ante-room of his house while he transacted business with others. This discourtesy was so open that McClellan's staff noticed it, and newspaper correspondents commented on it. The President was too keen not to see the situation, but he was strong enough to ignore it. It was a battle he wanted from McClellan, not deference.

"I will hold McClellan's horse, if he will only bring us success," he said one day.

Extra Member of the Cabinet

G. H. Giddings was selected as the bearer of a message from the President to Governor Sam Houston, of Texas. A conflict had arisen there between the Southern party and the Governor, Sam Houston, and on March 18 the latter had been deposed. When Mr. Lincoln heard of this, he decided to try to get a message to the Governor, offering United States support if he would put himself at the head of the Union party of the State.

Mr. Giddings thus told of his interview with the President:

"He said to me that the message was of such importance that, before handing it to me, he would read it to me. Before beginning to read he said, 'This is a confidential and secret message. No one besides my Cabinet and myself knows anything about it, and we are all sworn to secrecy. I am going to swear you in as one of my Cabinet.'

"And then he said to me in a jocular way, 'Hold up your right hand,' which I did.

"'Now,' said he, consider yourself a member of my Cabinet.'"

How Lincoln Was Abused

With the possible exception of President Washington, whose political opponents did not hesitate to rob the vocabulary of vulgarity and wickedness whenever they desired to vilify the Chief Magistrate, Lincoln was the most and "best" abused man who ever held office in the United States. During the first half of his initial term there was no epithet which was not applied to him.

One newspaper in New York habitually characterized him as "that hideous baboon at the other end of the avenue," and declared that "Barnum should buy and exhibit him as a zoological curiosity."

Although the President did not, to all appearances, exhibit annoyance because of the various diatribes printed and spoken, yet the fact is that his life was so cruelly embittered by these and other expressions quite as virulent, that he often declared to those most intimate with him, "I would rather be dead than, as President, thus abused in the house of my friends."

How "Fighting Joe" Was Appointed

General "Joe" Hooker, the fourth commander of the noble but unfortunate Army of the Potomac, was appointed to that position by President Lincoln in January, 1863. General Scott, for some reason, disliked Hooker and would not appoint him. Hooker, after some months of discouraging waiting, decided to return to California, and called to pay his respects to President Lincoln. He was introduced as Captain Hooker, and to the surprise of the President began the following speech:

"Mr. President, my friend makes a mistake. I am not Captain Hooker, but was once Lieutenant-Colonel Hooker of the regular army. I was lately a farmer in California, but since the Rebellion broke out I have been trying to get into service, but I find I am not wanted.

"I am about to return home; but before going, I was anxious to pay my respects to you, and express my wishes for your personal welfare and success in quelling this Rebellion. And I want to say to you a word more.

"I was at Bull Run the other day, Mr. President, and it is no vanity in me to say, I am a darned sight better general than you had on the field."

This was said, not in the tone of a braggart, but of a man who knew what he was talking about. Hooker did not return to California, but in a few weeks Captain Hooker received from the President a commission as Brigadier-General Hooker.

Kept His Courage Up

The President, like old King Saul, when his term was about to expire, was in a quandary concerning a further lease of the Presidential office. He consulted again the "prophetess" of Georgetown, immortalized by his patronage.

She retired to an inner chamber, and, after raising and consulting more than a dozen of distinguished spirits from Hades, she returned to the reception-parlor, where the chief magistrate awaited her, and declared that General Grant would capture Richmond, and that "Honest Old Abe" would be next President.

She, however, as the report goes, told him to beware of Chase.

A Fortune-Teller's Prediction

Lincoln had been born and reared among people who were believers in premonitions and supernatural appearances all his life, and he once declared to his friends that he was "from boyhood superstitious."

He at one time said to Judge Arnold that "the near approach of the important events of his life were indicated by a presentiment or a strange dream, or in some other mysterious way it was impressed upon him that something important was to occur." This was earlier than 1850.

It is said that on his second visit to New Orleans, Lincoln and his companion, John Hanks, visited an old fortune-teller—a voodoo negress. Tradition says that "during the interview she became very much excited, and after various predictions, exclaimed: 'You will be President, and all the negroes will be free.'"

That the old voodoo negress should have foretold that the visitor would be President is not at all incredible. She doubtless told this to many aspiring lads, but Lincoln, so it is avowed, took the prophecy seriously.

Too Much Powder

So great was Lincoln's anxiety for the success of the Union arms that he considered no labor on his part too arduous, and spent much of his time in looking after even the small details.

Admiral Dahlgren was sent for one morning by the President, who said "Well, captain, here's a letter about some new powder."

After reading the letter he showed the sample of powder, and remarked that he had burned some of it, and did not believe it was a good article—here was too much residuum.

"I will show you," he said; and getting a small piece of paper, placed thereupon some of the powder, then went to the fire and with the tongs picked up a coal, which he blew, clapped it on the powder, and after the resulting explosion, added, "You see there is too much left there."

Sleep Standing Up

McClellan was a thorn in Lincoln's side—"always up in the air," as the President put it—and yet he hesitated to remove him. "The Young Napoleon" was a good organizer, but no fighter. Lincoln sent him everything necessary in the way of men, ammunition, artillery and equipments, but he was forever unready.

Instead of making a forward movement at the time expected, he would notify the President that he must have more men. These were given him as rapidly as possible, and then would come a demand for more horses, more this and that, usually winding up with a demand for still "more men."

Lincoln bore it all in patience for a long time, but one day, when he had received another request for more men, he made a vigorous protest.

"If I gave McClellan all the men he asks for," said the President, "they couldn't find room to lie down. They'd have to sleep standing up."

Should Have Fought Another Battle

General Meade, after the great victory at Gettysburg, was again face to face with General Lee shortly afterwards at Williamsport, and even the former's warmest friends agree that he might have won in another battle, but he took no action. He was not a "pushing" man like Grant. It was this negligence on the part of Meade that lost him the rank of Lieutenant-General, conferred upon General Sheridan.

A friend of Meade's, speaking to President Lincoln and intimating that Meade should have, after that battle, been made Commander-in-Chief of the Union Armies, received this reply from Lincoln:

"Now, don't misunderstand me about General Meade. I am profoundly grateful down to the bottom of my boots for what he did at Gettysburg, but I think that if I had been General Meade I would have fought another battle."

Lincoln Upbraided Lamon

In one of his reminiscences of Lincoln, Ward Lamon tells how keenly the President-elect always regretted the "sneaking in act" when he made the celebrated "midnight ride," which he took under protest, and landed him in Washington known to but a few. Lamon says:

"The President was convinced that he committed a grave mistake in listening to the solicitations of a 'professional spy' and of friends too easily alarmed, and frequently upbraided me for having aided him to degrade himself at the very moment in all his life when his behavior should have exhibited the utmost dignity and composure.

"Neither he nor the country generally then understood the true facts concerning the dangers to his life. It is now an acknowledged fact that there never was a moment from the day he crossed the Maryland line, up to the time of his assassination, that he was not in danger of death by violence, and that his life was spared until the night of the 14th of April, 1865, only through the ceaseless and watchful care of the guards thrown around him."

Marked Out a Few Words

President Lincoln was calm and unmoved when England and France were blustering and threatening war. At Lincoln's instance Secretary of State Seward notified the English Cabinet and the French Emperor that as ours was merely a family quarrel of a strictly private and confidential nature, there was no call for meddling; also that they would have a war on their hands in a very few minutes if they didn't keep their hands off.

Many of Seward's notes were couched in decidedly peppery terms, some expressions being so tart that President Lincoln ran his pen through them.

Lincoln Silences Seward

General Farnsworth told the writer nearly twenty years ago that, being in the War Office one day, Secretary Stanton told him that at the last Cabinet meeting he had learned a lesson he should never forget, and thought he had obtained an insight into Mr. Lincoln's wonderful power over the masses. The Secretary said a Cabinet meeting was called to consider our relations with England in regard to the Mason-Slidell affair. One after another of the Cabinet presented his views, and Mr. Seward read an elaborate diplomatic dispatch, which he had prepared.

Finally Mr. Lincoln read what he termed "a few brief remarks upon the subject," and asked the opinions of his auditors. They unanimously agreed that our side of the question needed no more argument than was contained in the President's "few brief remarks."

Mr. Seward said he would be glad to adopt the remarks, and, giving them more of the phraseology usual in diplomatic circles, send them to Lord Palmerston, the British premier.

"Then," said Secretary Stanton, "came the demonstration. The President, half wheeling in his seat, threw one leg over the chair-arm, and, holding the letter in his hand, said, 'Seward, do you suppose Palmerston will understand our position from that letter, just as it is?'

"'Certainly, Mr. President.'

"'Do you suppose the London Times will?'

"'Certainly.'

"'Do you suppose the average Englishman of affairs will?'

"'Certainly; it cannot be mistaken in England.'

"'Do you suppose that a hackman out on his box (pointing to the street) will understand it?'

"'Very readily, Mr. President.'

"'Very well, Seward, I guess we'll let her slide just as she is.'

"And the letter did 'slide,' and settled the whole business in a manner that was effective."

Brought the Husband Up

One morning President Lincoln asked Major Eckert, on duty at the White House, "Who is that woman crying out in the hall? What is the matter with her?"

Eckert said it was a woman who had come a long distance expecting to go down to the army to see her husband. An order had gone out a short time before to allow no women in the army, except in special cases.

Mr. Lincoln sat moodily for a moment after hearing this story, and suddenly looking up, said, "Let's send her down. You write the order, Major."

Major Eckert hesitated a moment, and replied, "Would it not be better for Colonel Hardie to write the order?"

"Yes," said Mr. Lincoln, "that is better; let Hardie write it."

The major went out, and soon returned, saying, "Mr. President, would it not be better in this case to let the woman's husband come to Washington?"

Mr. Lincoln's face lighted up with pleasure. "Yes, yes," was the President's answer in a relieved tone; "that's the best way; bring him up."

The order was written, and the man was sent to Washington.

No War Without Blood-Letting

"You can't carry on war without blood-letting," said Lincoln one day.

The President, although almost feminine in his kind-heartedness, knew not only this, but also that large bodies of soldiers in camp were at the mercy of diseases of every sort, the result being a heavy casualty list.

Of the (estimated) half-million men of the Union armies who gave up their lives in the War of the Rebellion—1861-65—fully seventy-five per cent died of disease. The soldiers killed upon the field of battle constituted a comparatively small proportion of the casualties.

Lincoln's Two Difficulties

London "Punch" caricatured President Lincoln in every possible way, holding him and the Union cause up to the ridicule of the world so far as it could. On August 23rd, 1862, its cartoon entitled "Lincoln's Two Difficulties" had the text underneath: LINCOLN: "What? No money! No men!" "Punch" desired to create the impression that the Washington Government was in a bad way, lacking both money and men for the purpose of putting down the Rebellion; that the United States Treasury was bankrupt, and the people of the North so devoid of patriotism that they would not send men for the army to assist in destroying the Confederacy. The truth is, that when this cartoon was printed the North had five hundred thousand men in the field, and, before the War closed, had provided fully two million and a half troops. The report of the Secretary of the Treasury which showed the financial affairs and situation of the United States up to July, 1862. The receipts of the National Government for the year ending June 30th, 1862, were $10,000,000 in excess of the expenditures, although the War was costing the country $2,000,000 per day; the credit of the United States was good, and business matters were in a satisfactory state. The Navy, by August 23rd, 1862, had received eighteen thousand additional men, and was in fine shape;

the people of the North stood ready to supply anything the Government needed, so that, all things taken together, the "Punch" cartoon was not exactly true, as the facts and figures abundantly proved.

White Elephant on His Hands

An old and intimate friend from Springfield called on President Lincoln and found him much depressed.

The President was reclining on a sofa, but rising suddenly he said to his friend:

"You know better than any man living that from my boyhood up my ambition was to be President. I am President of one part of this divided country at least; but look at me! Oh, I wish I had never been born!

"I've a white elephant on my hands—one hard to manage. With a fire in my front and rear to contend with, the jealousies of the military commanders, and not receiving that cordial co-operative support from Congress that could reasonably be expected with an active and formidable enemy in the field threatening the very life-blood of the Government, my position is anything but a bed of roses."

When Lincoln and Grant Clashed

Ward Lamon, one of President Lincoln's law partners, and his most intimate friend in Washington, has this to relate:

"I am not aware that there was ever a serious discord or misunderstanding between Mr. Lincoln and General Grant, except on a single occasion. From the commencement of the struggle, Lincoln's policy was to break the backbone of the Confederacy by depriving it of its principal means of subsistence.

"Cotton was its vital aliment; deprive it of this, and the rebellion must necessarily collapse. The Hon. Elihu B. Washburne from the outset was opposed to any contraband traffic with the Confederates.

"Lincoln had given permits and passes through the lines to two persons—Mr. Joseph Mattox of Maryland and General Singleton of

Illinois—to enable them to bring cotton and other Southern products from Virginia. Washburne heard of it, called immediately on Mr. Lincoln, and, after remonstrating with him on the impropriety of such a demarche, threatened to have General Grant countermand the permits if they were not revoked.

"Naturally, both became excited. Lincoln declared that he did not believe General Grant would take upon himself the responsibility of such an act. 'I will show you, sir; I will show you whether Grant will do it or not,' responded Mr. Washburne, as he abruptly withdrew.

"By the next boat, subsequent to this interview, the Congressman left Washington for the headquarters of General Grant. He returned shortly afterward to the city, and so likewise did Mattox and Singleton. Grant had countermanded the permits.

"Under all the circumstances, it was, naturally, a source of exultation to Mr. Washburne and his friends, and of corresponding surprise and mortification to the President. The latter, however, said nothing further than this:

"'I wonder when General Grant changed his mind on this subject? He was the first man, after the commencement of this War, to grant a permit for the passage of cotton through the lines, and that to his own father.'

"The President, however, never showed any resentment toward General Grant.

"In referring afterwards to the subject, the President said: 'It made me feel my insignificance keenly at the moment; but if my friends Washburne, Henry Wilson and others derive pleasure from so unworthy a victory over me, I leave them to its full enjoyment.'

"This ripple on the otherwise unruffled current of their intercourse did not disturb the personal relations between Lincoln and Grant; but there was little cordiality between the President and Messrs. Washburne and Wilson afterwards."

Won James Gordon Bennett's Support

The story as to how President Lincoln won the support of James Gordon Bennett, Sr., founder of the New York Herald, is a most interesting one. It was one of Lincoln's shrewdest political acts, and was brought about by the tender, in an autograph letter, of the French Mission to Bennett.

The New York Times was the only paper in the metropolis which supported him heartily, and President Lincoln knew how important it was to have the support of the Herald. He therefore, according to the way Colonel McClure tells it, carefully studied how to bring its editor into close touch with himself.

The outlook for Lincoln's re-election was not promising. Bennett had strongly advocated the nomination of General McClellan by the Democrats, and that was ominous of hostility to Lincoln; and when McClellan was nominated he was accepted on all sides as a most formidable candidate.

It was in this emergency that Lincoln's political sagacity served him sufficiently to win the Herald to his cause, and it was done by the confidential tender of the French Mission. Bennett did not break over to Lincoln at once, but he went by gradual approaches.

His first step was to declare in favor of an entirely new candidate, which was an utter impossibility. He opened a "leader" in the Herald on the subject in this way: "Lincoln has proved a failure; McClellan has proved a failure; Fremont has proved a failure; let us have a new candidate."

Lincoln, McClellan and Fremont were then all in the field as nominated candidates, and the Fremont defection was a serious threat to Lincoln. Of course, neither Lincoln nor McClellan declined, and the Herald, failing to get the new man it knew to be an impossibility, squarely advocated Lincoln's re-election.

Without consulting any one, and without any public announcement: whatever, Lincoln wrote to Bennett, asking him to accept the mission to France. The offer was declined. Bennett valued the offer very much more than the office, and from that day until the day of the President's death he was one of Lincoln's most appreciative friends and hearty supporters on his own independent line.

Stood by the "Silent Man"

Once, in reply to a delegation, which visited the White House, the members of which were unusually vociferous in their demands that the Silent Man (as General Grant was called) should be relieved from duty, the President remarked:

"What I want and what the people want is generals who will fight battles and win victories.

"Grant has done this, and I propose to stand by him."

This declaration found its way into the newspapers, and Lincoln was upheld by the people of the North, who, also, wanted "generals who will fight battles and win victories."

A Very Brainy Nubbin

President Lincoln and Secretary of State Seward met Alexander H. Stephens, Vice-President of the Confederacy, on February 2nd, 1865, on the River Queen, at Fortress Monroe. Stephens was enveloped in overcoats and shawls, and had the appearance of a fair-sized man. He began to take off one wrapping after another, until the small, shriveled old man stood before them.

Lincoln quietly said to Seward: "This is the largest shucking for so small a nubbin that I ever saw."

President Lincoln had a friendly conference, but presented his ultimatum that the one and only condition of peace was that Confederates "must cease their resistance."

Sent to His "Friends"

During the Civil War, Clement L. Vallandigham, of Ohio, had shown himself, in the National House of Representatives and elsewhere, one of the bitterest and most outspoken of all the men of that class which insisted that "the war was a failure." He declared that it was the design of "those in power to establish a despotism," and that they had "no intention of restoring the Union." He denounced the conscription which had been ordered, and declared that men who submitted to be drafted into the army were "unworthy to be called free men." He spoke of the President as "King Lincoln."

Such utterances at this time, when the Government was exerting itself to the utmost to recruit the armies, were dangerous, and Vallandigham was arrested, tried by court-martial at Cincinnati, and sentenced to be placed in confinement during the war.

General Burnside, in command at Cincinnati, approved the sentence, and ordered that he be sent to Fort Warren, in Boston Harbor; but the President ordered that he be sent "beyond our lines into those of his friends." He was therefore escorted to the Confederate lines in Tennessee, thence going to Richmond. He did not meet with a very cordial reception there, and finally sought refuge in Canada.

Vallandigham died in a most peculiar way some years after the close of the War, and it was thought by many that his death was the result of premeditation upon his part.

Go Down with Colors Flying

In August, 1864, the President called for five hundred thousand more men. The country was much depressed. The Confederates had, in comparatively small force, only a short time before, been to the very gates of Washington, and returned almost unharmed.

The Presidential election was impending. Many thought another call for men at such a time would insure, if not destroy, Mr. Lincoln's chances for re-election. A friend said as much to him one day, after the President had told him of his purpose to make such a call.

"As to my re-election," replied Mr. Lincoln, "it matters not. We must have the men. If I go down, I intend to go, like the Cumberland, with my colors flying!"

All Were Tragedies

A cartoon was published in "Harper's Weekly" on January 31st, 1863, the explanatory text, underneath, reading in this way:

MANAGER LINCOLN: "Ladies and gentlemen, I regret to say that the tragedy entitled 'The Army of the Potomac' has been withdrawn on account of quarrels among the leading performers, and I have substituted three new and striking farces, or burlesques, one, entitled 'The Repulse of Vicksburg,' by the well-known favorite, E. M. Stanton, Esq., and the others, 'The Loss of the Harriet Lane,' and 'The Exploits of the Alabama'—a very sweet thing in farces, I assure you—by the veteran composer, Gideon Welles. (Unbounded applause by the Copperheads)."

In July, after this cartoon appeared, the Army of the Potomac defeated Lee at Gettysburg, and sounded the death-knell of the Confederacy; General Hooker, with his corps from this Army opened the Tennessee River, thus affording some relief to the Union troops in Chattanooga; Hooker's men also captured Lookout Mountain, and assisted in taking Missionary Ridge.

General Grant converted the farce "The Repulse of Vicksburg" into a tragedy for the Copperheads, taking that stronghold on July 4th, and Captain Winslow, with the Union man-of-war Kearsarge, meeting the Confederate privateer Alabama, off the coast of France, near Cherbourg, fought the famous ship to a finish and sunk her. Thus the tragedy of "The Army of the Potomac" was given after all, and Playwright Stanton and Composer Welles were vindicated, their compositions having been received by the public with great favor.

"He's the Best of Us"

Secretary of State Seward did not appreciate President Lincoln's ability until he had been associated with him for quite a time, but he was awakened to a full realization of the greatness of the Chief Executive "all of a sudden."

Having submitted "Some Thoughts for the President's Consideration"—a lengthy paper intended as an outline of the policy, both domestic and foreign, the Administration should pursue—he was not more surprised at the magnanimity and kindness of President Lincoln's reply than the thorough mastery of the subject displayed by the President.

A few months later, when the Secretary had begun to understand Mr. Lincoln, he was quick and generous to acknowledge his power.

"Executive force and vigor are rare qualities," he wrote to Mrs. Seward. "The President is the best of us."

How Lincoln "Composed"

Superintendent Chandler, of the Telegraph Office in the War Department, once told how President Lincoln wrote telegrams. Said he:

"Mr. Lincoln frequently wrote telegrams in my office. His method of composition was slow and laborious. It was evident that he thought out what he was going to say before he touched his pen to the paper. He would sit looking out of the window, his left elbow on the table, his hand scratching his temple, his lips moving, and frequently he spoke the sentence aloud or in a half whisper.

"After he was satisfied that he had the proper expression, he would write it out. If one examines the originals of Mr. Lincoln's telegrams and letters, he will find very few erasures and very little interlining. This was because he had them definitely in his mind before writing them.

"In this he was the exact opposite of Mr. Stanton, who wrote with feverish haste, often scratching out words, and interlining frequently. Sometimes he would seize a sheet which he had filled, and impatiently tear it into pieces."

Hamlin Might Do It

Several United States Senators urged President Lincoln to muster Southern slaves into the Union Army. Lincoln replied:

"Gentlemen, I have put thousands of muskets into the hands of loyal citizens of Tennessee, Kentucky, and Western North Carolina. They have said they could defend themselves, if they had guns. I have given them the guns. Now, these men do not believe in mustering-in the negro. If I do it, these thousands of muskets will be turned against us. We should lose more than we should gain."

Being still further urged, President Lincoln gave them this answer:

"Gentlemen," he said, "I can't do it. I can't see it as you do. You may be right, and I may be wrong; but I'll tell you what I can do; I can resign in favor of Mr. Hamlin. Perhaps Mr. Hamlin could do it."

The matter ended there, for the time being.

The Gun Shot Better

The President took a lively interest in all new firearm improvements and inventions, and it sometimes happened that, when an inventor could get nobody else in the Government to listen to him, the President would personally test his gun. A former clerk in the Navy Department tells an incident illustrative.

He had stayed late one night at his desk, when he heard someone striding up and down the hall muttering: "I do wonder if they have gone already and left the building all alone." Looking out, the clerk was surprised to see the President.

"Good evening," said Mr. Lincoln. "I was just looking for that man who goes shooting with me sometimes."

The clerk knew Mr. Lincoln referred to a certain messenger of the Ordnance Department who had been accustomed to going with him to test weapons, but as this man had gone home, the clerk offered his services. Together they went to the lawn south of the White House, where Mr. Lincoln fixed up a target cut from a sheet of white Congressional notepaper.

"Then pacing off a distance of about eighty or a hundred feet," writes the clerk, "he raised the rifle to a level, took a quick aim, and drove the round of seven shots in quick succession, the bullets shooting all around the target like a Gatling gun and one striking near the center.

"'I believe I can make this gun shoot better,' said Mr. Lincoln, after we had looked at the result of the first fire. With this he took from his vest pocket a small wooden sight which he had whittled from a pine stick, and adjusted it over the sight of the carbine. He then shot two rounds, and of the fourteen bullets nearly a dozen hit the paper!"

Lenient with Mcclellan

General McClellan, aside from his lack of aggressiveness, fretted the President greatly with his complaints about military matters, his obtrusive criticism regarding political matters, and especially at his insulting declaration to the Secretary of War, dated June 28th, 1862, just after his retreat to the James River.

General Halleck was made Commander-in-Chief of the Union forces in July, 1862, and September 1st McClellan was called to Washington. The day before he had written his wife that "as a matter of self-respect, I cannot go there." President Lincoln and General Halleck called at McClellan's house, and the President said: "As a favor to me, I wish you would take command of the fortifications of Washington and all the troops for the defense of the capital."

Lincoln thought highly of McClellan's ability as an organizer and his strength in defense, yet any other President would have had him court-martialed for using this language, which appeared in McClellan's letter of June 28th:

"If I save this army now, I tell you plainly that I owe no thanks to you or to any other person in Washington. You have done your best to sacrifice this army."

This letter, although addressed to the Secretary of War, distinctly embraced the President in the grave charge of conspiracy to defeat McClellan's army and sacrifice thousands of the lives of his soldiers.

Didn't Want a Military Reputation

Lincoln was averse to being put up as a military hero.

When General Cass was a candidate for the Presidency his friends sought to endow him with a military reputation.

Lincoln, at that time a representative in Congress, delivered a speech before the House, which, in its allusion to Mr. Cass, was exquisitely sarcastic and irresistibly humorous:

"By the way, Mr. Speaker," said Lincoln, "do you know I am a military hero?

"Yes, sir, in the days of the Black Hawk War, I fought, bled, and came away.

"Speaking of General Cass's career reminds me of my own.

"I was not at Stillman's defeat, but I was about as near it as Cass to Hull's surrender; and like him I saw the place very soon afterwards.

"It is quite certain I did not break my sword, for I had none to break, but I bent my musket pretty badly on one occasion.

"If General Cass went in advance of me picking whortleberries, I guess I surpassed him in charging upon the wild onion.

"If he saw any live, fighting Indians, it was more than I did, but I had a good many bloody struggles with the mosquitoes, and although I never fainted from loss of blood, I can truly say that I was often very hungry."

Lincoln concluded by saying that if he ever turned Democrat and should run for the Presidency, he hoped they would not make fun of him by attempting to make him a military hero.

"Surrender No Slave"

About March, 1862, General Benjamin F. Butler, in command at Fortress Monroe, advised President Lincoln that he had determined to regard all slaves coming into his camps as contraband of war, and to employ their labor under fair compensation, and Secretary of War Stanton replied to him, in behalf of the President, approving his course, and saying, "You are not to interfere between master and slave on the one hand, nor surrender slaves who may come within your lines."

This was a significant milestone of progress to the great end that was thereafter to be reached.

Conscripting Dead Men

Mr. Lincoln being found fault with for making another "call," said that if the country required it, he would continue to do so until the matter stood as described by a Western provost marshal, who says:

"I listened a short time since to a butternut-clad individual, who succeeded in making good his escape, expatiate most eloquently on the rigidness with which the conscription was enforced south of the Tennessee River. His response to a question propounded by a citizen ran somewhat in this wise:

"'Do they conscript close over the river?'

"'Stranger, I should think they did! They take every man who hasn't been dead more than two days!'

"If this is correct, the Confederacy has at least a ghost of a chance left."

And of another, a Methodist minister in Kansas, living on a small salary, who was greatly troubled to get his quarterly instalment. He at last told the non-paying trustees that he must have his money, as he was suffering for the necessaries of life.

"Money!" replied the trustees; "you preach for money? We thought you preached for the good of souls!"

"Souls!" responded the reverend; "I can't eat souls; and if I could it would take a thousand such as yours to make a meal!"

"That soul is the point, sir," said the President.

Lincoln's Rejected Manuscript

On February 5th, 1865, President Lincoln formulated a message to Congress, proposing the payment of $400,000,000 to the South as compensation for slaves lost by emancipation, and submitted it to his Cabinet, only to be unanimously rejected.

Lincoln sadly accepted the decision, and filed away the manuscript message, together with this indorsement thereon, to which his signature was added: "February 5, 1865. To-day these papers, which explain themselves, were drawn up and submitted to the Cabinet unanimously disapproved by them."

When the proposed message was disapproved, Lincoln soberly asked: "How long will the war last?"

To this none could make answer, and he added: "We are spending now, in carrying on the war, $3,000,000 a day, which will amount to all this money, besides all the lives."

Lincoln as a Story Writer

In his youth, Mr. Lincoln once got an idea for a thrilling, romantic story. One day, in Springfield, he was sitting with his feet on the window sill, chatting with an acquaintance, when he suddenly changed the drift of the conversation by saying: "Did you ever write out a story in your mind? I did when I was a little codger. One day a wagon with a lady and two girls and a man broke down near us, and while they were fixing up, they cooked in our kitchen. The woman had books and read us stories, and they were the first I had ever heard. I took a great fancy to one of the girls; and when they were gone I thought of her a great deal, and one day when I was sitting out in the sun by the house I wrote out a story in my mind. I thought I took my father's horse and followed the wagon, and finally I found it, and they were surprised to see me. I talked with the girl, and persuaded her to elope with me; and that night I put her on my horse, and we started off across the prairie. After several hours we came to a camp; and when we rode up we found it was the one we had left a few hours before, and went in. The next night we tried again, and the same thing happened—the horse came back to the same place; and then we concluded that we ought not to elope. I stayed until I had persuaded her father to give her to me. I always meant to write that story out and publish it, and I began once; but I concluded that it was not much of a story. But I think that was the beginning of love with me."

Lincoln's Ideas on Crossing a River When He Got to It

Lincoln's reply to a Springfield (Illinois) clergyman, who asked him what was to be his policy on the slavery question was most apt:

"Well, your question is rather a cool one, but I will answer it by telling you a story:

"You know Father B., the old Methodist preacher? and you know Fox River and its freshets?

"Well, once in the presence of Father B., a young Methodist was worrying about Fox River, and expressing fears that he should be prevented from fulfilling some of his appointments by a freshet in the river.

"Father B. checked him in his gravest manner. Said he:

"'Young man, I have always made it a rule in my life not to cross Fox River till I get to it.'

"And," said the President, "I am not going to worry myself over the slavery question till I get to it."

A few days afterward a Methodist minister called on the President, and on being presented to him, said, simply:

"Mr. President, I have come to tell you that I think we have got to Fox River!"

Lincoln thanked the clergyman, and laughed heartily.

President Nominated First

The day of Lincoln's second nomination for the Presidency he forgot all about the Republican National Convention, sitting at Baltimore, and wandered over to the War Department. While there, a telegram came announcing the nomination of Johnson as Vice-President.

"What," said Lincoln to the operator, "do they nominate a Vice-President before they do a President?"

"Why," replied the astonished official, "have you not heard of your own nomination? It was sent to the White House two hours ago."

"It is all right," replied the President; "I shall probably find it on my return."

"Them Gilliteens"

The illustrated newspapers of the United States and England had a good deal of fun, not only with President Lincoln, but the latter's Cabinet officers and military commanders as well. It was said by these funny publications that the President had set up a guillotine in his "back-yard," where all those who offended were beheaded with both neatness, and despatch. "Harper's Weekly" of January 3rd,

1863, contained a cartoon labeled "Those Guillotines; a Little Incident at the White House," the personages figuring in the "incident" being Secretary of War Stanton and a Union general who had been unfortunate enough to lose a battle to the Confederates. Beneath the cartoon was the following dialogue:

SERVANT: "If ye plase, sir, them Gilliteens has arrove." MR. LINCOLN: "All right, Michael. Now, gentlemen, will you be kind enough to step out in the back-yard?"

The hair and whiskers of Secretary of War Stanton are ruffled and awry, and his features are not calm and undisturbed, indicating that he has an idea of what's the matter in that back-yard; the countenance of the officer in the rear of the Secretary of War wears rather an anxious, or worried, look, and his hair isn't combed smoothly, either.

President Lincoln's frequent changes among army commanders—before he found Grant, Sherman and Sheridan—afforded an opportunity the caricaturists did not neglect, and some very clever cartoons were the consequence.

"Consider the Sympathy of Lincoln"

Consider the sympathy of Abraham Lincoln. Do you know the story of William Scott, private? He was a boy from a Vermont farm.

There had been a long march, and the night succeeding it he had stood on picket. The next day there had been another long march, and that night William Scott had volunteered to stand guard in the place of a sick comrade who had been drawn for the duty.

It was too much for William Scott. He was too tired. He had been found sleeping on his beat.

The army was at Chain Bridge. It was in a dangerous neighborhood. Discipline must be kept.

William Scott was apprehended, tried by court-martial, sentenced to be shot. News of the case was carried to Lincoln. William Scott was a prisoner in his tent, expecting to be shot next day.

But the flaps of his tent were parted, and Lincoln stood before him. Scott said:

"The President was the kindest man I had ever seen; I knew him at once by a Lincoln medal I had long worn.

"I was scared at first, for I had never before talked with a great man; but Mr. Lincoln was so easy with me, so gentle, that I soon forgot my fright.

"He asked me all about the people at home, the neighbors, the farm, and where I went to school, and who my schoolmates were. Then he asked me about mother and how she looked; and I was glad I could take her photograph from my bosom and show it to him.

"He said how thankful I ought to be that my mother still lived, and how, if he were in my place, he would try to make her a proud mother, and never cause her a sorrow or a tear.

"I cannot remember it all, but every word was so kind.

"He had said nothing yet about that dreadful next morning; I thought it must be that he was so kind-hearted that he didn't like to speak of it.

"But why did he say so much about my mother, and my not causing her a sorrow or a tear, when I knew that I must die the next morning?

"But I supposed that was something that would have to go unexplained; and so I determined to brace up and tell him that I did not feel a bit guilty, and ask him wouldn't he fix it so that the firing party would not be from our regiment.

"That was going to be the hardest of all—to die by the hands of my comrades.

"Just as I was going to ask him this favor, he stood up, and he says to me:

"'My boy, stand up here and look me in the face.'

"I did as he bade me.

"'My boy,' he said, 'you are not going to be shot to-morrow. I believe you when you tell me that you could not keep awake.

"'I am going to trust you, and send you back to your regiment.

"'But I have been put to a good deal of trouble on your account.

"'I have had to come up here from Washington when I have got a great deal to do; and what I want to know is, how are you going to pay my bill?'

"There was a big lump in my throat; I could scarcely speak. I had expected to die, you see, and had kind of got used to thinking that way.

"To have it all changed in a minute! But I got it crowded down, and managed to say:

"'I am grateful, Mr. Lincoln! I hope I am as grateful as ever a man can be to you for saving my life.

"'But it comes upon me sudden and unexpected like. I didn't lay out for it at all; but there is some way to pay you, and I will find it after a little.

"'There is the bounty in the savings bank; I guess we could borrow some money on the mortgage of the farm.'

"'There was my pay was something, and if he would wait until pay-day I was sure the boys would help; so I thought we could make it up if it wasn't more than five or six hundred dollars.

"'But it is a great deal more than that,' he said.

"Then I said I didn't just see how, but I was sure I would find some way—if I lived.

"Then Mr. Lincoln put his hands on my shoulders, and looked into my face as if he was sorry, and said; "'My boy, my bill is a very large one. Your friends cannot pay it, nor your bounty, nor the farm, nor all your comrades!

"'There is only one man in all the world who can pay it, and his name is William Scott!

"'If from this day William Scott does his duty, so that, if I was there when he comes to die, he can look me in the face as he does now, and say, I have kept my promise, and I have done my duty as a soldier, then my debt will be paid.

"'Will you make that promise and try to keep it?"

The promise was given. Thenceforward there never was such a soldier as William Scott.

This is the record of the end. It was after one of the awful battles of the Peninsula. He was shot all to pieces. He said:

"Boys, I shall never see another battle. I supposed this would be my last. I haven't much to say.

"You all know what you can tell them at home about me.

"I have tried to do the right thing! If any of you ever have the chance I wish you would tell President Lincoln that I have never forgotten the kind words he said to me at the Chain Bridge; that I have tried to be a good soldier and true to the flag; that I should have paid my whole debt to him if I had lived; and that now, when I know that I am dying, I think of his kind face, and thank him again, because he gave me the chance to fall like a soldier in battle, and not like a coward, by the hands of my comrades."

What wonder that Secretary Stanton said, as he gazed upon the tall form and kindly face as he lay there, smitten down by the assassin's bullet, "There lies the most perfect ruler of men who ever lived."

Saved a Life

One day during the Black Hawk War a poor old Indian came into the camp with a paper of safe conduct from General Lewis Cass in his possession. The members of Lincoln's company were greatly exasperated by late Indian barbarities, among them the horrible murder of a number of women and children, and were about to kill him; they said the safe-conduct paper was a forgery, and approached the old savage with muskets cocked to shoot him.

Lincoln rushed forward, struck up the weapons with his hands, and standing in front of the victim, declared to the Indian that he should not be killed. It was with great difficulty that the men could be kept from their purpose, but the courage and firmness of Lincoln thwarted them.

Lincoln was physically one of the bravest of men, as his company discovered.

Lincoln Played Ball

Frank P. Blair, of Chicago, tells an incident, showing Mr. Lincoln's love for children and how thoroughly he entered into all of their sports:

"During the war my grandfather, Francis P. Blair, Sr., lived at Silver Springs, north of Washington, seven miles from the White House. It was a magnificent place of four or five hundred acres, with an extensive lawn in the rear of the house. The grandchildren gathered there frequently.

"There were eight or ten of us, our ages ranging from eight to twelve years. Although I was but seven or eight years of age, Mr. Lincoln's visits were of such importance to us boys as to leave a clear impression on my memory. He drove out to the place quite frequently. We boys, for hours at a time played 'town ball' on the vast lawn, and Mr. Lincoln would join ardently in the sport. I remember vividly how he ran with the children; how long were his strides, and how far his coat-tails stuck out behind, and how we tried to hit him with the ball, as he ran the bases. He entered into the spirit of the play as completely as any of us, and we invariably hailed his coming with delight."

His Passes to Richmond Not Honored

A man called upon the President and solicited a pass for Richmond.

"Well," said the President, "I would be very happy to oblige, if my passes were respected; but the fact is, sir, I have, within the past two years, given passes to two hundred and fifty thousand men to go to Richmond, and not one has got there yet."

The applicant quietly and respectfully withdrew on his tiptoes.

"Public Hangman" for the United States

A certain United States Senator, who believed that every man who believed in secession should be hanged, asked the President what he intended to do when the War was over.

"Reconstruct the machinery of this Government," quickly replied Lincoln.

"You are certainly crazy," was the Senator's heated response. "You talk as if treason was not henceforth to be made odious, but that the traitors, cutthroats and authors of this War should not only go unpunished, but receive encouragement to repeat their treason with impunity! They should be hanged higher than Haman, sir! Yes, higher than any malefactor the world has ever known!"

The President was entirely unmoved, but, after a moment's pause, put a question which all but drove his visitor insane.

"Now, Senator, suppose that when this hanging arrangement has been agreed upon, you accept the post of Chief Executioner. If you will take the office, I will make you a brigadier general and Public Hangman for the United States. That would just about suit you, wouldn't it?"

"I am a gentleman, sir," returned the Senator, "and I certainly thought you knew me better than to believe me capable of doing such dirty work. You are jesting, Mr. President."

The President was extremely patient, exhibiting no signs of ire, and to this bit of temper on the part of the Senator responded:

"You speak of being a gentleman; yet you forget that in this free country all men are equal, the vagrant and the gentleman standing on the same ground when it comes to rights and duties, particularly in time of war. Therefore, being a gentleman, as you claim, and a law-abiding citizen, I trust, you are not exempt from doing even the dirty work at which your high spirit revolts."

This was too much for the Senator, who quitted the room abruptly, and never again showed his face in the White House while Lincoln occupied it.

"He won't bother me again," was the President's remark as he departed.

Few, but Boisterous

Lincoln was a very quiet man, and went about his business in a quiet way, making the least noise possible. He heartily disliked those boisterous people who were constantly deluging him with advice, and shouting at the tops of their voices whenever they appeared at the White House. "These noisy people create a great clamor," said he one day, in conversation with some personal friends, "and remind me, by the way, of a good story I heard out in Illinois while I was practicing, or trying to practice, some law there. I will say, though, that I practiced more law than I ever got paid for.

"A fellow who lived just out of town, on the bank of a large marsh, conceived a big idea in the money-making line. He took it to a prominent merchant, and began to develop his plans and specifications. 'There are at least ten million frogs in that marsh near me, an' I'll just arrest a couple of carloads of them and hand them over to you. You can send them to the big cities and make lots of money for both of us. Frogs' legs are great delicacies in the big towns, an' not very plentiful. It won't take me more'n two or three days to pick 'em. They make so much noise my family can't sleep, and by this deal I'll get rid of a nuisance and gather in some cash.'

"The merchant agreed to the proposition, promised the fellow he would pay him well for the two carloads. Two days passed, then three, and finally two weeks were gone before the fellow showed up again, carrying a small basket. He looked weary and 'done up,' and he wasn't talkative a bit. He threw the basket on the counter with the remark, 'There's your frogs.'

"'You haven't two carloads in that basket, have you?' inquired the merchant.

"'No,' was the reply, 'and there ain't no two carloads in all this blasted world.'

"'I thought you said there were at least ten millions of 'em in that marsh near you, according to the noise they made,' observed the merchant. 'Your people couldn't sleep because of 'em.'

"'Well,' said the fellow, 'accordin' to the noise they made, there was, I thought, a hundred million of 'em, but when I had waded and swum that there marsh day and night fer two blessed weeks, I couldn't harvest but six. There's two or three left yet, an' the marsh is as noisy as it uster be. We haven't catched up on any of our lost sleep yet. Now, you can have these here six, an' I won't charge you a cent fer 'em.'

"You can see by this little yarn," remarked the President, "that these boisterous people make too much noise in proportion to their numbers."

Keep Pegging Away

Being asked one time by an "anxious" visitor as to what he would do in certain contingencies—provided the rebellion was not subdued after three or four years of effort on the part of the Government?

"Oh," replied the President, "there is no alternative but to keep 'pegging' away!"

Beware of the Tail

After the issue of the Emancipation Proclamation, Governor Morgan, of New York, was at the White House one day, when the President said:

"I do not agree with those who say that slavery is dead. We are like whalers who have been long on a chase—we have at last got the harpoon into the monster, but we must now look how we steer, or, with one 'flop' of his tail, he will yet send us all into eternity!"

"Lincoln's Dream"

President Lincoln was depicted as a headsman in a cartoon printed in "Frank Leslie's Illustrated Newspaper," on February 14, 1863, the title of the picture being "Lincoln's Dreams; or, There's a Good Time Coming."

The cartoon represents, on the right, the Union Generals who had been defeated by the Confederates in battle, and had suffered decapitation in consequence—McDowell, who lost at Bull Run; McClellan, who failed to take Richmond, when within twelve miles of that city and no opposition, comparatively; and Burnside, who was so badly whipped at Fredericksburg. To the left of the block, where the President is standing with the bloody axe in his hand, are shown the members of the Cabinet—Secretary of State Seward, Secretary of War Stanton, Secretary of the Navy Welles, and others—each awaiting his turn. This part of the "Dream" was never realized, however, as the President did not decapitate any of his Cabinet officers.

It was the idea of the cartoonist to hold Lincoln up as a man who would not countenance failure upon the part of subordinates, but visit the severest punishment upon those commanders who did not win victories. After Burnside's defeat at Fredericksburg, he was relieved by Hooker, who suffered disaster at Chancellorsville; Hooker was relieved by Meade, who won at Gettysburg, but was refused promotion because he did not follow up and crush Lee; Rosecrans was all but defeated at Chickamauga, and gave way to Grant, who, of all the Union commanders, had never suffered defeat. Grant was Lincoln's ideal fighting man, and the "Old Commander" was never superseded.

There Was No Need of a Story

Dr. Hovey, of Dansville, New York, thought he would call and see the President.

Upon arriving at the White House he found the President on horseback, ready for a start.

Approaching him, he said:

"President Lincoln, I thought I would call and see you before leaving the city, and hear you tell a story."

The President greeted him pleasantly, and asked where he was from.

"From Western New York."

"Well, that's a good enough country without stories," replied the President, and off he rode.

Lincoln a Man of Simple Habits

Lincoln's habits at the White House were as simple as they were at his old home in Illinois.

He never alluded to himself as "President," or as occupying "the Presidency."

His office he always designated as "the place."

"Call me Lincoln," said he to a friend; "Mr. President" had become so very tiresome to him.

"If you see a newsboy down the street, send him up this way," said he to a passenger, as he stood waiting for the morning news at his gate.

Friends cautioned him about exposing himself so openly in the midst of enemies; but he never heeded them.

He frequently walked the streets at night, entirely unprotected; and felt any check upon his movements a great annoyance.

He delighted to see his familiar Western friends; and he gave them always a cordial welcome.

He met them on the old footing, and fell at once into the accustomed habits of talk and story-telling.

An old acquaintance, with his wife, visited Washington. Mr. and Mrs. Lincoln proposed to these friends a ride in the Presidential carriage.

It should be stated in advance that the two men had probably never seen each other with gloves on in their lives, unless when they were used as protection from the cold.

The question of each—Lincoln at the White House, and his friend at the hotel—was, whether he should wear gloves.

Of course the ladies urged gloves; but Lincoln only put his in his pocket, to be used or not, according to the circumstances.

When the Presidential party arrived at the hotel, to take in their friends, they found the gentleman, overcome by his wife's persuasions, very handsomely gloved.

The moment he took his seat he began to draw off the clinging kids, while Lincoln began to draw his on!

"No! no! no!" protested his friend, tugging at his gloves. "It is none of my doings; put up your gloves, Mr. Lincoln."

So the two old friends were on even and easy terms, and had their ride after their old fashion.

His Last Speech

President Lincoln was reading the draft of a speech. Edward, the conservative but dignified butler of the White House, was seen struggling with Tad and trying to drag him back from the window from which was waving a Confederate flag, captured in some fight and given to the boy. Edward conquered and Tad, rushing to find his father, met him coming forward to make, as it proved, his last speech.

The speech began with these words, "We meet this evening, not in sorrow, but in gladness of heart." Having his speech written in loose leaves, and being compelled to hold a candle in the other hand, he would let the loose leaves drop to the floor one by one. "Tad" picked them up as they fell, and impatiently called for more as they fell from his father's hand.

Forgot Everything He Knew Before

President Lincoln, while entertaining a few select friends, is said to have related the following anecdote of a man who knew too much:

He was a careful, painstaking fellow, who always wanted to be absolutely exact, and as a result he frequently got the ill-will of his less careful superiors.

During the administration of President Jackson there was a singular young gentleman employed in the Public Postoffice in Washington.

His name was G.; he was from Tennessee, the son of a widow, a neighbor of the President, on which account the old hero had a kind feeling for him, and always got him out of difficulties with some of the higher officials, to whom his singular interference was distasteful.

Among other things, it is said of him that while employed in the General Postoffice, on one occasion he had to copy a letter to Major H., a high official, in answer to an application made by an old gentleman in Virginia or Pennsylvania, for the establishment of a new postoffice.

The writer of the letter said the application could not be granted, in consequence of the applicant's "proximity" to another office.

When the letter came into G.'s hand to copy, being a great stickler for plainness, he altered "proximity" to "nearness to."

Major H. observed it, and asked G. why he altered his letter.

"Why," replied G., "because I don't think the man would understand what you mean by proximity."

"Well," said Major H., "try him; put in the 'proximity' again."

In a few days a letter was received from the applicant, in which he very indignantly said that his father had fought for liberty in the second war for independence, and he should like to have the name of the scoundrel who brought the charge of proximity or anything else wrong against him.

"There," said G., "did I not say so?"

G. carried his improvements so far that Mr. Berry, the Postmaster-General, said to him: "I don't want you any longer; you know too much."

Poor G. went out, but his old friend got him another place.

This time G.'s ideas underwent a change. He was one day very busy writing, when a stranger called in and asked him where the Patent Office was.

"I don't know," said G.

"Can you tell me where the Treasury Department is?" said the stranger.

"No," said G.

"Nor the President's house?"

"No."

The stranger finally asked him if he knew where the Capitol was.

"No," replied G.

"Do you live in Washington, sir?"

"Yes, sir," said G.

"Good Lord! and don't you know where the Patent Office, Treasury, President's house and Capitol are?"

"Stranger," said G., "I was turned out of the postoffice for knowing too much. I don't mean to offend in that way again."

"I am paid for keeping this book.

"I believe I know that much; but if you find me knowing anything more you may take my head."

"Good morning," said the stranger.

Lincoln Believed in Education

"That every man may receive at least a moderate education, and thereby be enabled to read the histories of his own and other countries, by which he may duly appreciate the value of our free institutions, appears to be an object of vital importance; even on this account alone, to say nothing of the advantages and satisfaction to be derived from all being able to read the Scriptures and other works, both of a religious and moral nature, for themselves.

"For my part, I desire to see the time when education, by its means, morality, sobriety, enterprise and integrity, shall become much more general than at present, and should be gratified to have it in my power to contribute something to the advancement of any measure which might have a tendency to accelerate the happy period."

Lincoln on the Dred Scott Decision

In a speech at Springfield, Illinois, June 26th, 1857, Lincoln referred to the decision of Chief Justice Roger B. Taney, of the United States Supreme Court, in the Dred Scott case, in this manner:

"The Chief justice does not directly assert, but plainly assumes as a fact, that the public estimate of the black man is more favorable now than it was in the days of the Revolution.

"In those days, by common consent, the spread of the black man's bondage in the new countries was prohibited; but now Congress decides that it will not continue the prohibition, and the Supreme Court decides that it could not if it would.

"In those days, our Declaration of Independence was held sacred by all, and thought to include all; but now, to aid in making the bondage of the negro universal and eternal, it is assailed and sneered at, and constructed and hawked at, and torn, till, if its framers could rise from their graves, they could not at all recognize it.

"All the powers of earth seem combining against the slave; Mammon is after him, ambition follows, philosophy follows, and the theology of the day is fast joining the cry."

Lincoln Made Many Notable Speeches

Abraham Lincoln made many notable addresses and speeches during his career previous to the time of his election to the Presidency.

However, beautiful in thought and expression as they were, they were not appreciated by those who heard and read them until after the people of the United States and the world had come to understand the man who delivered them.

Lincoln had the rare and valuable faculty of putting the most sublime feeling into his speeches; and he never found it necessary to incumber his wisest, wittiest and most famous sayings with a weakening mass of words.

He put his thoughts into the simplest language, so that all might comprehend, and he never said anything which was not full of the deepest meaning.

What Ailed the Boys

Mr. Roland Diller, who was one of Mr. Lincoln's neighbors in Springfield, tells the following:

"I was called to the door one day by the cries of children in the street, and there was Mr. Lincoln, striding by with two of his boys, both of whom were wailing aloud. 'Why, Mr. Lincoln, what's the matter with the boys?' I asked.

"'Just what's the matter with the whole world,' Lincoln replied. 'I've got three walnuts, and each wants two.'"

Tad's Confederate Flag

One of the prettiest incidents in the closing days of the Civil War occurred when the troops, 'marching home again,' passed in grand form, if with well-worn uniforms and tattered bunting, before the White House.

Naturally, an immense crowd had assembled on the streets, the lawns, porches, balconies, and windows, even those of the executive mansion itself being crowded to excess. A central figure was that of the President, Abraham Lincoln, who, with bared head, unfurled and waved our Nation's flag in the midst of lusty cheers.

But suddenly there was an unexpected sight.

A small boy leaned forward and sent streaming to the air the banner of the boys in gray. It was an old flag which had been captured from the Confederates, and which the urchin, the President's second son, Tad, had obtained possession of and considered an additional triumph to unfurl on this all-important day.

Vainly did the servant who had followed him to the window plead with him to desist. No, Master Tad, Pet of the White House, was not to be prevented from adding to the loyal demonstration of the hour.

To his surprise, however, the crowd viewed it differently. Had it floated from any other window in the capital that day, no doubt it would have been the target of contempt and abuse; but when the President, understanding what had happened, turned, with a smile on his grand, plain face, and showed his approval by a gesture and expression, cheer after cheer rent the air.

Called Blessings on the American Women

President Lincoln attended a Ladies' Fair for the benefit of the Union soldiers, at Washington, March 16th, 1864.

In his remarks he said:

"I appear to say but a word.

"This extraordinary war in which we are engaged falls heavily upon all classes of people, but the most heavily upon the soldiers. For it has been said, 'All that a man hath will he give for his life,' and, while all contribute of their substance, the soldier puts his life at stake, and often yields it up in his country's cause.

"The highest merit, then, is due the soldiers.

"In this extraordinary war extraordinary developments have manifested themselves such as have not been seen in former wars; and among these manifestations nothing has been more remarkable than these fairs for the relief of suffering soldiers and their families, and the chief agents in these fairs are the women of America!

"I am not accustomed to the use of language of eulogy; I have never studied the art of paying compliments to women; but I must say that if all that has been said by orators and poets since the creation of the world in praise of women were applied to the women of America, it would not do them justice for their conduct during the war.

"I will close by saying, God bless the women of America!"

Lincoln's "Order No. 252"

After the United States had enlisted former negro slaves as soldiers to fight alongside the Northern troops for the maintenance of the integrity of the Union, so great was the indignation of the Confederate Government that President Davis declared he would not recognize blacks captured in battle and in uniform as prisoners of war. This meant that he would have them returned to their previous owners, have them flogged and fined for running away from their masters, or even shot if he felt like it. This attitude of the President of the Confederate States of America led to the promulgation of President Lincoln's famous "Order No. 252," which, in effect, was a notification to the commanding officers of the Southern forces that if negro prisoners of war were not treated as such, the Union commanders would retaliate. "Harper's Weekly" of August 15th, 1863, contained a clever cartoon representing President Lincoln holding the South by the collar, while "Old Abe" shouts the following words of warning to Jeff Davis, who, cat-o'-nine-tails in hand, is in pursuit of a terrified little negro boy:

MR. LINCOLN: "Look here, Jeff Davis! If you lay a finger on that boy, to hurt him, I'll lick this ugly cub of yours within an inch of his life!"

Much to the surprise of the Confederates, the negro soldiers fought valiantly; they were fearless when well led, obeyed orders without hesitation, were amenable to discipline, and were eager and anxious, at all times, to do their duty. In battle they were formidable opponents, and in using the bayonet were the equal of the best trained troops. The Southerners hated them beyond power of expression.

Talked to the Negroes of Richmond

The President walked through the streets of Richmond—without a guard except a few seamen—in company with his son "Tad," and Admiral Porter, on April 4th, 1865, the day following the evacuation of the city.

Colored people gathered about him on every side, eager to see and thank their liberator. Mr. Lincoln addressed the following remarks to one of these gatherings:

"My poor friends, you are free—free as air. You can cast off the name of slave and trample upon it; it will come to you no more.

"Liberty is your birthright. God gave it to you as He gave it to others, and it is a sin that you have been deprived of it for so many years.

"But you must try to deserve this priceless boon. Let the world see that you merit it, and are able to maintain it by your good work.

"Don't let your joy carry you into excesses; learn the laws, and obey them. Obey God's commandments, and thank Him for giving you liberty, for to Him you owe all things.

"There, now, let me pass on; I have but little time to spare.

"I want to see the Capitol, and must return at once to Washington to secure to you that liberty which you seem to prize so highly."

"Abe" Added a Saving Clause

Lincoln fell in love with Miss Mary S. Owens about 1833 or so, and, while she was attracted toward him she was not passionately fond of him.

Lincoln's letter of proposal of marriage, sent by him to Miss Owens, while singular, unique, and decidedly unconventional, was certainly not very ardent. He, after the fashion of the lawyer, presented the matter very cautiously, and pleaded his own cause; then presented her side of the case, advised her not "to do it," and agreed to abide by her decision.

Miss Owens respected Lincoln, but promptly rejected him—really very much to "Abe's" relief.

How "Jack" Was "Done Up"

Not far from New Salem, Illinois, at a place called Clary's Grove, a gang of frontier ruffians had established headquarters, and the champion wrestler of "The Grove" was "Jack" Armstrong, a bully of the worst type.

Learning that Abraham was something of a wrestler himself, "Jack" sent him a challenge. At that time and in that community a refusal would have resulted in social and business ostracism, not to mention the stigma of cowardice which would attach.

It was a great day for New Salem and "The Grove" when Lincoln and Armstrong met. Settlers within a radius of fifty miles flocked to the scene, and the wagers laid were heavy and many. Armstrong proved a weakling in the hands of the powerful Kentuckian, and "Jack's" adherents were about to mob Lincoln when the latter's friends saved him from probable death by rushing to the rescue.

Angels Couldn't Swear It Right

The President was once speaking about an attack made on him by the Congressional Committee on the Conduct of the War for a certain alleged blunder in the Southwest—the matter involved being one which had fallen directly under the observation of the army officer to whom he was talking, who possessed official evidence completely upsetting all the conclusions of the Committee.

"Might it not be well for me," queried the officer, "to set this matter right in a letter to some paper, stating the facts as they actually transpired?"

"Oh, no," replied the President, "at least, not now. If I were to try to read, much less answer, all the attacks made on me, this shop might as well be closed for any other business. I do the very best I know how the very best I can; and I mean to keep doing so until the end. If the end brings me out all right, what is said against me won't amount to anything. If the end brings me out wrong, ten thousand angels swearing I was right would make no difference."

"Must Go, and Go to Stay"

Ward Hill Lamon was President Lincoln's Cerberus, his watch dog, guardian, friend, companion and confidant. Some days before Lincoln's departure for Washington to be inaugurated, he wrote to Lamon at Bloomington, that he desired to see him at once. He went to Springfield, and Lincoln said:

"Hill, on the 11th I go to Washington, and I want you to go along with me. Our friends have already asked me to send you as Consul to Paris. You know I would cheerfully give you anything for which our friends may ask or which you may desire, but it looks as if we might have war.

"In that case I want you with me. In fact, I must have you. So get yourself ready and come along. It will be handy to have you around. If there is to be a fight, I want you to help me to do my share of it, as you have done in times past. You must go, and go to stay."

This is Lamon's version of it.

Lincoln Wasn't Buying Nominations

To a party who wished to be empowered to negotiate reward for promises of influence in the Chicago Convention, 1860, Mr. Lincoln replied:

"No, gentlemen; I have not asked the nomination, and I will not now buy it with pledges.

"If I am nominated and elected, I shall not go into the Presidency as the tool of this man or that man, or as the property of any factor or clique."

He Envied the Soldier at the Front

After some very bad news had come in from the army in the field, Lincoln remarked to Schuyler Colfax:

"How willingly would I exchange places to-day with the soldier who sleeps on the ground in the Army of the Potomac!"

Don't Trust Too Far

In the campaign of 1852, Lincoln, in reply to Douglas' speech, wherein he spoke of confidence in Providence, replied: "Let us stand by our candidate (General Scott) as faithfully as he has always stood by our country, and I much doubt if we do not perceive a slight abatement of Judge Douglas' confidence in Providence as well as the people. I suspect that confidence is not more firmly fixed with the judge than it was with the old woman whose horse ran away with her in a buggy. She said she 'trusted in Providence till the britchen broke,' and then she 'didn't know what in airth to do.'"

He'd "Risk the Dictatorship"

Lincoln's great generosity to his leaders was shown when, in January, 1863, he assigned "Fighting Joe" Hooker to the command of the Army of the Potomac. Hooker had believed in a military dictatorship, and it was an open secret that McClellan might have become such had he possessed the nerve. Lincoln, however, was not bothered by this prattle, as he did not think enough of it to relieve McClellan of his command. The President said to Hooker:

"I have heard, in such a way as to believe it, of your recently saying that both the army and the Government needed a dictator. Of course, it was not for this, but in spite of it, that I have given you the command. Only those generals who gain success can be dictators.

"What I now ask of you is military success, and I will risk the dictatorship."

Lincoln also believed Hooker had not given cordial support to General Burnside when he was in command of the army. In Lincoln's own peculiarly plain language, he told Hooker that he had done "a great wrong to the country and to a most meritorious and honorable brother officer."

"Major General, I Reckon"

At one time the President had the appointment of a large additional number of brigadier and major generals. Among the immense number of applications, Mr. Lincoln came upon one wherein the claims of a certain worthy (not in the service at all), "for a generalship" were glowingly set forth. But the applicant didn't specify whether he wanted to be brigadier or major general.

The President observed this difficulty, and solved it by a lucid indorsement. The clerk, on receiving the paper again, found written across its back, "Major General, I reckon. A. Lincoln."

Would See the Tracks

Judge Herndon, Lincoln's law partner, said that he never saw Lincoln more cheerful than on the day previous to his departure from Springfield for Washington, and Judge Gillespie, who visited him a few days earlier, found him in excellent spirits.

"I told him that I believed it would do him good to get down to Washington," said Herndon.

"I know it will," Lincoln replied. "I only wish I could have got there to lock the door before the horse was stolen. But when I get to the spot, I can find the tracks."

"Abe" Gave Her a "Sure Tip"

If all the days Lincoln attended school were added together, they would not make a single year's time, and he never studied grammar or geography or any of the higher branches. His first teacher in Indiana was Hazel Dorsey, who opened a school in a log schoolhouse a mile and a half from the Lincoln cabin. The building had holes for windows, which were covered over with greased paper to admit light. The roof was just high enough for a man to stand erect. It did not take long to demonstrate that "Abe" was superior to any scholar in his class. His next teacher was Andrew Crawford, who taught in the winter of 1822-3, in the same little schoolhouse. "Abe" was an excellent speller, and it is said that he liked to show off his knowledge, especially if he could help out his less fortunate schoolmates. One day the teacher gave out the word "defied." A large class was on the floor, but it seemed that no one would be able to spell it. The teacher declared he would keep the whole class in all day and night if "defied" was not spelled correctly.

When the word came around to Katy Roby, she was standing where she could see young "Abe." She started, "d-e-f," and while trying to decide whether to spell the word with an "i" or a "y," she noticed that Abe had his finger on his eye and a smile on his face, and instantly took the hint. She spelled the word correctly and school was dismissed.

The President Had Knowledge of Him

Lincoln never forgot anyone or anything.

At one of the afternoon receptions at the White House a stranger shook hands with him, and, as he did so, remarked casually, that he was elected to Congress about the time Mr. Lincoln's term as representative expired, which happened many years before.

"Yes," said the President, "You are from—" (mentioning the State). "I remember reading of your election in a newspaper one morning on a steamboat going down to Mount Vernon."

At another time a gentleman addressed him, saying, "I presume, Mr. President, you have forgotten me?"

"No," was the prompt reply; "your name is Flood. I saw you last, twelve years ago, at—" (naming the place and the occasion).

"I am glad to see," he continued, "that the Flood goes on."

Subsequent to his re-election a deputation of bankers from various sections were introduced one day by the Secretary of the Treasury.

After a few moments of general conversation, Lincoln turned to one of them and said:

"Your district did not give me so strong a vote at the last election as it did in 1860."

"I think, sir, that you must be mistaken," replied the banker. "I have the impression that your majority was considerably increased at the last election."

"No," rejoined the President, "you fell off about six hundred votes."

Then taking down from the bookcase the official canvass of 1860 and 1864, he referred to the vote of the district named, and proved to be quite right in his assertion.

Only Half a Man

As President Lincoln, arm in arm with ex-President Buchanan, entered the Capitol, and passed into the Senate Chamber, filled to overflowing with Senators, members of the Diplomatic Corps, and visitors, the contrast between the two men struck every observer.

"Mr. Buchanan was so withered and bowed with age," wrote George W. Julian, of Indiana, who was among the spectators, "that in contrast with the towering form of Mr. Lincoln he seemed little more than half a man."

Grant Congratulated Lincoln

As soon as the result of the Presidential election of 1864 was known, General Grant telegraphed from City Point his congratulations, and added that "the election having passed off quietly . . . is a victory worth more to the country than a battle won."

"Brutus and Caesar"

London "Punch" persistently maintained throughout the War for the Union that the question of what to do with the blacks was the most bothersome of all the problems President Lincoln had to solve. "Punch" thought the Rebellion had its origin in an effort to determine whether there should or should not be slavery in the United States, and was fought with this as the main end in view. "Punch" of August 15th, 1863, contained a cartoon, the title being "Brutus and Caesar."

President Lincoln was pictured as Brutus, while the ghost of Caesar, which appeared in the tent of the American Brutus during the dark hours of the night, was represented in the shape of a husky and anything but ghost-like African, whose complexion would tend to make the blackest tar look like skimmed milk in comparison. This was the text below the cartoon: (From the American Edition of Shakespeare.) The Tent of Brutus (Lincoln). Night. Enter the Ghost of Caesar.

BRUTUS: "Wall, now! Do tell! Who's you?"

CAESAR: "I am dy ebil genus, Massa Linking. Dis child am awful impressional!"

"Punch's" cartoons were decidedly unfriendly in tone toward President Lincoln, some of them being not only objectionable in the display of bad taste, but offensive and vulgar. It is true that after the assassination of the President, "Punch," in illustrations, paid marked and deserved tribute to the memory of the Great Emancipator, but it had little that was good to say of him while he was among the living and engaged in carrying out the great work for which he was destined to win eternal fame.

How Stanton Got into the Cabinet

President Lincoln, well aware of Stanton's unfriendliness, was surprised when Secretary of the Treasury Chase told him that Stanton had expressed the opinion that the arrest of the Confederate Commissioners, Mason and Slidell, was legal and justified by international law. The President asked Secretary Chase to invite Stanton to the White House, and Stanton came. Mr. Lincoln thanked him for the opinion he had expressed, and asked him to put it in writing.

Stanton complied, the President read it carefully, and, after putting it away, astounded Stanton by offering him the portfolio of War. Stanton was a Democrat, had been one of the President's most persistent vilifiers, and could not realize, at first, that Lincoln meant what he said. He managed, however to say:

"I am both surprised and embarrassed, Mr. President, and would ask a couple of days to consider this most important matter."

Lincoln fully understood what was going on in Stanton's mind, and then said:

"This is a very critical period in the life of the nation, Mr. Stanton, as you are well aware, and I well know you are as much interested in sustaining the government as myself or any other man. This is no time to consider mere party issues. The life of the nation is in danger. I need the best counsellors around me. I have every confidence in your judgment, and have concluded to ask you to become one of my counsellors. The office of the Secretary of War will soon be vacant, and I am anxious to have you take Mr. Cameron's place."

Stanton decided to accept.

"Abe" Like His Father

"Abe" Lincoln's father was never at loss for an answer. An old neighbor of Thomas Lincoln—"Abe's" father—was passing the Lincoln farm one day, when he saw "Abe's" father grubbing up some hazelnut bushes, and said to him: "Why, Grandpap, I thought you wanted to sell your farm?"

"And so I do," he replied, "but I ain't goin' to let my farm know it."

"'Abe's' jes' like his father," the old ones would say.

"No Moon at All"

One of the most notable of Lincoln's law cases was that in which he defended William D. Armstrong, charged with murder. The case was one which was watched during its progress with intense interest, and it had a most dramatic ending.

The defendant was the son of Jack and Hannah Armstrong. The father was dead, but Hannah, who had been very motherly and helpful to Lincoln during his life at New Salem, was still living, and asked Lincoln to defend him. Young Armstrong had been a wild lad, and was often in bad company.

The principal witness had sworn that he saw young Armstrong strike the fatal blow, the moon being very bright at the time.

Lincoln brought forward the almanac, which showed that at the time the murder was committed there was no moon at all. In his argument, Lincoln's speech was so feelingly made that at its close all the men in the jury-box were in tears. It was just half an hour when the jury returned a verdict of acquittal.

Lincoln would accept no fee except the thanks of the anxious mother.

"Abe" a Superb Mimic

Lincoln's reading in his early days embraced a wide range. He was particularly fond of all stories containing fun, wit and humor, and every one of these he came across he learned by heart, thus adding to his personal store.

He improved as a reciter and retailer of the stories he had read and heard, and as the reciter of tales of his own invention, and he had ready and eager auditors.

Judge Herndon, in his "Abraham Lincoln," relates that as a mimic Lincoln was unequalled. An old neighbor said: "His laugh was striking. Such awkward gestures belonged to no other man. They attracted universal attention, from the old and sedate down to the schoolboy. Then, in a few moments, he was as calm and thoughtful as a judge on the bench, and as ready to give advice on the most important matters; fun and gravity grew on him alike."

Why He Was Called "Honest Abe"

During the year Lincoln was in Denton Offutt's store at New Salem, that gentleman, whose business was somewhat widely and unwisely spread about the country, ceased to prosper in his finances and finally failed. The store was shut up, the mill was closed, and Abraham Lincoln was out of business.

The year had been one of great advance, in many respects. He had made new and valuable acquaintances, read many books, mastered the grammar of his own tongue, won multitudes of friends, and became ready for a step still further in advance.

Those who could appreciate brains respected him, and those whose ideas of a man related to his muscles were devoted to him. It was while he was performing the work of the store that he acquired the sobriquet of "Honest Abe"—a characterization he never dishonored, and an abbreviation that he never outgrew.

He was judge, arbitrator, referee, umpire, authority, in all disputes, games and matches of man-flesh, horse-flesh, a pacificator in all quarrels; everybody's friend; the best-natured, the most sensible, the best-informed, the most modest and unassuming, the kindest, gentlest, roughest, strongest, best fellow in all New Salem and the region round about.

"Abe's" Name Remained on the Sign

Enduring friendship and love of old associations were prominent characteristics of President Lincoln. When about to leave Springfield for Washington, he went to the dingy little law office which had sheltered his saddest hours.

He sat down on the couch, and said to his law partner, Judge Herndon:

"Billy, you and I have been together for more than twenty years, and have never passed a word. Will you let my name stay on the old sign until I come back from Washington?"

The tears started to Herndon's eyes. He put out his hand. "Mr. Lincoln," said he, "I never will have any other partner while you live"; and to the day of assassination, all the doings of the firm were in the name of "Lincoln & Herndon."

Very Homely at First Sight

Early in January, 1861, Colonel Alex. K. McClure, of Philadelphia, received a telegram from President-elect Lincoln, asking him (McClure) to visit him at Springfield, Illinois. Colonel McClure described his disappointment at first sight of Lincoln in these words:

"I went directly from the depot to Lincoln's house and rang the bell, which was answered by Lincoln himself opening the door. I doubt whether a wholly concealed my disappointment at meeting him.

"Tall, gaunt, ungainly, ill clad, with a homeliness of manner that was unique in itself, I confess that my heart sank within me as I remembered that this was the man chosen by a great nation to become its ruler in the gravest period of its history.

"I remember his dress as if it were but yesterday—snuff-colored and slouchy pantaloons, open black vest, held by a few brass buttons; straight or evening dresscoat, with tightly fitting sleeves to exaggerate his long, bony arms, and all supplemented by an awkwardness that was uncommon among men of intelligence.

"Such was the picture I met in the person of Abraham Lincoln. We sat down in his plainly furnished parlor, and were uninterrupted during the nearly four hours that I remained with him, and little by little, as his earnestness, sincerity and candor were developed in conversation, I forgot all the grotesque qualities which so confounded me when I first greeted him."

The Man to Trust

"If a man is honest in his mind," said Lincoln one day, long before he became President, "you are pretty safe in trusting him."

"Wuz Goin' Ter Be 'Hitched'"

"Abe's" nephew—or one of them—related a story in connection with Lincoln's first love (Anne Rutledge), and his subsequent marriage to Miss Mary Todd. This nephew was a plain, every-day farmer, and thought everything of his uncle, whose greatness he quite thoroughly appreciated, although he did not pose to any extreme as the relative of a President of the United States.

Said he one day, in telling his story:

"Us child'en, w'en we heerd Uncle 'Abe' wuz a-goin' to be married, axed Gran'ma ef Uncle 'Abe' never hed hed a gal afore, an' she says, sez she, 'Well, "Abe" wuz never a han' nohow to run 'round visitin' much, or go with the gals, neither, but he did fall in love with a Anne Rutledge, who lived out near Springfield, an' after she died he'd come home an' ev'ry time he'd talk 'bout her, he cried dreadful. He never could talk of her nohow 'thout he'd jes' cry an' cry, like a young feller.'

"Onct he tol' Gran'ma they wuz goin' ter be hitched, they havin' promised each other, an' thet is all we ever heered 'bout it. But, so it wuz, that arter Uncle 'Abe' hed got over his mournin,' he wuz married ter a woman w'ich hed lived down in Kentuck.

"Uncle 'Abe' hisself tol' us he wuz married the nex' time he come up ter our place, an' w'en we ast him why he didn't bring his wife up to see us, he said: 'She's very busy and can't come.'

"But we knowed better'n that. He wuz too proud to bring her up,'cause nothin' would suit her, nohow. She wuzn't raised the way we wuz, an' wuz different from us, and we heerd, tu, she wuz as proud as cud be.

"No, an' he never brought none uv the child'en, neither.

"But then, Uncle 'Abe,' he wuzn't to blame. We never thought he wuz stuck up."

He Proposed to Save the Union

Replying to an editorial written by Horace Greeley, the President wrote:

"My paramount object is to save the Union, and not either to save or to destroy slavery.

"If I could save the Union without freeing any slave, I would do it.

"If I could save it by freeing all the slaves, I would do it; and if I could do it by freeing some and leaving others alone, I would also do that.

"What I do about slavery and the colored race, I do because I believe it helps to save this Union; and what I forbear, I forbear because I do not believe it would help to save the Union.

"I shall do less whenever I shall believe what I am doing hurts the cause, and I shall do more whenever I believe doing more will help the cause."

The Same Old Rum

One of President Lincoln's friends, visiting at the White House, was finding considerable fault with the constant agitation in Congress of the slavery question. He remarked that, after the adoption of the Emancipation policy, he had hoped for something new.

"There was a man down in Maine," said the President, in reply, "who kept a grocery store, and a lot of fellows used to loaf around for their toddy. He only gave 'em New England rum, and they drank pretty considerable of it. But after awhile they began to get tired of that, and kept asking for something new—something new—all the time. Well, one night, when the whole crowd were around, the grocer brought out his glasses, and says he, 'I've got something New for you to drink, boys, now.'

"'Honor bright?' said they.

"'Honor bright,' says he, and with that he sets out a jug. 'Thar' says he, 'that's something new; it's New England rum!' says he.

"Now," remarked the President, in conclusion, "I guess we're a good deal like that crowd, and Congress is a good deal like that store-keeper!"

Saved Lincoln's Life

When Mr. Lincoln was quite a small boy he met with an accident that almost cost him his life. He was saved by Austin Gollaher, a young playmate. Mr. Gollaher lived to be more than ninety years of age, and to the day of his death related with great pride his boyhood association with Lincoln.

"Yes," Mr. Gollaher once said, "the story that I once saved Abraham Lincoln's life is true. He and I had been going to school together for a year or more, and had become greatly attached to each other. Then school disbanded on account of there being so few scholars, and we did not see each other much for a long while.

"One Sunday my mother visited the Lincolns, and I was taken along. 'Abe' and I played around all day. Finally, we concluded to cross the creek to hunt for some partridges young Lincoln had seen the day before. The creek was swollen by a recent rain, and, in crossing on the narrow footlog, 'Abe' fell in. Neither of us could swim. I got a long pole and held it out to 'Abe,' who grabbed it. Then I pulled him ashore.

"He was almost dead, and I was badly scared. I rolled and pounded him in good earnest. Then I got him by the arms and shook him, the water meanwhile pouring out of his mouth. By this means I succeeded in bringing him to, and he was soon all right.

"Then a new difficulty confronted us. If our mothers discovered our wet clothes they would whip us. This we dreaded from experience, and determined to avoid. It was June, the sun was very warm, and we soon dried our clothing by spreading it on the rocks about us. We promised never to tell the story, and I never did until after Lincoln's tragic end."

Would Not Recall a Single Word

In conversation with some friends at the White House on New Year's evening, 1863, President Lincoln said, concerning his Emancipation Proclamation:

"The signature looks a little tremulous, for my hand was tired, but my resolution was firm.

"I told them in September, if they did not return to their allegiance, and cease murdering our soldiers, I would strike at this pillar of their strength.

"And now the promise shall be kept, and not one word of it will I ever recall."

Old Broom Best After All

During the time the enemies of General Grant were making their bitterest attacks upon him, and demanding that the President remove him from command, "Frank Leslie's Illustrated Newspaper," of June 13, 1863, came out with a cartoon under which was the following:

OLD ABE: "Greeley be hanged! I want no more new brooms. I begin to think that the worst thing about my old ones was in not being handled right."

The old broom the President holds in his right hand is labeled "Grant." The latter had captured Fort Donelson, defeated the Confederates at Shiloh, Iuka, Port Gibson, and other places, and had

Vicksburg in his iron grasp. When the demand was made that Lincoln depose Grant, the President answered, "I can't spare this man; he fights!" Grant never lost a battle and when he found the enemy he always fought him. McClellan, Burnside, Pope and Hooker had been found wanting, so Lincoln pinned his faith to Grant. As noted in the cartoon, Horace Greeley, editor of the New York Tribune, Thurlow Weed, and others wanted Lincoln to try some other new brooms, but President Lincoln was wearied with defeats, and wanted a few victories to offset them. Therefore; he stood by Grant, who gave him victories.

God with a Little "G"

> *Abraham Lincoln*
> *his hand and pen*
> *he will be good*
> *but god Knows When*

These lines were found written in young Lincoln's own hand at the bottom of a page whereon he had been ciphering. Lincoln always wrote a clear, regular "fist." In this instance he evidently did not appreciate the sacredness of the name of the Deity, when he used a little "g."

Lincoln once said he did not remember the time when he could not write.

"Abe's" Log

It was the custom in Sangamon for the "menfolks" to gather at noon and in the evening, when resting, in a convenient lane near the mill. They had rolled out a long peeled log, on which they lounged while they whittled and talked.

Lincoln had not been long in Sangamon before he joined this circle. At once he became a favorite by his jokes and good-humor. As soon as he appeared at the assembly ground the men would start him to story-telling. So irresistibly droll were his "yarns" that whenever he'd end up in his unexpected way the boys on the log would whoop and roll off. The result of the rolling off was to polish the log like a mirror. The men, recognizing Lincoln's part in this polishing, christened their seat "Abe's log."

Long after Lincoln had disappeared from Sangamon, "Abe's log" remained, and until it had rotted away people pointed it out, and repeated the droll stories of the stranger.

It Was a Fine Fizzle

President Lincoln, in company with General Grant, was inspecting the Dutch Gap Canal at City Point. "Grant, do you know what this reminds me of? Out in Springfield, Ill., there was a blacksmith who, not having much to do, took a piece of soft iron and attempted to weld it into an agricultural implement, but discovered that the iron would not hold out; then he concluded it would make a claw hammer; but having too much iron, attempted to make an ax, but decided after working awhile that there was not enough iron left. Finally, becoming disgusted, he filled the forge full of coal and brought the iron to a white heat; then with his tongs he lifted it from the bed of coals, and thrusting it into a tub of water near by, exclaimed: 'Well, if I can't make anything else of you, I will make a fizzle, anyhow.'" "I was afraid that was about what we had done with the Dutch Gap Canal," said General Grant.

A Teetotaler

When Lincoln was in the Black Hawk War as captain, the volunteer soldiers drank in with delight the jests and stories of the tall captain. Aesop's Fables were given a new dress, and the tales of the wild adventures that he had brought from Kentucky and Indiana were many, but his inspiration was never stimulated by recourse to the whisky jug.

When his grateful and delighted auditors pressed this on him he had one reply: "Thank you, I never drink it."

Not to "Open Shop" There

President Lincoln was passing down Pennsylvania avenue in Washington one day, when a man came running after him, hailed him, and thrust a bundle of papers in his hands.

It angered him not a little, and he pitched the papers back, saying, "I'm not going to open shop here."

We Have Liberty of All Kinds

Lincoln delivered a remarkable speech at Springfield, Illinois, when but twenty-eight years of age, upon the liberty possessed by the people of the United States.

In part, he said:

"In the great journal of things happening under the sun, we, the American people, find our account running under date of the nineteenth century of the Christian era.

"We find ourselves in the peaceful possession of the fairest portion of the earth as regards extent of territory, fertility of soil, and salubrity of climate.

"We find ourselves under the government of a system of political institutions conducing more essentially to the ends of civil and religious liberty than any of which history of former times tells us.

"We, when mounting the stage of existence, found ourselves the legal inheritors of these fundamental blessings.

"We toiled not in the acquisition or establishment of them; they are a legacy bequeathed to us by a once hardy, brave, and patriotic, but now lamented and departed race of ancestors.

"Theirs was the task (and nobly did they perform it) to possess themselves, us, of this goodly land, to uprear upon its hills and valleys a political edifice of liberty and equal rights; 'tis ours to transmit these—the former unprofaned by the foot of an intruder, the latter undecayed by the lapse of time and untorn by usurpation—to the generation that fate shall permit the world to know.

"This task, gratitude to our fathers, justice to ourselves, duty to posterity—all imperatively require us faithfully to perform.

"How, then, shall we perform it? At what point shall we expect the approach of danger?

"Shall we expect some trans-Atlantic military giant to step the ocean and crush us at a blow?

"Never! All the armies of Europe, Asia and Africa, combined, with all the treasures of the earth (our own excepted) in their military chest, with a Bonaparte for a commander, could not, by force, take a drink from the Ohio, or make a track on the Blue Ridge, in a trial of a thousand years.

"At what point, then, is this approach of danger to be expected?

"I answer, if ever it reach us, it must spring up amongst us. It cannot come from abroad.

"If destruction be our lot, we must ourselves be its author and finisher.

"As a nation of freemen, we must live through all time or die by suicide.

"I hope I am not over-wary; but, if I am not, there is even now something of ill-omen amongst us.

"I mean the increasing disregard for law which pervades the country, the disposition to substitute the wild and furious passions in lieu of the sober judgment of courts, and the worse than savage mobs for the executive ministers of justice.

"This disposition is awfully fearful in any community, and that it now exists in ours, though grating to our feelings to admit it, it would be a violation of truth and an insult to deny.

"Accounts of outrages committed by mobs form the every-day news of the times.

"They have pervaded the country from New England to Louisiana; they are neither peculiar to the eternal snows of the former, nor the burning sun of the latter.

"They are not the creatures of climate, neither are they confined to the slave-holding or non-slave-holding States.

"Alike they spring up among the pleasure-hunting Southerners and the order-loving citizens of the land of steady habits.

"Whatever, then, their cause may be, it is common to the whole country.

"Many great and good men, sufficiently qualified for any task they may undertake, may ever be found, whose ambition would aspire to nothing beyond a seat in Congress, a gubernatorial or Presidential chair; but such belong not to the family of the lion, or the tribe of the eagle.

"What! Think you these places would satisfy an Alexander, a Caesar, or a Napoleon? Never!

"Towering genius disdains a beaten path. It seeks regions hitherto unexplored.

"It seeks no distinction in adding story to story upon the monuments of fame, erected to the memory of others.

"It denies that it is glory enough to serve under any chief.

"It scorns to tread in the footpaths of any predecessor, however illustrious.

"It thirsts and burns for distinction, and, if possible, it will have it, whether at the expense of emancipating the slaves or enslaving freemen.

"Another reason which once was, but which to the same extent is now no more, has done much in maintaining our institutions thus far.

"I mean the powerful influence which the interesting scenes of the Revolution had upon the passions of the people, as distinguished from their judgment.

"But these histories are gone. They can be read no more forever. They were a fortress of strength.

"But what the invading foeman could never do, the silent artillery of time has done, the levelling of the walls.

"They were a forest of giant oaks, but the all-resisting hurricane swept over them and left only here and there a lone trunk, despoiled of its verdure, shorn of its foliage, unshading and unshaded, to murmur in a few more gentle breezes and to combat with its mutilated limbs a few more rude storms, then to sink and be no more.

"They were the pillars of the temple of liberty, and now that they have crumbled away, that temple must fall, unless we, the descendants, supply the places with pillars hewn from the same solid quarry of sober reason.

"Passion has helped us, but can do so no more. It will in future be our enemy.

"Reason—cold, calculating, unimpassioned reason—must furnish all the materials for our support and defense.

"Let those materials be molded into general intelligence, sound morality, and, in particular, a reverence for the Constitution and the laws; and then our country shall continue to improve, and our nation, revering his name, and permitting no hostile foot to pass or desecrate his resting-place, shall be the first to hear the last trump that shall awaken our Washington.

"Upon these let the proud fabric of freedom rest as the rock of its basis, and as truly as has been said of the only greater institution, 'the gates of hell shall not prevail against it.'"

Tom Corwin's Latest Story

One of Mr. Lincoln's warm friends was Dr. Robert Boal, of Lacon, Illinois. Telling of a visit he paid to the White House soon after Mr. Lincoln's inauguration, he said: "I found him the same Lincoln as a struggling lawyer and politician that I did in Washington as President of the United States, yet there was a dignity and self-possession about him in his high official authority. I paid him a second call in the evening. He had thrown off his reserve somewhat, and would walk up and down the room with his hands to his sides and laugh at the joke he was telling, or at one that was told to him. I remember one story he told to me on this occasion.

"Tom Corwin, of Ohio, had been down to Alexandria, Va., that day and had come back and told Lincoln a story which pleased him so much that he broke out in a hearty laugh and said: 'I must tell you Tom Corwin's latest. Tom met an old man at Alexandria who knew George Washington, and he told Tom that George Washington often swore. Now, Corwin's father had always held the father of our country up as a faultless person and told his son to follow in his footsteps.

"'"Well," said Corwin, "when I heard that George Washington was addicted to the vices and infirmities of man, I felt so relieved that I just shouted for joy."'"

"Catch 'Em and Cheat 'Em"

The lawyers on the circuit traveled by Lincoln got together one night and tried him on the charge of accepting fees which tended to lower the established rates. It was the understood rule that a lawyer should accept all the client could be induced to pay. The tribunal was known as "The Ogmathorial Court."

Ward Lamon, his law partner at the time, tells about it:

"Lincoln was found guilty and fined for his awful crime against the pockets of his brethren of the bar. The fine he paid with great good humor, and then kept the crowd of lawyers in uproarious laughter until after midnight.

"He persisted in his revolt, however, declaring that with his consent his firm should never during its life, or after its dissolution, deserve the reputation enjoyed by those shining lights of the profession, 'Catch 'em and Cheat 'em.'"

A Juryman's Scorn

Lincoln had assisted in the prosecution of a man who had robbed his neighbor's hen roosts. Jogging home along the highway with the foreman of the jury that had convicted the hen stealer, he was complimented by Lincoln on the zeal and ability of the prosecution, and remarked: "Why, when the country was young, and I was stronger than I am now, I didn't mind packing off a sheep now and again, but stealing hens!" The good man's scorn could not find words to express his opinion of a man who would steal hens.

He "Broke" to Win

A lawyer, who was a stranger to Mr. Lincoln, once expressed to General Linder the opinion that Mr. Lincoln's practice of telling stories to the jury was a waste of time.

"Don't lay that flattering unction to your soul," Linder answered; "Lincoln is like Tansey's horse, he 'breaks to win.'"

Wanted Her Children Back

On the 3rd of January, 1863, "Harper's Weekly" appeared with a cartoon representing Columbia indignantly demanding of President Lincoln and Secretary of War Stanton that they restore to her those of her sons killed in battle. Below the picture is the reading matter:

COLUMBIA: "Where are my 15,000 sons—murdered at Fredericksburg?"

LINCOLN: "This reminds me of a little joke—"

COLUMBIA: "Go tell your joke at Springfield!!"

The battle of Fredericksburg was fought on December 13th, 1862, between General Burnside, commanding the Army of the Potomac, and General Lee's force. The Union troops, time and again, assaulted the heights where the Confederates had taken position, but were driven back with frightful losses. The enemy, being behind breastworks, suffered comparatively little. At the beginning of the fight the Confederate line was broken, but the result of the engagement was disastrous to the Union cause. Burnside had one thousand one hundred and fifty-two killed, nine thousand one hundred and one wounded, and three thousand two hundred and thirty-four missing, a total of thirteen thousand seven hundred and seventy-one. General Lee's losses, all told, were not much more than five thousand men.

Burnside had succeeded McClellan in command of the Army of the Potomac, mainly, it was said, through the influence of Secretary of War Stanton. Three months before, McClellan had defeated Lee at Antietam, the bloodiest battle of the War, Lee's losses footing up more than thirteen thousand men. At Fredericksburg, Burnside had about one hundred and twenty thousand men; at Antietam, McClellan had about eighty thousand. It has been maintained that Burnside should not have fought this battle, the chances of success being so few.

Six Feet Four at Seventeen

"Abe's" school teacher, Crawford, endeavored to teach his pupils some of the manners of the "polite society" of Indiana—1823 or so. This was a part of his system:

One of the pupils would retire, and then come in as a stranger, and another pupil would have to introduce him to all the members of the school n what was considered "good manners."

As "Abe" wore a linsey-woolsey shirt, buckskin breeches which were too short and very tight, and low shoes, and was tall and awkward, he no doubt created considerable merriment when his turn came. He was growing at a fearful rate; he was fifteen years of age, and two years later attained his full height of six feet four inches.

Had Respect for the Eggs

Early in 1831, "Abe" was one of the guests of honor at a boat-launching, he and two others having built the craft. The affair was a notable one, people being present from the territory surrounding. A large party came from Springfield with an ample supply of whisky, to give the boat and its builders a send-off. It was a sort of bipartisan mass-meeting, but there was one prevailing spirit, that born of rye and corn. Speeches were made in the best of feeling, some in favor of Andrew Jackson and some in favor of Henry Clay. Abraham Lincoln, the cook, told a number of funny stories, and it is recorded that they were not of too refined a character to suit the taste of his audience. A sleight-of-hand performer was present, and among other tricks performed, he fried some eggs in Lincoln's hat. Judge Herndon says, as explanatory to the delay in passing up the hat for the experiment, Lincoln drolly observed: "It was out of respect for the eggs, not care for my hat."

How Was the Milk Upset?

William G. Greene, an old-time friend of Lincoln, was a student at Illinois College, and one summer brought home with him, on a vacation, Richard Yates (afterwards Governor of Illinois) and some other boys, and, in order to entertain them, took them up to see Lincoln.

He found him in his usual position and at his usual occupation— flat on his back, on a cellar door, reading a newspaper. This was the manner in which a President of the United States and a Governor of Illinois became acquainted with each other.

Greene says Lincoln repeated the whole of Burns, and a large quantity of Shakespeare for the entertainment of the college boys, and, in return, was invited to dine with them on bread and milk. How he managed to upset his bowl of milk is not a matter of history, but the fact is that he did so, as is the further fact that Greene's mother, who loved Lincoln, tried to smooth over the accident and relieve the young man's embarrassment.

"Pulled Fodder" for a Book

Once "Abe" borrowed Weems' "Life of Washington" from Joseph Crawford, a neighbor. "Abe" devoured it; read it and re-read it, and when asleep put it by him between the logs of the wall. One night a rain storm wet it through and ruined it.

"I've no money," said "Abe," when reporting the disaster to Crawford, "but I'll work it out."

"All right," was Crawford's response; "you pull fodder for three days, an' the book is your'n."

"Abe" pulled the fodder, but he never forgave Crawford for putting so much work upon him. He never lost an opportunity to crack a joke at his expense, and the name "Blue-nose Crawford" "Abe" applied to him stuck to him throughout his life.

Praises His Rival for Office

When Mr. Lincoln was a candidate for the Legislature, it was the practice at that date in Illinois for two rival candidates to travel over the district together. The custom led to much good-natured raillery between them; and in such contests Lincoln was rarely, if ever, worsted. He could even turn the generosity of a rival to account by his whimsical treatment.

On one occasion, says Mr. Weir, a former resident of Sangamon county, he had driven out from Springfield in company with a political opponent to engage in joint debate. The carriage, it seems, belonged to his opponent. In addressing the gathering of farmers that met them, Lincoln was lavish in praise of the generosity of his friend.

"I am too poor to own a carriage," he said, "but my friend has generously invited me to ride with him. I want you to vote for me if you will; but if not then vote for my opponent, for he is a fine man."

His extravagant and persistent praise of his opponent appealed to the sense of humor in his rural audience, to whom his inability to own a carriage was by no means a disqualification.

One Thing "Abe" Didn't Love

Lincoln admitted that he was not particularly energetic when it came to real hard work.

"My father," said he one day, "taught me how to work, but not to love it. I never did like to work, and I don't deny it. I'd rather read, tell stories, crack jokes, talk, laugh—anything but work."

The Modesty of Genius

The opening of the year 1860 found Mr. Lincoln's name freely mentioned in connection with the Republican nomination for the Presidency. To be classed with Seward, Chase, McLean, and other celebrities, was enough to stimulate any Illinois lawyer's pride; but in Mr. Lincoln's case, if it had any such effect, he was most artful in concealing it. Now and then, some ardent friend, an editor, for example, would run his name up to the masthead, but in all cases he discouraged the attempt.

"In regard to the matter you spoke of," he answered one man who proposed his name, "I beg you will not give it a further mention. Seriously, I do not think I am fit for the Presidency."

Why She Married Him

There was a "social" at Lincoln's house in Springfield, and "Abe" introduced his wife to Ward Lamon, his law partner. Lamon tells the story in these words:

"After introducing me to Mrs. Lincoln, he left us in conversation. I remarked to her that her husband was a great favorite in the eastern part of the State, where I had been stopping.

"'Yes,' she replied, 'he is a great favorite everywhere. He is to be President of the United States some day; if I had not thought so I never would have married him, for you can see he is not pretty.

"'But look at him, doesn't he look as if he would make a magnificent President?'"

Niagara Falls

The following article on Niagara Falls, in Mr. Lincoln's handwriting, was found among his papers after his death:

"Niagara Falls! By what mysterious power is it that millions and millions are drawn from all parts of the world to gaze upon Niagara Falls? There is no mystery about the thing itself. Every effect is just as any intelligent man, knowing the causes, would anticipate without seeing it. If the water moving onward in a great river reaches a point where there is a perpendicular jog of a hundred feet in descent in the bottom of the river, it is plain the water will have a violent and continuous plunge at that point. It is also plain, the water, thus plunging, will foam and roar, and send up a mist continuously, in which last, during sunshine, there will be perpetual rainbows. The mere physical of Niagara Falls is only this. Yet this is really a very small part of that world's wonder. Its power to excite reflection and emotion is its great charm. The geologist will demonstrate that the plunge, or fall, was once at Lake Ontario, and has worn its way back to its present position; he will ascertain how fast it is wearing now, and so get a basis for determining how long it has been wearing back from Lake Ontario, and finally demonstrate by it that this world is at least fourteen thousand years old. A philosopher of a slightly different turn will say, 'Niagara Falls is only the lip of the basin out of which pours all the surplus water which rains down on two or three hundred thousand square miles of the earth's surface.' He will estimate with approximate accuracy that five hundred thousand tons of water fall with their full weight a distance of a hundred feet each minute—thus exerting a force equal to the lifting of the same weight, through the same space, in the same time.

"But still there is more. It calls up the indefinite past. When Columbus first sought this continent—when Christ suffered on the cross—when Moses led Israel through the Red Sea—nay, even when Adam first came from the hand of his Maker; then, as now, Niagara was roaring here. The eyes of that species of extinct giants whose bones fill the mounds of America have gazed on Niagara, as ours do now. Contemporary with the first race of men, and older than the first man, Niagara is strong and fresh to-day as ten thousand years ago. The Mammoth and Mastodon, so long dead that fragments of their monstrous bones alone testify that they ever lived, have gazed on Niagara—in that long, long time never still for a single moment (never dried), never froze, never slept, never rested."

Made It Hot for Lincoln

A lady relative, who lived for two years with the Lincolns, said that Mr. Lincoln was in the habit of lying on the floor with the back of a chair for a pillow when he read.

One evening, when in this position in the hall, a knock was heard at the front door, and, although in his shirtsleeves, he answered the call. Two ladies were at the door, whom he invited into the parlor, notifying them in his open, familiar way, that he would "trot the women folks out."

Mrs. Lincoln, from an adjoining room, witnessed the ladies' entrance, and, overhearing her husband's jocose expression, her indignation was so instantaneous she made the situation exceedingly interesting for him, and he was glad to retreat from the house. He did not return till very late at night, and then slipped quietly in at a rear door.

Wouldn't Hold Title Against Him

During the rebellion the Austrian Minister to the United States Government introduced to the President a count, a subject of the Austrian government, who was desirous of obtaining a position in the American army.

Being introduced by the accredited Minister of Austria he required no further recommendation to secure the appointment; but, fearing that his importance might not be fully appreciated by the republican President, the count was particular in impressing the fact upon him that he bore that title, and that his family was ancient and highly respectable.

President Lincoln listened with attention, until this unnecessary commendation was mentioned; then, with a merry twinkle in his eye, he tapped the aristocratic sprig of hereditary nobility on the shoulder in the most fatherly way, as if the gentleman had made a confession of some unfortunate circumstance connected with his lineage, for which he was in no way responsible, and said:

"Never mind, you shall be treated with just as much consideration for all that. I will see to it that your bearing a title shan't hurt you."

Only One Life to Live

A young man living in Kentucky had been enticed into the rebel army. After a few months he became disgusted, and managed to make his way back home. Soon after his arrival, the Union officer in command of the military stationed in the town had him arrested as a rebel spy, and, after a military trial he was condemned to be hanged.

President Lincoln was seen by one of his friends from Kentucky, who explained his errand and asked for mercy. "Oh, yes, I understand; someone has been crying, and worked upon your feelings, and you have come here to work on mine."

His friend then went more into detail, and assured him of his belief in the truth of the story. After some deliberation, Mr. Lincoln, evidently scarcely more than half convinced, but still preferring to err on the side of mercy, replied:

"If a man had more than one life, I think a little hanging would not hurt this one; but after he is once dead we cannot bring him back, no matter how sorry we may be; so the boy shall be pardoned."

And a reprieve was given on the spot.

Couldn't Locate His Birthplace

While the celebrated artist, Hicks, was engaged in painting Mr. Lincoln's portrait, just after the former's first nomination for the Presidency, he asked the great statesman if he could point out the precise spot where he was born.

Lincoln thought the matter over for a day or two, and then gave the artist the following memorandum:

"Springfield, Ill., June 14, 1860

"I was born February 12, 1809, in then Hardin county, Kentucky, at a point within the now county of Larue, a mile or a mile and a half from where Rodgen's mill now is. My parents being dead, and my own memory not serving, I know no means of identifying the precise locality. It was on Nolen Creek.

"A. LINCOLN."

"Sambo" Was "Afeared"

In his message to Congress in December, 1864, just after his re-election, President Lincoln, in his message of December 6th, let himself out, in plain, unmistakable terms, to the effect that the freedmen should never be placed in bondage again. "Frank Leslie's Illustrated Newspaper" of December 24th, 1864, printed a cartoon, the text underneath running in this way:

UNCLE ABE: "Sambo, you are not handsome, any more than myself, but as to sending you back to your old master, I'm not the man to do it—and, what's more, I won't." (Vice President's message.)

Congress, at the previous sitting, had neglected to pass the resolution for the Constitutional amendment prohibiting slavery, but, on the 31st of January, 1865, the resolution was finally adopted, and the United States Constitution soon had the new feature as one of its clauses, the necessary number of State Legislatures approving it. President Lincoln regarded the passage of this resolution by Congress as most important, as the amendment, in his mind, covered whatever defects a rigid construction of the Constitution might find in his Emancipation Proclamation.

After the latter was issued, negroes were allowed to enlist in the Army, and they fought well and bravely. After the War, in the reorganization of the Regular Army, four regiments of colored men were provided for—the Ninth and Tenth Cavalry and the Twenty-fourth and Twenty-fifth Infantry. In the cartoon, Sambo has evidently been asking "Uncle Abe" as to the probability or possibility of his being again enslaved.

When Money Might Be Used

Some Lincoln enthusiast in Kansas, with much more pretensions than power, wrote him in March, 1860 proposing to furnish a Lincoln delegation from that State to the Chicago Convention, and suggesting that Lincoln should pay the legitimate expenses of organizing, electing, and taking to the convention the promised Lincoln delegates.

To this Lincoln replied that "in the main, the use of money is wrong, but for certain objects in a political contest the use of some is both right and indispensable." And he added: "If you shall be appointed a delegate to Chicago, I will furnish $100 to bear the expenses of the trip."

He heard nothing further from the Kansas man until he saw an announcement in the newspapers that Kansas had elected delegates and instructed them for Seward.

"Abe" Was No Beauty

Lincoln's military service in the Back Hawk war had increased his popularity at New Salem, and he was put up as a candidate for the Legislature.

A. Y. Ellis describes his personal appearance at this time as follows: "He wore a mixed jean coat, claw-hammer style, short in the sleeves and bob-tailed; in fact, it was so short in the tail that he could not sit on it; flax and tow linen pantaloons and a straw hat. I think he wore a vest, but do not remember how it looked; he wore pot-metal boots."

"He's Just Beautiful"

Lincoln's great love for children easily won their confidence.

A little girl, who had been told that the President was very homely, was taken by her father to see the President at the White House.

Lincoln took her upon his knee and chatted with her for a moment in his merry way, when she turned to her father and exclaimed:

"Oh, Pa! he isn't ugly at all; he's just beautiful!"

Big Enough Hog for Him

To a curiosity-seeker who desired a permit to pass the lines to visit the field of Bull Run, after the first battle, Lincoln made the following reply:

"A man in Cortlandt county raised a porker of such unusual size that strangers went out of their way to see it.

"One of them the other day met the old gentleman and inquired about the animal.

"'Wall, yes,' the old fellow said, 'I've got such a critter, mi'ty big un; but I guess I'll have to charge you about a shillin' for lookin' at him.'

"The stranger looked at the old man for a minute or so, pulled out the desired coin, handed it to him and started to go off. 'Hold on,' said the other, 'don't you want to see the hog?'

"'No,' said the stranger; 'I have seen as big a hog as I want to see!'

"And you will find that fact the case with yourself, if you should happen to see a few live rebels there as well as dead ones."

"Abe" Offers a Speech for Something to Eat

When Lincoln's special train from Springfield to Washington reached the Illinois State line, there was a stop for dinner. There was such a crowd that Lincoln could scarcely reach the dining-room. "Gentlemen," said he, as he surveyed the crowd, "if you will make me a little path, so that I can get through and get something to eat, I will make you a speech when I get back."

They Understood Each Other

When complaints were made to President Lincoln by victims of Secretary of War Stanton's harshness, rudeness, and refusal to be obliging—particularly in cases where Secretary Stanton had refused to honor Lincoln's passes through the lines—the President would often remark to this effect: "I cannot always be sure that permits given by me ought to be granted. There is an understanding between myself and Stanton that when I send a request to him which cannot consistently be granted, he is to refuse to honor it. This he sometimes does."

Few Fence Rails Left

"There won't be a tar barrel left in Illinois to-night," said Senator Stephen A. Douglas, in Washington, to his Senatorial friends, who asked him, when the news of the nomination of Lincoln reached them, "Who is this man Lincoln, anyhow?"

Douglas was right. Not only the tar barrels, but half the fences of the State of Illinois went up in the fire of rejoicing.

The "Great Snow" of 1830-31

In explanation of Lincoln's great popularity, D. W. Bartlett, in his "Life and Speeches of Abraham Lincoln," published in 1860 makes this statement of "Abe's" efficient service to his neighbors in the "Great Snow" of 1830-31:

"The deep snow which occurred in 1830-31 was one of the chief troubles endured by the early settlers of central and southern Illinois. Its consequences lasted through several years. The people were ill-prepared to meet it, as the weather had been mild and pleasant—unprecedentedly so up to Christmas—when a snow-storm set in which lasted two days, something never before known even among the traditions of the Indians, and never approached in the weather of any winter since.

"The pioneers who came into the State (then a territory) in 1800 say the average depth of snow was never, previous to 1830, more than knee-deep to an ordinary man, while it was breast-high all that winter. It became crusted over, so as, in some cases, to bear teams. Cattle and horses perished, the winter wheat was killed, the meager stock of provisions ran out, and during the three months' continuance of the snow, ice and continuous cold weather the most wealthy settlers came near starving, while some of the poor ones actually did. It was in the midst of such scenes that Abraham Lincoln attained his majority, and commenced his career of bold and manly independence. . . . .

"Communication between house and house was often entirely obstructed for teams, so that the young and strong men had to do all the traveling on foot; carrying from one neighbor what of his store he could spare to another, and bringing back in return something of his store sorely needed. Men living five, ten, twenty and thirty miles apart were called 'neighbors' then. Young Lincoln was always ready to perform these acts of humanity, and was foremost in the counsels of the settlers when their troubles seemed gathering like a thick cloud about them."

Creditor Paid Debtors Debt

A certain rich man in Springfield, Illinois, sued a poor attorney for $2.50, and Lincoln was asked to prosecute the case. Lincoln urged the creditor to let the matter drop, adding, "You can make nothing out of him, and it will cost you a good deal more than the debt to bring suit." The creditor was still determined to have his way, and threatened to seek some other attorney. Lincoln then said, "Well, if you are determined that suit should be brought, I will bring it; but my charge will be $10."

The money was paid him, and peremptory orders were given that the suit be brought that day. After the client's departure Lincoln went out of the office, returning in about an hour with an amused look on his face.

Asked what pleased him, he replied, "I brought suit against ——, and then hunted him up, told him what I had done, handed him half of the $10, and we went over to the squire's office. He confessed judgment and paid the bill."

Lincoln added that he didn't see any other way to make things satisfactory for his client as well as the other.

Helped Out the Soldiers

Judge Thomas B. Bryan, of Chicago, a member of the Union Defense Committee during the War, related the following concerning the original copy of the Emancipation Proclamation:

"I asked Mr. Lincoln for the original draft of the Proclamation," said Judge Bryan, "for the benefit of our Sanitary Fair, in 1865. He sent it and accompanied it with a note in which he said:

"'I had intended to keep this paper, but if it will help the soldiers, I give it to you.'

"The paper was put up at auction and brought $3,000. The buyer afterward sold it again to friends of Mr. Lincoln at a greatly advanced price, and it was placed in the rooms of the Chicago Historical Society, where it was burned in the great fire of 1871."

Every Fellow for Himself

An elegantly dressed young Virginian assured Lincoln that he had done a great deal of hard manual labor in his time. Much amused at this solemn declaration, Lincoln said:

"Oh, yes; you Virginians shed barrels of perspiration while standing off at a distance and superintending the work your slaves do for you. It is different with us. Here it is every fellow for himself, or he doesn't get there."

"Butcher-Knife Boys" at the Polls

When young Lincoln had fully demonstrated that he was the champion wrestler in the country surrounding New Salem, the men of "de gang" at Clary's Grove, whose leader "Abe" had downed, were his sworn political friends and allies.

Their work at the polls was remarkably effective. When the "Butcherknife boys," the "huge-pawed boys," and the "half-horse-half-alligator men" declared for a candidate the latter was never defeated.

No "Second Coming" for Springfield

Soon after the opening of Congress in 1861, Mr. Shannon, from California, made the customary call at the White House. In the conversation that ensued, Mr Shannon said: "Mr. President, I met an old friend of yours in California last summer, a Mr. Campbell, who had a good deal to say of your Springfield life."

"Ah!" returned Mr. Lincoln, "I am glad to hear of him. Campbell used to be a dry fellow in those days," he continued. "For a time he was Secretary of State. One day during the legislative vacation, a meek, cadaverous-looking man, with a white neck-cloth, introduced himself to him at his office, and, stating that he had been informed that Mr. C. had the letting of the hall of representatives, he wished to secure it, if possible, for a course of lectures he desired to deliver in Springfield.

"'May I ask,' said the Secretary, 'what is to be the subject of your lectures?'

"'Certainly,' was the reply, with a very solemn expression of countenance. 'The course I wish to deliver is on the Second Coming of our Lord.'

"'It is of no use,' said C.; 'if you will take my advice, you will not waste your time in this city. It is my private opinion that, if the Lord has been in Springfield once, He will never come the second time!'"

How He Won a Friend

J. S. Moulton, of Chicago, a master in chancery and influential in public affairs, looked upon the candidacy of Mr. Lincoln for President as something in the nature of a joke. He did not rate the Illinois man in the same class with the giants of the East. In fact he had expressed himself as by no means friendly to the Lincoln cause.

Still he had been a good friend to Lincoln and had often met him when the Springfield lawyer came to Chicago. Mr. Lincoln heard of Moulton's attitude, but did not see Moulton until after the election, when the President-elect came to Chicago and was tendered a reception at one of the big hotels.

Moulton went up in the line to pay his respects to the newly-elected chief magistrate, purely as a formality, he explained to his companions. As Moulton came along the line Mr. Lincoln grasped Moulton's hand with his right, and with his left took the master of chancery by the shoulder and pulled him out of the line.

"You don't belong in that line, Moulton," said Mr. Lincoln. "You belong here by me."

Everyone at the reception was a witness to the honoring of Moulton. From that hour every faculty that Moulton possessed was at the service of the President. A little act of kindness, skillfully bestowed, had won him; and he stayed on to the end.

Never Sued a Client

If a client did not pay, Lincoln did not believe in suing for the fee. When a fee was paid him his custom was to divide the money into two equal parts, put one part into his pocket, and the other into an envelope labeled "Herndon's share."

The Lincoln Household Goods

It is recorded that when "Abe" was born, the household goods of his father consisted of a few cooking utensils, a little bedding, some carpenter tools, and four hundred gallons of the fierce product of the mountain still.

Running the Machine

One of the cartoon-posters issued by the Democratic National Campaign Committee in the fall of 1864 had the legend "Running the Machine" printed beneath; the "machine" was Secretary Chase's "Greenback Mill," and the mill was turning out paper money by the million to satisfy the demands of greedy contractors. "Uncle Abe" is pictured as about to tell one of his funny stories, of which the scene "reminds" him; Secretary of War Stanton is receiving a message from the front, describing a great victory, in which one prisoner and one gun were taken; Secretary of State Seward is handing an order to a messenger for the arrest of a man who had called him a "humbug," the habeas corpus being suspended throughout the Union at that period; Secretary of the Navy Welles—the long-haired, long-bearded man at the head of the table—is figuring out a naval problem; at the side of the table, opposite "Uncle Abe," are seated two Government contractors, shouting for "more greenbacks," and at the extreme left is Secretary of the Treasury Fessenden (who succeeded Chase when the latter was made Chief Justice of the United States Supreme Court), who complains that he cannot satisfy the greed of the contractors for "more greenbacks," although he is grinding away at the mill day and night.

Was "Boss" When Necessary

Lincoln was the actual head of the administration, and whenever he chose to do so he controlled Secretary of War Stanton as well as the other Cabinet ministers.

Secretary Stanton on one occasion said: "Now, Mr. President, those are the facts and you must see that your order cannot be executed."

Lincoln replied in a somewhat positive tone: "Mr. Secretary, I reckon you'll have to execute the order."

Stanton replied with vigor: "Mr. President, I cannot do it. This order is an improper one, and I cannot execute it."

Lincoln fixed his eyes upon Stanton, and, in a firm voice and accent that clearly showed his determination, said: "Mr. Secretary, it will have to be done."

It was done.

"Rather Starve Than Swindle"

Ward Lamon, once Lincoln's law partner, relates a story which places Lincoln's high sense of honor in a prominent light. In a certain case, Lincoln and Lamon being retained by a gentleman named Scott, Lamon put the fee at $250, and Scott agreed to pay it. Says Lamon:

"Scott expected a contest, but, to his surprise, the case was tried inside of twenty minutes; our success was complete. Scott was satisfied, and cheerfully paid over the money to me inside the bar, Lincoln looking on. Scott then went out, and Lincoln asked, 'What did you charge that man?'

"I told him $250. Said he: 'Lamon, that is all wrong. The service was not worth that sum. Give him back at least half of it.'

"I protested that the fee was fixed in advance; that Scott was perfectly satisfied, and had so expressed himself. 'That may be,' retorted Lincoln, with a look of distress and of undisguised displeasure, 'but I am not satisfied. This is positively wrong. Go, call him back and return half the money at least, or I will not receive one cent of it for my share.'

"I did go, and Scott was astonished when I handed back half the fee.

"This conversation had attracted the attention of the lawyers and the court. Judge David Davis, then on our circuit bench (afterwards Associate Justice on the United States Supreme bench), called Lincoln to him. The Judge never could whisper, but in this instance he probably did his best. At all events, in attempting to whisper to Lincoln he trumpeted his rebuke in about these words, and in rasping tones that could be heard all over the court-room: 'Lincoln, I have been watching you and Lamon. You are impoverishing this bar by your picayune charges of fees, and the lawyers have reason to complain of you. You are now almost as poor as Lazarus, and if you don't make people pay you more for your services you will die as poor as Job's turkey!'

"Judge O. L. Davis, the leading lawyer in that part of the State, promptly applauded this malediction from the bench; but Lincoln was immovable.

"'That money,' said he, 'comes out of the pocket of a poor, demented girl, and I would rather starve than swindle her in this manner.'"

Don't Aim Too High

"Billy, don't shoot too high—aim lower, and the common people will understand you," Lincoln once said to a brother lawyer.

"They are the ones you want to reach—at least, they are the ones you ought to reach.

"The educated and refined people will understand you, anyway. If you aim too high, your idea will go over the heads of the masses, and only hit those who need no hitting."

Not Much at Rail-Splitting

One who afterward became one of Lincoln's most devoted friends and adherents tells this story regarding the manner in which Lincoln received him when they met for the first time:

"After a comical survey of my fashionable toggery,—my swallow-tail coat, white neck-cloth, and ruffled shirt (an astonishing outfit for a young limb of the law in that settlement), Lincoln said:

"'Going to try your hand at the law, are you? I should know at a glance that you were a Virginian; but I don't think you would succeed at splitting rails. That was my occupation at your age, and I don't think I have taken as much pleasure in anything else from that day to this.'"

Gave the Soldier the Preference

July 27th, 1863, Lincoln wrote the Postmaster-General:

"Yesterday little indorsements of mine went to you in two cases of postmasterships, sought for widows whose husbands have fallen in the battles of this war.

"These cases, occurring on the same day, brought me to reflect more attentively than what I had before done as to what is fairly due from us here in dispensing of patronage toward the men who, by fighting our battles, bear the chief burden of saving our country.

"My conclusion is that, other claims and qualifications being equal, they have the right, and this is especially applicable to the disabled soldier and the deceased soldier's family."

The President Was Not Scared

When told how uneasy all had been at his going to Richmond, Lincoln replied:

"Why, if any one else had been President and had gone to Richmond, I would have been alarmed; but I was not scared about myself a bit."

Jeff. Davis's Reply to Lincoln

On the 20th of July, 1864, Horace Greeley crossed into Canada to confer with refugee rebels at Niagara. He bore with him this paper from the President:

"To Whom It May Concern: Any proposition which embraces the restoration of peace, the integrity of the whole Union, and the abandonment of slavery, and which comes by and with an authority that can control the armies now at war with the United States, will be received and considered by the executive government of the United States, and will be met by liberal terms and other substantial and collateral points, and the bearer or bearers thereof shall have safe conduct both ways."

To this Jefferson Davis replied: "We are not fighting for slavery; we are fighting for independence."

Lincoln Was a Gentleman

Lincoln was compelled to contend with the results of the ill-judged zeal of politicians, who forced ahead his flatboat and rail-splitting record, with the homely surroundings of his earlier days, and thus, obscured for the time, the other fact that, always having the heart, he had long since acquired the manners of a true gentleman.

So, too, did he suffer from Eastern censors, who did not take those surroundings into account, and allowed nothing for his originality of character. One of these critics heard at Washington that Mr. Lincoln, in speaking at different times of some move or thing, said "it had petered out"; that some other one's plan "wouldn't gibe"; and being asked if the War and the cause of the Union were not a great care to him, replied:

"Yes, it is a heavy hog to hold."

The first two phrases are so familiar here in the West that they need no explanation. Of the last and more pioneer one it may be said that it had a special force, and was peculiarly Lincoln-like in the way applied by him.

In the early times in Illinois, those having hogs, did their own killing, assisted by their neighbors. Stripped of its hair, one held the carcass nearly perpendicular in the air, head down, while others put one point of the gambrel-bar through a slit in its hock, then over the string-pole, and the other point through the other hock, and so swung the animal clear of the ground. While all this was being done, it took a good man to "hold the hog," greasy, warmly moist, and weighing some two hundred pounds. And often those with the gambrel prolonged the strain, being provokingly slow, in hopes to make the holder drop his burden.

This latter thought is again expressed where President Lincoln, writing of the peace which he hoped would "come soon, to stay; and so come as to be worth the keeping in all future time," added that while there would "be some black men who can remember that with silent tongue and clenched teeth and steady eye, and well-poised bayonet, they have helped mankind on to this great consummation," he feared there would "be some white ones unable to forget that, with malignant heart and deceitful tongue, they had striven to hinder it."

He had two seemingly opposite elements little understood by strangers, and which those in more intimate relations with him find difficult to explain; an open, boyish tongue when in a happy mood, and with this a reserve of power, a force of thought that impressed itself without words on observers in his presence. With the cares of the nation on his mind, he became more meditative, and lost much of his lively ways remembered "back in Illinois."

His Poor Relations

One of the most beautiful traits of Mr. Lincoln's character was his considerate regard for the poor and obscure relatives he had left, plodding along in their humble ways of life. Wherever upon his circuit he found them, he always went to their dwellings, ate with them, and, when convenient, made their houses his home. He never assumed in their presence the slightest superiority to them. He gave them money when they needed it and he had it. Countless times he was known to leave his companions at the village hotel, after a hard day's work in the court-room, and spend the evening with these old friends and companions of his humbler days. On one occasion, when urged not to go, he replied, "Why, Aunt's heart would be broken if I should leave town without calling upon her"; yet, he was obliged to walk several miles to make the call.

Deserter's Sins Washed Out in Blood

This was the reply made by Lincoln to an application for the pardon of a soldier who had shown himself brave in war, had been severely wounded, but afterward deserted:

"Did you say he was once badly wounded?

"Then, as the Scriptures say that in the shedding of blood is the remission of sins, I guess we'll have to let him off this time."

Sure Cure for Boils

President Lincoln and Postmaster-General Blair were talking of the war.

"Blair," said the President, "did you ever know that fright has sometimes proven a cure for boils?" "No, Mr. President, how is that?" "I'll tell you. Not long ago when a colonel, with his cavalry,

heat of a quarrel, shot a young man named Ben Boyle and was arrested. My father was seriously ill with inflammatory rheumatism at the time, and could scarcely move hand or foot. He certainly could not defend Dan. I was his secretary, and I remember it was but a day or so after the shooting till letters of sympathy began to pour in. In the first bundle which I picked up there was a big letter, the handwriting on which I recognized as that of Mr. Lincoln. The letter was very sympathetic.

"'I know how you feel, Linder,' it said. 'I can understand your anger as a father, added to all the other sentiments. But may we not be in a measure to blame? We have talked about the defense of criminals before our children; about our success in defending them; have left the impression that the greater the crime, the greater the triumph of securing an acquittal. Dan knows your success as a criminal lawyer, and he depends on you, little knowing that of all cases you would be of least value in this.'

"He concluded by offering his services, an offer which touched my father to tears.

"Mr. Lincoln tried to have Dan released on bail, but Ben Boyle's family and friends declared the wounded man would die, and feeling had grown so bitter that the judge would not grant any bail. So the case was changed to Marshall county, but as Ben finally recovered it was dismissed."

Thought of Learning a Trade

Lincoln at one time thought seriously of learning the blacksmith's trade. He was without means, and felt the immediate necessity of undertaking some business that would give him bread. While entertaining this project an event occurred which, in his undetermined state of mind, seemed to open a way to success in another quarter.

Reuben Radford, keeper of a small store in the village of New Salem, had incurred the displeasure of the "Clary Grove Boys," who exercised their "regulating" prerogatives by irregularly breaking his windows. William G. Greene, a friend of young Lincoln, riding by Radford's store soon afterward, was hailed by him, and told that he intended to sell out. Mr. Greene went into the store, and offered him at random $400 for his stock, which offer was immediately accepted.

Lincoln "happened in" the next day, and being familiar with the value of the goods, Mr. Greene proposed to him to take an inventory of the stock, to see what sort of a bargain he had made. This he did, and it was found that the goods were worth $600.

Lincoln then made an offer of $125 for his bargain, with the proposition that he and a man named Berry, as his partner, take over Greene's notes given to Radford. Mr. Greene agreed to the arrangement, but Radford declined it, except on condition that Greene would be their security. Greene at last assented.

Lincoln was not afraid of the "Clary Grove Boys"; on the contrary, they had been his most ardent friends since the time he thrashed "Jack" Armstrong, champion bully of "The Grove"—but their custom was not heavy.

The business soon became a wreck; Greene had to not only assist in closing it up, but pay Radford's notes as well. Lincoln afterwards spoke of these notes, which he finally made good to Greene, as "the National Debt."

Lincoln Defends Fifteen Mrs. Nations

When Lincoln's sympathies were enlisted in any cause, he worked like a giant to win. At one time (about 1855) he was in attendance upon court at the little town of Clinton, Ill., and one of the cases on the docket was where fifteen women from a neighboring village were defendants, they having been indicted for trespass. Their offense, as duly set forth in the indictment, was that of swooping down upon one Tanner, the keeper of a saloon in the village, and knocking in the heads of his barrels. Lincoln was not employed in the case, but sat watching the trial as it proceeded.

In defending the ladies, their attorney seemed to evince a little want of tact, and this prompted one of the former to invite Mr. Lincoln to add a few words to the jury, if he thought he could aid their

cause. He was too gallant to refuse, and their attorney having consented, he made use of the following argument:

"In this case I would change the order of indictment and have it
read The State vs. Mr. Whiskey, instead of The State vs. The Ladies;
and touching these there are three laws: the law of self-protection;
the law of the land, or statute law; and the moral law, or law of God.

"First the law of self-protection is a law of necessity, as evinced
by our forefathers in casting the tea overboard and asserting their
right to the pursuit of life, liberty and happiness: In this case it is
the only defense the Ladies have, for Tanner neither feared God nor
regarded man.

"Second, the law of the land, or statute law, and Tanner is recreant
to both.

"Third, the moral law, or law of God, and this is probably a law
for the violation of which the jury can fix no punishment."

Lincoln gave some of his own observations on the ruinous effects
of whiskey in society, and demanded its early suppression.

After he had concluded, the Court, without awaiting the return of
the jury, dismissed the ladies, saying:

"Ladies, go home. I will require no bond of you, and if any fine is
ever wanted of you, we will let you know."

Avoided Even Appearance of Evil

Frank W. Tracy, President of the First National Bank of Spring-
field, tells a story illustrative of two traits in Mr. Lincoln's character.
Shortly after the National banking law went into effect the First
National of Springield was chartered, and Mr. Tracy wrote to Mr.
Lincoln, with whom he was well acquainted in a business way, and
tendered him an opportunity to subscribe for some of the stock.

In reply to the kindly offer Mr. Lincoln wrote, thanking Mr. Tracy,
but at the same time declining to subscribe. He said he recognized
that stock in a good National bank would be a good thing to hold,
but he did not feel that he ought, as President, profit from a law
which had been passed under his administration.

"He seemed to wish to avoid even the appearance of evil," said

Mr. Tracy, in telling of the incident. "And so the act proved both his unvarying probity and his unfailing policy."

War Didn't Admit of Holidays

Lincoln wrote a letter on October 2d, 1862, in which he observed:
"I sincerely wish war was a pleasanter and easier business than it is, but it does not admit of holidays."

"Neutrality"

Old John Bull got himself into a precious fine scrape when he went so far as to "play double" with the North, as well as the South, during the great American Civil War. In its issue of November 14th, 1863, London "Punch" printed a rather clever cartoon illustrating the predicament Bull had created for himself. John is being lectured by Mrs. North and Mrs. South—both good talkers and eminently able to hold their own in either social conversation, parliamentary debate or political argument—but he bears it with the best grace possible. This is the way the text underneath the picture runs:

MRS. NORTH. "How about the Alabama, you wicked old man?" MRS. SOUTH: "Where's my rams? Take back your precious consols—there!!" "Punch" had a good deal of fun with old John before it was through with him, but, as the Confederate privateer Alabama was sent beneath the waves of the ocean at Cherbourg by the Kearsarge, and Mrs. South had no need for any more rams, John got out of the difficulty without personal injury. It was a tight squeeze, though, for Mrs. North was in a fighting humor, and prepared to scratch or pull hair. The fact that the privateer Alabama, built at an English shipyard and manned almost entirely by English sailors, had managed to do about $10,000,000 worth of damage to United States commerce, was enough to make any one angry.

Days of Gladness Past

After the war was well on, a patriot woman of the West urged President Lincoln to make hospitals at the North where the sick from the Army of the Mississippi could revive in a more bracing air. Among other reasons, she said, feelingly: "If you grant my petition, you will be glad as long as you live."

With a look of sadness impossible to describe, the President said: "I shall never be glad any more."

Wouldn't Take the Money

Lincoln always regarded himself as the friend and protector of unfortunate clients, and such he would never press for pay for his services. A client named Cogdal was unfortunate in business, and gave a note in settlement of legal fees. Soon afterward he met with an accident by which he lost a hand. Meeting Lincoln some time after on the steps of the State-House, the kind lawyer asked him how he was getting along.

"Badly enough," replied Cogdal; "I am both broken up in business and crippled." Then he added, "I have been thinking about that note of yours."

Lincoln, who had probably known all about Cogdal's troubles, and had prepared himself for the meeting, took out his pocket-book, and saying, with a laugh, "Well, you needn't think any more about it," handed him the note.

Cogdal protesting, Lincoln said, "Even if you had the money, I would not take it," and hurried away.

Grant Held on All the Time

(Dispatch to General Grant, August 17th, 1864.)

"I have seen your dispatch expressing your unwillingness to break your hold where you are. Neither am I willing.

"Hold on with a bulldog grip."

Chewed the Cud in Solitude

As a student (if such a term could be applied to Lincoln), one who did not know him might have called him indolent. He would pick up a book and run rapidly over the pages, pausing here and there.

At the end of an hour—never more than two or three hours—he would close the book, stretch himself out on the office lounge, and then, with hands under his head and eyes shut, would digest the mental food he had just taken.

"Abe's" Yankee Ingenuity

War Governor Richard Yates (he was elected Governor of Illinois in 1860, when Lincoln was first elected President) told a good story at Springfield (Ill.) about Lincoln.

One day the latter was in the Sangamon River with his trousers rolled up five feet—more or less—trying to pilot a flatboat over a mill-dam. The boat was so full of water that it was hard to manage. Lincoln got the prow over, and then, instead of waiting to bail the water out, bored a hole through the projecting part and let it run out, affording a forcible illustration of the ready ingenuity of the future President.

Lincoln Paid Homage to Washington

The Martyr President thus spoke of Washington in the course of an address:

"Washington is the mightiest name on earth—long since the mightiest in the cause of civil liberty, still mightiest in moral reformation.

"On that name a eulogy is expected. It cannot be.

"To add brightness to the sun or glory to the name of Washington is alike impossible.

"Let none attempt it.

"In solemn awe pronounce the name, and, in its naked, deathless splendor, leave it shining on."

Stirred Even the Reporters

Lincoln's influence upon his audiences was wonderful. He could sway people at will, and nothing better illustrates his extraordinary power than he manner in which he stirred up the newspaper reporters by his Bloomingon speech.

Joseph Medill, editor of the Chicago Tribune, told the story:

"It was my journalistic duty, though a delegate to the convention, to make a 'longhand' report of the speeches delivered for the Tribune. I did make a few paragraphs of what Lincoln said in the first eight or ten minutes, but I became so absorbed in his magnetic oratory that I forgot myself and ceased to take notes, and joined with the convention in cheering and stamping and clapping to the end of his speech.

"I well remember that after Lincoln sat down and calm had succeeded the tempest, I waked out of a sort of hypnotic trance, and then thought of my report for the paper. There was nothing written but an abbreviated introduction.

"It was some sort of satisfaction to find that I had not been 'scooped,' as all the newspaper men present had been equally carried away by the excitement caused by the wonderful oration and had made no report or sketch of the speech."

When "Abe" Came in

When "Abe" was fourteen years of age, John Hanks journeyed from Kentucky to Indiana and lived with the Lincolns. He described "Abe's" habits thus:

"When Lincoln and I returned to the house from work, he would go to the cupboard, snatch a piece of corn-bread, take down a book, sit down on a chair, cock his legs up as high as his head, and read.

"He and I worked barefooted, grubbed it, plowed, mowed, cradled together; plowed corn, gathered it, and shucked corn. 'Abe' read constantly when he had an opportunity."

Eternal Fidelity to the Cause of Liberty

During the Harrison Presidential campaign of 1840, Lincoln said, in a speech at Springfield, Illinois:

"Many free countries have lost their liberty, and ours may lose hers; but if she shall, be it my proudest plume, not that I was last to desert, but that I never deserted her.

"I know that the great volcano at Washington, aroused and directed by the evil spirit that reigns there, is belching forth the lava of political corruption in a current broad and deep, which is sweeping with frightful velocity over the whole length and breadth of the land, bidding fair to leave unscathed no green spot or living thing.

"I cannot deny that all may be swept away. Broken by it, I, too, may be; bow to it I never will.

"The possibility that we may fail in the struggle ought not to deter us from the support of a cause which we believe to be just. It shall never deter me.

"If ever I feel the soul within me elevate and expand to those dimensions not wholly unworthy of its Almighty Architect, it is when I contemplate the cause of my country, deserted by all the world beside, and I standing up boldly alone, and hurling defiance at her victorious oppressors.

"Here, without contemplating consequences, before heaven, and in the face of the world, I swear eternal fidelity to the just cause, as I deem it, of the land of my life, my liberty, and my love; and who that thinks with me will not fearlessly adopt the oath that I take?

"Let none falter who thinks he is right, and we may succeed.

"But if, after all, we shall fail, be it so; we have the proud consolation of saying to our consciences, and to the departed shade of our country's freedom, that the cause approved of our judgment, and, adorned of our hearts in disaster, in chains, in death, we never faltered in defending."

"Abe's" "Defalcations"

Lincoln could not rest for as instant under the consciousness that, even unwittingly, he had defrauded anybody. On one occasion, while clerking in Offutt's store, at New Salem, he sold a woman a little bale of goods, amounting, by the reckoning, to $2.20. He received the money, and the woman went away.

On adding the items of the bill again to make himself sure of correctness, he found that he had taken six and a quarter cents too much.

It was night, and, closing and locking the store, he started out on foot, a distance of two or three miles, for the house of his defrauded customer, and, delivering to her the sum whose possession had so much troubled him, went home satisfied.

On another occasion, just as he was closing the store for the night, a woman entered and asked for half a pound of tea. The tea was weighed out and paid for, and the store was left for the night.

The next morning Lincoln, when about to begin the duties of the day, discovered a four-ounce weight on the scales. He saw at once that he had made a mistake, and, shutting the store, he took a long walk before breakfast to deliver the remainder of the tea.

These are very humble incidents, but they illustrate the man's perfect conscientiousness—his sensitive honesty—better, perhaps, than they would if they were of greater moment.

He Wasn't Guileless

Leonard Swett, of Chicago, whose counsels were doubtless among the most welcome to Lincoln, in summing up Lincoln's character, said:

"From the commencement of his life to its close I have sometimes doubted whether he ever asked anybody's advice about anything. He would listen to everybody; he would hear everybody; but he rarely, if ever, asked for opinions.

"As a politician and as President he arrived at all his conclusions from his own reflections, and when his conclusions were once formed he never doubted but what they were right.

"One great public mistake of his (Lincoln's) character, as generally received and acquiesced in, is that he is considered by the people of this country as a frank, guileless, and unsophisticated man. There never was a greater mistake.

"Beneath a smooth surface of candor and apparent declaration of all his thoughts and feelings he exercised the most exalted tact and wisest discrimination. He handled and moved men remotely as we do pieces upon a chess-board.

"He retained through life all the friends he ever had, and he made the wrath of his enemies to praise him. This was not by cunning or intrigue in the low acceptation of the term, but by far-seeing reason and discernment. He always told only enough of his plans and purposes to induce the belief that he had communicated all; yet he reserved enough to have communicated nothing."

Sweet, but Mild Revenge

When the United States found that a war with Black Hawk could not be dodged, Governor Reynolds, of Illinois, issued a call for volunteers, and among the companies that immediately responded was one from Menard county, Illinois. Many of these volunteers were from New Salem and Clary's Grove, and Lincoln, being out of business, was the first to enlist.

The company being full, the men held a meeting at Richland for the election of officers. Lincoln had won many hearts, and they told him that he must be their captain. It was an office to which he did not aspire, and for which he felt he had no special fitness; but he finally consented to be a candidate.

There was but one other candidate, a Mr. Kirkpatrick, who was one of the most influential men of the region. Previously, Kirkpatrick had been an employer of Lincoln, and was so overbearing in his treatment of the young man that the latter left him.

The simple mode of electing a captain adopted by the company was by placing the candidates apart, and telling the men to go and stand with the one they preferred. Lincoln and his competitor took their positions, and then the word was given. At least three out of every four went to Lincoln at once.

When it was seen by those who had arranged themselves with the other candidate that Lincoln was the choice of the majority of the company, they left their places, one by one, and came over to the successful side, until Lincoln's opponent in the friendly strife was left standing almost alone.

"I felt badly to see him cut so," says a witness of the scene.

Here was an opportunity for revenge. The humble laborer was his employer's captain, but the opportunity was never improved. Mr. Lincoln frequently confessed that no subsequent success of his life had given him half the satisfaction that this election did.

Didn't Trust the Court

In one of his many stories of Lincoln, his law partner, W. H. Herndon, told this as illustrating Lincoln's shrewdness as a lawyer:

"I was with Lincoln once and listened to an oral argument by him in which he rehearsed an extended history of the law. It was a carefully prepared and masterly discourse, but, as I thought, entirely useless. After he was through and we were walking home, I asked him why he went so far back in the history of the law. I presumed the court knew enough history.

"'That's where you're mistaken,' was his instant rejoinder. 'I dared not just the case on the presumption that the court knows everything—in fact I argued it on the presumption that the court didn't know anything,' a statement, which, when one reviews the decision of our appellate courts, is not so extravagant as one would at first suppose."

Handsomest Man on Earth

One day Thaddeus Stevens called at the White House with an elderly woman, whose son had been in the army, but for some offense had been court-martialed and sentenced to death. There were some extenuating circumstances, and after a full hearing the President turned to Stevens and said: "Mr. Stevens, do you think this is a case which will warrant my interference?"

"With my knowledge of the facts and the parties," was the reply, "I should have no hesitation in granting a pardon."

"Then," returned Mr. Lincoln, "I will pardon him," and proceeded forthwith to execute the paper.

The gratitude of the mother was too deep for expression, save by her tears, and not a word was said between her and Stevens until they were half way down the stairs on their passage out, when she suddenly broke forth in an excited manner with the words:

"I knew it was a copperhead lie!"

"What do you refer to, madam?" asked Stevens.

"Why, they told me he was an ugly-looking man," she replied, with vehemence. "He is the handsomest man I ever saw in my life."

That Coon Came Down

"Lincoln's Last Warning" was the title of a cartoon which appeared in "Harper's Weekly," on October 11, 1862. Under the picture was the text:

"Now if you don't come down I'll cut the tree from under you."

This illustration was peculiarly apt, as, on the 1st of January, 1863, President Lincoln issued his great Emancipation Proclamation, declaring all slaves in the United States forever free. "Old Abe" was a handy man with the axe, he having split many thousands of rails with its keen edge. As the "Slavery Coon" wouldn't heed the warning, Lincoln did cut the tree from under him, and so he came down to the ground with a heavy thump.

This Act of Emancipation put an end to the notion of the Southern slave holders that involuntary servitude was one of the "sacred institutions" on the Continent of North America. It also demonstrated that Lincoln was thoroughly in earnest when he declared that he would not only save the Union, but that he meant what he said in the speech wherein he asserted, "This Nation cannot exist half slave and half free."

Wrote "Pieces" When Very Young

At fifteen years of age "Abe" wrote "pieces," or compositions, and even some doggerel rhyme, which he recited, to the great amusement of his playmates.

One of his first compositions was against cruelty to animals. He was very much annoyed and pained at the conduct of the boys, who were in the habit of catching terrapins and putting coals of fire on their backs, which thoroughly disgusted Abraham.

"He would chide us," said "Nat" Grigsby, "tell us it was wrong, and would write against it."

When eighteen years old, "Abe" wrote a "piece" on "National Politics," and it so pleased a lawyer friend, named Pritchard, that the latter had it printed in an obscure paper, thereby adding much to the author's pride. "Abe" did not conceal his satisfaction. In this "piece" he wrote, among other things:

"The American government is the best form of government for an intelligent people. It ought to be kept sound, and preserved forever, that general education should be fostered and carried all over the country; that the Constitution should be saved, the Union perpetuated and the laws revered, respected and enforced."

"Try to Steer Her through"

John A. Logan and a friend of Illinois called upon Lincoln at Willard's Hotel, Washington, February 23d, the morning of his arrival, and urged a vigorous, firm policy.

Patiently listening, Lincoln replied seriously but cheerfully:

"As the country has placed me at the helm of the ship, I'll try to steer her through."

Grand, Gloomy and Peculiar

Lincoln was a marked and peculiar young man. People talked about him. His studious habits, his greed for information, his thorough mastery of the difficulties of every new position in which he was placed, his intelligence on all matters of public concern, his unwearying good-nature, his skill in telling a story, his great athletic power, his quaint, odd ways, his uncouth appearance—all tended to bring him in sharp contrast with the dull mediocrity by which he was surrounded.

Denton Offutt, his old employer, said, after having had a conversation with Lincoln, that the young man "had talent enough in him to make a President."

On the Way to Gettysburg

When Lincoln was on his way to the National Cemetery at Gettysburg, an old gentleman told him that his only son fell on Little Round Top at Gettysburg, and he was going to look at the spot. Mr. Lincoln replied: "You have been called on to make a terrible sacrifice for the Union, and a visit to that spot, I fear, will open your wounds afresh.

"But, oh, my dear sir, if we had reached the end of such sacrifices, and had nothing left for us to do but to place garlands on the graves of those who have already fallen, we could give thanks even amidst our tears; but when I think of the sacrifices of life yet to be offered, and the hearts and homes yet to be made desolate before this dreadful war is over, my heart is like lead within me, and I feel at times like hiding in deep darkness." At one of the stopping places of the train, a very beautiful child, having a bunch of rosebuds in her hand, was lifted up to an open window of the President's car. "Floweth for the President." The President stepped to the window, took the rosebuds, bent down and kissed the child, saying, "You are a sweet little rosebud yourself. I hope your life will open into perpetual beauty and goodness."

Stood Up the Longest

There was a rough gallantry among the young people; and Lincoln's old comrades and friends in Indiana have left many tales of how he "went to see the girls," of how he brought in the biggest back-log and made the brightest fire; of how the young people, sitting around it, watching the way the sparks flew, told their fortunes.

He helped pare apples, shell corn and crack nuts. He took the girls to meeting and to spelling school, though he was not often allowed to take part in the spelling-match, for the one who "chose first" always chose "Abe" Lincoln, and that was equivalent to winning, as the others knew that "he would stand up the longest."

A Mortifying Experience

A lady reader or elocutionist came to Springfield in 1857. A large crowd greeted her. Among other things she recited "Nothing to Wear," a piece in which is described the perplexities that beset "Miss Flora McFlimsy" in her efforts to appear fashionable.

In the midst of one stanza in which no effort is made to say anything particularly amusing, and during the reading of which the audience manifested the most respectful silence and attention, someone in the rear seats burst out with a loud, coarse laugh, a sudden and explosive guffaw.

It startled the speaker and audience, and kindled a storm of un-suppressed laughter and applause. Everybody looked back to ascertain the cause of the demonstration, and were greatly surprised to find that it was Mr. Lincoln.

He blushed and squirmed with the awkward diffidence of a schoolboy. What caused him to laugh, no one was able to explain. He was doubtless wrapped up in a brown study, and recalling some amusing episode, indulged in laughter without realizing his surroundings. The experience mortified him greatly.

No Halfway Business

Soon after Mr. Lincoln began to practice law at Springfield, he was engaged in a criminal case in which it was thought there was little chance of success. Throwing all his powers into it, he came off victorious, and promptly received for his services five hundred dollars. A legal friend, calling upon him the next morning, found him sitting before a table, upon which his money was spread out, counting it over and over.

"Look here, Judge," said he. "See what a heap of money I've got from this case. Did you ever see anything like it? Why, I never had so much money in my life before, put it all together." Then, crossing his arms upon the table, his manner sobering down, he added: "I have got just five hundred dollars; if it were only seven hundred and fifty, I would go directly and purchase a quarter section of land, and settle it upon my old step-mother."

His friend said that if the deficiency was all he needed, he would loan him the amount, taking his note, to which Mr. Lincoln instantly acceded.

His friend then said:

"Lincoln, I would do just what you have indicated. Your step-mother is getting old, and will not probably live many years. I would settle the property upon her for her use during her lifetime, to revert to you upon her death."

With much feeling, Mr. Lincoln replied:

"I shall do no such thing. It is a poor return at best for all the good woman's devotion and fidelity to me, and there is not going to be any halfway business about it." And so saying, he gathered up his money and proceeded forthwith to carry his long-cherished purpose into execution.

Discouraged Litigation

Lincoln believed in preventing unnecessary litigation, and carried out this in his practice. "Who was your guardian?" he asked a young man who came to him to complain that a part of the property left him had been withheld. "Enoch Kingsbury," replied the young man.

"I know Mr. Kingsbury," said Lincoln, "and he is not the man to have cheated you out of a cent, and I can't take the case, and advise you to drop the subject."

And it was dropped.

Going Home to Get Ready

Edwin M. Stanton was one of the attorneys in the great "reaper patent" case heard in Cincinnati in 1855, Lincoln also having been retained. The latter was rather anxious to deliver the argument on the general propositions of law applicable to the case, but it being decided to have Mr. Stanton do this, the Westerner made no complaint.

Speaking of Stanton's argument and the view Lincoln took of it, Ralph Emerson, a young lawyer who was present at the trial, said:

"The final summing up on our side was by Mr. Stanton, and though he took but about three hours in its delivery, he had devoted as many, if not more, weeks to its preparation. It was very able, and Mr. Lincoln was throughout the whole of it a rapt listener. Mr. Stanton closed his speech in a flight of impassioned eloquence.

"Then the court adjourned for the day, and Mr. Lincoln invited me to take a long walk with him. For block after block he walked rapidly forward, not saying a word, evidently deeply dejected.

"At last he turned suddenly to me, exclaiming, 'Emerson, I am going home.' A pause. 'I am going home to study law.'

"'Why,' I exclaimed, 'Mr. Lincoln, you stand at the head of the bar in Illinois now! What are you talking about?'

"'Ah, yes,' he said, 'I do occupy a good position there, and I think that I can get along with the way things are done there now. But these college-trained men, who have devoted their whole lives to study, are coming West, don't you see? And they study their cases as we never do. They have got as far as Cincinnati now. They will soon be in Illinois.'

"Another long pause; then stopping and turning toward me, his countenance suddenly assuming that look of strong determination which those who knew him best sometimes saw upon his face, he exclaimed, 'I am going home to study law! I am as good as any, of them, and when they get out to Illinois, I will be ready for them.'"

"The 'Rail-Sputter' Repairing the Union"

One of the posters which decorated the picturesque Presidential campaign of 1864, and assisted in making the period previous to the vote-casting a lively and memorable one, had the title, "The Rail-Splitter at Work Repairing the Union." As the title would indicate, the President is using the Vice-Presidential candidate on the Republican National ticket (Andrew Johnson) as an aid in the work. Johnson was, in early life, a tailor, and he is pictured as busily engaged in sewing up the rents made in the map of the Union by the secessionists.

Both men are thoroughly in earnest, and, as history relates, the torn places in the Union map were stitched together so nicely that no one could have told, by mere observation, that a tear had ever been made. Andrew Johnson, who succeeded Lincoln upon the assassination of the latter, was a remarkable man. Born in North Carolina, he removed to Tennessee when young, was Congressman, Governor, and United States Senator, being made military Governor of his State in 1862. A strong, stanch Union man, he was nominated for the Vice-Presidency on the Lincoln ticket to conciliate the War Democrats. After serving out his term as President, he was again elected United States Senator from Tennessee, but died shortly after taking his seat. But he was just the sort of a man to assist "Uncle Abe" in sewing up the torn places in the Union map, and as military Governor of Tennessee was a powerful factor in winning friends in the South to the Union cause.

"Find Out for Yourselves"

"Several of us lawyers," remarked one of his colleagues, "in the eastern end of the circuit, annoyed Lincoln once while he was holding court for Davis by attempting to defend against a note to which there were many makers. We had no legal, but a good moral defense, but what we wanted most of all was to stave it off till the next term of court by one expedient or another.

"We bothered 'the court' about it till late on Saturday, the day of adjournment. He adjourned for supper with nothing left but this case to dispose of. After supper he heard our twaddle for nearly an hour, and then made this odd entry.

"'L. D. Chaddon vs. J. D. Beasley et al. April Term, 1856. Champaign county Court. Plea in abatement by B. Z. Green, a defendant not served, filed Saturday at 11 o'clock a. m., April 24, 1856, stricken from the files by order of court. Demurrer to declaration, if there ever was one, overruled. Defendants who are served now, at 8 o'clock p. m., of the last day of the term, ask to plead to the merits, which is denied by the court on the ground that the offer comes too late, and therefore, as by nil dicet, judgment is rendered for Pl'ff. Clerk assess damages. A. Lincoln, Judge pro tem.'

"The lawyer who reads this singular entry will appreciate its oddity if no one else does. After making it, one of the lawyers, on recovering from his astonishment, ventured to enquire: 'Well, Lincoln, how can we get this case up again?'

"Lincoln eyed him quizzically for a moment, and then answered, 'You have all been so mighty smart about this case, you can find out how to take it up again yourselves.'"

Rough on the Negro

Mr. Lincoln, one day, was talking with the Rev. Dr. Sunderland about the Emancipation Proclamation and the future of the negro. Suddenly a ripple of amusement broke the solemn tone of his voice. "As for the negroes, Doctor, and what is going to become of them: I told Ben Wade the other day, that it made me think of a story I read in one of my first books, 'Aesop's Fables.' It was an old edition, and had curious rough wood cuts, one of which showed three white men scrubbing a negro in a potash kettle filled with cold water. The text explained that the men thought that by scrubbing the negro they might make him white. Just about the time they thought they were succeeding, he took cold and died. Now, I am afraid that by the time we get through this War the negro will catch cold and die."

Challenged All Comers

Personal encounters were of frequent occurrence in Gentryville in early days, and the prestige of having thrashed an opponent gave the victor marked social distinction. Green B. Taylor, with whom "Abe" worked the greater part of one winter on a farm, furnished an account of the noted fight between John Johnston, "Abe's" step-brother, and William Grigsby, in which stirring drama "Abe" himself played an important role before the curtain was rung down.

Taylor's father was the second for Johnston, and William Whitten officiated in a similar capacity for Grigsby. "They had a terrible fight," related Taylor, "and it soon became apparent that Grigsby was too much for Lincoln's man, Johnston. After they had fought a long time without interference, it having been agreed not to break the ring, 'Abe' burst through, caught Grigsby, threw him off and some feet away. There Grigsby stood, proud as Lucifer, and, swinging a bottle of liquor over his head, swore he was 'the big buck of the lick.'

"'If any one doubts it,' he shouted, 'he has only to come on and whet his horns.'"

A general engagement followed this challenge, but at the end of hostilities the field was cleared and the wounded retired amid the exultant shouts of their victors.

"Government Rests in Public Opinion"

Lincoln delivered a speech at a Republican banquet at Chicago, December 10th, 1856, just after the Presidential campaign of that year, in which he said:

"Our government rests in public opinion. Whoever can change public opinion can change the government practically just so much.

"Public opinion, on any subject, always has a 'central idea,' from which all its minor thoughts radiate.

"That 'central idea' in our political public opinion at the beginning was, and until recently has continued to be, 'the equality of man.'

"And although it has always submitted patiently to whatever of inequality there seemed to be as a matter of actual necessity, its constant working has been a steady progress toward the practical equality of all men.

"Let everyone who really believes, and is resolved, that free society is not and shall not be a failure, and who can conscientiously declare that in the past contest he has done only what he thought best—let every such one have charity to believe that every other one can say as much.

"Thus, let bygones be bygones; let party differences as nothing be, and with steady eye on the real issue, let us reinaugurate the good old 'central ideas' of the Republic.

"We can do it. The human heart is with us; God is with us.

"We shall never be able to declare that 'all States as States are equal,' nor yet that 'all citizens are equal,' but to renew the broader, better declaration, including both these and much more, that 'all men are created equal.'"

Hurry Might Make Trouble

Up to the very last moment of the life of the Confederacy, the London "Punch" had its fling at the United States. In a cartoon, printed February 18th, 1865, labeled "The Threatening Notice," "Punch" intimates that Uncle Sam is in somewhat of a hurry to serve notice on John Bull regarding the contentions in connection with the northern border of the United States.

Lincoln, however, as attorney for his revered Uncle, advises caution. Accordingly, he tells his Uncle, according to the text under the picture:

ATTORNEY LINCOLN: "Now, Uncle Sam, you're in a darned hurry to serve this here notice on John Bull. Now, it's my duty, as your attorney, to tell you that you may drive him to go over to that cuss, Davis." (Uncle Sam considers.) In this instance, President Lincoln is given credit for judgment and common sense, his advice to his Uncle Sam to be prudent being sound. There was trouble all along the Canadian border during the War, while Canada was the refuge of Northern conspirators and Southern spies, who, at times, crossed the line and inflicted great damage upon the States bordering on it. The plot to seize the great lake cities—Chicago, Milwaukee, Detroit, Cleveland, Buffalo and others—was figured out in Canada by the Southerners and Northern allies. President Lincoln, in his message to Congress in December, 1864, said the United States had given notice to England that, at the end of six months, this country would, if necessary, increase its naval armament upon the lakes. What Great Britain feared was the abrogation by the United States of all treaties regarding Canada. By previous stipulation, the United States and England were each to have but one war vessel on the Great Lakes.

Saw Himself Dead

This story cannot be repeated in Lincoln's own language, although he told it often enough to intimate friends; but, as it was never taken down by a stenographer in the martyred President's exact words, the reader must accept a simple narration of the strange occurrence.

It was not long after the first nomination of Lincoln for the Presidency, when he saw, or imagined he saw, the startling apparition. One day, feeling weary, he threw himself upon a lounge in one of the rooms of his house at Springfield to rest. Opposite the lounge upon which he was lying was a large, long mirror, and he could easily see the reflection of his form, full length.

Suddenly he saw, or imagined he saw, two Lincolns in the mirror, each lying full length upon the lounge, but they differed strangely in appearance. One was the natural Lincoln, full of life, vigor, energy and strength; the other was a dead Lincoln, the face white as marble, the limbs nerveless and lifeless, the body inert and still.

Lincoln was so impressed with this vision, which he considered merely an optical illusion, that he arose, put on his hat, and went out for a walk. Returning to the house, he determined to test the matter again—and the result was the same as before. He distinctly saw the two Lincolns—one living and the other dead.

He said nothing to his wife about this, she being, at that time, in a nervous condition, and apprehensive that some accident would surely befall her husband. She was particularly fearful that he might be the victim of an assassin. Lincoln always made light of her fears, but yet he was never easy in his mind afterwards.

To more thoroughly test the so-called "optical illusion," and prove, beyond the shadow of a doubt, whether it was a mere fanciful creation of the brain or a reflection upon the broad face of the mirror which might be seen at any time, Lincoln made frequent experiments. Each and every time the result was the same. He could not get away from the two Lincolns—one living and the other dead.

Lincoln never saw this forbidding reflection while in the White House. Time after time he placed a couch in front of a mirror at a distance from the glass where he could view his entire length while lying down, but the looking-glass in the Executive Mansion was faithful to its trust, and only the living Lincoln was observable.

The late Ward Lamon, once a law partner of Lincoln, and Marshal of the District of Columbia during his first administration, tells, in his "Recollections of Abraham Lincoln," of the dreams the President had—all foretelling death.

Lamon was Lincoln's most intimate friend, being, practically, his bodyguard, and slept in the White House. In reference to Lincoln's "death dreams," he says:

"How, it may be asked, could he make life tolerable, burdened as he was with that portentous horror, which, though visionary, and of trifling import in our eyes, was by his interpretation a premonition of impending doom? I answer in a word: His sense of duty to his country; his belief that 'the inevitable' is right; and his innate and irrepressible humor.

"But the most startling incident in the life of Mr. Lincoln was a dream he had only a few days before his assassination. To him it was a thing of deadly import, and certainly no vision was ever fashioned more exactly like a dread reality. Coupled with other dreams, with the mirror-scene and with other incidents, there was something about it so amazingly real, so true to the actual tragedy which occurred soon after, that more than mortal strength and wisdom would have been required to let it pass without a shudder or a pang.

"After worrying over it for some days, Mr. Lincoln seemed no longer able to keep the secret. I give it as nearly in his own words as I can, from notes which I made immediately after its recital. There were only two or three persons present.

"The President was in a melancholy, meditative mood, and had been silent for some time. Mrs. Lincoln, who was present, rallied him on his solemn visage and want of spirit. This seemed to arouse him, and, without seeming to notice her sally, he said, in slow and measured tones:

"'It seems strange how much there is in the Bible about dreams. There are, I think, some sixteen chapters in the Old Testament and four or five in the New, in which dreams are mentioned; and there are many other passages scattered throughout the book which refer to visions. In the old days, God and His angels came to men in their sleep and made themselves known in dreams.'

"Mrs. Lincoln here remarked, 'Why, you look dreadfully solemn; do you believe in dreams?'

"'I can't say that I do,' returned Mr. Lincoln; 'but I had one the other night which has haunted me ever since. After it occurred the first time, I opened the Bible, and, strange as it may appear, it was at the twenty-eighth chapter of Genesis, which relates the wonderful dream Jacob had. I turned to other passages, and seemed to encounter a dream or a vision wherever I looked. I kept on turning the leaves of the old book, and everywhere my eyes fell upon passages recording matters strangely in keeping with my own thoughts—supernatural visitations, dreams, visions, etc.'

"He now looked so serious and disturbed that Mrs. Lincoln exclaimed 'You frighten me! What is the matter?'

"'I am afraid,' said Mr. Lincoln, observing the effect his words had upon his wife, 'that I have done wrong to mention the subject at all; but somehow the thing has got possession of me, and, like Banquo's ghost, it will not down.'

"This only inflamed Mrs. Lincoln's curiosity the more, and while bravely disclaiming any belief in dreams, she strongly urged him to tell the dream which seemed to have such a hold upon him, being seconded in this by another listener. Mr. Lincoln hesitated, but at length commenced very deliberately, his brow overcast with a shade of melancholy.

"'About ten days ago,' said he, 'I retired very late. I had been up waiting for important dispatches from the front. I could not have been long in bed when I fell into a slumber, for I was weary. I soon began to dream. There seemed to be a deathlike stillness about me. Then I heard subdued sobs, as if a number of people were weeping.

"'I thought I left my bed and wandered down-stairs. There the silence was broken by the same pitiful sobbing, but the mourners were invisible. I went from room to room; no living person was in sight, but the same mournful sounds of distress met me as I passed along. It was light in all the rooms; every object was familiar to me; but where were all the people who were grieving as if their hearts would break? I was puzzled and alarmed. What could be the meaning of all this?

"'Determined to find the cause of a state of things so mysterious and so shocking, I kept on until I arrived at the East Room, which I entered. There I met with a sickening surprise. Before me was a catafalque, on which rested a corpse wrapped in funeral vestments. Around it were stationed soldiers who were acting as guards; and there was a throng of people, some gazing mournfully upon the corpse, whose face was covered, others weeping pitifully.

"'"Who is dead in the White House?" I demanded of one of the soldiers.

"'"The President," was his answer; "he was killed by an assassin."

"'Then came a loud burst of grief from the crowd, which awoke me from my dream. I slept no more that night; and although it was only a dream, I have been strangely annoyed by it ever since.'

"'That is horrid!' said Mrs. Lincoln. 'I wish you had not told it. I am glad I don't believe in dreams, or I should be in terror from this time forth.'

"'Well,' responded Mr. Lincoln, thoughtfully, 'it is only a dream, Mary. Let us say no more about it, and try to forget it.'

"This dream was so horrible, so real, and so in keeping with other dreams and threatening presentiments of his, that Mr. Lincoln was profoundly disturbed by it. During its recital he was grave, gloomy, and at times visibly pale, but perfectly calm. He spoke slowly, with measured accents and deep feeling.

"In conversations with me, he referred to it afterwards, closing one with this quotation from 'Hamlet': 'To sleep; perchance to dream! ay, there's the rub!' with a strong accent upon the last three words.

"Once the President alluded to this terrible dream with some show of playful humor. 'Hill,' said he, 'your apprehension of harm to me from some hidden enemy is downright foolishness. For a long time you have been trying to keep somebody-the Lord knows who—from killing me.

"'Don't you see how it will turn out? In this dream it was not me, but some other fellow, that was killed. It seems that this ghostly assassin tried his hand on someone else. And this reminds me of an old farmer in Illinois whose family were made sick by eating greens.

"'Some poisonous herb had got into the mess, and members of the family were in danger of dying. There was a half-witted boy in the family called Jake; and always afterward when they had greens the old man would say, "Now, afore we risk these greens, let's try 'em on Jake. If he stands 'em we're all right." Just so with me. As long as this imaginary assassin continues to exercise himself on others, I can stand it.'

"He then became serious and said: 'Well, let it go. I think the Lord in His own good time and way will work this out all right. God knows what is best.'

"These words he spoke with a sigh, and rather in a tone of soliloquy, as if hardly noting my presence.

"Mr. Lincoln had another remarkable dream, which was repeated so frequently during his occupancy of the White House that he came to regard it is a welcome visitor. It was of a pleasing and promising character, having nothing in it of the horrible.

"It was always an omen of a Union victory, and came with unerring certainty just before every military or naval engagement where our arms were crowned with success. In this dream he saw a ship sailing away rapidly, badly damaged, and our victorious vessels in close pursuit.

"He saw, also, the close of a battle on land, the enemy routed, and our forces in possession of vantage ground of inestimable importance. Mr. Lincoln stated it as a fact that he had this dream just before the battles of Antietam, Gettysburg, and other signal engagements throughout the War.

"The last time Mr. Lincoln had this dream was the night before his assassination. On the morning of that lamentable day there was a Cabinet meeting, at which General Grant was present. During an interval of general discussion, the President asked General Grant if he had any news from General Sherman, who was then confronting Johnston. The reply was in the negative, but the general added that he was in hourly expectation of a dispatch announcing Johnston's surrender.

"Mr. Lincoln then, with great impressiveness, said, 'We shall hear very soon, and the news will be important.'

"General Grant asked him why he thought so.

"'Because,' said Mr. Lincoln, 'I had a dream last night; and ever since this War began I have had the same dream just before every event of great national importance. It portends some important event which will happen very soon.'

"On the night of the fateful 14th of April, 1865, Mrs. Lincoln's first exclamation, after the President was shot, was, 'His dream was prophetic!'

"Lincoln was a believer in certain phases of the supernatural. Assured as he undoubtedly was by omens which, to his mind, were conclusive, that he would rise to greatness and power, he was as firmly convinced by the same tokens that he would be suddenly cut off at the height of his career and the fullness of his fame. He always believed that he would fall by the hand of an assassin.

"Mr. Lincoln had this further idea: Dreams, being natural occurrences, in the strictest sense, he held that their best interpreters are the common people; and this accounts, in great measure, for the profound respect he always had for the collective wisdom of plain people—'the children of Nature,' he called them—touching matters belonging to the domain of psychical mysteries. There was some basis of truth, he believed, for whatever obtained general credence among these 'children of Nature.'

"Concerning presentiments and dreams, Mr. Lincoln had a philosophy of his own, which, strange as it may appear, was in perfect harmony with his character in all other respects. He was no dabbler in divination—astrology, horoscopy, prophecy, ghostly lore, or witcheries of any sort."

Every Little Helped

As the time drew near at which Mr. Lincoln said he would issue the Emancipation Proclamation, some clergymen, who feared the President might change his mind, called on him to urge him to keep his promise.

"We were ushered into the Cabinet room," says Dr. Sunderland. "It was very dim, but one gas jet burning. As we entered, Mr. Lincoln was standing at the farther end of the long table, which filled the center of the room. As I stood by the door, I am so very short, that I was obliged to look up to see the President. Mr. Robbins introduced me, and I began at once by saying: 'I have come, Mr. President, to anticipate the new year with my respects, and if I may, to say to you a word about the serious condition of this country.'

"'Go ahead, Doctor,' replied the President; 'every little helps.' But I was too much in earnest to laugh at his sally at my smallness."

About to Lay Down the Burden

President Lincoln (at times) said he felt sure his life would end with the War. A correspondent of a Boston paper had an interview with him in July, 1864, and wrote regarding it:

"The President told me he was certain he should not outlast the rebellion. As will be remembered, there was dissension then among the Republican leaders. Many of his best friends had deserted him, and were talking of an opposition convention to nominate another candidate, and universal gloom was among the people.

"The North was tired of the War, and supposed an honorable peace attainable. Mr. Lincoln knew it was not—that any peace at that time would be only disunion. Speaking of it, he said: 'I have faith in the people. They will not consent to disunion. The danger is, they are misled. Let them know the truth, and the country is safe.'

"He looked haggard and careworn; and further on in the interview I remarked on his appearance, 'You are wearing yourself out with work.'

"'I can't work less,' he answered; 'but it isn't that—work never troubled me. Things look badly, and I can't avoid anxiety. Personally, I care nothing about a re-election, but if our divisions defeat us, I fear for the country.'

"When I suggested that right must eventually triumph, he replied, 'I grant that, but I may never live to see it. I feel a presentiment that I shall not outlast the rebellion. When it is over, my work will be done.'

"He never intimated, however, that he expected to be assassinated."

Lincoln Would Have Preferred Death

Horace Greeley said, some time after the death of President Lincoln:

"After the Civil War began, Lincoln's tenacity of purpose paralleled his former immobility; I believe he would have been nearly the last, if not the very last, man in America to recognize the Southern Confederacy had its armies been triumphant. He would have preferred death."

"Punch" and His Little Picture

London "Punch" was not satisfied with anything President Lincoln did. On December 3rd, 1864, after Mr. Lincoln's re-election to the Presidency, a cartoon appeared in one of the pages of that genial publication. Labeled "The Federal Phoenix," it attracted great attention at the time, and was particularly pleasing to the enemies of the United States, as it showed Lincoln as the Phoenix arising from the ashes of the Federal Constitution, the Public Credit, the Freedom of the Press, State Rights and the Commerce of the North American Republic.

President Lincoln's endorsement by the people of the United States meant that the Confederacy was to be crushed, no matter what the cost; that the Union of States was to be preserved, and that State Rights was a thing of the past. "Punch" wished to create the impression that President Lincoln's re-election was a personal victory; that he would set up a despotism, with himself at its head, and trample upon the Constitution of the United States and all the rights the citizens of the Republic ever possessed.

The result showed that "Punch" was suffering from an acute attack of needless alarm.

Fascinated by the Wonderful

Lincoln was particularly fascinated by the wonderful happenings recorded in history. He loved to read of those mighty events which had been foretold, and often brooded upon these subjects. His early convictions upon occult matters led him to read all books tending' to strengthen these convictions.

The following lines, in Byron's "Dream," were frequently quoted by him:

> *"Sleep hath its own world,*
> *A boundary between the things misnamed*
> *Death and existence: Sleep hath its own world*
> *And a wide realm of wild reality.*
> *And dreams in their development have breath,*
> *And tears and tortures, and the touch of joy;*
> *They leave a weight upon our waking thoughts,*
> *They take a weight from off our waking toils,*
> *They do divide our being."*

Those with whom he was associated in his early youth and young manhood, and with whom he was always in cordial sympathy, were thorough believers in presentiments and dreams; and so Lincoln drifted on through years of toil and exceptional hardship—meditative, aspiring, certain of his star, but appalled at times by its malignant aspect. Many times prior to his first election to the Presidency he was both elated and alarmed by what seemed to him a rent in the veil which hides from mortal view what the future holds.

He saw, or thought he saw, a vision of glory and of blood, himself the central figure in a scene which his fancy transformed from giddy enchantment to the most appalling tragedy.

"Why Don't They Come!"

The suspense of the days when the capital was isolated, the expected troops not arriving, and an hourly attack feared, wore on Mr. Lincoln greatly.

"I begin to believe," he said bitterly, one day, to some Massachusetts soldiers, "that there is no North. The Seventh Regiment is a myth. Rhode Island is another. You are the only real thing."

And again, after pacing the floor of his deserted office for a half-hour, he was heard to exclaim to himself, in an anguished tone: "Why don't they come! Why don't they come!"

Grant's Brand of Whiskey

Lincoln was not a man of impulse, and did nothing upon the spur of the moment; action with him was the result of deliberation and study. He took nothing for granted; he judged men by their performances and not their speech.

If a general lost battles, Lincoln lost confidence in him; if a commander was successful, Lincoln put him where he would be of the most service to the country.

"Grant is a drunkard," asserted powerful and influential politicians to the President at the White House time after time; "he is not himself half the time; he can't be relied upon, and it is a shame to have such a man in command of an army."

"So Grant gets drunk, does he?" queried Lincoln, addressing himself to one of the particularly active detractors of the soldier, who, at that period, was inflicting heavy damage upon the Confederates.

"Yes, he does, and I can prove it," was the reply.

"Well," returned Lincoln, with the faintest suspicion of a twinkle in his eye, "you needn't waste your time getting proof; you just find out, to oblige me, what brand of whiskey Grant drinks, because I want to send a barrel of it to each one of my generals."

That ended the crusade against Grant, so far as the question of drinking was concerned.

His Financial Standing

A New York firm applied to Abraham Lincoln, some years before he became President, for information as to the financial standing of one of his neighbors. Mr. Lincoln replied:

"I am well acquainted with Mr. —— and know his circumstances. First of all, he has a wife and baby; together they ought to be worth $50,000 to any man. Secondly, he has an office in which there is a table worth $1.50 and three chairs worth, say, $1. Last of all, there is in one corner a large rat hole, which will bear looking into. Respectfully, A. Lincoln."

The Dandy and the Boys

President Lincoln appointed as consul to a South American country a young man from Ohio who was a dandy. A wag met the new appointee on his way to the White House to thank the President. He was dressed in the most extravagant style. The wag horrified him by telling him that the country to which he was assigned was noted chiefly for the bugs that abounded there and made life unbearable.

"They'll bore a hole clean through you before a week has passed," was the comforting assurance of the wag as they parted at the White House steps. The new consul approached Lincoln with disappointment clearly written all over his face. Instead of joyously thanking the President, he told him the wag's story of the bugs. "I am informed, Mr. President," he said, "that the place is full of vermin and that they could eat me up in a week's time." "Well, young man," replied Lincoln, "if that's true, all I've got to say is that if such a thing happened they would leave a mighty good suit of clothes behind."

"Some Ugly Old Lawyer"

A. W. Swan, of Albuquerque, New Mexico, told this story on Lincoln, being an eyewitness of the scene:

"One day President Lincoln was met in the park between the White House and the War Department by an irate private soldier, who was swearing in a high key, cursing the Government from the President down. Mr. Lincoln paused and asked him what was the matter. 'Matter enough,' was the reply. 'I want my money. I have been discharged here, and can't get my pay.' Mr. Lincoln asked if he had his papers, saying that he used to practice law in a small way, and possibly could help him.

"My friend and I stepped behind some convenient shrubbery where we could watch the result. Mr. Lincoln took the papers from the hands of the crippled soldier, and sat down with him at the foot of a convenient tree, where he examined them carefully, and writing a line on the back, told the soldier to take them to Mr. Potts, Chief Clerk of the War Department, who would doubtless attend to the matter at once.

"After Mr. Lincoln had left the soldier, we stepped out and asked him if he knew whom he had been talking with. 'Some ugly old fellow who pretends to be a lawyer,' was the reply. My companion asked to see the papers, and on their being handed to him, pointed to the indorsement they had received: This indorsement read:

"'Mr. Potts, attend to this man's case at once and see that he gets his pay. A. L.'"

Good Memory of Names

The following story illustrates the power of Mr. Lincoln's memory of names and faces. When he was a comparatively young man, and a candidate for the Illinois Legislature, he made a personal canvass of the district. While "swinging around the circle" he stopped one day and took dinner with a farmer in Sangamon county.

Years afterward, when Mr. Lincoln had become President, a soldier came to call on him at the White House. At the first glance the Chief Executive said: "Yes, I remember; you used to live on the Danville road. I took dinner with you when I was running for the Legislature. I recollect that we stood talking out at the barnyard gate while I sharpened my jackknife."

"Y-a-a-s," drawled the soldier, "you did. But say, wherever did you put that whetstone? I looked for it a dozen times, but I never could find it after the day you used it. We allowed as how mabby you took it 'long with you."

"No," said Lincoln, looking serious and pushing away a lot of documents of state from the desk in front of him. "No, I put it on top of that gatepost—that high one."

"Well!" exclaimed the visitor, "mabby you did. Couldn't anybody else have put it there, and none of us ever thought of looking there for it."

The soldier was then on his way home, and when he got there the first thing he did was to look for the whetstone. And sure enough, there it was, just where Lincoln had laid it fifteen years before. The honest fellow wrote a letter to the Chief Magistrate, telling him that the whetstone had been found, and would never be lost again.

Settled Out of Court

When Abe Lincoln used to be drifting around the country, practicing law in Fulton and Menard counties, Illinois, an old fellow met him going to Lewiston, riding a horse which, while it was a serviceable enough animal, was not of the kind to be truthfully called a fine saddler. It was a weatherbeaten nag, patient and plodding, and it toiled along with Abe—and Abe's books, tucked away in saddlebags, lay heavy on the horse's flank.

"Hello, Uncle Tommy," said Abe.

"Hello, Abe," responded Uncle Tommy. "I'm powerful glad to see ye, Abe, fer I'm gwyne to have sumthin' fer ye at Lewiston co't, I reckon."

"How's that, Uncle Tommy?" said Abe.

"Well, Jim Adams, his land runs 'long o' mine, he's pesterin' me a heap an' I got to get the law on Jim, I reckon."

"Uncle Tommy, you haven't had any fights with Jim, have you?"

"No."

"He's a fair to middling neighbor, isn't he?"

"Only tollable, Abe."

"He's been a neighbor of yours for a long time, hasn't he?"

"Nigh on to fifteen year."

"Part of the time you get along all right, don't you?"

"I reckon we do, Abe."

"Well, now, Uncle Tommy, you see this horse of mine? He isn't as good a horse as I could straddle, and I sometimes get out of patience with him, but I know his faults. He does fairly well as horses go, and it might take me a long time to get used to some other horse's faults. For all horses have faults. You and Uncle Jimmy must put up with each other as I and my horse do with one another."

"I reckon, Abe," said Uncle Tommy, as he bit off about four ounces of Missouri plug. "I reckon you're about right."

And Abe Lincoln, with a smile on his gaunt face, rode on toward Lewiston.

The Five Points Sunday School

When Mr. Lincoln visited New York in 1860, he felt a great interest in many of the institutions for reforming criminals and saving the young from a life of crime. Among others, he visited, unattended, the Five Points House of Industry, and the superintendent of the Sabbath school there gave the following account of the event:

"One Sunday morning I saw a tall, remarkable-looking man enter the room and take a seat among us. He listened with fixed attention to our exercises, and his countenance expressed such genuine interest that I approached him and suggested that he might be willing to say something to the children. He accepted the invitation with evident pleasure, and coming forward began a simple address, which at once fascinated every little hearer and hushed the room into silence. His language was strikingly beautiful, and his tones musical with intense feeling. The little faces would droop into sad conviction when he uttered sentences of warning, and would brighten into sunshine as he spoke cheerful words of promise. Once or twice he attempted to close his remarks, but the imperative shout of, 'Go on! Oh, do go on!' would compel him to resume.

"As I looked upon the gaunt and sinewy frame of the stranger, and marked his powerful head and determined features, now touched into softness by the impressions of the moment, I felt an irrepressible curiosity to learn something more about him, and while he was quietly leaving the room, I begged to know his name. He courteously replied: 'It is Abraham Lincoln, from Illinois.'"

Sentinel Obeyed Orders

A slight variation of the traditional sentry story is related by C. C. Buel. It was a cold, blusterous winter night. Says Mr. Buel:

"Mr. Lincoln emerged from the front door, his lank figure bent over as he drew tightly about his shoulders the shawl which he employed for such protection; for he was on his way to the War Department, at the west corner of the grounds, where in times of battle he was wont to get the midnight dispatches from the field. As the blast struck him he thought of the numbness of the pacing sentry, and, turning to him, said: 'Young man, you've got a cold job to-night; step inside, and stand guard there.'

"'My orders keep me out here,' the soldier replied.

"'Yes,' said the President, in his argumentative tone; 'but your duty can be performed just as well inside as out here, and you'll oblige me by going in.'

"'I have been stationed outside,' the soldier answered, and resumed his beat.

"'Hold on there!' said Mr. Lincoln, as he turned back again; 'it occurs to me that I am Commander-in-Chief of the army, and I order you to go inside.'"

Why Lincoln Growed Whiskers

Perhaps the majority of people in the United States don't know why Lincoln "growed" whiskers after his first nomination for the Presidency. Before that time his face was clean shaven.

In the beautiful village of Westfield, Chautauqua county, New York, there lived, in 1860, little Grace Bedell. During the campaign of that year she saw a portrait of Lincoln, for whom she felt the love and reverence that was common in Republican families, and his smooth, homely face rather disappointed her. She said to her mother: "I think, mother, that Mr. Lincoln would look better if he wore whiskers, and I mean to write and tell him so."

The mother gave her permission.

Grace's father was a Republican; her two brothers were Democrats. Grace wrote at once to the "Hon. Abraham Lincoln, Esq., Springfield, Illinois," in which she told him how old she was, and where she lived; that she was a Republican; that she thought he would make a good President, but would look better if he would let his whiskers grow. If he would do so, she would try to coax her brothers to vote for him. She thought the rail fence around the picture of his cabin was very pretty. "If you have not time to answer my letter, will you allow your little girl to reply for you?"

Lincoln was much pleased with the letter, and decided to answer it, which he did at once, as follows:

"Springfield, Illinois, October 19, 1860.

"Miss Grace Bedell.

"My Dear Little Miss: Your very agreeable letter of the fifteenth is received. I regret the necessity of saying I have no daughter. I have three sons; one seventeen, one nine and one seven years of age. They, with their mother, constitute my whole family. As to the whiskers, having never worn any, do you not think people would call it a piece of silly affectation if I should begin it now? Your very sincere well-wisher, A. LINCOLN."

When on the journey to Washington to be inaugurated, Lincoln's train stopped at Westfield. He recollected his little correspondent and spoke of her to ex-Lieutenant Governor George W. Patterson, who called out and asked if Grace Bedell was present.

There was a large surging mass of people gathered about the train, but Grace was discovered at a distance; the crowd opened a pathway to the coach, and she came, timidly but gladly, to the President-elect, who told her that she might see that he had allowed his whiskers to grow at her request. Then, reaching out his long arms, he drew her up to him and kissed her. The act drew an enthusiastic demonstration of approval from the multitude.

Grace married a Kansas banker, and became Grace Bedell Billings.

Lincoln as a Dancer

Lincoln made his first appearance in society when he was first sent to Springfield, Ill., as a member of the State Legislature. It was not an imposing figure which he cut in a ballroom, but still he was occasionally to be found there. Miss Mary Todd, who afterward became his wife, was the magnet which drew the tall, awkward young man from his den. One evening Lincoln approached Miss Todd, and said, in his peculiar idiom:

"Miss Todd, I should like to dance with you the worst way." The young woman accepted the inevitable, and hobbled around the room with him. When she returned to her seat, one of her companions asked mischievously:

"Well, Mary, did he dance with you the worst way."

"Yes," she answered, "the very worst."

Simply Practical Humanity

An instance of young Lincoln's practical humanity at an early period of his life is recorded in this way:

One evening, while returning from a "raising" in his wide neighborhood, with a number of companions, he discovered a stray horse, with saddle and bridle upon him. The horse was recognized as belonging to a man who was accustomed to get drunk, and it was suspected at once that he was not far off. A short search only was necessary to confirm the belief.

The poor drunkard was found in a perfectly helpless condition, upon the chilly ground. Abraham's companions urged the cowardly policy of leaving him to his fate, but young Lincoln would not hear to the proposition.

At his request, the miserable sot was lifted on his shoulders, and he actually carried him eighty rods to the nearest house.

Sending word to his father that he should not be back that night, with the reason for his absence, he attended and nursed the man until the morning, and had the pleasure of believing that he had saved his life.

Happy Figures of Speech

On one occasion, exasperated at the discrepancy between the aggregate of troops forwarded to McClellan and the number that same general reported as having received, Lincoln exclaimed: "Sending men to that army is like shoveling fleas across a barnyard—half of them never get there."

To a politician who had criticised his course, he wrote: "Would you have me drop the War where it is, or would you prosecute it in future with elder stalk squirts charged with rosewater?"

When, on his first arrival in Washington as President, he found himself besieged by office-seekers, while the War was breaking out, he said: "I feel like a man letting lodgings at one end of his house while the other end is on fire."

A Few "Rhythmic Shots"

Ward Lamon, Marshal of the District of Columbia during Lincoln's time in Washington, accompanied the President everywhere. He was a good singer, and, when Lincoln was in one of his melancholy moods, would "fire a few rhythmic shots" at the President to cheer the latter. Lincoln keenly relished nonsense in the shape of witty or comic ditties. A parody of "A Life on the Ocean Wave" was always pleasing to him:

> *"Oh, a life on the ocean wave,*

> *And a home on the rolling deep!*
> *With ratlins fried three times a day*
> *And a leaky old berth for to sleep;*
> *Where the gray-beard cockroach roams,*
> *On thoughts of kind intent,*
> *And the raving bedbug comes*
> *The road the cockroach went."*

Lincoln could not control his laughter when he heard songs of this sort.

He was fond of negro melodies, too, and "The Blue-Tailed Fly" was a great favorite with him. He often called for that buzzing ballad when he and Lamon were alone, and he wanted to throw off the weight of public and private cares. The ballad of "The Blue-Tailed Fly" contained two verses, which ran:

> *"When I was young I used to wait*
> *At massa's table, 'n' hand de plate,*
> *An' pass de bottle when he was dry,*
> *An' brush away de blue-tailed fly.*
> *"Ol' Massa's dead; oh, let him rest!*
> *Dey say all things am for de best;*
> *But I can't forget until I die*
> *Ol' massa an' de blue-tailed fly."*

While humorous songs delighted the President, he also loved to listen to patriotic airs and ballads containing sentiment. He was fond of hearing "The Sword of Bunker Hill," "Ben Bolt," and "The Lament of the Irish Emigrant." His preference of the verses in the latter was this:

> *"I'm lonely now, Mary,*
> *For the poor make no new friends;*
> *But, oh, they love the better still*
> *The few our Father sends!*
> *And you were all I had, Mary,*
> *My blessing and my pride;*

There's nothing left to care for now,
Since my poor Mary died."

Those who knew Lincoln were well aware he was incapable of
so monstrous an act as that of wantonly insulting the dead, as was
charged in the infamous libel which asserted that he listened to a
comic song on the field of Antietam, before the dead were buried.

Old Man Glenn's Religion

Mr. Lincoln once remarked to a friend that his religion was like
that of an old man named Glenn, in Indiana, whom he heard speak
at a church meeting, and who said: "When I do good, I feel good;
when I do bad, I feel bad; and that's my religion."

Mrs. Lincoln herself has said that Mr. Lincoln had no faith—no
faith, in the usual acceptance of those words. "He never joined a
church; but still, as I believe, he was a religious man by nature. He
first seemed to think about the subject when our boy Willie died,
and then more than ever about the time he went to Gettysburg; but
it was a kind of poetry in his nature, and he never was a technical
Christian."

Last Acts of Mercy

During the afternoon preceding his assassination the President
signed a pardon for a soldier sentenced to be shot for desertion,
remarking as he did so, "Well, I think the boy can do us more good
above ground than under ground."

He also approved an application for the discharge, on taking the
oath of allegiance, of a rebel prisoner, in whose petition he wrote,
"Let it be done."

This act of mercy was his last official order.

Just Like Seward

The first corps of the army commanded by General Reynolds was once reviewed by the President on a beautiful plain at the north of Potomac Creek, about eight miles from Hooker's headquarters. The party rode thither in an ambulance over a rough corduroy road, and as they passed over some of the more difficult portions of the jolting way the ambulance driver, who sat well in front, occasionally let fly a volley of suppressed oaths at his wild team of six mules.

Finally, Mr. Lincoln, leaning forward, touched the man on the shoulder and said,

"Excuse me, my friend, are you an Episcopalian?"

The man, greatly startled, looked around and replied:

"No, Mr. President; I am a Methodist."

"Well," said Lincoln, "I thought you must be an Episcopalian, because you swear just like Governor Seward, who is a church warder."

A Cheerful Prospect

The first night after the departure of President-elect Lincoln from Springfield, on his way to Washington, was spent in Indianapolis. Governor Yates, O. H. Browning, Jesse K. Dubois, O. M. Hatch, Josiah Allen, of Indiana, and others, after taking leave of Mr. Lincoln to return to their respective homes, took Ward Lamon into a room, locked the door, and proceeded in the most solemn and impressive manner to instruct him as to his duties as the special guardian of Mr. Lincoln's person during the rest of his journey to Washington. Lamon tells the story as follows:

"The lesson was concluded by Uncle Jesse, as Mr. Dubois was commonly, called, who said:

"'Now, Lamon, we have regarded you as the Tom Hyer of Illinois, with Morrissey attachment. We intrust the sacred life of Mr. Lincoln to your keeping; and if you don't protect it, never return to Illinois, for we will murder you on sight.'"

Thought God Would Have Told Him

Professor Jonathan Baldwin Turner was one of the few men to whom Mr. Lincoln confided his intention to issue the Proclamation of Emancipation.

Mr. Lincoln told his Illinois friend of the visit of a delegation to him who claimed to have a message from God that the War would not be successful without the freeing of the negroes, to whom Mr. Lincoln replied: "Is it not a little strange that He should tell this to you, who have so little to do with it, and should not have told me, who has a great deal to do with it?"

At the same time he informed Professor Turner he had his Proclamation in his pocket.

Lincoln and a Bible Hero

A writer who heard Mr. Lincoln's famous speech delivered in New York after his nomination for President has left this record of the event:

"When Lincoln rose to speak, I was greatly disappointed. He was tall, tall, oh, so tall, and so angular and awkward that I had for an instant a feeling of pity for so ungainly a man. He began in a low tone of voice, as if he were used to speaking out of doors and was afraid of speaking too loud.

"He said 'Mr. Cheerman,' instead of 'Mr. Chairman,' and employed many other words with an old-fashioned pronunciation. I said to myself, 'Old fellow, you won't do; it is all very well for the Wild West, but this will never go down in New York.' But pretty soon he began to get into the subject; he straightened up, made regular and graceful gestures; his face lighted as with an inward fire; the whole man was transfigured.

"I forgot the clothing, his personal appearance, and his individual peculiarities. Presently, forgetting myself, I was on my feet with the rest, yelling like a wild Indian, cheering the wonderful man. In the close parts of his argument you could hear the gentle sizzling of the gas burners.

"When he reached a climax the thunders of applause were terrific. It was a great speech. When I came out of the hall my face was glowing with excitement and my frame all a-quiver. A friend, with his eyes aglow, asked me what I thought of 'Abe' Lincoln, the rail-splitter. I said, 'He's the greatest man since St. Paul.' And I think so yet."

Boy Was Cared for

President Lincoln one day noticed a small, pale, delicate-looking boy, about thirteen years old, among the number in the White House antechamber.

The President saw him standing there, looking so feeble and faint, and said: "Come here, my boy, and tell me what you want."

The boy advanced, placed his hand on the arm of the President's chair, and, with a bowed head and timid accents, said: "Mr. President, I have been a drummer boy in a regiment for two years, and my colonel got angry with me and turned me off. I was taken sick and have been a long time in the hospital."

The President discovered that the boy had no home, no father—he had died in the army—no mother.

"I have no father, no mother, no brothers, no sisters, and," bursting into tears, "no friends—nobody cares for me."

Lincoln's eyes filled with tears, and the boy's heart was soon made glad by a request to certain officials "to care for this poor boy."

The Jury Acquitted Him

One of the most noted murder cases in which Lincoln defended the accused was tried in August, 1859. The victim, Crafton, was a student in his own law office, the defendant, "Peachy" Harrison, was a grandson of Rev. Peter Cartwright; both were connected with the best families in the county; they were brothers in law, and had always been friends.

Senator John M. Palmer and General John A. McClelland were on the side of the prosecution. Among those who represented the defendant were Lincoln and Senator Shelby M. Cullom. The two young men had engaged in a political quarrel, and Crafton was stabbed to death by Harrison. The tragic pathos of a case which involved the deepest affections of almost an entire community reached its climax in the appearance in court of the venerable Peter Cartwright. Lincoln had beaten him for Congress in 1846.

Eccentric and aggressive as he was, he was honored far and wide; and when he arose to take the witness stand, his white hair crowned with this cruel sorrow, the most indifferent spectator felt that his examination would be unbearable.

It fell to Lincoln to question Cartwright. With the rarest gentleness he began to put his questions.

"How long have you known the prisoner?"

Cartwright's head dropped on his breast for a moment; then straightening himself, he passed his hand across his eyes and answered in a deep, quavering voice:

"I have known him since a babe, he laughed and cried on my knee."

The examination ended by Lincoln drawing from the witness the story of how Crafton had said to him, just before his death: "I am dying; I will soon part with all I love on earth, and I want you to say to my slayer that I forgive him. I want to leave this earth with a forgiveness of all who have in any way injured me."

This examination made a profound impression on the jury. Lincoln closed his argument by picturing the scene anew, appealing to the jury to practice the same forgiving spirit that the murdered man had shown on his death-bed. It was undoubtedly to his handling of the grandfather's evidence that Harrison's acquittal was due.

Took Nothing but Money

During the War Congress appropriated $10,000 to be expended by the President in defending United States Marshals in cases of arrests and seizures where the legality of their actions was tested in the courts. Previously the Marshals sought the assistance of the Attorney-General in defending them, but when they found that the President had a fund for that purpose they sought to control the money.

In speaking of these Marshals one day, Mr. Lincoln said:

"They are like a man in Illinois, whose cabin was burned down, and, according to the kindly custom of early days in the West, his neighbors all contributed something to start him again. In his case they had been so liberal that he soon found himself better off than before the fire, and he got proud. One day a neighbor brought him a bag of oats, but the fellow refused it with scorn.

"'No,' said he, 'I'm not taking oats now. I take nothing but money.'"

Naughty Boy Had to Take His Medicine

The resistance to the military draft of 1863 by the City of New York, the result of which was the killing of several thousand persons, was illustrated on August 29th, 1863, by "Frank Leslie's Illustrated Newspaper," over the title of "The Naughty Boy, Gotham, Who Would Not Take the Draft." Beneath was also the text:

MAMMY LINCOLN: "There now, you bad boy, acting that way, when your little sister Penn (State of Pennsylvania) takes hers like a lady!"

Horatio Seymour was then Governor of New York, and a prominent "the War is a failure" advocate. He was in Albany, the State capital, when the riots broke out in the City of New York, July 13th, and after the mob had burned the Colored Orphan Asylum and killed several hundred negroes, came to the city. He had only soft words for the rioters, promising them that the draft should be suspended. Then the Government sent several regiments of veterans, fresh from the field of Gettysburg, where they had assisted in defeating Lee.

These troops made short work of the brutal ruffians, shooting down three thousand or so of them, and the rioting was subdued. The "Naughty Boy Gotham" had to take his medicine, after all, but as the spirit of opposition to the War was still rampant, the President issued a proclamation suspending the writ of habeas corpus in all the States of the Union where the Government had control. This had a quieting effect upon those who were doing what they could in obstructing the Government.

Would Blow Them to H——

Mr. Lincoln had advised Lieutenant-General Winfield Scott, commanding the United States Army, of the threats of violence on inauguration day, 1861. General Scott was sick in bed at Washington when Adjutant-General Thomas Mather, of Illinois, called upon him in President-elect Lincoln's behalf, and the veteran commander was much wrought up. Said he to General Mather:

"Present my compliments to Mr. Lincoln when you return to Springfield, and tell him I expect him to come on to Washington as soon as he is ready; say to him that I will look after those Maryland and Virginia rangers myself. I will plant cannon at both ends of Pennsylvania avenue, and if any of them show their heads or raise a finger, I'll blow them to h——."

"Yankee" Goodness of Heart

One day, when the President was with the troops who were fighting at the front, the wounded, both Union and Confederate, began to pour in.

As one stretcher was passing Lincoln, he heard the voice of a lad calling to his mother in agonizing tones. His great heart filled. He forgot the crisis of the hour. Stopping the carriers, he knelt, and bending over him, asked: "What can I do for you, my poor child?"

"Oh, you will do nothing for me," he replied. "You are a Yankee. I cannot hope that my message to my mother will ever reach her."

Lincoln, in tears, his voice full of tenderest love, convinced the boy of his sincerity, and he gave his good-bye words without reserve.

The President directed them copied, and ordered that they be sent that night, with a flag of truce, into the enemy's lines.

Walked as He Talked

When Mr. Lincoln made his famous humorous speech in Congress ridiculing General Cass, he began to speak from notes, but, as he warmed up, he left his desk and his notes, to stride down the alley toward the Speaker's chair.

Occasionally, as he would complete a sentence amid shouts of laughter, he would return up the alley to his desk, consult his notes, take a sip of water and start off again.

Mr. Lincoln received many congratulations at the close, Democrats joining the Whigs in their complimentary comments.

One Democrat, however (who had been nicknamed "Sausage" Sawyer), didn't enthuse at all.

"Sawyer," asked an Eastern Representative, "how did you like the lanky Illinoisan's speech? Very able, wasn't it?"

"Well," replied Sawyer, "the speech was pretty good, but I hope he won't charge mileage on his travels while delivering it."

The Song Did the Business

The Virginia (Ill.) Enquirer, of March 1, 1879, tells this story:

"John McNamer was buried last Sunday, near Petersburg, Menard county. A long while ago he was Assessor and Treasurer of the County for several successive terms. Mr. McNamer was an early settler in that section, and, before the town of Petersburg was laid out, in business in Old Salem, a village that existed many years ago two miles south of the present site of Petersburg.

"'Abe' Lincoln was then postmaster of the place and sold whisky to its inhabitants. There are old-timers yet living in Menard who bought many a jug of corn-juice from 'Old Abe' when he lived at

Salem. It was here that Anne Rutledge dwelt, and in whose grave Lincoln wrote that his heart was buried.

"As the story runs, the fair and gentle Anne was originally John McNamer's sweetheart, but 'Abe' took a 'shine' to the young lady, and succeeded in heading off McNamer and won her affections. But Anne Rutledge died, and Lincoln went to Springfield, where he some time afterwards married.

"It is related that during the War a lady belonging to a prominent Kentucky family visited Washington to beg for her son's pardon, who was then in prison under sentence of death for belonging to a band of guerrillas who had committed many murders and outrages.

"With the mother was her daughter, a beautiful young lady, who was an accomplished musician. Mr. Lincoln received the visitors in his usual kind manner, and the mother made known the object of her visit, accompanying her plea with tears and sobs and all the customary romantic incidents.

"There were probably extenuating circumstances in favor of the young rebel prisoner, and while the President seemed to be deeply pondering the young lady moved to a piano near by and taking a seat commenced to sing 'Gentle Annie,' a very sweet and pathetic ballad which, before the War, was a familiar song in almost every household in the Union, and is not yet entirely forgotten, for that matter.

"It is to be presumed that the young lady sang the song with more plaintiveness and effect than 'Old Abe' had ever heard it in Springfield. During its rendition, he arose from his seat, crossed the room to a window in the westward, through which he gazed for several minutes with a 'sad, far-away look,' which has so often been noted as one of his peculiarities.

"His memory, no doubt, went back to the days of his humble life on the Sangamon, and with visions of Old Salem and its rustic people, who once gathered in his primitive store, came a picture of the 'Gentle Annie' of his youth, whose ashes had rested for many long years under the wild flowers and brambles of the old rural burying-ground, but whose spirit then, perhaps, guided him to the side of mercy.

"Be that as it may, President Lincoln drew a large red silk handkerchief from his coatpocket, with which he wiped his face vigorously. Then he turned, advanced quickly to his desk, wrote a brief note, which he handed to the lady, and informed her that it was the pardon she sought.

"The scene was no doubt touching in a great degree and proves that a nice song, well sung, has often a powerful influence in recalling tender recollections. It proves, also, that Abraham Lincoln was a man of fine feelings, and that, if the occurrence was a put-up job on the lady's part, it accomplished the purpose all the same."

A "Free for All"

Lincoln made a political speech at Pappsville, Illinois, when a candidate for the Legislature the first time. A free-for-all fight began soon after the opening of the meeting, and Lincoln, noticing one of his friends about to succumb to the energetic attack of an infuriated ruffian, edged his way through the crowd, and, seizing the bully by the neck and the seat of his trousers, threw him, by means of his strength and long arms, as one witness stoutly insists, "twelve feet away." Returning to the stand, and throwing aside his hat, he inaugurated his campaign with the following brief but pertinent declaration:

"Fellow-citizens, I presume you all know who I am. I am humble Abraham Lincoln. I have been solicited by many friends to become a candidate for the Legislature. My politics are short and sweet, like the old woman's dance. I am in favor of the national bank; I am in favor of the internal improvement system and a high protective tariff. These are my sentiments; if elected, I shall be thankful; if not, it will be all the same."

Three Infernal Bores

One day, when President Lincoln was alone and busily engaged on an important subject, involving vexation and anxiety, he was disturbed by the unwarranted intrusion of three men, who, without apology, proceeded to lay their claim before him.

The spokesman of the three reminded the President that they were the owners of some torpedo or other warlike invention which, if the government would only adopt it, would soon crush the rebellion.

"Now," said the spokesman, "we have been here to see you time and again; you have referred us to the Secretary of War, the Chief of Ordnance, and the General of the Army, and they give us no satisfaction. We have been kept here waiting, till money and patience are exhausted, and we now come to demand of you a final reply to our application."

Mr. Lincoln listened to this insolent tirade, and at its close the old twinkle came into his eye.

"You three gentlemen remind me of a story I once heard," said he, "of a poor little boy out West who had lost his mother. His father wanted to give him a religious education, and so placed him in the family of a clergyman, whom he directed to instruct the little fellow carefully in the Scriptures. Every day the boy had to commit to memory and recite one chapter of the Bible. Things proceeded smoothly until they reached that chapter which details the story of the trial of Shadrach, Meshach and Abednego in the fiery furnace. When asked to repeat these three names the boy said he had forgotten them.

"His teacher told him that he must learn them, and gave him another day to do so. The next day the boy again forgot them.

"'Now,' said the teacher, 'you have again failed to remember those names and you can go no farther until you have learned them. I will give you another day on this lesson, and if you don't repeat the names I will punish you.'

"A third time the boy came to recite, and got down to the stumbling block, when the clergyman said: 'Now tell me the names of the men in the fiery furnace.'

"'Oh,' said the boy, 'here come those three infernal bores! I wish the devil had them!'"

Having received their "final answer," the three patriots retired, and at the Cabinet meeting which followed, the President, in high good humor, related how he had dismissed his unwelcome visitors.

Lincoln's Men Were "Hustlers"

In the Chicago Convention of 1860 the fight for Seward was maintained with desperate resolve until the final ballot was taken. Thurlow Weed was the Seward leader, and he was simply incomparable as a master in handling a convention. With him were Governor Morgan, Henry J. Raymond, of the New York Times, with William M. Evarts as chairman of the New York delegation, whose speech nominating Seward was the most impressive utterance of his life. The Bates men (Bates was afterwards Lincoln's Attorney-General) were led by Frank Blair, the only Republican Congressman from a slave State, who was nothing if not heroic, aided by his brother Montgomery (afterwards Lincoln's Postmaster General), who was a politician of uncommon cunning. With them was Horace Greeley, who was chairman of the delegation from the then almost inaccessible State of Oregon.

It was Lincoln's friends, however, who were the "hustlers" of that battle. They had men for sober counsel like David Davis; men of supreme sagacity like Leonard Swett; men of tireless effort like Norman B. Judd; and they had what was more important than all—a seething multitude wild with enthusiasm for "Old Abe."

A Slow Horse

On one occasion when Mr. Lincoln was going to attend a political convention one of his rivals, a liveryman, provided him with a slow horse, hoping that he would not reach his destination in time. Mr. Lincoln got there, however, and when he returned with the horse he said: "You keep this horse for funerals, don't you?" "Oh, no," replied the liveryman. "Well, I'm glad of that, for if you did you'd never get a corpse to the grave in time for the resurrection."

Dodging "Browsing Presidents"

General McClellan, after being put in command of the Army, resented any "interference" by the President. Lincoln, in his anxiety to know the details of the work in the army, went frequently to Mc-Clellan's headquarters. That the President had a serious purpose in these visits McClellan did not see.

"I enclose a card just received from 'A. Lincoln,'" he wrote to his wife one day; "it shows too much deference to be seen outside."

In another letter to Mrs. McClellan he spoke of being "interrupted" by the President and Secretary Seward, "who had nothing in particular to say," and again of concealing himself "to dodge all enemies in shape of 'browsing' Presidents," etc.

"I am becoming daily more disgusted with this Administration— perfectly sick of it," he wrote early in October; and a few days later, "I was obliged to attend a meeting of the Cabinet at 8 P. M., and was bored and annoyed. There are some of the greatest geese in the Cabinet I have ever seen—enough to tax the patience of Job."

A Greenback Legend

At a Cabinet meeting once, the advisability of putting a legend on greenbacks similar to the In God We Trust legend on the silver coins was discussed, and the President was asked what his view was. He replied: "If you are going to put a legend on the greenback, I would suggest that of Peter and Paul: 'Silver and gold we have not, but what we have we'll give you.'"

God's Best Gift to Man

One of Mr. Lincoln's notable religious utterances was his reply to a deputation of colored people at Baltimore who presented him a Bible. He said:

"In regard to the great book, I have only to say it is the best gift which God has ever given man. All the good from the Savior of the world is communicated to us through this book. But for this book we could not know right from wrong. All those things desirable to man are contained in it."

Scalping in the Black Hawk War

When Lincoln was President he told this story of the Black Hawk War:

The only time he ever saw blood in this campaign, was one morning when, marching up a little valley that makes into the Rock River bottom, to reinforce a squad of outposts that were thought to be in danger, they came upon the tent occupied by the other party just at sunrise. The men had neglected to place any guard at night, and had been slaughtered in their sleep.

As the reinforcing party came up the slope on which the camp had been made, Lincoln saw them all lying with their heads towards the rising sun, and the round red spot that marked where they had been scalped gleamed more redly yet in the ruddy light of the sun. This scene years afterwards he recalled with a shudder.

Matrimonial Advice

For a while during the Civil War, General Fremont was without a command. One day in discussing Fremont's case with George W. Julian, President Lincoln said he did not know where to place him, and that it reminds him of the old man who advised his son to take a wife, to which the young man responded: "All right; whose wife shall I take?"

Owed Lots of Money

On April 14, 1865, a few hours previous to his assassination, President Lincoln sent a message by Congressman Schuyler Colfax, Vice-President during General Grant's first term, to the miners in the

Rocky Mountains and the regions bounded by the Pacific ocean, in which he said:

"Now that the Rebellion is overthrown, and we know pretty nearly the amount of our National debt, the more gold and silver we mine, we make the payment of that debt so much easier.

"Now I am going to encourage that in every possible way. We shall have hundreds of thousands of disbanded soldiers, and many have feared that their return home in such great numbers might paralyze industry by furnishing, suddenly, a greater supply of labor than there will be demand for. I am going to try to attract them to the hidden wealth of our mountain ranges, where there is room enough for all. Immigration, which even the War has not stopped, will land upon our shores hundreds of thousands more per year from overcrowded Europe. I intend to point them to the gold and silver that wait for them in the West.

"Tell the miners for me that I shall promote their interests to the utmost of my ability; because their prosperity as the prosperity of the nation; and," said he, his eye kindling with enthusiasm, "we shall prove, in a very few years, that we are indeed the treasury of the world."

"on the Lord's Side"

President Lincoln made a significant remark to a clergyman in the early days of the War.

"Let us have faith, Mr. President," said the minister, "that the Lord is on our side in this great struggle."

Mr. Lincoln quietly answered: "I am not at all concerned about that, for I know that the Lord is always on the side of the right; but it is my constant anxiety and prayer that I and this nation may be on the Lord's side."

Wanted to Be Near "Abe"

It was Lincoln's custom to hold an informal reception once a week, each caller taking his turn.

Upon one of these eventful days an old friend from Illinois stood in line for almost an hour. At last he was so near the President his voice could reach him, and, calling out to his old associate, he startled everyone by exclaiming, "Hallo, 'Abe'; how are ye? I'm in line and hev come for an orfice, too."

Lincoln singled out the man with the stentorian voice, and recognizing a particularly old friend, one whose wife had befriended him at a peculiarly trying time, the President responded to his greeting in a cordial manner, and told him "to hang onto himself and not kick the traces. Keep in line and you'll soon get here."

They met and shook hands with the old fervor and renewed their friendship.

The informal reception over, Lincoln sent for his old friend, and the latter began to urge his claims.

After having given him some good advice, Lincoln kindly told him he was incapable of holding any such position as he asked for. The disappointment of the Illinois friend was plainly shown, and with a perceptible tremor in his voice he said, "Martha's dead, the gal is married, and I've guv Jim the forty."

Then looking at Lincoln he came a little nearer and almost whispered, "I knowed I wasn't eddicated enough to git the place, but I kinder want to stay where I ken see 'Abe' Lincoln."

He was given employment in the White House grounds.

Afterwards the President said, "These brief interviews, stripped of even the semblance of ceremony, give me a better insight into the real character of the person and his true reason for seeking one."

Got His Foot in It

William H. Seward, idol of the Republicans of the East, six months after Lincoln had made his "Divided House" speech, delivered an address at Rochester, New York, containing this famous sentence:

"It is an irrepressible conflict between opposing and enduring forces, and it means that the United States must, and will, sooner or later, become either entirely a slave-holding nation, or entirely a free-labor nation."

Seward, who had simply followed in Lincoln's steps, was defeated for the Presidential nomination at the Republican National Convention of 1860, because he was "too radical," and Lincoln, who was still "radicaler," was named.

Saved by a Letter

The chief interest of the Illinois campaign of 1843 lay in the race for Congress in the Capital district, which was between Hardin—fiery, eloquent, and impetuous Democrat—and Lincoln—plain, practical, and ennobled Whig. The world knows the result. Lincoln was elected.

It is not so much his election as the manner in which he secured his nomination with which we have to deal. Before that ever-memorable spring Lincoln vacillated between the courts of Springfield, rated as a plain, honest, logical Whig, with no ambition higher politically than to occupy some good home office.

Late in the fall of 1842 his name began to be mentioned in connection with Congressional aspirations, which fact greatly annoyed the leaders of his political party, who had already selected as the Whig candidate E. D. Baker, afterward the gallant Colonel who fell so bravely and died such an honorable death on the battlefield of Ball's Bluff.

Despite all efforts of his opponents within his party, the name of the "gaunt rail-splitter" was hailed with acclaim by the masses, to whom he had endeared himself by his witticisms, honest tongue, and quaint philosophy when on the stump, or mingling with them in their homes.

The convention, which met in early spring, in the city of Springfield, was to be composed of the usual number of delegates. The contest for the nomination was spirited and exciting.

A few weeks before the meeting of the convention the fact was found by the leaders that the advantage lay with Lincoln, and that unless they pulled some very fine wires nothing could save Baker.

They attempted to play the game that has so often won, by "convincing" delegates under instructions for Lincoln to violate them, and vote for Baker. They had apparently succeeded.

"The best laid plans of mice and men gang aft agley." So it was in this case. Two days before the convention Lincoln received an intimation of this, and, late at night, wrote the following letter.

The letter was addressed to Martin Morris, who resided at Petersburg, an intimate friend of his, and by him circulated among those who were instructed for him at the county convention.

It had the desired effect. The convention met, the scheme of the conspirators miscarried, Lincoln was nominated, made a vigorous canvass, and was triumphantly elected, thus paving the way for his more extended and brilliant conquests.

This letter, Lincoln had often told his friends, gave him ultimately the Chief Magistracy of the nation. He has also said, that, had he been beaten before the convention, he would have been forever obscured. The following is a verbatim copy of the epistle:

"April 14, 1843.

"Friend Morris: I have heard it intimated that Baker is trying to get you or Miles, or both of you, to violate the instructions of the meeting that appointed you, and to go for him. I have insisted, and still insist, that this cannot be true.

"Sure Baker would not do the like. As well might Hardin ask me to vote for him in the convention.

"Again, it is said there will be an attempt to get instructions in your county requiring you to go for Baker. This is all wrong. Upon the same rule, why might I not fly from the decision against me at Sangamon and get up instructions to their delegates to go for me.

There are at least 1,200 Whigs in the county that took no part, and yet I would as soon stick my head in the fire as attempt it.

"Besides, if any one should get the nomination by such extraordinary means, all harmony in the district would inevitably be lost. Honest Whigs (and very nearly all of them are honest) would not quietly abide such enormities.

"I repeat, such an attempt on Baker's part cannot be true. Write me at Springfield how the matter is. Don't show or speak of this letter.

"A. LINCOLN."

Mr. Morris did show the letter, and Mr. Lincoln always thanked his stars that he did.

His Favorite Poem

Mr. Lincoln's favorite poem was "Oh! Why Should the Spirit of Mortal Be Proud?" written by William Knox, a Scotchman, although Mr. Lincoln never knew the author's name. He once said to a friend:

"This poem has been a great favorite with me for years. It was first shown to me, when a young man, by a friend. I afterward saw it and cut it from a newspaper and learned it by heart. I would give a great deal to know who wrote it, but I have never been able to ascertain."

> "Oh! why should the spirit of mortal be proud?—
> Like a swift-fleeing meteor, a fast-flying cloud,
> A flash of the lightning, a break of the wave,
> He passeth from life to his rest in the grave.
>
> "The leaves of the oak and the willow shall fade,
> Be scattered around, and together be laid;
> And the young and the old, and the low and the
>   high,
> Shall moulder to dust, and together shall lie.
>
> "The infant a mother attended and loved;
> The mother, that infant's affection who proved,
> The husband, that mother and infant who blessed
> —Each, all, are away to their dwellings of rest.

"The maid on whose cheek, on whose brow, in
    whose eye,
Shone beauty and pleasure—her triumphs are by;
And the memory of those who loved her and
    praised,
Are alike from the minds of the living erased.

"The hand of the king, that the sceptre hath borne,
The brow of the priest, that the mitre hath worn,
The eye of the sage, and the heart of the brave,
Are hidden and lost in the depths of the grave.

"The peasant, whose lot was to sow and to reap,
The herdsman, who climbed with his goats up the
    steep;
The beggar, who wandered in search of his bread,
Have faded away like the grass that we tread.

"The saint, who enjoyed the communion of heaven,
The sinner, who dared to remain unforgiven;
The wise and the foolish, the guilty and just,
Have quietly mingled their bones in the dust.

"So the multitude goes—like the flower or the weed
That withers away to let others succeed;
So the multitude comes—even those we behold,
To repeat every tale that has often been told:

"For we are the same our fathers have been;
We see the same sights our fathers have seen;
We drink the same stream, we view the same sun,
And run the same course our fathers have run.

"The thoughts we are thinking, our fathers would
    think;
From the death we are shrinking, our fathers
    would shrink;
To the life we are clinging, they also would cling
—But it speeds from us all like a bird on the wing.

"They loved—but the story we cannot unfold;

They scorned—but the heart of the haughty is cold;
They grieved—but no wail from their slumber will
        come;
They joyed—but the tongue of their gladness is
        dumb.

"They died—aye, they died—and we things that
        are now,
That walk on the turf that lies o'er their brow,
And make in their dwellings a transient abode,
Meet the things that they met on their pilgrimage
        road.

"Yea! hope and despondency, pleasure and pain,
Are mingled together in sunshine and rain;
And the smile and the tear, the song and the dirge,
Still follow each other, like surge upon surge.

"'Tis the wink of an eye,—' tis the draught of a
        breath;
—From the blossom of health to the paleness of
        death,
From the gilded saloon to the bier and the shroud:
—Oh! why should the spirit of mortal be proud?"

Five-Legged Calf

President Lincoln had great doubt as to his right to emancipate the slaves under the War power. In discussing the question, he used to liken the case to that of the boy who, when asked how many legs his calf would have if he called its tail a leg, replied, "five," to which the prompt response was made that calling the tail a leg would not make it a leg.

A Stage-Coach Story

The following is told by Thomas H. Nelson, of Terre Haute, Indiana, who was appointed minister to Chili by Lincoln:

Judge Abram Hammond, afterwards Governor of Indiana, and myself arranged to go from Terre Haute to Indianapolis in a stage-coach.

As we stepped in we discovered that the entire back seat was occupied by a long, lank individual, whose head seemed to protrude from one end of the coach and his feet from the other. He was the sole occupant, and was sleeping soundly. Hammond slapped him familiarly on the shoulder, and asked him if he had chartered the coach that day.

"Certainly not," and he at once took the front seat, politely giving us the place of honor and comfort. An odd-looking fellow he was, with a twenty-five cent hat, without vest or cravat. Regarding him as a good subject for merriment, we perpetrated several jokes.

He took them all with utmost innocence and good nature, and joined in the laugh, although at his own expense.

After an astounding display of wordy pyrotechnics, the dazed and bewildered stranger asked, "What will be the upshot of this comet business?"

Late in the evening we reached Indianapolis, and hurried to Browning's hotel, losing sight of the stranger altogether.

We retired to our room to brush our clothes. In a few minutes I descended to the portico, and there descried our long, gloomy fellow traveler in the center of an admiring group of lawyers, among whom were Judges McLean and Huntington, Albert S. White, and Richard W. Thompson, who seemed to be amused and interested in a story he was telling. I inquired of Browning, the landlord, who he was. "Abraham Lincoln, of Illinois, a member of Congress," was his response.

I was thunderstruck at the announcement. I hastened upstairs and told Hammond the startling news, and together we emerged from the hotel by a back door, and went down an alley to another house, thus avoiding further contact with our distinguished fellow traveler.

Years afterward, when the President-elect was on his way to

Washington, I was in the same hotel looking over the distinguished party, when a long arm reached to my shoulder, and a shrill voice exclaimed, "Hello, Nelson! do you think, after all, the whole world is going to follow the darned thing off?" The words were my own in answer to his question in the stage-coach. The speaker was Abraham Lincoln.

The "400" Gathered There

Lincoln had periods while "clerking" in the New Salem grocery store during which there was nothing for him to do, and was therefore in circumstances that made laziness almost inevitable. Had people come to him for goods, they would have found him willing to sell them. He sold all that he could, doubtless.

The store soon became the social center of the village. If the people did not care (or were unable) to buy goods, they liked to go where they could talk with their neighbors and listen to stories. These Lincoln gave them in abundance, and of a rare sort.

It was in these gatherings of the "Four Hundred" at the village store that Lincoln got his training as a debater. Public questions were discussed there daily and nightly, and Lincoln always took a prominent part in the discussions. Many of the debaters came to consider "Abe Linkin" as about the smartest man in the village.

Only Level-Headed Men Wanted

Lincoln wanted men of level heads for important commands. Not infrequently he gave his generals advice.

He appreciated Hooker's bravery, dash and activity, but was fearful of the results of what he denominated "swashing around."

This was one of his telegrams to Hooker:

"And now, beware of rashness; beware of rashness, but, with energy and sleepless vigilance, go forward and give us victories."

His Faith in the Monitor

When the Confederate iron-clad Merrimac was sent against the Union vessels in Hampton Roads President Lincoln expressed his belief in the Monitor to Captain Fox, the adviser of Captain Ericsson, who constructed the Monitor. "We have three of the most effective vessels in Hampton Roads, and any number of small craft that will hang on the stern of the Merrimac like small dogs on the haunches of a bear. They may not be able to tear her down, but they will interfere with the comfort of her voyage. Her trial trip will not be a pleasure trip, I am certain.

"We have had a big share of bad luck already, but I do not believe the future has any such misfortunes in store for us as you anticipate." Said Captain Fox: "If the Merrimac does not sink our ships, who is to prevent her from dropping her anchor in the Potomac, where that steamer lies," pointing to a steamer at anchor below the long bridge, "and throwing her hundred-pound shells into this room, or battering down the walls of the Capitol?"

"The Almighty, Captain," answered the President, excitedly, but without the least affectation. "I expect set-backs, defeats; we have had them and shall have them. They are common to all wars. But I have not the slightest fear of any result which shall fatally impair our military and naval strength, or give other powers any right to interfere in our quarrel. The destruction of the Capitol would do both.

"I do not fear it, for this is God's fight, and He will win it in His own good time. He will take care that our enemies will not push us too far.

"Speaking of iron-clads," said the President, "you do not seem to take the little Monitor into account. I believe in the Monitor and her commander. If Captain Worden does not give a good account of the Monitor and of himself, I shall have made a mistake in following my judgment for the first time since I have been here, Captain.

"I have not made a mistake in following my clear judgment of men since this War began. I followed that judgment when I gave Worden the command of the Monitor. I would make the appointment over again to-day. The Monitor should be in Hampton Roads now. She left New York eight days ago."

After the captain had again presented what he considered the possibilities of failure the President replied, "No, no, Captain, I respect your judgments as you have reason to know, but this time you are all wrong.

"The Monitor was one of my inspirations; I believed in her firmly when that energetic contractor first showed me Ericsson's plans. Captain Ericsson's plain but rather enthusiastic demonstration made my conversion permanent. It was called a floating battery then; I called it a raft. I caught some of the inventor's enthusiasm and it has been growing upon me. I thought then, and I am confident now, it is just what we want. I am sure that the Monitor is still afloat, and that she will yet give a good account of herself. Sometimes I think she may be the veritable sling with a stone that will yet smite the Merrimac Philistine in the forehead."

Soon was the President's judgment verified, for the "Fight of the Monitor and Merrimac" changed all the conditions of naval warfare.

After the victory was gained, the presiding Captain Fox and others went on board the Monitor, and Captain Worden was requested by the President to narrate the history of the encounter.

Captain Worden did so in a modest manner, and apologized for not being able better to provide for his guests. The President smilingly responded "Some charitable people say that old Bourbon is an indispensable element in the fighting qualities of some of our generals in the field, but, Captain, after the account that we have heard to-day, no one will say that any Dutch courage is needed on board the Monitor."

"It never has been, sir," modestly observed the captain.

Captain Fox then gave a description of what he saw of the engagement and described it as indescribably grand. Then, turning to the President, he continued, "Now standing here on the deck of this battle-scarred vessel, the first genuine iron-clad—the victor in the first fight of iron-clads—let me make a confession, and perform an act of simple justice.

"I never fully believed in armored vessels until I saw this battle.

"I know all the facts which united to give us the Monitor. I withhold no credit from Captain Ericsson, her inventor, but I know that the country is principally indebted for the construction of the vessel to President Lincoln, and for the success of her trial to Captain Worden, her commander."

Her Only Imperfection

At one time a certain Major Hill charged Lincoln with making defamatory remarks regarding Mrs. Hill.

Hill was insulting in his language to Lincoln who never lost his temper.

When he saw his chance to edge a word in, Lincoln denied emphatically using the language or anything like that attributed to him.

He entertained, he insisted, a high regard for Mrs. Hill, and the only thing he knew to her discredit was the fact that she was Major Hill's wife.

The Old Lady's Prophecy

Among those who called to congratulate Mr. Lincoln upon his nomination for President was an old lady, very plainly dressed. She knew Mr. Lincoln, but Mr. Lincoln did not at first recognize her. Then she undertook to recall to his memory certain incidents connected with his ride upon the circuit—especially his dining at her house upon the road at different times. Then he remembered her and her home.

Having fixed her own place in his recollection, she tried to recall to him a certain scanty dinner of bread and milk that he once ate at her house. He could not remember it—on the contrary, he only remembered that he had always fared well at her house.

"Well," she said, "one day you came along after we had got through dinner, and we had eaten up everything, and I could give you nothing but a bowl of bread and milk, and you ate it; and when you got up you said it was good enough for the President of the United States!"

The good woman had come in from the country, making a journey of eight or ten miles, to relate to Mr. Lincoln this incident, which, in her mind, had doubtless taken the form of a prophecy. Mr. Lincoln placed the honest creature at her ease, chatted with her of old times, and dismissed her in the most happy frame of mind.

How the Town of Lincoln, Ill., Was Named

The story of naming the town of Lincoln, the county seat of Logan county, Illinois, is thus given on good authority:

The first railroad had been built through the county, and a station was about to be located there. Lincoln, Virgil Hitchcock, Colonel R. B. Latham and several others were sitting on a pile of ties and talking about moving a county seat from Mount Pulaski. Mr. Lincoln rose and started to walk away, when Colonel Latham said: "Lincoln, if you will help us to get the county seat here, we will call the place Lincoln."

"All right, Latham," he replied.

Colonel Latham then deeded him a lot on the west side of the courthouse, and he owned it at the time he was elected President.

"Old Jeff's" Big Nightmare

"Jeff" Davis had a large and threatening nightmare in November, 1864, and what he saw in his troubled dreams was the long and lanky figure of Abraham Lincoln, who had just been endorsed by the people of the United States for another term in the White House at Washington. A cartoon from the issue of "Frank Leslie's Illustrated Newspaper" of December 3rd, 1864, depicted the scene, entitled "Jeff Davis' November Nightmare."

Davis had been told that McClellan, "the War is a failure" candidate for the Presidency, would have no difficulty whatever in defeating Lincoln; that negotiations with the Confederate officials for the cessation of hostilities would be entered into as soon as McClellan was seated in the Chief Executive's chair; that the Confederacy would, in all probability, be recognized as an independent government by the Washington Administration; that the "sacred institution" of slavery would continue to do business at the old stand; that the Confederacy would be one of the great nations of the world, and have all the "State Rights" and other things it wanted, with absolutely no interference whatever upon the part of the North.

Therefore, Lincoln's re-election was a rough, rude shock to Davis, who had not prepared himself for such an event. Six months from the date of that nightmare-dream he was a prisoner in the hands of the Union forces, and the Confederacy was a thing of the past.

Lincoln's Last Official Act

Probably the last official act of President Lincoln's life was the signing of the commission reappointing Alvin Saunders Governor of Nebraska.

"I saw Mr. Lincoln regarding the matter," said Governor Saunders, "and he told me to go home; that he would attend to it all right. I left Washington on the morning of the 14th, and while en route the news of the assassination on the evening of the same day reached me. I immediately wired back to find out what had become of my commission, and was told that the room had not been opened. When it was opened, the document was found lying on the desk.

"Mr. Lincoln signed it just before leaving for the theater that fatal evening, and left it lying there, unfolded.

"A note was found below the document as follows: 'Rather a lengthy commission, bestowing upon Mr. Alvin Saunders the official authority of Governor of the Territory of Nebraska.' Then came Lincoln's signature, which, with one exception, that of a penciled message on the back of a card sent up by a friend as Mr. Lincoln was dressing for the theater, was the very last signature of the martyred President."

The Lad Needed the Sleep

A personal friend of President Lincoln is authority for this:

"I called on him one day in the early part of the War. He had just written a pardon for a young man who had been sentenced to be shot for sleeping at his post. He remarked as he read it to me:

"'I could not think of going into eternity with the blood of the poor young man on my skirts.' Then he added:

"'It is not to be wondered at that a boy, raised on a farm, probably in the habit of going to bed at dark, should, when required to watch, fall asleep; and I cannot consent to shoot him for such an act.'"

"Massa Linkum Like De Lord!"

By the Act of Emancipation President Lincoln built for himself forever the first place in the affections of the African race in this country. The love and reverence manifested for him by many of these people has, on some occasions, almost reached adoration. One day Colonel McKaye, of New York, who had been one of a committee to investigate the condition of the freedmen, upon his return from Hilton Head and Beaufort called upon the President, and in the course of the interview said that up to the time of the arrival among them in the South of the Union forces they had no knowledge of any other power. Their masters fled upon the approach of our soldiers, and this gave the slaves the conception of a power greater than their masters exercised. This power they called "Massa Linkum."

Colonel McKaye said their place of worship was a large building they called "the praise house," and the leader of the "meeting," a venerable black man, was known as "the praise man."

On a certain day, when there was quite a large gathering of the people, considerable confusion was created by different persons attempting to tell who and what "Massa Linkum" was. In the midst of the excitement the white-headed leader commanded silence. "Brederen," said he, "you don't know nosen' what you'se talkin' 'bout. Now, you just listen to me. Massa Linkum, he ebery whar. He know ebery ting."

Then, solemnly looking up, he added: "He walk de earf like de Lord!"

How Lincoln Took the News

One of Lincoln's most dearly loved friends, United States Senator Edward D. Baker, of Oregon, Colonel of the Seventy-first Pennsylvania, a former townsman of Mr. Lincoln, was killed at the battle of Ball's Bluff, in October, 1861. The President went to General McClellan's headquarters to hear the news, and a friend thus described the effect it had upon him:

"We could hear the click of the telegraph in the adjoining room and low conversation between the President and General McClellan, succeeded by silence, excepting the click, click of the instrument, which went on with its tale of disaster.

"Five minutes passed, and then Mr. Lincoln, unattended, with bowed head and tears rolling down his furrowed cheeks, his face pale and wan, his breast heaving with emotion, passed through the room. He almost fell as he stepped into the street. We sprang involuntarily from our seats to render assistance, but he did not fall.

"With both hands pressed upon his heart, he walked down the street, not returning the salute of the sentinel pacing his beat before the door."

Profanity as a Safety-Valve

Lincoln never indulged in profanity, but confessed that when Lee was beaten at Malvern Hill, after seven days of fighting, and Richmond, but twelve miles away, was at McClellan's mercy, he felt very much like swearing when he learned that the Union general had retired to Harrison's Landing.

Lee was so confident his opponent would not go to Richmond that he took his army into Maryland—a move he would not have made had an energetic fighting man been in McClellan's place.

It is true McClellan followed and defeated Lee in the bloodiest battle of the War—Antietam—afterwards following him into Virginia; but Lincoln could not bring himself to forgive the general's inaction before Richmond.

Why We Won at Gettysburg

President Lincoln said to General Sickles, just after the victory of Gettysburg: "The fact is, General, in the stress and pinch of the campaign there, I went to my room, and got down on my knees and prayed God Almighty for victory at Gettysburg. I told Him that this was His country, and the war was His war, but that we really couldn't stand another Fredericksburg or Chancellorsville. And then and there I made a solemn vow with my Maker that if He would stand by you boys at Gettysburg I would stand by Him. And He did, and I will! And after this I felt that God Almighty had taken the whole thing into His hands."

Had to Wait for Him

President Lincoln, having arranged to go to New York, was late for his train, much to the disgust of those who were to accompany him, and all were compelled to wait several hours until the next train steamed out of the station. President Lincoln was much amused at the dissatisfaction displayed, and then ventured the remark that the situation reminded him of "a little story." Said he:

"Out in Illinois, a convict who had murdered his cellmate was sentenced to be hanged. On the day set for the execution, crowds lined the roads leading to the spot where the scaffold had been erected, and there was much jostling and excitement. The condemned man took matters coolly, and as one batch of perspiring, anxious men rushed past the cart in which he was riding, he called out, 'Don't be in a hurry, boys. You've got plenty of time. There won't be any fun until I get there.'

"That's the condition of things now," concluded the President; "there won't be any fun at New York until I get there."

President and Cabinet Joined in Prayer

On the day the news of General Lee's surrender at Appomattox Court-House was received, so an intimate friend of President Lincoln relates, the Cabinet meeting was held an hour earlier than usual. Neither the President nor any member of the Cabinet was able, for a time, to give utterance to his feelings. At the suggestion of Mr. Lincoln all dropped on their knees, and offered, in silence and in tears, their humble and heartfelt acknowledgments to the Almighty for the triumph He had granted to the National cause.

Believed He Was a Christian

Mr. Lincoln was much impressed with the devotion and earnestness of purpose manifested by a certain lady of the "Christian Commission" during the War, and on one occasion, after she had discharged the object of her visit, said to her:

"Madam, I have formed a high opinion of your Christian character, and now, as we are alone, I have a mind to ask you to give me in brief your idea of what constitutes a true religious experience."

The lady replied at some length, stating that, in her judgment, it consisted of a conviction of one's own sinfulness and weakness, and a personal need of the Saviour for strength and support; that views of mere doctrine might and would differ, but when one was really brought to feel his need of divine help, and to seek the aid of the Holy Spirit for strength and guidance, it was satisfactory evidence of his having been born again. This was the substance of her reply.

When she had, concluded Mr. Lincoln was very thoughtful for a few moments. He at length said, very earnestly: "If what you have told me is really a correct view of this great subject I think I can say with sincerity that I hope I am a Christian. I had lived," he continued, "until my boy Willie died without fully realizing these things. That blow overwhelmed me. It showed me my weakness as I had never felt it before, and if I can take what you have stated as a test I think I can safely say that I know something of that change of which you speak; and I will further add that it has been my intention for some time, at a suitable opportunity, to make a public religious profession."

With the Help of God

Mr. Lincoln once remarked to Mr. Noah Brooks, one of his most intimate personal friends: "I should be the most presumptuous blockhead upon this footstool if I for one day thought that I could discharge the duties which have come upon me, since I came to this place, without the aid and enlightenment of One who is stronger and wiser than all others."

He said on another occasion: "I am very sure that if I do not go away from here a wiser man, I shall go away a better man, from having learned here what a very poor sort of a man I am."

Turned Tears to Smiles

One night Schuyler Colfax left all other business to go to the White House to ask the President to respite the son of a constituent, who was sentenced to be shot, at Davenport, for desertion. Mr. Lincoln heard the story with his usual patience, though he was wearied out with incessant calls, and anxious for rest, and then replied:

"Some of our generals complain that I impair discipline and subordination in the army by my pardons and respites, but it makes me rested, after a hard day's work, if I can find some good excuse for saving a man's life, and I go to bed happy as I think how joyous the signing of my name will make him and his family and his friends."

And with a happy smile beaming over that care-furrowed face, he signed that name that saved that life.

Lincoln's Last Written Words

As the President and Mrs. Lincoln were leaving the White House, a few minutes before eight o'clock, on the evening of April 14th, 1865, Lincoln wrote this note:

"Allow Mr. Ashmun and friend to come to see me at 9 o'clock a. m., to-morrow, April 15th, 1865."

Women Plead for Pardons

One day during the War an attractively and handsomely dressed woman called on President Lincoln to procure the release from prison of a relation in whom she professed the deepest interest.

She was a good talker, and her winning ways seemed to make a deep impression on the President. After listening to her story, he wrote a few words on a card: "This woman, dear Stanton, is a little smarter than she looks to be," enclosed it in an envelope and directed her to take it to the Secretary of War.

On the same day another woman called, more humble in appearance, more plainly clad. It was the old story.

Father and son both in the army, the former in prison. Could not the latter be discharged from the army and sent home to help his mother?

A few strokes of the pen, a gentle nod of the head, and the little woman, her eyes filling with tears and expressing a grateful acknowledgment her tongue, could not utter, passed out.

A lady so thankful for the release of her husband was in the act of kneeling in thankfulness. "Get up," he said, "don't kneel to me, but thank God and go."

An old lady for the same reason came forward with tears in her eyes to express her gratitude. "Good-bye, Mr. Lincoln," said she; "I shall probably never see you again till we meet in heaven." She had the President's hand in hers, and he was deeply moved. He instantly took her right hand in both of his, and, following her to the door, said, "I am afraid with all my troubles I shall never get to the resting-place you speak of; but if I do, I am sure I shall find you. That you wish me to get there is, I believe, the best wish you could make for me. Good-bye."

Then the President remarked to a friend, "It is more than many can often say, that in doing right one has made two people happy in one day. Speed, die when I may, I want it said of me by those who know me best, that I have always plucked a thistle and planted a flower when I thought a flower would grow."

Lincoln Wished to See Richmond

The President remarked to Admiral David D. Porter, while on board the flagship Malvern, on the James River, in front of Richmond, the day the city surrendered:

"Thank God that I have lived to see this!

"It seems to me that I have been dreaming a horrid dream for four years, and now the nightmare is gone.

"I wish to see Richmond."

Spoken Like a Christian

Frederick Douglass told, in these words, of his first interview with President Lincoln:

"I approached him with trepidation as to how this great man might receive me; but one word and look from him banished all my fears and set me perfectly at ease. I have often said since that meeting that it was much easier to see and converse with a great man than it was with a small man.

"On that occasion he said:

"'Douglass, you need not tell me who you are. Mr. Seward has told me all about you.'

"I then saw that there was no reason to tell him my personal story, however interesting it might be to myself or others, so I told him at once the object of my visit. It was to get some expression from him upon three points:

"1. Equal pay to colored soldiers.

"2. Their promotion when they had earned it on the battle-field.

"3. Should they be taken prisoners and enslaved or hanged, as Jefferson Davis had threatened, an equal number of Confederate prisoners should be executed within our lines.

"A declaration to that effect I thought would prevent the execution of the rebel threat. To all but the last, President Lincoln assented. He argued, however, that neither equal pay nor promotion could be granted at once. He said that in view of existing prejudices it was a great step forward to employ colored troops at all; that it was necessary to avoid everything that would offend this prejudice and increase opposition to the measure.

"He detailed the steps by which white soldiers were reconciled to the employment of colored troops; how these were first employed as laborers; how it was thought they should not be armed or uniformed like white soldiers; how they should only be made to wear a peculiar uniform; how they should be employed to hold forts and arsenals in sickly locations, and not enter the field like other soldiers.

"With all these restrictions and limitations he easily made me see that much would be gained when the colored man loomed before the country as a full-fledged United States soldier to fight, flourish or fall in defense of the united republic. The great soul of Lincoln halted only when he came to the point of retaliation.

"The thought of hanging men in cold blood, even though the rebels should murder a few of the colored prisoners, was a horror from which he shrank.

"'Oh, Douglass! I cannot do that. If I could get hold of the actual murderers of colored prisoners I would retaliate; but to hang those who have no hand in such murders, I cannot.'

"The contemplation of such an act brought to his countenance such an expression of sadness and pity that it made it hard for me to press my point, though I told him it would tend to save rather than destroy life. He, however, insisted that this work of blood, once begun, would be hard to stop—that such violence would beget violence. He argued more like a disciple of Christ than a commander-in-chief of the army and navy of a warlike nation already involved in a terrible war.

"How sad and strange the fate of this great and good man, the saviour of his country, the embodiment of human charity, whose heart, though strong, was as tender as a heart of childhood; who always tempered justice with mercy; who sought to supplant the sword with counsel of reason, to suppress passion by kindness and moderation; who had a sigh for every human grief and a tear for every human woe, should at last perish by the hand of a desperate assassin, against whom no thought of malice had ever entered his heart!"

"Lincoln Goes in When the Quakers Are Out"

One of the campaign songs of 1860 which will never be forgotten was Whittier's "The Quakers Are Out:—"

> *"Give the flags to the winds!*
> *Set the hills all aflame!*
> *Make way for the man with*
> *The Patriarch's name!*
> *Away with misgivings—away*
> *With all doubt,*
> *For Lincoln goes in when the*
> *Quakers are out!"*

Speaking of this song (with which he was greatly pleased) one day at the White House, the President said: "It reminds me of a little story I heard years ago out in Illinois. A political campaign was on, and the atmosphere was kept at a high temperature. Several fights had already occurred, many men having been seriously hurt, and the prospects were that the result would be close. One of the candidates was a professional politician with a huge wart on his nose, this disfigurement having earned for him the nickname of 'Warty.' His opponent was a young lawyer who wore 'biled' shirts, 'was shaved by a barber, and had his clothes made to fit him.

"Now, 'Warty' was of Quaker stock, and around election time made a great parade of the fact. When there were no campaigns in progress he was anything but Quakerish in his language or actions. The young lawyer didn't know what the inside of a meeting house looked like.

"Well, the night before election-day the two candidates came together at a joint debate, both being on the speakers' platform. The young lawyer had to speak after 'Warty,' and his reputation suffered at the hands of the Quaker, who told the many Friends present what a wicked fellow the young man was—never went to church, swore, drank, smoked and gambled.

"After 'Warty' had finished the other arose and faced the audience. 'I'm not a good man,' said he, 'and what my opponent has said about me is true enough, but I'm always the same. I don't profess religion when I run for office, and then turn around and associate with bad people when the campaign's over. I'm no hypocrite. I don't sing many psalms. Neither does my opponent; and, talking about singing, I'd just like to hear my friend who is running against me sing the song—for the benefit of this audience—I heard him sing the night after he was nominated. I yield the floor to him:

"Of course 'Warty' refused, his Quaker supporters grew suspicious, and when they turned out at the polls the following day they voted for the wicked young lawyer.

"So, it's true that when 'the Quakers are out' the man they support is apt to go in."

Had Confidence in Him—"but—"

"General Blank asks for more men," said Secretary of War Stanton to the President one day, showing the latter a telegram from the commander named appealing for re-enforcements.

"I guess he's killed off enough men, hasn't he?" queried the President.

"I don't mean Confederates—our own men. What's the use in sending volunteers down to him if they're only used to fill graves?"

"His dispatch seems to imply that, in his opinion, you have not the confidence in him he thinks he deserves," the War Secretary went on to say, as he looked over the telegram again.

"Oh," was the President's reply, "he needn't lose any of his sleep on that account. Just telegraph him to that effect; also, that I don't propose to send him any more men."

How Hominy Was Originated

During the progress of a Cabinet meeting the subject of food for the men in the Army happened to come up. From that the conversation changed to the study of the Latin language.

"I studied Latin once," said Mr. Lincoln, in a casual way.

"Were you interested in it?" asked Mr. Seward, the Secretary of State.

"Well, yes. I saw some very curious things," was the President's rejoinder.

"What?" asked Secretary Seward.

"Well, there's the word hominy, for instance. We have just ordered a lot of that stuff for the troops. I see how the word originated. I notice it came from the Latin word homo—a man.

"When we decline homo, it is:

"'Homo—a man.

"'Hominis—of man.

"'Homini—for man.'

"So you see, hominy, being 'for man,' comes from the Latin. I guess those soldiers who don't know Latin will get along with it all right—though I won't rest real easy until I hear from the Commissary Department on it."

His Idea's Old, After All

One day, while listening to one of the wise men who had called at the White House to unload a large cargo of advice, the President interjected a remark to the effect that he had a great reverence for learning.

"This is not," President Lincoln explained, "because I am not an educated man. I feel the need of reading. It is a loss to a man not to have grown up among books."

"Men of force," the visitor answered, "can get on pretty well without books. They do their own thinking instead of adopting what other men think."

"Yes," said Mr. Lincoln, "but books serve to show a man that those original thoughts of his aren't very new, after all."

This was a point the caller was not willing to debate, and so he cut his call short.

Lincoln's First Speech

Lincoln made his first speech when he was a mere boy, going barefoot, his trousers held up by one suspender, and his shock of hair sticking through a hole in the crown of his cheap straw hat.

"Abe," in company with Dennis Hanks, attended a political meeting, which was addressed by a typical stump speaker—one of those loud-voiced fellows who shouted at the top of his voice and waved his arms wildly.

At the conclusion of the speech, which did not meet the views either of "Abe" or Dennis, the latter declared that "Abe" could make a better speech than that. Whereupon he got a dry-goods box and called on "Abe" to reply to the campaign orator.

Lincoln threw his old straw hat on the ground, and, mounting the dry-goods box, delivered a speech which held the attention of the crowd and won him considerable applause. Even the campaign orator admitted that it was a fine speech and answered every point in his own "oration."

Dennis Hanks, who thought "Abe" was about the greatest man that ever lived, was delighted, and he often told how young "Abe" got the better of the trained campaign speaker.

"Abe Wanted No Sneakin' 'Round"

It was in 1830, when "Abe" was just twenty-one years of age, that the Lincoln family moved from Gentryville, Indiana, to near Decatur, Illinois, their household goods being packed in a wagon drawn by four oxen driven by "Abe."

The winter previous the latter had "worked" in a country store in Gentryville and before undertaking the journey he invested all the money he had—some thirty dollars—in notions, such as needles, pins, thread, buttons and other domestic necessities. These he sold to families along the route and made a profit of about one hundred per cent.

This mercantile adventure of his youth "reminded" the President of a very clever story while the members of the Cabinet were one day solemnly debating a rather serious international problem. The President was in the minority, as was frequently the case, and he was "in a hole," as he afterwards expressed it. He didn't want to argue the points raised, preferring to settle the matter in a hurry, and an apt story was his only salvation.

Suddenly the President's fact brightened. "Gentlemen," said he, addressing those seated at the Cabinet table, "the situation just now reminds me of a fix I got into some thirty years or so ago when I was peddling 'notions' on the way from Indiana to Illinois. I didn't have a large stock, but I charged large prices, and I made money. Perhaps you don't see what I am driving at?"

Secretary of State Seward was wearing a most gloomy expression of countenance; Secretary of War Stanton was savage and inclined to be morose; Secretary of the Treasury Chase was indifferent and cynical, while the others of the Presidential advisers resigned themselves to the hearing of the inevitable "story."

"I don't propose to argue this matter," the President went on to say, "because arguments have no effect upon men whose opinions are fixed and whose minds are made up. But this little story of mine will make some things which now are in the dark show up more clearly."

There was another pause, and the Cabinet officers, maintaining their previous silence, began wondering if the President himself really knew what he was "driving at."

"Just before we left Indiana and crossed into Illinois," continued Mr. Lincoln solemnly, speaking in a grave tone of voice, "we came across a small farmhouse full of nothing but children. These ranged in years from seventeen years to seventeen months, and all were in tears. The mother of the family was red-headed and red-faced, and the whip she held in her right hand led to the inference that she had been chastising her brood. The father of the family, a meek-looking, mild-mannered, tow-headed chap, was standing in the front door-way, awaiting—to all appearances—his turn to feel the thong.

"I thought there wasn't much use in asking the head of that house if she wanted any 'notions.' She was too busy. It was evident an insurrection had been in progress, but it was pretty well quelled when I got there. The mother had about suppressed it with an iron hand, but she was not running any risks. She kept a keen and wary eye upon all the children, not forgetting an occasional glance at the 'old man' in the doorway.

"She saw me as I came up, and from her look I thought she was of the opinion that I intended to interfere. Advancing to the doorway, and roughly pushing her husband aside, she demanded my business.

"'Nothing, madame,' I answered as gently as possible; 'I merely dropped in as I came along to see how things were going.'

"'Well, you needn't wait,' was the reply in an irritated way; 'there's trouble here, an' lots of it, too, but I kin manage my own affairs without the help of outsiders. This is jest a family row, but I'll teach these brats their places ef I hev to lick the hide off ev'ry one of them. I don't do much talkin,' but I run this house, an' I don't want no one sneakin' round tryin' to find out how I do it, either.'

"That's the case here with us," the President said in conclusion. "We must let the other nations know that we propose to settle our family row in our own way, and 'teach these brats their places' (the seceding States) if we have to 'lick the hide off' of each and every one of them. And, like the old woman, we don't want any 'sneakin' 'round' by other countries who would like to find out how we are to do it, either.

"Now, Seward, you write some diplomatic notes to that effect." And the Cabinet session closed.

Didn't Even Need Stilts

As the President considered it his duty to keep in touch with all the improvements in the armament of the vessels belonging to the United States Navy, he was necessarily interested in the various types of these floating fortresses. Not only was it required of the Navy Department to furnish seagoing warships, deep-draught vessels for the great rivers and the lakes, but this Department also found use for little gunboats which could creep along in the shallowest of water and attack the Confederates in by-places and swamps.

The consequence of the interest taken by Mr. Lincoln in the Navy was that he was besieged, day and night, by steamboat contractors, each one eager to sell his product to the Washington Government. All sorts of experiments were tried, some being dire failures, while others were more than fairly successful. More than once had these tiny war vessels proved themselves of great service, and the United States Government had a large number of them built.

There was one particular contractor who bothered the President more than all the others put together. He was constantly impressing upon Mr. Lincoln the great superiority of his boats, because they would run in such shallow water.

"Oh, yes," replied the President, "I've no doubt they'll run anywhere where the ground is a little moist!"

"How Do You Get Out of This Place?"

"It seems to me," remarked the President one day while reading, over some of the appealing telegrams sent to the War Department by General McClellan, "that McClellan has been wandering around and has sort of got lost. He's been hollering for help ever since he went South—wants somebody to come to his deliverance and get him out of the place he's got into.

"He reminds me of the story of a man out in Illinois who, in company with a number of friends, visited the State penitentiary. They wandered all through the institution and saw everything, but just about the time to depart this particular man became separated from his friends and couldn't find his way out.

"He roamed up and down one corridor after another, becoming more desperate all the time, when, at last, he came across a convict who was looking out from between the bars of his cell-door. Here was salvation at last. Hurrying up to the prisoner he hastily asked,

"'Say! How do you get out of this place?'"

"Tad" Introduces "Our Friends"

President Lincoln often avoided interviews with delegations representing various States, especially when he knew the objects of their errands, and was aware he could not grant their requests. This was the case with several commissioners from Kentucky, who were put off from day to day.

They were about to give up in despair, and were leaving the White House lobby, their speech being interspersed with vehement and uncomplimentary terms concerning "Old Abe," when "Tad" happened along. He caught at these words, and asked one of them if they wanted to see "Old Abe," laughing at the same time.

"Yes," he replied.

"Wait a minute," said "Tad," and rushed into his father's office. Said he, "Papa, may I introduce some friends to you?"

His father, always indulgent and ready to make him happy, kindly said, "Yes, my son, I will see your friends."

"Tad" went to the Kentuckians again, and asked a very dignified looking gentleman of the party his name. He was told his name. He then said, "Come, gentlemen," and they followed him.

Leading them up to the President, "Tad," with much dignity, said, "Papa, let me introduce to you Judge ——, of Kentucky"; and quickly added, "Now Judge, you introduce the other gentlemen."

The introductions were gone through with, and they turned out to be the gentlemen Mr. Lincoln had been avoiding for a week. Mr. Lincoln reached for the boy, took him in his lap, kissed him, and told him it was all right, and that he had introduced his friend like a little gentleman as he was. Tad was eleven years old at this time.

The President was pleased with Tad's diplomacy, and often laughed at the incident as he told others of it. One day while caressing the boy, he asked him why he called those gentlemen "his friends." "Well," said Tad, "I had seen them so often, and they looked so good and sorry, and said they were from Kentucky, that I thought they must be our friends." "That is right, my son," said Mr. Lincoln; "I would have the whole human race your friends and mine, if it were possible."

Mixed Up Worse Than Before

The President told a story which most beautifully illustrated the muddled situation of affairs at the time McClellan's fate was hanging in the balance. McClellan's work was not satisfactory, but the President hesitated to remove him; the general was so slow that the Confederates marched all around him; and, to add to the dilemma, the President could not find a suitable man to take McClellan's place.

The latter was a political, as well as a military, factor; his friends threatened that, if he was removed, many war Democrats would cast their influence with the South, etc. It was, altogether, a sad mix-up, and the President, for a time, was at his wits' end. He was assailed on all sides with advice, but none of it was worth acting upon.

"This situation reminds me," said the President at a Cabinet meeting one day not long before the appointment of General Halleck as McClellan's successor in command of the Union forces, "of a Union man in Kentucky whose two sons enlisted in the Federal Army. His wife was of Confederate sympathies. His nearest neighbor was a Confederate in feeling, and his two sons were fighting under Lee. This neighbor's wife was a Union woman and it nearly broke her heart to know that her sons were arrayed against the Union.

"Finally, the two men, after each had talked the matter over with his wife, agreed to obtain divorces; this they, did, and the Union man and Union woman were wedded, as were the Confederate man and the Confederate woman—the men swapped wives, in short. But this didn't seem to help matters any, for the sons of the Union woman were still fighting for the South, and the sons of the Confederate woman continued in the Federal Army; the Union husband couldn't get along with his Union wife, and the Confederate husband and his Confederate wife couldn't agree upon anything, being forever fussing and quarreling.

"It's the same thing with the Army. It doesn't seem worth while to secure divorces and then marry the Army and McClellan to others, for they won't get along any better than they do now, and there'll only be a new set of heartaches started. I think we'd better wait; perhaps a real fighting general will come along some of these days, and then we'll all be happy. If you go to mixing in a mix-up, you only make the muddle worse."

"Long Abe's" Feet "Protruded over"

George M. Pullman, the great sleeping-car builder, once told a joke in which Lincoln was the prominent figure. In fact, there wouldn't have been any joke had it not been for "Long Abe." At the time of the occurrence, which was the foundation for the joke— and Pullman admitted that the latter was on him—Pullman was the conductor of his only sleeping-car. The latter was an experiment, and Pullman was doing everything possible to get the railroads to take hold of it.

"One night," said Pullman in telling the story, "as we were about going out of Chicago—this was long before Lincoln was what you might call a renowned man—a long, lean, ugly man, with a wart on his cheek, came into the depot. He paid me fifty cents, and half a berth was assigned him. Then he took off his coat and vest and hung them up, and they fitted the peg about as well as they fitted him. Then he kicked off his boots, which were of surprising length, turned into the berth, and, undoubtedly having an easy conscience, was sleeping like a healthy baby before the car left the depot.

"Pretty soon along came another passenger and paid his fifty cents. In two minutes he was back at me, angry as a wet hen.

"'There's a man in that berth of mine,' said he, hotly, 'and he's about ten feet high. How am I going to sleep there, I'd like to know? Go and look at him.'

"In I went—mad, too. The tall, lank man's knees were under his chin, his arms were stretched across the bed and his feet were stored comfortably—for him. I shook him until he awoke, and then told him if he wanted the whole berth he would have to pay $1.

"'My dear sir,' said the tall man, 'a contract is a contract. I have paid you fifty cents for half this berth, and, as you see, I'm occupying it. There's the other half,' pointing to a strip about six inches wide. 'Sell that and don't disturb me again.'

"And so saying, the man with a wart on his face went to sleep again. He was Abraham Lincoln, and he never grew any shorter afterward. We became great friends, and often laughed over the incident."

Could Lick Any Man in the Crowd

When the enemies of General Grant were bothering the President with emphatic and repeated demands that the "Silent Man" be removed from command, Mr. Lincoln remained firm. He would not consent to lose the services of so valuable a soldier. "Grant fights," said he in response to the charges made that Grant was a butcher, a drunkard, an incompetent and a general who did not know his business.

"That reminds me of a story," President Lincoln said one day to a delegation of the "Grant-is-no-good" style.

"Out in my State of Illinois there was a man nominated for sheriff of the county. He was a good man for the office, brave, determined and honest, but not much of an orator. In fact, he couldn't talk at all; he couldn't make a speech to save his life.

"His friends knew he was a man who would preserve the peace of the county and perform the duties devolving upon him all right, but the people of the county didn't know it. They wanted him to come out boldly on the platform at political meetings and state his convictions and principles; they had been used to speeches from candidates, and were somewhat suspicious of a man who was afraid to open his mouth.

"At last the candidate consented to make a speech, and his friends were delighted. The candidate was on hand, and, when he was called upon, advanced to the front and faced the crowd. There was a glitter in his eye that wasn't pleasing, and the way he walked out to the front of the stand showed that he knew just what he wanted to say.

"'Feller Citizens,' was his beginning, the words spoken quietly, 'I'm not a speakin' man; I ain't no orator, an' I never stood up before a lot of people in my life before; I'm not goin' to make no speech, 'xcept to say that I can lick any man in the crowd!'"

His Way to a Child's Heart

Charles E. Anthony's one meeting with Mr. Lincoln presents an interesting contrast to those of the men who shared the emancipator's interest in public affairs. It was in the latter part of the winter of 1861, a short time before Mr. Lincoln left for his inauguration at Washington. Judge Anthony went to the Sherman House, where the President-elect was stopping, and took with him his son, Charles, then but a little boy. Charles played about the room as a child will, looking at whatever interested him for the time, and when the interview with his father was over he was ready to go.

But Mr. Lincoln, ever interested in little children, called the lad to him and took him upon his great knee.

"My impression of him all the time I had been playing about the room," said Mr. Anthony, "was that he was a terribly homely man. I was rather repelled. But no sooner did he speak to me than the expression of his face changed completely, or, rather, my view of it changed. It at once became kindly and attractive. He asked me some questions, seeming instantly to find in the turmoil of all the great questions that must have been heavy upon him, the very ones that would go to the thought of a child. I answered him without hesitation, and after a moment he patted my shoulder and said:

"'Well, you'll be a man before your mother yet,' and put me down.

"I had never before heard the homely old expression, and it puzzled me for a time. After a moment I understood it, but he looked at me while I was puzzling over it, and seemed to be amused, as no doubt he was."

The incident simply illustrates the ease and readiness with which Lincoln could turn from the mighty questions before the nation, give a moment's interested attention to a child, and return at once to matters of state.

"Left It the Women to Howl About Me"

Donn Piatt, one of the brightest newspaper writers in the country, told a good story on the President in regard to the refusal of the latter to sanction the death penalty in cases of desertion from the Union Army.

"There was far more policy in this course," said Piatt, "than kind feeling. To assert the contrary is to detract from Lincoln's force of character, as well as intellect. Our War President was not lost in his high admiration of brigadiers and major-generals, and had a positive dislike for their methods and the despotism upon which an army is based. He knew that he was dependent upon volunteers for soldiers, and to force upon such men as those the stern discipline of the Regular Army was to render the service unpopular. And it pleased him to be the source of mercy, as well as the fountain of honor, in this direction.

"I was sitting with General Dan Tyler, of Connecticut, in the antechamber of the War Department, shortly after the adjournment of the Buell Court of Inquiry, of which we had been members, when President Lincoln came in from the room of Secretary Stanton. Seeing us, he said: 'Well, gentlemen, have you any matter worth reporting?'

"'I think so, Mr. President,' replied General Tyler. 'We had it proven that Bragg, with less than ten thousand men, drove your eighty-three thousand men under Buell back from before Chattanooga, down to the Ohio at Louisville, marched around us twice, then doubled us up at Perryville, and finally got out of the State of Kentucky with all his plunder.'

"'Now, Tyler,' returned the President, 'what is the meaning of all this; what is the lesson? Don't our men march as well, and fight as well, as these rebels? If not, there is a fault somewhere. We are all of the same family—same sort.'

"'Yes, there is a lesson,' replied General Tyler; 'we are of the same sort, but subject to different handling. Bragg's little force was superior to our larger number because he had it under control. If a man left his ranks, he was punished; if he deserted, he was shot. We had nothing of that sort. If we attempt to shoot a deserter you pardon him, and our army is without discipline.'

"The President looked perplexed. 'Why do you interfere?' continued General Tyler. 'Congress has taken from you all responsibility.'

"'Yes,' answered the President impatiently, 'Congress has taken the responsibility and left the women to howl all about me,' and so he strode away."

He'd Ruin All the Other Convicts

One of the droll stories brought into play by the President as an ally in support of his contention, proved most effective. Politics was rife among the generals of the Union Army, and there was more "wire-pulling" to prevent the advancement of fellow commanders than the laying of plans to defeat the Confedcrates in battle.

However, when it so happened that the name of a particularly unpopular general was sent to the Senate for confirmation, the protest against his promotion was almost unanimous. The nomination didn't seem to please anyone. Generals who were enemies before conferred together for the purpose of bringing every possible influence to bear upon the Senate and securing the rejection of the hated leader's name. The President was surprised. He had never known such unanimity before.

"You remind me," said the President to a delegation of officers which called upon him one day to present a fresh protest to him regarding the nomination, "of a visit a certain Governor paid to the Penitentiary of his State. It had been announced that the Governor would hear the story of every inmate of the institution, and was prepared to rectify, either by commutation or pardon, any wrongs that had been done to any prisoner.

"One by one the convicts appeared before His Excellency, and each one maintained that he was an innocent man, who had been sent to prison because the police didn't like him, or his friends and relatives wanted his property, or he was too popular, etc., etc. The last prisoner to appear was an individual who was not all prepossessing. His face was against him; his eyes were shifty; he didn't have the appearance of an honest man, and he didn't act like one.

"'Well,' asked the Governor, impatiently, 'I suppose you're innocent like the rest of these fellows?'

"'No, Governor,' was the unexpected answer; 'I was guilty of the crime they charged against me, and I got just what I deserved.'

"When he had recovered from his astonishment, the Governor, looking the fellow squarely in the face, remarked with emphasis: 'I'll have to pardon you, because I don't want to leave so bad a man as you are in the company of such innocent sufferers as I have discovered your fellow-convicts to be. You might corrupt them and teach them wicked tricks. As soon as I get back to the capital, I'll have the papers made out.'

"You gentlemen," continued the President, "ought to be glad that so bad a man, as you represent this officer to be, is to get his promotion, for then you won't be forced to associate with him and suffer the contamination of his presence and influence. I will do all I can to have the Senate confirm him."

And he was confirmed.

In a Hopeless Minority

The President was often in opposition to the general public sentiment of the North upon certain questions of policy, but he bided his time, and things usually came out as he wanted them. It was Lincoln's opinion, from the first, that apology and reparation to England must be made by the United States because of the arrest, upon the high seas, of the Confederate Commissioners, Mason and Slidell. The country, however (the Northern States), was wild for a conflict with England.

"One war at a time," quietly remarked the President at a Cabinet meeting, where he found the majority of his advisers unfavorably disposed to "backing down." But one member of the Cabinet was a really strong supporter of the President in his attitude.

"I am reminded," the President said after the various arguments had been put forward by the members of the Cabinet, "of a fellow out in my State of Illinois who happened to stray into a church while a revival meeting was in progress. To be truthful, this individual was not entirely sober, and with that instinct which seems to impel all men in his condition to assume a prominent part in proceedings, he walked up the aisle to the very front pew.

"All noticed him, but he did not care; for awhile he joined audibly in the singing, said 'Amen' at the close of the prayers, but, drowsiness overcoming him, he went to sleep. Before the meeting closed, the pastor asked the usual question—'Who are on the Lord's side?'—and the congregation arose en masse. When he asked, 'Who are on the side of the Devil?' the sleeper was about waking up. He heard a portion of the interrogatory, and, seeing the minister on his feet, arose.

"'I don't exactly understand the question,' he said, 'but I'll stand by you, parson, to the last. But it seems to me,' he added, 'that we're in a hopeless minority.'

"I'm in a hopeless minority now," said the President, "and I'll have to admit it."

"Did Ye Ask Morrissey Yet?"

John Morrissey, the noted prize fighter, was the "Boss" of Tammany Hall during the Civil War period. It pleased his fancy to go to Congress, and his obedient constituents sent him there. Morrissey was such an absolute despot that the New York City democracy could not make a move without his consent, and many of the Tammanyites were so afraid of him that they would not even enter into business ventures without consulting the autocrat.

President Lincoln had been seriously annoyed by some of his generals, who were afraid to make the slightest move before asking advice from Washington. One commander, in particular, was so cautious that he telegraphed the War Department upon the slightest pretext, the result being that his troops were lying in camp doing nothing, when they should have been in the field.

"This general reminds me," the President said one day while talking to Secretary Stanton, at the War Department, "of a story I once heard about a Tammany man. He happened to meet a friend, also a member of Tammany, on the street, and in the course of the talk the friend, who was beaming with smiles and good nature, told the other Tammanyite that he was going to be married.

"This first Tammany man looked more serious than men usually do upon hearing of the impending happiness of a friend. In fact, his face seemed to take on a look of anxiety and worry.

"'Ain't you glad to know that I'm to get married?' demanded the second Tammanyite, somewhat in a huff.

"'Of course I am,' was the reply; 'but,' putting his mouth close to the ear of the other, 'have ye asked Morrissey yet?'

"Now, this general of whom we are speaking, wouldn't dare order out the guard without asking Morrissey," concluded the President.

Got the Laugh on Douglas

At one time, when Lincoln and Douglas were "stumping" Illinois, they met at a certain town, and it was agreed that they would have a joint debate. Douglas was the first speaker, and in the course of his talk remarked that in early life, his father, who, he said, was an excellent cooper by trade, apprenticed him out to learn the cabinet business.

This was too good for Lincoln to let pass, so when his turn came to reply, he said:

"I had understood before that Mr. Douglas had been bound out to learn the cabinet-making business, which is all well enough, but I was not aware until now that his father was a cooper. I have no doubt, however, that he was one, and I am certain, also, that he was a very good one, for (here Lincoln gently bowed toward Douglas) he has made one of the best whiskey casks I have ever seen."

As Douglas was a short heavy-set man, and occasionally imbibed, the pith of the joke was at once apparent, and most heartily enjoyed by all.

On another occasion, Douglas made a point against Lincoln by telling the crowd that when he first knew Lincoln he was a "grocery-keeper," and sold whiskey, cigars, etc.

"Mr. L.," he said, "was a very good bar-tender!" This brought the laugh on Lincoln, whose reply, however, soon came, and then the laugh was on the other side.

"What Mr. Douglas has said, gentlemen," replied Lincoln, "is true enough; I did keep a grocery and I did sell cotton, candles and cigars, and sometimes whiskey; but I remember in those days that Mr. Douglas was one of my best customers."

"I can also say this; that I have since left my side of the counter, while Mr. Douglas still sticks to his!"

This brought such a storm of cheers and laughter that Douglas was unable to reply.

"Fixed Up" a Bit for the "City Folks"

Mrs. Lincoln knew her husband was not "pretty," but she liked to have him presentable when he appeared before the public. Stephen Fiske, in "When Lincoln Was First Inaugurated," tells of Mrs. Lincoln's anxiety to have the President-elect "smoothed down" a little when receiving a delegation that was to greet them upon reaching New York City.

"The train stopped," writes Mr. Fiske, "and through the windows immense crowds could be seen; the cheering drowning the blowing off of steam of the locomotive. Then Mrs. Lincoln opened her handbag and said:

"'Abraham, I must fix you up a bit for these city folks.'

"Mr. Lincoln gently lifted her upon the seat before him; she parted, combed and brushed his hair and arranged his black necktie.

"'Do I look nice now, mother?' he affectionately asked.

"'Well, you'll do, Abraham,' replied Mrs. Lincoln critically. So he kissed her and lifted her down from the seat, and turned to meet Mayor Wood, courtly and suave, and to have his hand shaken by the other New York officials."

Even Rebels Ought to Be Saved

The Rev. Mr. Shrigley, of Philadelphia, a Universalist, had been nominated for hospital chaplain, and a protesting delegation went to Washington to see President Lincoln on the subject.

"We have called, Mr. President, to confer with you in regard to the appointment of Mr. Shrigley, of Philadelphia, as hospital chaplain."

The President responded: "Oh, yes, gentlemen. I have sent his name to the Senate, and he will no doubt be confirmed at an early date." One of the young men replied: "We have not come to ask for the appointment, but to solicit you to withdraw the nomination."

"Ah!" said Lincoln, "that alters the case; but on what grounds do you wish the nomination withdrawn?"

The answer was: "Mr. Shrigley is not sound in his theological opinions."

The President inquired: "On what question is the gentleman unsound?"

Response: "He does not believe in endless punishment; not only so, sir, but he believes that even the rebels themselves will be finally saved."

"Is that so?" inquired the President.

The members of the committee responded, "Yes, yes.'

"Well, gentlemen, if that be so, and there is any way under Heaven whereby the rebels can be saved, then, for God's sake and their sakes, let the man be appointed."

The Rev. Mr. Shrigley was appointed, and served until the close of the war.

Tried to Do What Seemed Best

John M. Palmer, Major-General in the Volunteer Army, Governor of the State of Illinois, and United States Senator from the Sucker State, became acquainted with Lincoln in 1839, and the last time he saw the President was at the White House in February, 1865. Senator Palmer told the story of his interview as follows:

"I had come to Washington at the request of the Governor, to complain that Illinois had been credited with 18,000 too few troops. I saw Mr. Lincoln one afternoon, and he asked me to come again in the morning.

"Next morning I sat in the ante-room while several officers were relieved. At length I was told to enter the President's room. Mr. Lincoln was in the hands of the barber.

"'Come in, Palmer,' he called out, 'come in. You're home folks. I can shave before you. I couldn't before those others, and I have to do it some time.'

"We chatted about various matters, and at length I said:

"'Well, Mr. Lincoln, if anybody had told me that in a great crisis like this the people were going out to a little one-horse town and pick out a one-horse lawyer for President I wouldn't have believed it.'

"Mr. Lincoln whirled about in his chair, his face white with lather, a towel under his chin. At first I thought he was angry. Sweeping the barber away he leaned forward, and, placing one hand on my knee, said:

"'Neither would I. But it was time when a man with a policy would have been fatal to the country. I have never had a policy. I have simply tried to do what seemed best each day, as each day came.'"

"Holding a Candle to the Czar"

England was anything but pleased when the Czar Alexander, of Russia, showed his friendship for the United States by sending a strong fleet to this country with the accompanying suggestion that Uncle Sam, through his representative, President Lincoln, could do whatever he saw fit with the ironclads and the munitions of war they had stowed away in their holds.

London "Punch," on November 7th, 1863, printed a cartoon with the caption "Holding a candle to the * * * * *." (Much the same thing.)

Of course, this was a covert sneer, intended to convey the impression that President Lincoln, in order to secure the support and friendship of the Emperor of Russia as long as the War of the Rebellion lasted, was willing to do all sorts of menial offices, even to the extent of holding the candle and lighting His Most Gracious Majesty, the White Czar, to his imperial bed-chamber.

It is a somewhat remarkable fact that the Emperor Alexander, who tendered inestimable aid to the President of the United States, was the Lincoln of Russia, having given freedom to millions of serfs in his empire; and, further than that, he was, like Lincoln, the victim of assassination. He was literally blown to pieces by a bomb thrown under his carriage while riding through the streets near the Winter Palace at St. Petersburg.

Nashville Was Not Surrendered

"I was told a mighty good story," said the President one day at a Cabinet meeting, "by Colonel Granville Moody, 'the fighting Methodist parson,' as they used to call him in Tennessee. I happened to meet Moody in Philadelphia, where he was attending a conference.

"The story was about 'Andy' Johnson and General Buell. Colonel Moody happened to be in Nashville the day it was reported that Buell had decided to evacuate the city. The rebels, strongly reinforced, were said to be within two days' march of the capital. Of course, the city was greatly excited. Moody said he went in search of Johnson at the edge of the evening and found him at his office closeted with two gentlemen, who were walking the floor with him, one on each side. As he entered they retired, leaving him alone with Johnson, who came up to him, manifesting intense feeling, and said:

"'Moody, we are sold out. Buell is a traitor. He is going to evacuate the city, and in forty-eight hours we will all be in the hands of the rebels!'

"Then he commenced pacing the floor again, twisting his hands and chafing like a caged tiger, utterly insensible to his friend's entreaties to become calm. Suddenly he turned and said:

"'Moody, can you pray?'

"'That is my business, sir, as a minister of the gospel,' returned the colonel.

"'Well, Moody, I wish you would pray,' said Johnson, and instantly both went down upon their knees at opposite sides of the room.

"As the prayer waxed fervent, Johnson began to respond in true Methodist style. Presently he crawled over on his hands and knees to Moody's side and put his arms over him, manifesting the deepest emotion.

"Closing the prayer with a hearty 'amen' from each, they arose.

"Johnson took a long breath, and said, with emphasis:

"'Moody, I feel better.'

"Shortly afterward he asked:

"'Will you stand by me?'

"'Certainly I will,' was the answer.

"'Well, Moody, I can depend upon you; you are one in a hundred thousand.'

"He then commenced pacing the floor again. Suddenly he wheeled, the current of his thought having changed, and said:

"'Oh, Moody, I don't want you to think I have become a religious man because I asked you to pray. I am sorry to say it, I am not, and never pretended to be religious. No one knows this better than you, but, Moody, there is one thing about it, I do believe in Almighty God, and I believe also in the Bible, and I say, d—n me if Nashville shall be surrendered!'

"And Nashville was not surrendered!"

He Couldn't Wait for the Colonel

General Fisk, attending a reception at the White House, saw waiting in the ante-room a poor old man from Tennessee, and learned that he had been waiting three or four days to get an audience, on which probably depended the life of his son, under sentence of death for some military offense.

General Fisk wrote his case in outline on a card and sent it in, with a special request that the President would see the man. In a moment the order came; and past impatient senators, governors and generals, the old man went.

He showed his papers to Mr. Lincoln, who said he would look into the case and give him the result next day.

The old man, in an agony of apprehension, looked up into the President's sympathetic face and actually cried out:

"To-morrow may be too late! My son is under sentence of death! It ought to be decided now!"

His streaming tears told how much he was moved.

"Come," said Mr. Lincoln, "wait a bit and I'll tell you a story"; and then he told the old man General Fisk's story about the swearing driver, as follows:

"The general had begun his military life as a colonel, and when he raised his regiment in Missouri he proposed to his men that he should do all the swearing of the regiment. They assented; and for months no instance was known of the violation of the promise.

"The colonel had a teamster named John Todd, who, as roads were not always the best, had some difficulty in commanding his temper and his tongue.

"John happened to be driving a mule team through a series of mudholes a little worse than usual, when, unable to restrain himself any longer, he burst forth into a volley of energetic oaths.

"The colonel took notice of the offense and brought John to account.

"'John,' said he, 'didn't you promise to let me do all the swearing of the regiment?'

"'Yes, I did, colonel,' he replied, 'but the fact was, the swearing had to be done then or not at all, and you weren't there to do it.'"

As he told the story the old man forgot his boy, and both the President and his listener had a hearty laugh together at its conclusion.

Then he wrote a few words which the old man read, and in which he found new occasion for tears; but the tears were tears of joy, for the words saved the life of his son.

Lincoln Pronounced This Story Funny

The President was heard to declare one day that the story given below was one of the funniest he ever heard.

One of General Fremont's batteries of eight Parrott guns, supported by a squadron of horse commanded by Major Richards, was in sharp conflict with a battery of the enemy near at hand. Shells and shot were flying thick and fast, when the commander of the battery, a German, one of Fremont's staff, rode suddenly up to the cavalry, exclaiming, in loud and excited terms, "Pring up de shackasses! Pring up de shackasses! For Cot's sake, hurry up de shackasses, im-me-di-ate-ly!"

The necessity of this order, though not quite apparent, will be more obvious when it is remembered that "shackasses" are mules, carry mountain howitzers, which are fired from the backs of that much-abused but valuable animal; and the immediate occasion for the "shackasses" was that two regiments of rebel infantry were at that moment discovered ascending a hill immediately behind our batteries.

The "shackasses," with the howitzers loaded with grape and canister, were soon on the ground.

The mules squared themselves, as they well knew how, for the shock.

A terrific volley was poured into the advancing column, which immediately broke and retreated.

Two hundred and seventy-eight dead bodies were found in the ravine next day, piled closely together as they fell, the effects of that volley from the backs of the "shackasses."

Joke Was on Lincoln

Mr. Lincoln enjoyed a joke at his own expense. Said he: "In the days when I used to be in the circuit, I was accosted in the cars by a stranger, who said, 'Excuse me, sir, but I have an article in my possession which belongs to you.' 'How is that?' I asked, considerably astonished.

"The stranger took a jackknife from his pocket. 'This knife,' said he, 'was placed in my hands some years ago, with the injunction that I was to keep it until I had found a man uglier than myself. I have carried it from that time to this. Allow me to say, sir, that I think you are fairly entitled to the property.'"

The Other One Was Worse

It so happened that an official of the War Department had escaped serious punishment for a rather flagrant offense, by showing where grosser irregularities existed in the management of a certain bureau of the Department. So valuable was the information furnished that the culprit who "gave the snap away" was not even discharged.

"That reminds me," the President said, when the case was laid before him, "of a story about Daniel Webster, when the latter was a boy.

"When quite young, at school, Daniel was one day guilty of a gross violation of the rules. He was detected in the act, and called up by the teacher for punishment.

"This was to be the old-fashioned 'feruling' of the hand. His hands happened to be very dirty.

"Knowing this, on the way to the teacher's desk, he spit upon the palm of his right hand, wiping it off upon the side of his pantaloons.

"'Give me your hand, sir,' said the teacher, very sternly.

"Out went the right hand, partly cleansed. The teacher looked at it a moment, and said:

"'Daniel, if you will find another hand in this school-room as filthy as that, I will let you off this time!'

"Instantly from behind the back came the left hand.

"'Here it is, sir,' was the ready reply.

"'That will do,' said the teacher, 'for this time; you can take your seat, sir.'"

"I'd a Been Missed by Myse'f"

The President did not consider that every soldier who ran away in battle, or did not stand firmly to receive a bayonet charge, was a coward. He was of opinion that self-preservation was the first law of Nature, but he didn't want this statute construed too liberally by the troops.

At the same time he took occasion to illustrate a point he wished to make by a story in connection with a darky who was a member of the Ninth Illinois Infantry Regiment. This regiment was one of those engaged at the capture of Fort Donelson. It behaved gallantly, and lost as heavily as any.

"Upon the hurricane-deck of one of our gunboats," said the President in telling the story, "I saw an elderly darky, with a very philosophical and retrospective cast of countenance, squatted upon his bundle, toasting his shins against the chimney, and apparently plunged into a state of profound meditation.

"As the negro rather interested me, I made some inquiries, and found that he had really been with the Ninth Illinois Infantry at

Donelson. and began to ask him some questions about the capture of the place.

"'Were you in the fight?'

"'Had a little taste of it, sa.'

"'Stood your ground, did you?'

"'No, sa, I runs.'

"'Run at the first fire, did you?

"'Yes, sa, and would hab run soona, had I knowd it war comin.'"

"'Why, that wasn't very creditable to your courage.'

"'Dat isn't my line, sa—cookin's my profeshun.'

"'Well, but have you no regard for your reputation?'

"'Reputation's nuffin to me by de side ob life.'

"'Do you consider your life worth more than other people's?'

"'It's worth more to me, sa.'

"'Then you must value it very highly?'

"'Yes, sa, I does, more dan all dis wuld, more dan a million ob dollars, sa, for what would dat be wuth to a man wid de bref out ob him? Self-preserbation am de fust law wid me.'

"'But why should you act upon a different rule from other men?'

"'Different men set different values on their lives; mine is not in de market.'

"'But if you lost it you would have the satisfaction of knowing that you died for your country.'

"'Dat no satisfaction when feelin's gone.'

"'Then patriotism and honor are nothing to you?'

"'Nufin whatever, sa—I regard them as among the vanities.'

"'If our soldiers were like you, traitors might have broken up the government without resistance.'

"'Yes, sa, dar would hab been no help for it. I wouldn't put my life in de scale 'g'inst any gobernment dat eber existed, for no gobernment could replace de loss to me.'

"'Do you think any of your company would have missed you if you had been killed?'

"'Maybe not, sa—a dead man ain't much to dese sogers—but I'd a missed myse'f, and dat was de p'int wid me.'

"I only tell this story," concluded the President, "in order to illustrate the result of the tactics of some of the Union generals who would be sadly 'missed' by themselves, if no one else, if they ever got out of the Army."

It All "Depended" Upon the Effect

President Lincoln and some members of his Cabinet were with a part of the Army some distance south of the National Capital at one time, when Secretary of War Stanton remarked that just before he left Washington he had received a telegram from General Mitchell, in Alabama. General Mitchell asked instructions in regard to a certain emergency that had arisen.

The Secretary said he did not precisely understand the emergency as explained by General Mitchell, but had answered back, "All right; go ahead."

"Now," he said, as he turned to Mr. Lincoln, "Mr. President, if I have made an error in not understanding him correctly, I will have to get you to countermand the order."

"Well," exclaimed President Lincoln, "that is very much like the happening on the occasion of a certain horse sale I remember that took place at the cross-roads down in Kentucky, when I was a boy.

"A particularly fine horse was to be sold, and the people in large numbers had gathered together. They had a small boy to ride the horse up and down while the spectators examined the horse's points.

"At last one man whispered to the boy as he went by: 'Look here, boy, hain't that horse got the splints?'

"The boy replied: 'Mister, I don't know what the splints is, but if it's good for him, he has got it; if it ain't good for him, he ain't got it.'

"Now," said President Lincoln, "if this was good for Mitchell, it was all right; but if it was not, I have got to countermand it."

Too Swift to Stay in the Army

There were strange, queer, odd things and happenings in the Army at times, but, as a rule, the President did not allow them to worry him. He had enough to bother about.

A quartermaster having neglected to present his accounts in proper shape, and the matter being deemed of sufficient importance to bring it to the attention of the President, the latter remarked:

"Now this instance reminds me of a little story I heard only a short time ago. A certain general's purse was getting low, and he said it was probable he might be obliged to draw on his banker for some money.

"'How much do you want, father?' asked his son, who had been with him a few days.

"'I think I shall send for a couple of hundred,' replied the general.

"'Why, father,' said his son, very quietly, 'I can let you have it.'

"'You can let me have it! Where did you get so much money?

"'I won it playing draw-poker with your staff, sir!' replied the youth.

"The earliest morning train bore the young man toward his home, and I've been wondering if that boy and that quartermaster had happened to meet at the same table."

Admired the Strong Man

Governor Hoyt of Wisconsin tells a story of Mr. Lincoln's great admiration for physical strength. Mr. Lincoln, in 1859, made a speech at the Wisconsin State Agricultural Fair. After the speech, in company with the Governor, he strolled about the grounds, looking at the exhibits. They came to a place where a professional "strong man" was tossing cannon balls in the air and catching them on his arms and juggling with them as though they were light as baseballs. Mr. Lincoln had never before seen such an exhibition, and he was greatly surprised and interested.

When the performance was over, Governor Hoyt, seeing Mr. Lincoln's interest, asked him to go up and be introduced to the athlete.

He did so, and, as he stood looking down musingly on the man, who was very short, and evidently wondering that one so much smaller than he could be so much stronger, he suddenly broke out with one of his quaint speeches. "Why," he said, "why, I could lick salt off the top of your hat."

Wished the Army Charged Like That

A prominent volunteer officer who, early in the War, was on duty in Washington and often carried reports to Secretary Stanton at the War Department, told a characteristic story on President Lincoln. Said he:

"I was with several other young officers, also carrying reports to the War Department, and one morning we were late. In this instance we were in a desperate hurry to deliver the papers, in order to be able to catch the train returning to camp.

"On the winding, dark staircase of the old War Department, which many will remember, it was our misfortune, while taking about three stairs at a time, to run a certain head like a catapult into the body of the President, striking him in the region of the right lower vest pocket.

"The usual surprised and relaxed grunt of a man thus assailed came promptly.

"We quickly sent an apology in the direction of the dimly seen form, feeling that the ungracious shock was expensive, even to the humblest clerk in the department.

"A second glance revealed to us the President as the victim of the collision. Then followed a special tender of 'ten thousand pardons,' and the President's reply:

"'One's enough; I wish the whole army would charge like that.'"

"Uncle Abraham" Had Everything Ready

"You can't do anything with them Southern fellows," the old man at the table was saying.

"If they get whipped, they'll retreat to them Southern swamps and bayous along with the fishes and crocodiles. You haven't got the fish-nets made that'll catch 'em."

"Look here, old gentleman," remarked President Lincoln, who was sitting alongside, "we've got just the nets for traitors, in the bayous or anywhere."

"Hey? What nets?"

"Bayou-nets!" and "Uncle Abraham" pointed his joke with his fork, spearing a fishball savagely.

Not as Smooth as He Looked

Mr. Lincoln's skill in parrying troublesome questions was wonderful. Once he received a call from Congressman John Ganson, of Buffalo, one of the ablest lawyers in New York, who, although a Democrat, supported all of Mr. Lincoln's war measures. Mr. Ganson wanted explanations. Mr. Ganson was very bald with a perfectly smooth face. He had a most direct and aggressive way of stating his views or of demanding what he thought he was entitled to. He said: "Mr. Lincoln, I have supported all of your measures and think I am entitled to your confidence. We are voting and acting in the dark in Congress, and I demand to know—think I have the right to ask and to know—what is the present situation, and what are the prospects and conditions of the several campaigns and armies."

Mr. Lincoln looked at him critically for a moment and then said: "Ganson, how clean you shave!"

Most men would have been offended, but Ganson was too broad and intelligent a man not to see the point and retire at once, satisfied, from the field.

A Small Crop

Chauncey M. Depew says that Mr. Lincoln told him the following story, which he claimed was one of the best two things he ever originated: He was trying a case in Illinois where he appeared for a prisoner charged with aggravated assault and battery. The complainant had told a horrible story of the attack, which his appearance fully justified, when the District Attorney handed the witness over to Mr. Lincoln, for cross-examination. Mr. Lincoln said he had no testimony, and unless he could break down the complainant's story he saw no way out. He had come to the conclusion that the witness was a bumptious man, who rather prided himself upon his smartness in repartee and, so, after looking at him for some minutes, he said:

"Well, my friend, how much ground did you and my client here fight over?"

The fellow answered: "About six acres."

"Well," said Mr. Lincoln, "don't you think that this is an almighty small crop of fight to gather from such a big piece of ground?"

The jury laughed. The Court and District-Attorney and complainant all joined in, and the case was laughed out of court.

"Never Regret What You Don't Write"

A simple remark one of the party might make would remind Mr. Lincoln of an apropos story.

Secretary of the Treasury Chase happened to remark, "Oh, I am so sorry that I did not write a letter to Mr. So-and-so before I left home!"

President Lincoln promptly responded:

"Chase, never regret what you don't write; it is what you do write that you are often called upon to feel sorry for."

A Vain General

In an interview between President Lincoln and Petroleum V. Nasby, the name came up of a recently deceased politician of Illinois whose merit was blemished by great vanity. His funeral was very largely attended.

"If General —— had known how big a funeral he would have had," said Mr. Lincoln, "he would have died years ago."

Death Bed Repentance

A Senator, who was calling upon Mr. Lincoln, mentioned the name of a most virulent and dishonest official; one, who, though very brilliant, was very bad.

"It's a good thing for B——" said Mr. Lincoln, "that there is such a thing as a deathbed repentance."

No Cause for Pride

A member of Congress from Ohio came into Mr. Lincoln's presence in a state of unutterable intoxication, and sinking into a chair, exclaimed in tones that welled up fuzzy through the gallon or more of whiskey that he contained, "Oh, 'why should (hic) the spirit of mortal be proud?'"

"My dear sir," said the President, regarding him closely, "I see no reason whatever."

Chapter 2

The Story of Lincoln's Life

"'The Short and Simple Annals of the Poor'"

When Abraham Lincoln once was asked to tell the story of his life, he replied:

"It is contained in one line of Gray's 'Elegy in a Country Church-yard':

"'The short and simple annals of the poor.'"

That was true at the time he said it, as everything else he said was Truth, but he was then only at the beginning of a career that was to glorify him as one of the heroes of the world, and place his name forever beside the immortal name of the mighty Washington.

Many great men, particularly those of America, began life in humbleness and poverty, but none ever came from such depths or rose to such a height as Abraham Lincoln.

His birthplace, in Hardin county, Kentucky, was but a wilderness, and Spencer county, Indiana, to which the Lincoln family removed when Abraham was in his eighth year, was a wilder and still more uncivilized region.

The little red schoolhouse which now so thickly adorns the country hillside had not yet been built. There were scattered log school-houses, but they were few and far between. In several of these Mr. Lincoln got the rudiments of an education—an education that was never finished, for to the day of his death he was a student and a seeker after knowledge.

Some records of his schoolboy days are still left us. One is a book made and bound by Lincoln himself, in which he had written the table of weights and measures, and the sums to be worked out therefrom. This was his arithmetic, for he was too poor to own a printed copy.

A Youthful Poet

On one of the pages of this quaint book he had written these four lines of schoolboy doggerel:

> *"Abraham Lincoln,*
> *His Hand and Pen,*
> *He Will be Good,*
> *But God knows when."*

The poetic spirit was strong in the young scholar just then for on another page of the same book he had written these two verses, which are supposed to have been original with him:

> *"Time, what an empty vapor 'tis,*
> *And days, how swift they are;*
> *Swift as an Indian arrow*
> *Fly on like a shooting star.*
>
> *The present moment just is here,*
> *Then slides away in haste,*
> *That we can never say they're ours,*
> *But only say they're past."*

Another specimen of the poetical, or rhyming ability, is found in the following couplet, written by him for his friend, Joseph C. Richardson:

> *"Good boys who to their books apply,*
> *Will all be great men by and by."*

In all, Lincoln's "schooling" did not amount to a year's time, but he was a constant student outside of the schoolhouse. He read all the books he could borrow, and it was his chief delight during the day to lie under the shade of some tree, or at night in front of an open fireplace, reading and studying. His favorite books were the Bible and Aesop's fables, which he kept always within reach and read time and again.

The first law book he ever read was "The Statutes of Indiana," and it was from this work that he derived his ambition to be a lawyer.

Made Speeches When a Boy

When he was but a barefoot boy he would often make political speeches to the boys in the neighborhood, and when he had reached young manhood and was engaged in the labor of chopping wood or splitting rails he continued this practice of speech-making with only the stumps and surrounding trees for hearers.

At the age of seventeen he had attained his full height of six feet four inches and it was at this time he engaged as a ferry boatman on the Ohio river, at thirty-seven cents a day.

That he was seriously beginning to think of public affairs even at this early age is shown by the fact that about this time he wrote a composition on the American Government, urging the necessity for preserving the Constitution and perpetuating the Union. A Rockport lawyer, by the name of Pickert, who read this composition, declared that "the world couldn't beat it."

When the dreaded disease, known as the "milk-sick" created such havoc in Indiana in 1829, the father of Abraham Lincoln, who was of a roving disposition, sought and found a new home in Illinois, locating near the town of Decatur, in Macon county, on a bluff overlooking the Sangamon river. A short time thereafter Abraham Lincoln came of age, and having done his duty to his father, began life on his own account.

His first employer was a man named Denton Offut, who engaged Lincoln, together with his step-brother and John Hanks, to take a boat-load of stock and provisions to New Orleans. Offut was so well pleased with the energy and skill that Lincoln displayed on this trip that he engaged him as clerk in a store which Offut opened a few months later at New Salem.

It was while clerking for Offut that Lincoln performed many of those marvelous feats of strength for which he was noted in his youth, and displayed his wonderful skill as a wrestler. In addition to being six feet four inches high he now weighed two hundred and fourteen pounds. And his strength and skill were so great combined that he could out-wrestle and out-lift any man in that section of the country.

During his clerkship in Offut's store Lincoln continued to read and study and made considerable progress in grammar and mathematics. Offut failed in business and disappeared from the village. In the language of Lincoln he "petered out," and his tall, muscular clerk had to seek other employment.

Assistant Pilot on a Steamboat

In his first public speech, which had already been delivered, Lincoln had contended that the Sangamon river was navigable, and it now fell to his lot to assist in giving practical proof of his argument. A steamboat had arrived at New Salem from Cincinnati, and Lincoln was hired as an assistant in piloting the vessel through the uncertain channel of the Sangamon river to the Illinois river. The way was obstructed by a milldam. Lincoln insisted to the owners of the dam that under the Federal Constitution and laws no one had a right to dam up or obstruct a navigable stream and as he had already proved that the Sangamon was navigable a portion of the dam was torn away and the boat passed safely through.

"Captain Lincoln" Pleased Him

At this period in his career the Blackhawk War broke out, and Lincoln was one of the first to respond to Governor Reynold's call for a thousand mounted volunteers to assist the United States troops in driving Blackhawk back across the Mississippi. Lincoln enlisted in the company from Sangamon county and was elected captain. He often remarked that this gave him greater pleasure than anything that had happened in his life up to this time. He had, however, no opportunities in this war to perform any distinguished service.

Upon his return from the Blackhawk War, in which, as he said afterward, in a humorous speech, when in Congress, that he "fought, bled and came away," he was an unsuccessful candidate for the Legislature. This was the only time in his life, as he himself has said, that he was ever beaten by the people. Although defeated, in his own town of New Salem he received all of the two hundred and eight votes cast except three.

Failure as a Business Man

Lincoln's next business venture was with William Berry in a general store, under the firm name of Lincoln & Berry, but did not take long to show that he was not adapted for a business career. The firm failed, Berry died and the debts of the firm fell entirely upon Lincoln. Many of these debts he might have escaped legally, but he assumed them all and it was not until fifteen years later that the last indebtedness of Lincoln & Berry was discharged. During his membership in this firm he had applied himself to the study of law, beginning at the beginning, that is with Blackstone. Now that he had nothing to do he spent much of his time lying under the shade of a tree poring over law books, borrowed from a comrade in the Blackhawk War, who was then a practicing lawyer at Springfield.

Gains Fame as a Story Teller

It was about this time, too, that Lincoln's fame as a story-teller began to spread far and wide. His sayings and his jokes were repeated throughout that section of the country, and he was famous as a story-teller before anyone ever heard of him as a lawyer or a politician.

It required no little moral courage to resist the temptation that beset an idle young man on every hand at that time, for drinking and carousing were of daily and nightly occurrence. Lincoln never drank intoxicating liquors, nor did he at that time use tobacco, but in any sports that called for skill or muscle he took a lively interest, even in horse races and cock fights.

Surveyor with No Strings on Him

John Calhoun was at that time surveyor of Sangamon county. He had been a lawyer and had noticed the studious Lincoln. Needing an assistant he offered the place to Lincoln. The average young man without any regular employment and hard-pressed for means to pay his board as Lincoln was, would have jumped at the opportunity, but a question of principle was involved which had to be settled before Lincoln would accept. Calhoun was a Democrat and Lincoln was a Whig, therefore Lincoln said, "I will take the office if I can be perfectly free in my political actions, but if my sentiments or even expression of them are to be abridged in any way, I would not have it or any other office."

With this understanding he accepted the office and began to study books on surveying, furnished him by his employer. He was not a natural mathematician, and in working out his most difficult problems he sought the assistance of Mentor Graham, a famous schoolmaster in those days, who had previously assisted Lincoln in his studies. He soon became a competent surveyor, however, and was noted for the accurate way in which he ran his lines and located his corners.

Surveying was not as profitable then as it has since become, and the young surveyor often had to take his pay in some article other than money. One old settler relates that for a survey made for him by Lincoln he paid two buckskins, which Hannah Armstrong "foxed" on his pants so that the briars would not wear them out.

About this time, 1833, he was made postmaster at New Salem, the first Federal office he ever held. Although the postoffice was located in a store, Lincoln usually carried the mail around in his hat and distributed it to people when he met them.

A Member of the Legislature

The following year Lincoln again ran for the Legislature, this time as an avowed Whig. Of the four successful candidates, Lincoln received the second highest number of votes.

When Lincoln went to take his seat in the Legislature at Vandalia he was so poor that he was obliged to borrow $200 to buy suitable clothes and uphold the dignity of his new position. He took little part in the proceedings, keeping in the background, but forming many lasting acquaintances and friendships.

Two years later, when he was again a candidate for the same office, there were more political issues to be met, and Lincoln met them with characteristic honesty and boldness. During the campaign he issued the following letter:

"New Salem, June 13, 1836.

"To the Editor of The Journal:

"In your paper of last Saturday I see a communication over the signature of 'Many Voters' in which the candidates who are announced in the journal are called upon to 'show their hands.' Agreed. Here's mine:

"I go for all sharing the privileges of the government who assist in bearing its burdens. Consequently, I go for admitting all whites to the right of suffrage who pay taxes or bear arms (by no means excluding females).

"If elected, I shall consider the whole people of Sangamon my constituents, as well those that oppose as those that support me.

"While acting as their Representative, I shall be governed by their will on all subjects upon which I have the means of knowing what their will is; and upon all others I shall do what my own judgment teaches me will best advance their interests. Whether elected or not, I go for distributing the proceeds of the sales of public lands to the several States to enable our State, in common with others, to dig canals and construct railroads without borrowing money and paying the interest on it.

"If alive on the first Monday in November, I shall vote for Hugh L. White, for President.

"Very respectfully,

"A. LINCOLN."

This was just the sort of letter to win the support of the plain-spoken voters of Sangamon county. Lincoln not only received more votes than any other candidate on the Legislative ticket, but the county which had always been Democratic was turned Whig.

The Famous "Long Nine"

The other candidates elected with Lincoln were Ninian W. Edwards, John Dawson, Andrew McCormick, "Dan" Stone, William F. Elkin, Robert L. Wilson, "Joe" Fletcher, and Archer G. Herndon. These were known as the "Long Nine." Their average height was six feet, and average weight two hundred pounds.

This Legislature was one of the most famous that ever convened in Illinois. Bonds to the amount of $12,000,000 were voted to assist in building thirteen hundred miles of railroad, to widen and deepen all the streams in the State and to dig a canal from the Illinois river to Lake Michigan. Lincoln favored all these plans, but in justice to him it must be said that the people he represented were also in favor of them.

It was at this session that the State capital was changed from Vandalia to Springfield. Lincoln, as the leader of the "Long Nine," had charge of the bill and after a long and bitter struggle succeeded in passing it.

Begins to Oppose Slavery

At this early stage in his career Abraham Lincoln began his opposition to slavery which eventually resulted in his giving liberty to four million human beings. This Legislature passed the following resolutions on slavery:

"Resolved by the General Assembly, of the State of Illinois: That we highly disapprove of the formation of Abolition societies and of the doctrines promulgated by them.

"That the right of property in slaves is sacred to the slave-holding

States by the Federal Constitution, and that they cannot be deprived of that right without their consent,

"That the General Government cannot abolish slavery in the District of Columbia against the consent of the citizens of said district without a manifest breach of good faith."

Against this resolution Lincoln entered a protest, but only succeeded in getting one man in the Legislature to sign the protest with him.

The protest was as follows:

"Resolutions upon the subject of domestic slavery having passed both branches of the General Assembly at its present session, the undersigned hereby protest against the passage of the same.

"They believe that the institution of slavery is founded on both injustice and bad policy, but that the promulgation of abolition doctrines tends rather to increase than abate its evils.

"They believe that the Congress of the United States has no power under the Constitution to interfere with the institution of slavery in the different States.

"They believe that the Congress of the United States has the power under the Constitution to abolish slavery in the District of Columbia, but that the power ought not to be exercised unless at the request of the people of the District.

"The difference between these opinions and those contained in the above resolutions is their reason for entering this protest.

"DAN STONE, "A. LINCOLN,

"Representatives from the county of Sangamon."

Begins to Practice Law

At the end of this session of the Legislature, Mr. Lincoln decided to remove to Springfield and practice law. He entered the office of John T. Stuart, a former comrade in the Blackhawk War, and in March, 1837, was licensed to practice.

Stephen T. Logan was judge of the Circuit Court, and Stephen A. Douglas, who was destined to become Lincoln's greatest political opponent, was prosecuting attorney. When Lincoln was not in his

law office his headquarters were in the store of his friend Joshua
F. Speed, in which gathered all the youthful orators and statesmen
of that day, and where many exciting arguments and discussions
were held. Lincoln and Douglas both took part in the discussion
held in Speed's store. Douglas was the acknowledged leader of the
Democratic side and Lincoln was rapidly coming to the front as a
leader among the Whig debaters. One evening in the midst of a
heated argument Douglas, or "the Little Giant," as he was called,
exclaimed:

"This store is no place to talk politics."

His First Joint Debate

Arrangements were at once made for a joint debate between the
leading Democrats and Whigs to take place in a local church. The
Democrats were represented by Douglas, Calhoun, Lamborn and
Thomas. The Whig speakers were Judge Logan, Colonel E. D. Baker,
Mr. Browning and Lincoln. This discussion was the forerunner of the
famous joint-debate between Lincoln and Douglas, which took place
some years later and attracted the attention of the people throughout the United States. Although Mr. Lincoln was the last speaker in
the first discussion held, his speech attracted more attention than
any of the others and added much to his reputation as a public
debater.

Mr. Lincoln's last campaign for the Legislature was in 1840. In
the same year he was made an elector on the Harrison presidential
ticket, and in his canvass of the State frequently met the Democratic
champion, Douglas, in debate. After 1840 Mr. Lincoln declined re-
election to the Legislature, but he was a presidential elector on the
Whig tickets of 1844 and 1852, and on the Republican ticket for the
State at large in 1856.

Marries a Springfield Belle

Among the social belles of Springfield was Mary Todd, a handsome and cultivated girl of the illustrious descent which could be traced back to the sixth century, to whom Mr. Lincoln was married in 1842. Stephen A. Douglas was his competitor in love as well as in politics. He courted Mary Todd until it became evident that she preferred Mr. Lincoln.

Previous to his marriage Mr. Lincoln had two love affairs, one of them so serious that it left an impression upon his whole future life. One of the objects of his affection was Miss Mary Owen, of Green county, Kentucky, who decided that Mr. Lincoln "was deficient in those little links which make up the chain of woman's happiness." The affair ended without any damage to Mr. Lincoln's heart or the heart of the lady.

Story of Anne Rutledge

Lincoln's first love, however, had a sad termination. The object of his affections at that time was Anne Rutledge, whose father was one of the founders of New Salem. Like Miss Owen, Miss Rutledge was also born in Kentucky, and was gifted with the beauty and graces that distinguish many Southern women. At the time that Mr. Lincoln and Anne Rutledge were engaged to be married, he thought himself too poor to properly support a wife, and they decided to wait until such time as he could better his financial condition. A short time thereafter Miss Rutledge was attacked with a fatal illness, and her death was such a blow to her intended husband that for a long time his friends feared that he would lose his mind.

His Duel with Shields

Just previous to his marriage with Mary Todd, Mr. Lincoln was challenged to fight a duel by James Shields, then Auditor of State. The challenge grew out of some humorous letters concerning Shields, published in a local paper. The first of these letters was written by Mr. Lincoln. The others by Mary Todd and her sister. Mr. Lincoln acknowledged the authorship of the letters without naming the ladies, and agreed to meet Shields on the field of honor. As he had the choice of weapons he named broadswords, and actually went to the place selected for the duel.

The duel was never fought. Mutual friends got together and patched up an understanding between Mr. Lincoln and the hot-headed Irishman.

Forms New Partnership

Before this time Mr. Lincoln had dissolved partnership with Stuart and entered into a law partnership with Judge Logan. In 1843 both Lincoln and Logan were candidates for nomination for Congress and the personal ill-will caused by their rivalry resulted in the dissolution of the firm and the formation of a new law firm of Lincoln & Herndon, which continued, nominally at least, until Mr. Lincoln's death.

The congressional nomination, however, went to Edward D. Baker, who was elected. Two years later the principal candidates for the Whig nomination for Congress were Mr. Lincoln and his former law partner, Judge Logan. Party sentiment was so strongly in favor of Lincoln that Judge Logan withdrew and Lincoln was nominated unanimously. The campaign that followed was one of the most memorable and interesting ever held in Illinois.

Defeats Peter Cartwright for Congress

Mr. Lincoln's opponent on the Democratic ticket was no less a person than old Peter Cartwright, the famous Methodist preacher and circuit rider. Cartwright had preached to almost every congregation in the district and had a strong following in all the churches. Mr. Lincoln did not underestimate the strength of his great rival. He abandoned his law business entirely and gave his whole attention to the canvass. This time Mr. Lincoln was victorious and was elected by a large majority.

When Lincoln took his seat in Congress, in 1847, he was the only Whig member from Illinois. His great political rival, Douglas, was in the Senate. The Mexican War had already broken out, which, in common with his party, he had opposed. Later in life he was charged with having opposed the voting of supplies to the American troops in Mexico, but this was a falsehood which he easily disproved. He was strongly opposed to the War, but after it was once begun he urged its vigorous prosecution and voted with the Democrats on all measures concerning the care and pay of the soldiers. His opposition to the War, however, cost him a re-election; it cost his party the congressional district, which was carried by the Democrats in 1848. Lincoln's former law partner, Judge Logan, secured the Whig nomination that year and was defeated.

Makes Speeches for "Old Zach"

In the national convention at Philadelphia, in 1848, Mr. Lincoln was a delegate and advocated the nomination of General Taylor.

After the nomination of General Taylor, or "Old Zach," or "rough and Ready," as he was called, Mr. Lincoln made a tour of New York and several New England States, making speeches for his candidate.

Mr. Lincoln went to New England in this campaign on account of the great defection in the Whig party. General Taylor's nomination was unsatisfactory to the free-soil element, and such leaders as Henry Wilson, Charles Francis Adams, Charles Allen, Charles Sumner, Stephen C. Phillips, Richard H. Dana, Jr., and Anson Burlingame, were in open revolt. Mr. Lincoln's speeches were confined largely to a defense of General Taylor, but at the same time he denounced the free-soilers for helping to elect Cass. Among other things he said that the free-soilers had but one principle and that they reminded him of the Yankee peddler going to sell a pair of pantaloons and describing them as "large enough for any man, and small enough for any boy."

It is an odd fact in history that the prominent Whigs of Massachusetts at that time became the opponents of Mr. Lincoln's election to the presidency and the policy of his administration, while the free-soilers, whom he denounced, were among his strongest supporters, advisers and followers.

At the second session of Congress Mr. Lincoln's one act of consequence was the introduction of a bill providing for the gradual emancipation of the slaves in the District of Columbia. Joshua R. Giddings, the great antislavery agitator, and one or two lesser lights supported it, but the bill was laid on the table.

After General Taylor's election Mr. Lincoln had the distribution of Federal patronage in his own Congressional district, and this added much to his political importance, although it was a ceaseless source of worry to him.

Declines a High Office

Just before the close of his term in Congress Mr. Lincoln was an applicant for the office of Commissioner of the General Land Office, but was unsuccessful. He had been such a factor in General Taylor's election that the administration thought something was due him, and after his return to Illinois he was called to Washington and offered the Governorship of the Territory of Oregon. It is likely he would have accepted this had not Mrs. Lincoln put her foot down with an emphatic no.

He declined a partnership with a well-known Chicago lawyer and returning to his Springfield home resumed the practice of law.

From this time until the repeal of the Missouri Compromise, which opened the way for the admission of slavery into the territories, Mr. Lincoln devoted himself more industriously than ever to the practice of law, and during those five years he was probably a greater student than he had ever been before. His partner, W. H. Herndon, has told of the changes that took place in the courts and in the methods of practice while Mr. Lincoln was away.

Lincoln as a Lawyer

When he returned to active practice he saw at once that the courts had grown more learned and dignified and that the bar relied more upon method and system and a knowledge of the statute law than upon the stump speech method of early days.

Mr. Herndon tells us that Lincoln would lie in bed and read by candle light, sometimes until two o'clock in the morning, while his famous colleagues, Davis, Logan, Swett, Edwards and Herndon, were soundly and sometimes loudly sleeping. He read and reread the statutes and books of practice, devoured Shakespeare, who was always a favorite of his, and studied Euclid so diligently that he could easily demonstrate all the propositions contained in the six books.

Mr. Lincoln detested office work. He left all that to his partner. He disliked to draw up legal papers or to write letters. The firm of which he was a member kept no books. When either Lincoln or Herndon received a fee they divided the money then and there. If his partner were not in the office at the time Mr. Lincoln would wrap up half of the fee in a sheet of paper, on which he would write, "Herndon's half," giving the name of the case, and place it in his partner's desk.

But in court, arguing a case, pleading to the jury and laying down the law, Lincoln was in his element. Even when he had a weak case he was a strong antagonist, and when he had right and justice on his side, as he nearly always had, no one could beat him.

He liked an outdoor life, hence he was fond of riding the circuit. He enjoyed the company of other men, liked discussion and argument, loved to tell stories and to hear them, laughing as heartily at his own stories as he did at those that were told to him.

Telling Stories on the Circuit

The court circuit in those days was the scene of many a story-telling joust, in which Lincoln was always the chief. Frequently he would sit up until after midnight reeling off story after story, each one followed by roars of laughter that could be heard all over the country tavern, in which the story-telling group was gathered. Every type of character would be represented in these groups, from the learned judge on the bench down to the village loafer.

Lincoln's favorite attitude was to sit with his long legs propped up on the rail of the stove, or with his feet against the wall, and thus he would sit for hours entertaining a crowd, or being entertained.

One circuit judge was so fond of Lincoln's stories that he often would sit up until midnight listening to them, and then declare that he had laughed so much he believed his ribs were shaken loose.

The great success of Abraham Lincoln as a trial lawyer was due to a number of facts. He would not take a case if he believed that the law and justice were on the other side. When he addressed a jury he made them feel that he only wanted fair play and justice. He did not talk over their heads, but got right down to a friendly tone such as we use in ordinary conversation, and talked at them, appealing to their honesty and common sense.

And making his argument plain by telling a story or two that brought the matter clearly within their understanding.

When he did not know the law in a particular case he never pretended to know it. If there were no precedents to cover a case he would state his side plainly and fairly; he would tell the jury what he believed was right for them to do, and then conclude with his favorite expression, "it seems to me that this ought to be the law."

Some time before the repeal of the Missouri Compromise a lawyer friend said to him: "Lincoln, the time is near at hand when we shall have to be all Abolitionists or all Democrats."

"When that time comes my mind is made up," he replied, "for I believe the slavery question never can be compromised."

The Lion Is Aroused to Action

While Lincoln took a mild interest in politics, he was not a candidate for office, except as a presidential elector, from the time of leaving Congress until the repeal of the Missouri Compromise. This repeal Legislation was the work of Lincoln's political antagonist, Stephen A. Douglas, and aroused Mr. Lincoln to action as the lion is roused by some foe worthy of his great strength and courage.

Mr. Douglas argued that the true intent and meaning of the act was not to legislate slavery into any territory or state, nor to exclude it therefrom, but to leave the people perfectly free to form and regulate their domestic institutions in their own way.

"Douglas' argument amounts to this," said Mr. Lincoln, "that if any one man chooses to enslave another no third man shall be allowed to object."

After the adjournment of Congress Mr. Douglas returned to Illinois and began to defend his action in the repeal of the Missouri Compromise. His most important speech was made at Springfield, and Mr. Lincoln was selected to answer it. That speech alone was sufficient to make Mr. Lincoln the leader of anti-Slavery sentiment in the West, and some of the men who heard it declared that it was the greatest speech he ever made.

With the repeal of the Missouri Compromise the Whig party began to break up, the majority of its members who were pronounced Abolitionists began to form the nucleus of the Republican party. Before this party was formed, however, Mr. Lincoln was induced to follow Douglas around the State and reply to him, but after one meeting at Peoria, where they both spoke, they entered into an agreement to return to their homes and make no more speeches during the campaign.

Seeks a Seat in the Senate

Mr. Lincoln made no secret at this time of his ambition to represent Illinois in the United States Senate. Against his protest he was nominated and elected to the Legislature, but resigned his seat. His old rival, James Shields, with whom he was once near to a duel, was then senator, and his term was to expire the following year.

A letter, written by Mr. Lincoln to a friend in Paris, Illinois, at this time is interesting and significant. He wrote:

"I have a suspicion that a Whig has been elected to the Legislature from Eagar. If this is not so, why, then, 'nix cum arous;' but if it is so, then could you not make a mark with him for me for United States senator? I really have some chance."

Another candidate besides Mr. Lincoln was seeking the seat in the United States Senate, soon to be vacated by Mr. Shields. This was Lyman Trumbull, an anti-slavery Democrat. When the Legislature met it was found that Mr. Lincoln lacked five votes of an election, while Mr. Trumbull had but five supporters. After several ballots Mr. Lincoln feared that Trumbull's votes would be given to a Democratic candidate and he determined to sacrifice himself for the principle at stake. Accordingly he instructed his friends in the Legislature to vote for Judge Trumbull, which they did, resulting in Trumbull's election.

The Abolitionists in the West had become very radical in their views, and did not hesitate to talk of opposing the extension of slavery by the use of force if necessary. Mr. Lincoln, on the other hand, was conservative and counseled moderation. In the meantime many outrages, growing out of the extension of slavery, were being perpetrated on the borders of Kansas and Missouri, and they no doubt influenced Mr. Lincoln to take a more radical stand against the slavery question.

An incident occurred at this time which had great effect in this direction. The son of a colored woman in Springfield had gone South to work. He was born free, but did not have his free papers with him. He was arrested and would have been sold into slavery to pay his prison expenses, had not Mr. Lincoln and some friends purchased his liberty. Previous to this Mr. Lincoln had tried to secure the boy's release through the Governor of Illinois, but the Governor informed him that nothing could be done.

Then it was that Mr. Lincoln rose to his full height and exclaimed:

"Governor, I'll make the ground in this country too hot for the foot of a slave, whether you have the legal power to secure the release of this boy or not."

Helps to Organize the Republican Party

The year after Mr. Trumbull's election to the Senate the Republican party was formally organized. A state convention of that party was called to meet at Bloomington May 29, 1856. The call for this convention was signed by many Springfield Whigs, and among the names was that of Abraham Lincoln. Mr. Lincoln's name had been signed to the call by his law partner, but when he was informed of this action he endorsed it fully. Among the famous men who took part in this convention were Abraham Lincoln, Lyman Trumbull, David Davis, Leonard Swett, Richard Yates, Norman, B. Judd and Owen Lovejoy, the Alton editor, whose life, like Lincoln's, finally paid the penalty for his Abolition views. The party nominated for Governor, Wm. H. Bissell, a veteran of the Mexican War, and adopted a platform ringing with anti-slavery sentiment.

Mr. Lincoln was the greatest power in the campaign that followed. He was one of the Fremont Presidential electors, and he went to work with all his might to spread the new party gospel and make votes for the old "Path-Finder of the Rocky Mountains."

An amusing incident followed close after the Bloomington convention. A meeting was called at Springfield to ratify the action at Bloomington. Only three persons attended—Mr. Lincoln, his law partner and a man named John Paine. Mr. Lincoln made a speech to his colleagues, in which, among other things, he said: "While all seems dead, the age itself is not. It liveth as sure as our Maker liveth."

In this campaign Mr. Lincoln was in general demand not only in his own state, but in Indiana, Iowa and Wisconsin as well.

The result of that Presidential campaign was the election of

Buchanan as President, Bissell as Governor, leaving Mr. Lincoln the undisputed leader of the new party. Hence it was that two years later he was the inevitable man to oppose Judge Douglas in the campaign for United States Senator.

The Rail-Splitter vs. the Little Giant

No record of Abraham Lincoln's career would be complete without the story of the memorable joint debates between the "Rail-Splitter of the Sangamon Valley" and the "Little Giant." The opening lines in Mr. Lincoln's speech to the Republican Convention were not only prophetic of the coming rebellion, but they clearly made the issue between the Republican and Democratic parties for two Presidential campaigns to follow. The memorable sentences were as follows:

"A house divided against itself cannot stand. I believe this Government cannot endure permanently half slave and half free. I do not expect the Union to be dissolved; I do not expect the house to fall; but I do expect it will cease to be divided. It will become all the one thing or the other. Either the opponents of slavery will arrest the further spread of it and place it where the public mind shall rest in the belief that it is in the course of ultimate extinction, or its advocates will push it forward till it becomes alike lawful in all the states, old as well as new, North as well as South."

It is universally conceded that this speech contained the most important utterances of Mr. Lincoln's life.

Previous to its delivery, the Democratic convention had endorsed Mr. Douglas for re-election to the Senate, and the Republican convention had resolved that "Abraham Lincoln is our first and only choice for United States Senator, to fill the vacancy about to be created by the expiration of Mr. Douglas' term of office."

Before Judge Douglas had made many speeches in this Senatorial campaign, Mr. Lincoln challenged him to a joint debate, which was accepted, and seven memorable meetings between these two great leaders followed. The places and dates were: Ottawa, August 21st; Freeport, August 27th; Jonesboro, September 15th; Charleston,

September 18th; Galesburg, October 7th; Quincy, October 13th; and Alton, October 15th.

The debates not only attracted the attention of the people in the state of Illinois, but aroused an interest throughout the whole country equal to that of a Presidential election.

Like Crowds at a Circus

All the meetings of the joint debate were attended by immense crowds of people. They came in all sorts of vehicles, on horseback, and many walked weary miles on foot to hear these two great leaders discuss the issues of the campaign. There had never been political meetings held under such unusual conditions as these, and there probably never will be again. At every place the speakers were met by great crowds of their friends and escorted to the platforms in the open air where the debates were held. The processions that escorted the speakers were most unique. They carried flags and banners and were preceded by bands of music. The people discharged cannons when they had them, and, when they did not, blacksmiths' anvils were made to take their places.

Oftentimes a part of the escort would be mounted, and in most of the processions were chariots containing young ladies representing the different states of the Union designated by banners they carried. Besides the bands, there was usually vocal music. Patriotic songs were the order of the day, the "Star-Spangled Banner" and "Hail Columbia" being great favorites.

So far as the crowds were concerned, these joint debates took on the appearance of a circus day, and this comparison was strengthened by the sale of lemonade, fruit, melons and confectionery on the outskirts of the gatherings.

At Ottawa, after his speech, Mr. Lincoln was carried around on the shoulders of his enthusiastic supporters, who did not put him down until they reached the place where he was to spend the night.

In the joint debates, each of the candidates asked the other a series of questions. Judge Douglas' replies to Mr. Lincoln's shrewd questions helped Douglas to win the Senatorial election, but they lost him the support of the South in the campaign for President two years thereafter. Mr. Lincoln was told when he framed his questions that if Douglas answered them in the way it was believed he would that the answers would make him Senator.

"That may be," said Mr. Lincoln, "but if he takes that shoot he never can be President."

The prophecy was correct. Mr. Douglas was elected Senator, but two years later only carried one state—Missouri—for President.

His Buckeye Campaign

After the close of this canvass, Mr. Lincoln again devoted himself to the practice of his profession, but he was destined to remain but a short time in retirement. In the fall of 1859 Mr. Douglas went to Ohio to stump the state for his friend, Mr. Pugh, the Democratic candidate for Governor. The Ohio Republicans at once asked Mr. Lincoln to come to the state and reply to the "Little Giant." He accepted the invitation and made two masterly speeches in the campaign. In one of them, delivered at Cincinnati, he prophesied the outcome of the rebellion if the Southern people attempted to divide the Union by force.

Addressing himself particularly to the Kentuckians in the audience, he said:

"I have told you what we mean to do. I want to know, now, when that thing takes place, what do you mean to do? I often hear it intimated that you mean to divide the Union whenever a Republican, or anything like it, is elected President of the United States. [A Voice—"That is so."] 'That is so,' one of them says; I wonder if he is a Kentuckian? [A Voice—"He is a Douglas man."] Well, then, I want to know what you are going to do with your half of it?

"Are you going to split the Ohio down through, and push your half off a piece? Or are you going to keep it right alongside of us outrageous fellows? Or are you going to build up a wall some way between your country, and ours, by which that movable property of yours can't come over here any more, to the danger of your losing it? Do you think you can better yourselves on that subject by leaving us here under no obligation whatever to return those specimens of your movable property that come hither?

"You have divided the Union because we would not do right with you, as you think, upon that subject; when we cease to be under obligations to do anything for you, how much better off do you think you will be? Will you make war upon us and kill us all? Why, gentlemen, I think you are as gallant and as brave men as live; that you can fight as bravely in a good cause, man for man, as any other people living; that you have shown yourselves capable of this upon various occasions; but, man for man, you are not better than we are, and there are not so many of you as there are of us.

"You will never make much of a hand at whipping us. If we were fewer in numbers than you, I think that you could whip us; if we were equal, it would likely be a drawn battle; but, being inferior in numbers, you will make nothing by attempting to master us.

"But perhaps I have addressed myself as long, or longer, to the Kentuckians than I ought to have done, inasmuch as I have said that, whatever course you take, we intend in the end to beat you."

First Visit to New York

Later in the year Mr. Lincoln also spoke in Kansas, where he was received with great enthusiasm, and in February of the following year he made his great speech in Cooper Union, New York, to an immense gathering, presided over by William Cullen Bryant, the poet, who was then editor of the New York Evening Post. There was great curiosity to see the Western rail-splitter who had so lately met the famous "Little Giant" of the West in debate, and Mr. Lincoln's speech was listened to by many of the ablest men in the East.

This speech won for him many supporters in the Presidential campaign that followed, for his hearers at once recognized his wonderful ability to deal with the questions then uppermost in the public mind.

First Nomination for President

The Republican National Convention of 1860 met in Chicago, May 16, in an immense building called the "Wigwam." The leading candidates for President were William H. Seward of New York and Abraham Lincoln of Illinois. Among others spoken of were Salmon P. Chase of Ohio and Simon Cameron of Pennsylvania.

On the first ballot for President, Mr. Seward received one hundred and seventy-three and one-half votes; Mr. Lincoln, one hundred and two votes, the others scattering. On the first ballot, Vermont had divided her vote, but on the second the chairman of the Vermont delegation announced: "Vermont casts her ten votes for the young giant of the West—Abraham Lincoln."

This was the turning point in the convention toward Mr. Lincoln's nomination. The second ballot resulted: Seward, one hundred and eighty-four and one-half; Lincoln, one hundred and eighty-one. On the third ballot, Mr. Lincoln received two hundred and thirty votes. One and one-half votes more would nominate him. Before the ballot was announced, Ohio made a change of four votes in favor of Mr. Lincoln, making him the nominee for President.

Other states tried to follow Ohio's example, but it was a long time before any of the delegates could make themselves heard. Cannons planted on top of the wigwam were roaring and booming; the large crowd in the wigwam and the immense throng outside were cheering at the top of their lungs, while bands were playing victorious airs.

When order had been restored, it was announced that on the third ballot Abraham Lincoln of Illinois had received three hundred and fifty-four votes and was nominated by the Republican party to the office of President of the United States.

Mr. Lincoln heard the news of his nomination while sitting in a newspaper office in Springfield, and hurried home to tell his wife.

As Mr. Lincoln had predicted, Judge Douglas' position on slavery in the territories lost him the support of the South, and when the Democratic convention met at Charleston, the slave-holding states forced the nomination of John C. Breckinridge. A considerable number of people who did not agree with either party nominated John Bell of Tennessee.

In the election which followed, Mr. Lincoln carried all of the free states, except New Jersey, which was divided between himself and Douglas; Breckinridge carried all the slave states, except Kentucky, Tennessee and Virginia, which went for Bell, and Missouri gave its vote to Douglas.

Formation of the Southern Confederacy

The election was scarcely over before it was evident that the Southern States did not intend to abide by the result, and that a conspiracy was on foot to divide the Union. Before the Presidential election even, the Secretary of War in President Buchanan's Cabinet had removed one hundred and fifty thousand muskets from Government armories in the North and sent them to Government armories in the South.

Before Mr. Lincoln had prepared his inaugural address, South Carolina, which took the lead in the secession movement, had declared through her Legislature her separation from the Union. Before Mr. Lincoln took his seat, other Southern States had followed the example of South Carolina, and a convention had been held at Montgomery, Alabama, which had elected Jefferson Davis President of the new Confederacy, and Alexander H. Stevens, of Georgia, Vice-President.

Southern men in the Cabinet, Senate and House had resigned their seats and gone home, and Southern States were demanding that Southern forts and Government property in their section should be turned over to them.

Between his election and inauguration, Mr. Lincoln remained silent, reserving his opinions and a declaration of his policy for his inaugural address.

Before Mr. Lincoln's departure from Springfield for Washington, threats had been freely made that he would never reach the capital alive, and, in fact, a conspiracy was then on foot to take his life in the city of Baltimore.

Mr. Lincoln left Springfield on February 11th, in company with his wife and three sons, his brother-in-law, Dr. W. S. Wallace; David Davis, Norman B. Judd, Elmer E. Elsworth, Ward H. Lamon, Colonel E. V. Sunder of the United States Army, and the President's two secretaries.

Good-Bye to the Old Folk

Early in February, before leaving for Washington, Mr. Lincoln slipped away from Springfield and paid a visit to his aged step-mother in Coles county. He also paid a visit to the unmarked grave of his father and ordered a suitable stone to mark the spot.

Before leaving Springfield, he made an address to his fellow-townsmen, in which he displayed sincere sorrow at parting from them.

"Friends," he said, "no one who has never been placed in a like position can understand my feelings at this hour, nor the oppressive sadness I feel at this parting. For more than a quarter of a century I have lived among you, and during all that time I have received nothing but kindness at your hands. Here I have lived from my youth until now I am an old man. Here the most sacred ties of earth were assumed. Here all my children were born, and here one of them lies buried.

"To you, dear friends, I owe all that I have, all that I am. All the strange, checkered past seems to crowd now upon my mind. To-day I leave you. I go to assume a task more difficult than that which devolved upon Washington. Unless the great God who assisted him shall be with and aid me, I must fail; but if the same omniscient mind and almighty arm that directed and protected him shall guide and support me, I shall not fail—I shall succeed. Let us all pray that the God of our fathers may not forsake us now.

"To Him I commend you all. Permit me to ask that with equal sincerity and faith you will invoke His wisdom and guidance for me. With these words I must leave you, for how long I know not. Friends, one and all, I must now bid you an affectionate farewell."

The journey from Springfield to Philadelphia was a continuous ovation for Mr. Lincoln. Crowds assembled to meet him at the various places along the way, and he made them short speeches, full of humor and good feeling. At Harrisburg, Pa., the party was met by Allan Pinkerton, who knew of the plot in Baltimore to take the life of Mr. Lincoln.

The "Secret Passage" to Washington

Throughout his entire life, Abraham Lincoln's physical courage was as great and superb as his moral courage. When Mr. Pinkerton and Mr. Judd urged the President-elect to leave for Washington that night, he positively refused to do it. He said he had made an engagement to assist at a flag raising in the forenoon of the next day and to show himself to the people of Harrisburg in the afternoon, and that he intended to keep both engagements.

At Philadelphia the Presidential party was met by Mr. Seward's son, Frederick, who had been sent to warn Mr. Lincoln of the plot against his life. Mr. Judd, Mr. Pinkerton and Mr. Lamon figured out a plan to take Mr. Lincoln through Baltimore between midnight and daybreak, when the would-be assassins would not be expecting him, and this plan was carried out so thoroughly that even the conductor on the train did not know the President-elect was on board.

Mr. Lincoln was put into his berth and the curtains drawn. He was supposed to be a sick man. When the conductor came around, Mr. Pinkerton handed him the "sick man's" ticket and he passed on without question.

When the train reached Baltimore, at half-past three o'clock in the morning, it was met by one of Mr. Pinkerton's detectives, who reported that everything was "all right," and in a short time the party was speeding on to the national capital, where rooms had been engaged for Mr. Lincoln and his guard at Willard's Hotel.

Mr. Lincoln always regretted this "secret passage" to Washington, for it was repugnant to a man of his high courage. He had agreed to the plan simply because all of his friends urged it as the best thing to do.

Now that all the facts are known, it is assured that his friends were right, and that there never was a moment from the day he crossed the Maryland line until his assassination that his life was not in danger, and was only saved as long as it was by the constant vigilance of those who were guarding him.

His Eloquent Inaugural Address

The wonderful eloquence of Abraham Lincoln—clear, sincere, natural—found grand expression in his first inaugural address, in which he not only outlined his policy toward the States in rebellion, but made that beautiful and eloquent plea for conciliation. The closing sentences of Mr. Lincoln's first inaugural address deservedly take rank with his Gettysburg speech:

"In your hands, my dissatisfied fellow-countrymen," he said, "and not in mine, is the momentous issue of civil war. The Government will not assail you.

"You can have no conflict without being yourselves the aggressors. You have no oath registered in heaven to destroy the Government, while I shall have the most solemn one to 'preserve, protect and defend' it.

"I am loath to close. We are not enemies, but friends. We must not be enemies. Though passion may have strained, it must not break our bonds of affection.

"The mystic cord of memory, stretching from every battle-field and patriot grave to every living heart and hearthstone all over this broad land, will yet swell the chorus of the Union, when again touched, as surely they will be, by the better angels of our nature."

Follows Precedent of Washington

In selecting his Cabinet, Mr. Lincoln, consciously or unconsciously, followed a precedent established by Washington, of selecting men of almost opposite opinions. His Cabinet was composed of William H. Seward of New York, Secretary of State; Salmon P. Chase of Ohio, Secretary of the Treasury; Simon Cameron of Pennsylvania, Secretary of War; Gideon E. Welles of Connecticut, Secretary of the Navy; Caleb B. Smith of Indiana, Secretary of the Interior; Montgomery Blair of Maryland, Postmaster-General; Edward Bates of Missouri, Attorney-General.

Mr. Chase, although an anti-slavery leader, was a States-Rights Federal Republican, while Mr. Seward was a Whig, without having connected himself with the anti-slavery movement.

Mr. Chase and Mr. Seward, the leading men of Mr. Lincoln's Cabinet, were as widely apart and antagonistic in their views as were Jefferson, the Democrat, and Hamilton, the Federalist, the two leaders in Washington's Cabinet. But in bringing together these two strong men as his chief advisers, both of whom had been rival candidates for the Presidency, Mr. Lincoln gave another example of his own greatness and self-reliance, and put them both in a position to render greater service to the Government than they could have done, probably, as President.

Mr. Lincoln had been in office little more than five weeks when the War of the Rebellion began by the firing on Fort Sumter.

Greater Diplomat Than Seward

The War of the Rebellion revealed to the people—in fact, to the whole world—the many sides of Abraham Lincoln's character. It showed him as a real ruler of men—not a ruler by the mere power of might, but by the power of a great brain. In his Cabinet were the ablest men in the country, yet they all knew that Lincoln was abler than any of them.

Mr. Seward, the Secretary of State, was a man famed in statesmanship and diplomacy. During the early stages of the Civil War, when France and England were seeking an excuse to interfere and help the Southern Confederacy, Mr. Seward wrote a letter to our minister in London, Charles Francis Adams, instructing him concerning the attitude of the Federal government on the question of interference, which would undoubtedly have brought about a war with England if Abraham Lincoln had not corrected and amended the letter. He did this, too, without yielding a point or sacrificing in any way his own dignity or that of the country.

Lincoln a Great General

Throughout the four years of war, Mr. Lincoln spent a great deal of time in the War Department, receiving news from the front and conferring with Secretary of War Stanton concerning military affairs.

Mr. Lincoln's War Secretary, Edwin M. Stanton, who had succeeded Simon Cameron, was a man of wonderful personality and iron will. It is generally conceded that no other man could have managed the great War Secretary so well as Lincoln. Stanton had his way in most matters, but when there was an important difference of opinion he always found Lincoln was the master.

Although Mr. Lincoln's communications to the generals in the field were oftener in the nature of suggestions than positive orders, every military leader recognized Mr. Lincoln's ability in military operations. In the early stages of the war, Mr. Lincoln followed closely every plan and movement of McClellan, and the correspondence between them proves Mr. Lincoln to have been far the abler general of the two. He kept close watch of Burnside, too, and when he gave the command of the Army of the Potomac to "Fighting Joe" Hooker he also gave that general some fatherly counsel and advice which was of great benefit to him as a commander.

Absolute Confidence in Grant

It was not until General Grant had been made Commander-in-Chief that President Lincoln felt he had at last found a general who did not need much advice. He was the first to recognize that Grant was a great military leader, and when he once felt sure of this fact nothing could shake his confidence in that general. Delegation after delegation called at the White House and asked for Grant's removal from the head of the army. They accused him of being a butcher, a drunkard, a man without sense or feeling.

President Lincoln listened to all of these attacks, but he always had an apt answer to silence Grant's enemies. Grant was doing what Lincoln wanted done from the first—he was fighting and winning victories, and victories are the only things that count in war.

Reasons for Freeing the Slaves

The crowning act of Lincoln's career as President was the emancipation of the slaves. All of his life he had believed in gradual emancipation, but all of his plans contemplated payment to the slaveholders. While he had always been opposed to slavery, he did not take any steps to use it as a war measure until about the middle of 1862. His chief object was to preserve the Union.

He wrote to Horace Greeley that if he could save the Union without freeing any of the slaves he would do it; that if he could save it by freeing some and leaving the others in slavery he would do that; that if it became necessary to free all the slaves in order to save the Union he would take that course.

The anti-slavery men were continually urging Mr. Lincoln to set the slaves free, but he paid no attention to their petitions and demands until he felt that emancipation would help him to preserve the Union of the States.

The outlook for the Union cause grew darker and darker in 1862, and Mr. Lincoln began to think, as he expressed it, that he must "change his tactics or lose the game." Accordingly he decided to issue the Emancipation Proclamation as soon as the Union army won a substantial victory. The battle of Antietam, on September 17, gave him the opportunity he sought. He told Secretary Chase that he had made a solemn vow before God that if General Lee should be driven back from Pennsylvania he would crown the result by a declaration of freedom to the slaves.

On the twenty-second of that month he issued a proclamation stating that at the end of one hundred days he would issue another proclamation declaring all slaves within any State or Territory to be forever free, which was done in the form of the famous Emancipation Proclamation.

Hard to Refuse Pardons

In the conduct of the war and in his purpose to maintain the Union, Abraham Lincoln exhibited a will of iron and determination that could not be shaken, but in his daily contact with the mothers, wives and daughters begging for the life of some soldier who had been condemned to death for desertion or sleeping on duty he was as gentle and weak as a woman.

It was a difficult matter for him to refuse a pardon if the slightest excuse could be found for granting it.

Secretary Stanton and the commanding generals were loud in declaring that Mr. Lincoln would destroy the discipline of the army by his wholesale pardoning of condemned soldiers, but when we come to examine the individual cases we find that Lincoln was nearly always right, and when he erred it was always on the side of humanity.

During the four years of the long struggle for the preservation of the Union, Mr. Lincoln kept "open shop," as he expressed it, where the general public could always see him and make known their wants and complaints. Even the private soldier was not denied admittance to the President's private office, and no request or complaint was too small or trivial to enlist his sympathy and interest.

A Fun-Loving and Humor-Loving Man

It was once said of Shakespeare that the great mind that conceived the tragedies of "Hamlet," "Macbeth," etc., would have lost its reason if it had not found vent in the sparkling humor of such comedies as "The Merry Wives of Windsor" and "The Comedy of Errors."

The great strain on the mind of Abraham Lincoln produced by four years of civil war might likewise have overcome his reason had it not found vent in the yarns and stories he constantly told. No more fun-loving or humor-loving man than Abraham Lincoln ever lived. He enjoyed a joke even when it was on himself, and probably, while he got his greatest enjoyment from telling stories, he had a keen appreciation of the humor in those that were told him.

His favorite humorous writer was David R. Locke, better known as "Petroleum V. Nasby," whose political satires were quite famous in their day. Nearly every prominent man who has written his recollections of Lincoln has told how the President, in the middle of a conversation on some serious subject, would suddenly stop and ask his hearer if he ever read the Nasby letters.

Then he would take from his desk a pamphlet containing the letters and proceed to read them, laughing heartily at all the good points they contained. There is probably no better evidence of Mr. Lincoln's love of humor and appreciation of it than his letter to Nasby, in which he said: "For the ability to write these things I would gladly trade places with you."

Mr. Lincoln was re-elected President in 1864. His opponent on the Democratic ticket was General George B. McClellan, whose command of the Army of the Potomac had been so unsatisfactory at the beginning of the war. Mr. Lincoln's election was almost unanimous, as McClellan carried but three States—Delaware, Kentucky and New Jersey.

General Grant, in a telegram of congratulation, said that it was "a victory worth more to the country than a battle won."

The war was fast drawing to a close. The black war clouds were breaking and rolling away. Sherman had made his famous march to the sea. Through swamp and ravine, Grant was rapidly tightening the lines around Richmond. Thomas had won his title of the "Rock of Chickamauga." Sheridan had won his spurs as the great modern cavalry commander, and had cleaned out the Shenandoah Valley. Sherman was coming back from his famous march to join Grant at Richmond.

The Confederacy was without a navy. The Kearsarge had sunk the Alabama, and Farragut had fought and won the famous victory in Mobile Bay. It was certain that Lee would soon have to evacuate Richmond only to fall into the hands of Grant.

Lincoln saw the dawn of peace. When he came to deliver his second inaugural address, it contained no note of victory, no exultation over a fallen foe. On the contrary, it breathed the spirit of brotherly love and of prayer for an early peace: "With malice toward none, with charity for all, with firmness in the right as God gives us to see the right, let us finish the work we are in, to bind up the nation's wounds, to care for him who shall have borne the battle and for his widow and his orphans, to do all which may achieve and cherish a just and lasting peace among ourselves and with all nations."

Not long thereafter, General Lee evacuated Richmond with about half of his original army, closely pursued by Grant. The boys in blue overtook their brothers in gray at Appomattox Court House, and there, beneath the warm rays of an April sun, the great Confederate general made his final surrender. The war was over, the American flag was floated over all the territory of the United States, and peace was now a reality. Mr. Lincoln visited Richmond and the final scenes of the war and then returned to Washington to carry out his announced plan of "binding up the nation's wounds."

He had now reached the climax of his career and touched the highest point of his greatness. His great task was over, and the heavy burden that had so long worn upon his heart was lifted.

While the whole nation was rejoicing over the return of peace, the Saviour of the Union was stricken down by the hand of an assassin.

Warnings of His Tragic Death

From early youth, Mr. Lincoln had presentiments that he would die a violent death, or, rather, that his final days would be marked by some great tragic event. From the time of his first election to the Presidency, his closest friends had tried to make him understand that he was in constant danger of assassination, but, notwithstanding his presentiments, he had such splendid courage that he only laughed at their fears.

During the summer months he lived at the Soldiers' Home, some miles from Washington, and frequently made the trip between the White House and the Home without a guard or escort. Secretary of War Stanton and Ward Lamon, Marshal of the District, were almost constantly alarmed over Mr. Lincoln's carelessness in exposing himself to the danger of assassination.

They warned him time and again, and provided suitable bodyguards to attend him. But Mr. Lincoln would often give the guards the slip, and, mounting his favorite riding horse, "Old Abe," would set out alone after dark from the White House for the Soldiers' Home.

While riding to the Home one night, he was fired upon by someone in ambush, the bullet passing through his high hat. Mr. Lincoln would not admit that the man who fired the shot had tried to kill him. He always attributed it to an accident, and begged his friends to say nothing about it.

Now that all the circumstances of the assassination are known, it is plain that there was a deep-laid and well-conceived plot to kill Mr. Lincoln long before the crime was actually committed. When Mr. Lincoln was delivering his second inaugural address on the steps of the Capitol, an excited individual tried to force his way through the guards in the building to get on the platform with Mr. Lincoln.

It was afterward learned that this man was John Wilkes Booth, who afterwards assassinated Mr. Lincoln in Ford's Theatre, on the night of the 14th of April.

Lincoln at the Theatre

The manager of the theatre had invited the President to witness a performance of a new play known as "Our American Cousin," in which the famous actress, Laura Keane, was playing. Mr. Lincoln was particularly fond of the theatre. He loved Shakespeare's plays above all others and never missed a chance to see the leading Shakespearean actors.

As "Our American Cousin" was a new play, the President did not care particularly to see it, but as Mrs. Lincoln was anxious to go, he consented and accepted the invitation.

General Grant was in Washington at the time, and as he was extremely anxious about the personal safety of the President, he reported every day regularly at the White House. Mr. Lincoln invited General Grant and his wife to accompany him and Mrs. Lincoln to the theatre on the night of the assassination, and the general accepted, but while they were talking he received a note from Mrs. Grant saying that she wished to leave Washington that evening to visit her daughter in Burlington. General Grant made his excuses to the President and left to accompany Mrs. Grant to the railway station. It afterwards became known that it was also a part of the plot to assassinate General Grant, and only Mrs. Grant's departure from Washington that evening prevented the attempt from being made.

General Grant afterwards said that as he and Mrs. Grant were riding along Pennsylvania avenue to the railway station a horseman rode rapidly by at a gallop, and, wheeling his horse, rode back, peering into their carriage as he passed.

Mrs. Grant remarked to the general: "That is the very man who sat near us at luncheon to-day and tried to overhear our conversation. He was so rude, you remember, as to cause us to leave the dining-room. Here he is again, riding after us."

General Grant attributed the action of the man to idle curiosity, but learned afterward that the horseman was John Wilkes Booth.

Lamon's Remarkable Request

Probably one reason why Mr. Lincoln did not particularly care to go to the theatre that night was a sort of half promise he had made to his friend and bodyguard, Marshal Lamon. Two days previous he had sent Lamon to Richmond on business connected with a call of a convention for reconstruction. Before leaving, Mr. Lamon saw Mr. Usher, the Secretary of the Interior, and asked him to persuade Mr. Lincoln to use more caution about his personal safety, and to go out as little as possible while Lamon was absent. Together they went to see Mr. Lincoln, and Lamon asked the President if he would make him a promise.

"I think I can venture to say I will," said Mr. Lincoln. "What is it?"

"Promise me that you will not go out after night while I am gone," said Mr. Lamon, "particularly to the theatre."

Mr. Lincoln turned to Mr. Usher and said: "Usher, this boy is a monomaniac on the subject of my safety. I can hear him or hear of his being around at all times in the night, to prevent somebody from murdering me. He thinks I shall be killed, and we think he is going crazy. What does any one want to assassinate me for? If any one wants to do so, he can do it any day or night if he is ready to give his life for mine. It is nonsense."

Mr. Usher said to Mr. Lincoln that it was well to heed Lamon's warning, as he was thrown among people from whom he had better opportunities to know about such matters than almost any one.

"Well," said Mr. Lincoln to Lamon, "I promise to do the best I can toward it."

How Lincoln Was Murdered

The assassination of President Lincoln was most carefully planned, even to the smallest detail. The box set apart for the President's party was a double one in the second tier at the left of the stage. The box had two doors with spring locks, but Booth had loosened the screws with which they were fastened so that it was impossible to secure them from the inside. In one door he had bored a hole with a gimlet, so that he could see what was going on inside the box.

An employee of the theatre by the name of Spangler, who was an accomplice of the assassin, had even arranged the seats in the box to suit the purposes of Booth.

On the fateful night the theatre was packed. The Presidential party arrived a few minutes after nine o'clock, and consisted of the President and Mrs. Lincoln, Miss Harris and Major Rathbone, daughter and stepson of Senator Harris of New York. The immense audience rose to its feet and cheered the President as he passed to his box.

Booth came into the theatre about ten o'clock. He had not only, planned to kill the President, but he had also planned to escape into Maryland, and a swift horse, saddled and ready for the journey, was tied in the rear of the theatre. For a few minutes he pretended to be interested in the performance, and then gradually made his way back to the door of the President's box.

Before reaching there, however, he was confronted by one of the President's messengers, who had been stationed at the end of the passage leading to the boxes to prevent any one from intruding. To this man Booth handed a card saying that the President had sent for him, and was permitted to enter.

Once inside the hallway leading to the boxes, he closed the hall door and fastened it by a bar prepared for the occasion, so that it was impossible to open it from without. Then he quickly entered the box through the right-hand door. The President was sitting in an easy armchair in the left-hand corner of the box nearest the audience. He was leaning on one hand and with the other had hold of a portion of the drapery. There was a smile on his face. The other members of the party were intently watching the performance on the stage.

The assassin carried in his right hand a small silver-mounted derringer pistol and in his left a long double-edged dagger. He placed the pistol just behind the President's left ear and fired.

Mr. Lincoln bent slightly forward and his eyes closed, but in every other respect his attitude remained unchanged.

The report of the pistol startled Major Rathbone, who sprang to his feet. The murderer was then about six feet from the President, and Rathbone grappled with him, but was shaken off. Dropping his pistol, Booth struck at Rathbone with the dagger and inflicted a severe wound. The assassin then placed his left hand lightly on the railing of the box and jumped to the stage, eight or nine feet below.

Booth Brandishes His Dagger and Escapes

The box was draped with the American flag, and, in jumping, Booth's spurs caught in the folds, tearing down the flag, the assassin falling heavily to the stage and spraining his ankle. He arose, however, and walked theatrically across the stage, brandished his knife and shouted, "Sic semper tyrannis!" and then added, "The South is avenged."

For the moment the audience was horrified and incapable of action. One man only, a lawyer named Stuart, had sufficient presence of mind to leap upon the stage and attempt to capture the assassin. Booth went to the rear door of the stage, where his horse was held in readiness for him, and, leaping into the saddle, dashed through the streets toward Virginia. Miss Keane rushed to the President's box with water and stimulants, and medical aid was summoned.

By this time the audience realized the tragedy that had been enacted, and then followed a scene such as has never been witnessed in any public gathering in this country. Women wept, shrieked and fainted; men raved and swore, and horror was depicted on every face. Before the audience could be gotten out of the theatre, horsemen were dashing through the streets and the telegraph was carrying the terrible details of the tragedy throughout the nation.

Walt Whitman's Description

Walt Whitman, the poet, has sketched in graphic language the scenes of that most eventful fourteenth of April. His account of the assassination has become historic, and is herewith given:

"The day (April 14, 1865) seems to have been a pleasant one throughout the whole land—the moral atmosphere pleasant, too—the long storm, so dark, so fratricidal, full of blood and doubt and gloom, over and ended at last by the sunrise of such an absolute national victory, and utter breaking down of secessionism—we almost doubted our senses! Lee had capitulated, beneath the apple tree at Appomattox. The other armies, the flanges of the revolt, swiftly followed.

"And could it really be, then? Out of all the affairs of this world of woe and passion, of failure and disorder and dismay, was there really come the confirmed, unerring sign of peace, like a shaft of pure light—of rightful rule—of God?

"But I must not dwell on accessories. The deed hastens. The popular afternoon paper, the little Evening Star, had scattered all over its third page, divided among the advertisements in a sensational manner in a hundred different places:

"'The President and his lady will be at the theatre this evening.'

"Lincoln was fond of the theatre. I have myself seen him there several times. I remember thinking how funny it was that he, the leading actor in the greatest and stormiest drama known to real history's stage, through centuries, should sit there and be so completely interested in those human jackstraws, moving about with their silly little gestures, foreign spirit, and flatulent text.

"So the day, as I say, was propitious. Early herbage, early flowers, were out. I remember where I was stopping at the time, the season being advanced, there were many lilacs in full bloom.

"By one of those caprices that enter and give tinge to events without being a part of them, I find myself always reminded of the great tragedy of this day by the sight and odor of these blossoms. It never fails.

"On this occasion the theatre was crowded, many ladies in rich

and gay costumes, officers in their uniforms, many well-known citizens, young folks, the usual cluster of gas lights, the usual mag-
netism of so many people, cheerful with perfumes, music of violins
and flutes—and over all, that saturating, that vast, vague wonder,
Victory, the nation's victory, the triumph of the Union, filling the
air, the thought, the sense, with exhilaration more than all the perfumes.

"The President came betimes, and, with his wife, witnessed the
play from the large stage boxes of the second tier, two thrown
into one, and profusely draped with the national flag. The acts
and scenes of the piece—one of those singularly witless compositions which have at the least the merit of giving entire relief to
an audience engaged in mental action or business excitements and
cares during the day, as it makes not the slightest call on either
the moral, emotional, esthetic or spiritual nature—a piece in which
among other characters, so called, a Yankee—certainly such a one
as was never seen, or at least like it ever seen in North America, is
introduced in England, with a varied fol-de-rol of talk, plot, scenery,
and such phantasmagoria as goes to make up a modern popular
drama—had progressed perhaps through a couple of its acts, when,
in the midst of this comedy, or tragedy, or non-such, or whatever it is
to be called, and to offset it, or finish it out, as if in Nature's and the
Great Muse's mockery of these poor mimics, comes interpolated that
scene, not really or exactly to be described at all (for on the many
hundreds who were there it seems to this hour to have left little but
a passing blur, a dream, a blotch)—and yet partially described as I
now proceed to give it:

"There is a scene in the play, representing the modern parlor, in
which two unprecedented ladies are informed by the unprecedented
and impossible Yankee that he is not a man of fortune, and therefore
undesirable for marriage-catching purposes; after which, the comments being finished, the dramatic trio make exit, leaving the stage
clear for a moment.

"There was a pause, a hush, as it were. At this period came the
death of Abraham Lincoln.

"Great as that was, with all its manifold train circling around it,
and stretching into the future for many a century, in the politics,

history, art, etc., of the New World, in point of fact, the main thing, the actual murder, transpired with the quiet and simplicity of any commonest occurrence—the bursting of a bud or pod in the growth of vegetation, for instance.

"Through the general hum following the stage pause, with the change of positions, etc., came the muffled sound of a pistol shot, which not one-hundredth part of the audience heard at the time—and yet a moment's hush—somehow, surely a vague, startled thrill—and then, through the ornamented, draperied, starred and striped space-way of the President's box, a sudden figure, a man, raises himself with hands and feet, stands a moment on the railing, leaps below to the stage, falls out of position, catching his boot heel in the copious drapery (the American flag), falls on one knee, quickly recovers himself, rises as if nothing had happened (he really sprains his ankle, unfelt then)—and the figure, Booth, the murderer, dressed in plain black broadcloth, bareheaded, with a full head of glossy, raven hair, and his eyes, like some mad animal's, flashing with light and resolution, yet with a certain strange calmness holds aloft in one hand a large knife—walks along not much back of the footlights—turns fully towards the audience, his face of statuesque beauty, lit by those basilisk eyes, flashing with desperation, perhaps insanity—launches out in a firm and steady voice the words, 'Sic semper tyrannis'—and then walks with neither slow nor very rapid pace diagonally across to the back of the stage, and disappears.

"(Had not all this terrible scene—making the mimic ones preposterous—had it not all been rehearsed, in blank, by Booth, beforehand?)

"A moment's hush, incredulous—a scream—a cry of murder— Mrs. Lincoln leaning out of the box, with ashy cheeks and lips, with involuntary cry, pointing to the retreating figure, 'He has killed the President!'

"And still a moment's strange, incredulous suspense—and then the deluge!—then that mixture of horror, noises, uncertainty—the sound, somewhere back, of a horse's hoofs clattering with speed— the people burst through chairs and railings, and break them up— that noise adds to the queerness of the scene—there is inextricable confusion and terror—women faint—quite feeble persons fall, and are trampled on—many cries of agony are heard—the broad stage suddenly fills to suffocation with a dense and motley crowd, like some horrible carnival—the audience rush generally upon it— at least the strong men do—the actors and actresses are there in their play costumes and painted faces, with mortal fright showing through the rouge—some trembling, some in tears—the screams and calls, confused talk—redoubled, trebled—two or three manage to pass up water from the stage to the President's box, others try to clamber up, etc., etc.

"In the midst of all this the soldiers of the President's Guard, with others, suddenly drawn to the scene, burst in—some two hundred altogether—they storm the house, through all the tiers, especially the upper ones—inflamed with fury, literally charging the audience with fixed bayonets, muskets and pistols, shouting, 'Clear out! clear out!'

"Such a wild scene, or a suggestion of it, rather, inside the play-house that night!

"Outside, too, in the atmosphere of shock and craze, crowds of people filled with frenzy, ready to seize any outlet for it, came near committing murder several times on innocent individuals.

"One such case was particularly exciting. The infuriated crowd, through some chance, got started against one man, either for words he uttered, or perhaps without any cause at all, and were proceeding to hang him at once to a neighboring lamp-post, when he was rescued by a few heroic policemen, who placed him in their midst and fought their way slowly and amid great peril toward the station-house.

"It was a fitting episode of the whole affair. The crowd rushing and eddying to and fro, the night, the yells, the pale faces, many frightened people trying in vain to extricate themselves, the attacked man, not yet freed from the jaws of death, looking like a corpse; the silent, resolute half-dozen policemen, with no weapons but their little clubs, yet stern and steady through all those eddying swarms, made, indeed, a fitting side scene to the grand tragedy of the murder. They gained the station-house with the protected man, whom they placed in security for the night, and discharged in the morning.

"And in the midst of that night pandemonium of senseless hate, infuriated soldiers, the audience and the crowd—the stage, and all its actors and actresses, its paint pots, spangles, gas-light—the life-blood from those veins, the best and sweetest of the land, drips slowly down, and death's ooze already begins its little bubbles on the lips.

"Such, hurriedly sketched, were the accompaniments of the death of President Lincoln. So suddenly, and in murder and horror unsurpassed, he was taken from us. But his death was painless."

The assassin's bullet did not produce instant death, but the President never again became conscious. He was carried to a house opposite the theatre, where he died the next morning. In the meantime the authorities had become aware of the wide-reaching conspiracy, and the capital was in a state of terror.

On the night of the President's assassination, Mr. Seward, Secretary of State, was attacked while in bed with a broken arm, by Booth's fellow-conspirators, and badly wounded.

The conspirators had also planned to take the lives of Vice-President Johnson and Secretary Stanton. Booth had called on Vice-President Johnson the day before, and, not finding him in, left a card.

Secretary Stanton acted with his usual promptness and courage. During the period of excitement he acted as President, and directed the plans for the capture of Booth.

Among other things, he issued the following reward:

REWARD OFFERED BY SECRETARY STANTON. War Department, Washington, April 20, 1865. Major-General John A. Dix, New York:

The murderer of our late beloved President, Abraham Lincoln, is still at large. Fifty thousand dollars reward will be paid by this Department for his apprehension, in addition to any reward offered by municipal authorities or State Executives.

Twenty-five thousand dollars reward will be paid for the apprehension of G. W. Atzerodt, sometimes called "Port Tobacco," one of Booth's accomplices. Twenty-five thousand dollars reward will be paid for the apprehension of David C. Herold, another of Booth's accomplices.

A liberal reward will be paid for any information that shall conduce to the arrest of either the above-named criminals or their accomplices.

All persons harboring or secreting the said persons, or either of them, or aiding or assisting their concealment or escape, will be treated as accomplices in the murder of the President and the attempted assassination of the Secretary of State, and shall be subject to trial before a military commission, and the punishment of death.

Let the stain of innocent blood be removed from the land by the arrest and punishment of the murderers.

All good citizens are exhorted to aid public justice on this occasion. Every man should consider his own conscience charged with this solemn duty, and rest neither night nor day until it be accomplished.

EDWIN M. STANTON, Secretary of War.

Booth Found in a Barn

Booth, accompanied by David C. Herold, a fellow-conspirator, finally made his way into Maryland, where eleven days after the assassination the two were discovered in a barn on Garrett's farm near Port Royal on the Rappahannock. The barn was surrounded by a squad of cavalrymen, who called upon the assassins to surrender. Herold gave himself up and was roundly cursed and abused by Booth, who declared that he would never be taken alive.

The cavalrymen then set fire to the barn and as the flames leaped up the figure of the assassin could be plainly seen, although the wall of fire prevented him from seeing the soldiers. Colonel Conger saw him standing upright upon a crutch with a carbine in his hands.

When the fire first blazed up Booth crept on his hands and knees to the spot, evidently for the purpose of shooting the man who had applied the torch, but the blaze prevented him from seeing anyone. Then it seemed as if he were preparing to extinguish the flames, but seeing the impossibility of this he started toward the door with his carbine held ready for action.

His eyes shone with the light of fever, but he was pale as death and his general appearance was haggard and unkempt. He had shaved off his mustache and his hair was closely cropped. Both he and Herold wore the uniforms of Confederate soldiers.

Booth Shot by "Boston" Corbett

The last orders given to the squad pursuing Booth were: "Don't shoot Booth, but take him alive." Just as Booth started to the door of the barn this order was disobeyed by a sergeant named Boston Corbett, who fired through a crevice and shot Booth in the neck. The wounded man was carried out of the barn and died four hours afterward on the grass where they had laid him. Before he died he whispered to Lieutenant Baker, "Tell mother I died for my country; I thought I did for the best." What became of Booth's body has always been and probably always will be a mystery. Many different stories have been told concerning his final resting place, but all that is known positively is that the body was first taken to Washington and a post-mortem examination of it held on the Monitor Montauk. On the night of April 27th it was turned over to two men who took it in a rowboat and disposed of it secretly. How they disposed of it none but themselves know and they have never told.

Fate of the Conspirators

The conspiracy to assassinate the President involved altogether twenty-five people. Among the number captured and tried were David C. Herold, G. W. Atzerodt, Louis Payne, Edward Spangler, Michael O'Loughlin, Samuel Arnold, Mrs. Surratt and Dr. Samuel Mudd, a physician, who set Booth's leg, which was sprained by his fall from the stage box. Of these Herold, Atzerodt, Payne and Mrs. Surratt were hanged. Dr. Mudd was deported to the Dry Tortugas.

While there an epidemic of yellow fever broke out and he rendered such good service that he was granted a pardon and died a number of years ago in Maryland.

John Surratt, the son of the woman who was hanged, made his escape to Italy, where he became one of the Papal guards in the Vatican at Rome. His presence there was discovered by Archbishop Hughes, and, although there were no extradition laws to cover his case, the Italian Government gave him up to the United States authorities.

He had two trials. At the first the jury disagreed; the long delay before his second trial allowed him to escape by pleading the statute of limitation. Spangler and O'Loughlin were sent to the Dry Tortugas and served their time.

Ford, the owner of the theatre in which the President was assassinated, was a Southern sympathizer, and when he attempted to reopen his theatre after the great national tragedy, Secretary Stanton refused to allow it. The Government afterward bought the theatre and turned it into a National museum.

President Lincoln was buried at Springfield, and on the day of his funeral there was universal grief.

Henry Ward Beecher's Eulogy

No final words of that great life can be more fitly spoken than the eulogy pronounced by Henry Ward Beecher:

"And now the martyr is moving in triumphal march, mightier than when alive. The nation rises up at every stage of his coming. Cities and States are his pall-bearers, and the cannon speaks the hours with solemn progression. Dead, dead, dead, he yet speaketh.

"Is Washington dead? Is Hampden dead? Is any man that was ever fit to live dead? Disenthralled of flesh, risen to the unobstructed sphere where passion never comes, he begins his illimitable work. His life is now grafted upon the infinite, and will be fruitful as no earthly life can be.

"Pass on, thou that hast overcome. Ye people, behold the martyr whose blood, as so many articulate words, pleads for fidelity, for law, for liberty."

Abraham Lincoln's Family

Abraham Lincoln was married on November 4, 1842, to Miss Mary Todd, four sons being the issue of the union.

Robert Todd, born August 1, 1843, removed to Chicago after his father's death, practiced law, and became wealthy; in 1881 he was appointed Secretary of War by President Garfield, and served through President Arthur's term; was made Minister to England in 1889, and served four years; became counsel for the Pullman Palace Car Company, and succeeded to the presidency of that corporation upon the death of George M. Pullman.

Edward Baker, born March 10, 1846, died in infancy.

William Wallace, born December 21, 1850, died in the White House in February, 1862.

Thomas (known as "Tad"), born April 4, 1853, died in 1871.

Mrs. Lincoln died in her sixty-fourth year at the home of her sister, Mrs. Ninian W. Edwards, at Springfield, Illinois, in 1882. She was the daughter of Robert S. Todd, of Kentucky. Her great-uncle, John Todd, and her grandfather, Levi Todd, accompanied General George Rogers Clark to Illinois, and were present at the capture of Kaskaskia and Vincennes. In December, 1778, John Todd was appointed by Patrick Henry, Governor of Virginia, to be lieutenant of the County of Illinois, then a part of Virginia. Colonel John Todd was one of the original proprietors of the town of Lexington, Kentucky. While encamped on the site of the present city, he heard of the opening battle of the Revolution, and named his infant settlement in its honor.

Mrs. Lincoln was a proud, ambitious woman, well-educated, speaking French fluently, and familiar with the ways of the best society in Lexington, Kentucky, where she was born December 13, 1818. She was a pupil of Madame Mantelli, whose celebrated seminary in Lexington was directly opposite the residence of Henry Clay. The conversation at the seminary was carried on entirely in French.

She visited Springfield, Illinois, in 1837, remained three months and then returned to her native State. In 1839 she made Springfield her permanent home. She lived with her eldest sister, Elizabeth, wife of Ninian W. Edwards, Lincoln's colleague in the Legislature, and it was not strange she and Lincoln should meet. Stephen A. Douglas was also a friend of the Edwards family, and a suitor for her hand, but she rejected him to accept the future President. She was one of the belles of the town.

She is thus described at the time she made her home in Springfield—1839:

"She was of the average height, weighing about a hundred and thirty pounds. She was rather compactly built, had a well rounded face, rich dark-brown hair, and bluish-gray eyes. In her bearing she was proud, but handsome and vivacious; she was a good conversationalist, using with equal fluency the French and English languages.

"When she used a pen, its point was sure to be sharp, and she wrote with wit and ability. She not only had a quick intellect but an intuitive judgment of men and their motives. Ordinarily she was affable and even charming in her manners; but when offended or antagonized she could be very bitter and sarcastic.

"In her figure and physical proportions, in education, bearing, temperament, history—in everything she was the exact reverse of Lincoln."

That Mrs. Lincoln was very proud of her husband there is no doubt; and it is probable that she married him largely from motives of ambition. She knew Lincoln better than he knew himself; she instinctively felt that he would occupy a proud position some day, and it is a matter of record that she told Ward Lamon, her husband's law partner, that "Mr. Lincoln will yet be President of the United States."

Mrs. Lincoln was decidedly pro-slavery in her views, but this never disturbed Lincoln. In various ways they were unlike. Her fearless, witty, and austere nature had nothing in common with the calm, imperturbable, and simple ways of her thoughtful and absent-minded husband. She was bright and sparkling in conversation, and fit to grace any drawing-room. She well knew that to marry Lincoln meant not a life of luxury and ease, for Lincoln was not a man to accumulate wealth; but in him she saw position in society, prominence in the world, and the grandest social distinction. By that means her ambition was certainly satisfied, for nineteen years after her marriage she was "the first lady of the land," and the mistress of the White House.

After his marriage, by dint of untiring efforts and the recognition of influential friends, the couple managed through rare frugality to move along.

In Lincoln's struggles, both in the law and for political advancement, his wife shared his sacrifices. She was a plucky little woman, and in fact endowed with a more restless ambition than he. She was gifted with a rare insight into the motives that actuate mankind, and there is no doubt that much of Lincoln's success was in a measure attributable to her acuteness and the stimulus of her influence.

His election to Congress within four years after their marriage afforded her extreme gratification. She loved power and prominence, and was inordinately proud of her tall and ungainly husband. She saw in him bright prospects ahead, and his every move was watched by her with the closest interest. If to other persons he seemed homely, to her he was the embodiment of noble manhood, and each succeeding day impressed upon her the wisdom of her choice of Lincoln over Douglas—if in reality she ever seriously accepted the latter's attentions.

"Mr. Lincoln may not be as handsome a figure," she said one day in Lincoln's law office during her husband's absence, when the conversation turned on Douglas, "but the people are perhaps not aware that his heart is as large as his arms are long."

Lincoln Monument at Springfield

The remains of Abraham Lincoln rest beneath a magnificent monument in Oak Ridge Cemetery, Springfield, Ill. Before they were deposited in their final resting place they were moved many times.

On May 4, 1865, all that was mortal of Abraham Lincoln was deposited in the receiving vault at the cemetery, until a tomb could be built. In 1876 thieves made an unsuccessful attempt to steal the remains. From the tomb the body of the martyred President was removed later to the monument.

A flight of iron steps, commencing about fifty yards east of the vault, ascends in a curved line to the monument, an elevation of more than fifty feet.

Excavation for this monument commenced September 9, 1869.

It is built of granite, from quarries at Biddeford, Maine. The rough ashlers were shipped to Quincy, Massachusetts, where they were dressed and numbered, thence shipped to Springfield. It is 721 feet from east to west, 119 1/2 feet from north to south, and 100 feet high. The total cost is about $230,000 to May 1, 1885. All the statuary is orange-colored bronze. The whole monument was designed by Larkin G. Mead; the statuary was modeled in plaster by him in Florence, Italy, and cast by the Ames Manufacturing Company, of Chicopee, Massachusetts. A statue of Lincoln and Coat of Arms were first placed on the monument; the statue was unveiled and the monument dedicated October 15, 1874. Infantry and Naval Groups were put on in September, 1877, an Artillery Group, April 13, 1882, and a Cavalry Group, March 13, 1883.

The principal front of the monument is on the south side, the statue of Lincoln being on that side of the obelisk, over Memorial Hall. On the east side are three tablets, upon which are the letters U. S. A. To the right of that, and beginning with Virginia, we find the abbreviations of the original thirteen States. Next comes Vermont, the first state admitted after the Union was perfected, the States following in the order they were admitted, ending with Nebraska on the east, thus forming the cordon of thirty-seven States composing the United States of America when the monument was erected. The new States admitted since the monument was built have been added.

The statue of Lincoln is just above the Coat of Arms of the United States. The grand climax is indicated by President Lincoln, with his left hand holding out as a golden scepter the emancipation Proclamation, while in his right he holds the pen with which he has just written it. The right hand is resting on another badge of authority, the American flag, thrown over the fasces. At the foot of the fasces lies a wreath of laurel, with which to crown the President as the victor over slavery and rebellion.

On March 10, 1900, President Lincoln's body was removed to a temporary vault to permit of alterations to the monument. The shaft was made twenty feet higher, and other changes were made costing $100,000.

April 24, 1901. the body was again transferred to the monument without public ceremony.

Lincoln Chronology

Abraham Lincoln, the great story-telling president, whose Emancipation Proclamation freed more than four million slaves, was a keen politician, profound statesman, shrewd diplomatist, a thorough judge of men and possessed of an intuitive knowledge of affairs. He was the first Chief Executive to die at the hands of an assassin. Without school education he rose to power by sheer merit and will-power. Born in a Kentucky log cabin in 1809, his surroundings being squalid, his chances for advancement were apparently hopeless. President Lincoln died April 15th, 1865, having been shot by J. Wilkes Booth the night before.

1806—Marriage of Thomas Lincoln and Nancy Hanks, June 12th, Washington County, Kentucky.

1809—Born February 12th, Hardin (now La Rue County), Kentucky.

1816—Family Removed to Perry County, Indiana.

1818—Death of Abraham's Mother, Nancy Hanks Lincoln.

1819—Second Marriage Thomas Lincoln; Married Sally Bush Johnston, December 2nd, at Elizabethtown, Kentucky.

1830—Lincoln Family Removed to Illinois, Locating in Macon County.

1831—Abraham Located at New Salem.

1832—Abraham a Captain in the Black Hawk War.

1833—Appointed Postmaster at New Salem.

1834—Abraham as a Surveyor. First Election to the Legislature.

1835—Love Romance with Anne Rutledge.

1836—Second Election to the Legislature.

1837—Licensed to Practice Law.

1838—Third Election to the Legislature.

1840—Presidential Elector on Harrison Ticket. Fourth Election to the Legislature.

1842—Married November 4th, to Mary Todd. "Duel" with General Shields.

1843—Birth of Robert Todd Lincoln, August 1st.

1846—Elected to Congress. Birth of Edward Baker Lincoln, March 10th.

1848—Delegate to the Philadelphia National Convention.

1850—Birth of William Wallace Lincoln, December 2nd.

1853—Birth of Thomas Lincoln, April 4th.

1856—Assists in Formation Republican Party.

1858—Joint Debater with Stephen A. Douglas. Defeated for the United States Senate.

1860—Nominated and Elected to the Presidency.

1861—Inaugurated as President, March 4th. 1863-Issued Emancipation Proclamation.

1864—Re-elected to the Presidency.

1865—Assassinated by J. Wilkes Booth, April 14th. Died April 15th. Remains Interred at Springfield, Illinois, May 4th.

www.ingramcontent.com/pod-product-compliance
Lightning Source LLC
Chambersburg PA
CBHW021210090426
42740CB00006B/178